EPISCOPAL MINISTRY

EPISCOPAL MINISTRY

The Report of the
Archbishops' Group on
The Episcopate

1990

CHURCH HOUSE PUBLISHING

Church House, Great Smith Street, London SW1P 3NZ

Published 1990 for the General Synod of the Church of England by
Church House Publishing

GS 944

British Library Cataloguing in Publication Data

Archbishops' Group on the Episcopate

Episcopal Ministry: The Report of the Archbishops' Group on the
Episcopate

1. Theology, doctrinal – episcopacy
2. Episcopacy and Christian Union
3. Anglican Communion

I   Title

ISBN 0-7151-3736-0

Typeset by Upper Case, Cambridge
Printed in England by Rapier Press Ltd

CONTENTS

Preface by the Chairman

To rebuke agitators, to comfort the faint-hearted, to take care of
the weak, to confute enemies, to take heed of snares, to teach the
uneducated, to waken the sluggish, to hold back the quarrelsome,
to put the conceited in their place, to appease the militant, to give
help to the poor, to liberate the oppressed, to encourage the good,
to endure the evil, and - O - to love them all.

> Augustine, Bishop of Hippo (354-430)
> on his office as bishop

To fulfil a pastoral ministry of oversight of the kind described by St.
Augustine, a bishop must have many and varied qualities; but, above all, the
ability to exercise authority as a spiritual leader.

Within an episcopal church it can readily be accepted that a bishop is
a leader and person of authority in the Church. However, the very existence
of the episcopate gives rise to many questions about the origin and functions
of bishops. Who appointed the first bishops? Have the functions of bishops
always remained the same? Must a bishop always be a man? What part does
a bishop play in representing his diocese within the collegiality of bishops in
the wider Church? In this Report we have addressed these and other
questions. In its preparation we have had it very much in mind that all
office in the Church is subordinate to and exists to serve the Word of God.

We were appointed as a Group by the Archbishops of Canterbury and
York at the request of the Standing Committee of the General Synod of the
Church of England, with the intention that we should identify and examine
the theological issues bearing upon the ordination of women to the
episcopate. The need for a study of this subject lay in the fact that, while
there had been extensive consideration in England of the issue of women and
the priesthood, not much attention had been given to the issue of women and
the episcopate. It was considered appropriate that a Report should be

available in case the issue of women and the episcopate arose in the context of the General Synod's consideration of women and the priesthood; and also so that it could form one element in the Church of England's contribution to the documentation for the 1988 Lambeth Conference.

At our first meeting in January 1986 we formed the view that it would be prudent and desirable to examine the theological issues bearing upon the ordination of women to the episcopate in the context of, and as part of, a general study of the nature and function of episcopal ministry. The Archbishops of Canterbury and York agreed to such an extension of our terms of reference in July 1986. Since then our terms of reference have been:

> To consider the nature and function of the episcopate in the Church, including a particular examination of the theological issues bearing upon the ordination of women to the episcopate.

Recognising that our new terms of reference would enable us to examine in depth the theology of *episcope* (the ministry of oversight) the Archbishops considered it appropriate to enlarge our membership so that matters of concern to the Dioceses Commission, particularly in relation to the role of a suffragan bishop,[1] could be brought to the attention of and be considered by our Group.

The time-scale for production of this Report has been affected both by external events and by the breadth of subject matter covered by our terms of reference. It proved impracticable to have it ready in time for the 1988 Lambeth Conference.

Events moved much more rapidly than had been anticipated, and within a few weeks of our Group's formation we found that the prospect of a woman being consecrated as a bishop had become a major issue demanding and receiving urgent consideration within the Anglican Communion at the request of the Primates.

The Episcopal Church in the United States of America, which had then had ten years' experience of women in the presbyterate, sent the following resolution to the Primates' Meeting in Toronto in March 1986:

---

[1] See Chapter 11 C.

The majority of the members of the House do not intend to withhold consent to the election of a Bishop of this Church on the grounds of gender and now call upon the Presiding Bishop to communicate this intention to the Primates of the Anglican Communion and seek the advice of the Episcopate of the Anglican Communion through the Primates at the earliest possible date.

The Primates welcomed the request of ECUSA for consultation, seeing it as indicating that the Episcopal Church in the United States of America recognised the consequences its action would have in the life of the wider Anglican family, and ecumenically. The Primates asked the Archbishop of Canterbury to set up a small Working Party to gather together the reactions of the Anglican Provinces to the admission of women to the episcopate. Such a Working Party, under the Chairmanship of the Archbishop of Brisbane, the Most Reverend John Grindrod, duly invited the views of the Provinces.

It was at this stage that our proposed programme of work became affected by the setting up of the Primates' Working Party. Before we had been able to embark on our general study, we were asked by the House of Bishops in the autumn of 1986 to prepare a memorandum by June 1987, setting out our interim comments on the theological issues relating to the ordination of women to the episcopate. This was with a view to assisting the House of Bishops in England to prepare their response to the Primates' Working Party.

We did not wish to be unco-operative but it was with some reluctance that we agreed to prepare such a memorandum. We did so agree on the understanding that it could do no more than represent the Group's provisional views on the theological issues relating to women in the episcopate. Misgivings were expressed about attempting to deal with the specific issues relating to women before we had had a chance to form a common mind on a theology of the episcopal ministry. When we came to discuss the content of the memorandum we found that our misgivings had been justified. We recognised that members of the Group had been appointed by the Archbishops to represent fairly the divergence of views within the Church of England on the question whether women may be ordained to the priestly ministry. It was hardly surprising, therefore, that views were strongly expressed and that heated exchanges took place, which made it apparent that in the absence of any unanimity on the subject of ordination of women to the priesthood there was no prospect of unanimity at that stage of our deliberations on the proper emphasis to place on issues relating to the ordination of women to the episcopate.

Despite the efforts of our Group to agree upon the final content of the memorandum helpfully prepared by Dr. George Carey, then Principal of Trinity College, Bristol, it proved impossible for members to do so, notwithstanding that many of us had offered contributions to, and suggestions for, the paper, which had undergone three revisions. The memorandum[2] was therefore forwarded to the House of Bishops under Dr. Carey's name, not as emanating from the Group as a whole.

The absence from the memorandum of any provisional conclusions on the part of our Group was attributable to our reluctance to put forward views at such an early stage in our deliberations, with the risk that they might mistakenly be treated as final and definitive. Furthermore, we were conscious of the limited time-scale which had unexpectedly been imposed upon us when we had been asked to consider a subject which had not previously been given detailed consideration.

Since the preparation of our memorandum, our work has covered a wide area, as we have examined the development of the ministry of oversight in various forms within the Church, and have reflected upon the nature of episcopal ministry past and present.

As a Group we had the privilege of having a private meeting in July 1989 with the Most Reverend Robert Eames, Archbishop of Armagh, when we were able to discuss with him the Report of the Archbishop of Canterbury's Commission on Communion and Women in the Episcopate, which was produced under his chairmanship. His Commission,[3] like our Group, reflects differing theological views on the question of the ordination of women to the priesthood and the episcopate.

We make no secret of the fact that both at the beginning of our work and more recently when we have returned to the subject again, the issue has been painfully divisive between us. However, such differences of opinion as we have had on this issue have not arisen in other areas we have discussed, where we have in general achieved a consensus; nor have they affected the fellowship amongst the Group as we have worked and prayed together.

---

[2] Printed here as Appendix III (a). As an amalgam of views, it should not, on the other hand, be regarded as necessarily fully or accurately representing Dr. Carey's own personal view.

[3] With which our Group has three members or consultants in common.

We were saddened by the death in 1987 of one of our members, the Reverend Canon Dr. Gareth Bennett. We were fortunate to have received from him a number of papers, which have greatly helped us in the preparation of the Report.

In addition to receiving a helpful Memorandum of Evidence from the Dioceses Commission, a sub-committee of our Group met the chairman and representatives of the Dioceses Commission so that we could be fully informed as to matters concerning them.

Because of the breadth of knowledge and experience within our Group and the extensive literature available to us, we did not ask for formal submissions of evidence. We are, however, grateful for a number of letters which we have received from diocesan and suffragan bishops.

We wish to record our appreciation for the invaluable assistance which we have received from our consultants throughout our work. We particularly wish to thank Canon Professor Henry Chadwick for all his comments and contributions; Canon Christopher Hill for his help with the ecumenical and other chapters; Sir Derek Pattinson for his advice and contributions; Dr. Mary Tanner for her guidance throughout our deliberations, for her contributions to the text and assistance with earlier drafting of the Report. We are especially grateful to Dr. Gillian Evans, who joined us by invitation as a consultant, and has not only made contributions to the text but has cheerfully and admirably undertaken the unenviable task of editing the Report prior to publication.

The Report is the result of the joint effort of members of the Group. Where appropriate we have submitted sections for scrutiny and comment by experts or asked them for portions of draft text, and we gratefully acknowledge the help we have received in this way from Canon Donald Allchin, Professor Owen Chadwick, Professor Patrick Collinson, the Reverend Martin Cressey, Mgr. Gérard Daucourt, the Reverend Dr. John Fenwick, the Reverend Dr. Brian Ferme, the Reverend Bernard Green, Canon Dr. John Halliburton, Canon John Hind, Professor Morna Hooker, the Reverend Paul McPartlan, Colin Podmore, the Reverend Dr. William Rusch, the Reverend Dietrich Schuld de Verny, Dr. David Thompson, the Reverend Albert van der Hoek and the Reverend Dr. Edward Yarnold. We should also like to thank Canon S. Van Culin for permission to reproduce a portion of the Report of the Eames Commission (1989) in Appendix III (b).

We are indebted to our secretary, Derek Fullarton, upon whom we have been able to rely with confidence to arrange our meetings and keep an accurate record of them. We are grateful to Marian Marle for all the typing assistance she has given to him, and to Valerie Howes and Anne Tyler for their typing of some of the first drafts of parts of the Report. Finally, we most warmly thank Fiona Wilson for her skill and patience in preparing a complicated succession of revised typescripts of this Report and for typesetting the final pages.

Sheila Cameron.

Chairman

The Archbishops' Group on the Episcopate

The following were appointed to the Group:

as Chairman:
Chancellor Sheila Cameron Q.C., Vicar General of the Province of
    Canterbury and Chancellor of the Diocese of Chelmsford

as Members:
The Reverend Dr. Mary Barr, Parish Deacon of Holy Trinity Church,
    Cambridge and Cambridge Pastorate Chaplain
Canon G.V. Bennett (until his death in 1987)
The Right Reverend Cyril Bowles (Bishop of Derby until 1987)
The Right Reverend George Carey, Bishop of Bath and Wells
Miss Ruth Etchells (Principal of St. John's College, Durham until 1988)
Canon Roger Greenacre, Chancellor of Chichester Cathedral
The Right Reverend David Hope, Bishop of Wakefield
The Very Reverend John Moses, Provost of Chelmsford
The Right Reverend William Persson, Bishop of Doncaster
Jane Williams

as Consultants:
Canon Professor Henry Chadwick, K.B.E., Master of Peterhouse,
    Cambridge
Dr. G.R. Evans, University Lecturer and Fellow of Fitzwilliam College,
    Cambridge (by invitation)
Canon Christopher Hill, Precentor of St. Paul's Cathedral (Secretary for
    Ecumenical Affairs to the Archbishop of Canterbury, until 1989)
Sir Derek Pattinson (Secretary-General of the General Synod of the Church
    of England until 1990)
Dr. Mary Tanner, Deputy Secretary of the Board for Mission and Unity

as Secretary:
Mr. Derek Fullarton (Private Secretary to the Secretary-General of the
    General Synod until 1988), on secondment from the Church
    Commissioners

Abbreviations

AR	Anglican-Reformed Conversations: *God's Reign and our Unity*, London and Edinburgh, 1984
ARCIC	Anglican-Roman Catholic International Commission, *The Final Report*, London, 1982
AL	Anglican-Lutheran Conversations
AO	Anglican-Orthodox Conversations
BEM	Baptism, Eucharist and Ministry, World Council of Churches, Lima Report, 1982, in *Growth*
Bishops: But What Kind?	*Bishops: But What Kind?*, ed. P. Moore, London, 1982
BR	Baptist-Reformed Conversations
Cardwell, *Synodalia*	*Synodalia*, ed. E. Cardwell, London, 1842, 2 vols.
CCSL	Corpus Christianorum Series Latina
Episcopacy Asserted	Jeremy Taylor, *Episcopacy Asserted*, in *Works*, ed. C.P. Eden, London, 1847-54, Vol. V
Growth	*Growth in Agreement: Reports and Agreed Statements of Ecumenical Conversations on a World Level*, ed. H. Meyer and L. Vischer, New York/Geneva, 1984
GS	General Synod papers
LRC	Lutheran-Roman Catholic Conversations: *The Ministry in the Church*, 1981

MRC   Methodist-Roman Catholic Conversations: Denver
                    Report 1971; Dublin Report, 1976

Niagara   *The Niagara Report*, London, 1988

ORC   Roman Catholic-Orthodox Conversations: *The
                    Sacrament of Order in the Sacramental Structure of
                    the Church*, New Valamo, 1988

Piepkorn   A.C. Piepkorn, *Profiles in Belief*, II, New York,
                    1978

RRC   Reformed-Roman Catholic Conversations

1

Setting the scene

i

1.   The ministry of oversight (*episcope*), whose beginnings we see in the New Testament, has been a continuing feature of the life of the whole Church. There have been changes in the character and understanding of *episcope* through the centuries, occasioned by the particular needs of the Church and its mission in differing cultural contexts. At every stage in the development of episcopal ministry in practice, contemporary circumstances and models drawn from changing systems of philosophical and political thought have influenced the ways in which the role of the bishop has been understood. These historical events are part of the Church's life in the world and thus integral to its being. In some periods of history human frailty has distorted the exercise of oversight and there have been calls for reform. While the Church of England shared in many aspects of the Continental Reformation, it nevertheless retained the threefold pattern of ministry in the sixteenth century, and in all ecumenical conversations Anglicans have maintained their commitment to the historic episcopate.

2.   The style of ministerial oversight today is not everywhere the same. Nor should it be. Yet in recent decades, there has been an increasing openness to one another's thinking, in both episcopal and non-episcopal Churches, and growing mutual understanding and rapprochement. We have believed it to be of the first importance that our Report should seek to make a contribution to this movement towards unity.

3.   In the vicissitudes of practice and thinking about the episcopate there can be traced consistent realities, sometimes expressed in part, or with a specific emphasis. There is a profound continuity. It is with a strong sense both of the continuity, and of the varying character of the Church's needs, that we have set our Report in a broad context. Our brief has been to look at the episcopate. Some of the questions arising today about the nature and working of episcopacy are domestic: relations between Church and State; the balance of episcopal and synodical authority in the government of the Church; the special responsibility of bishops, both individually and corporately, for the guardianship of faith and order in the Church of

England; the role of English bishops in addressing the complex political, social and economic issues of today's world; the size of dioceses; the procedure for the appointment of bishops; jurisdiction; the role of the suffragan or area bishop within the diocese. Others have a wider reference. Recent consecrations of women as bishops in the United States of America and in New Zealand have raised afresh questions both about the nature of episcopal office and the powers of Provinces to make independent decisions in matters of order. That in its turn has led to discussion of the corporate authority of bishops in the Provinces, and in the Anglican Communion as a whole. Ecumenical conversations are prompting fresh thinking worldwide about apostolic succession, collegiality, conciliarity, primacy; and these are far from irrelevant at home in the running of local ecumenical schemes.

4.   We have tried, then, to provide a study, as a complement to the recent Reports on the Diaconate[1] and *The Priesthood of the Ordained Ministry*,[2] of which the Church of England will be able to make use in its reflections on the theology and practice of episcopacy amidst the challenges with which we find ourselves faced; but which will also keep clearly before us the great responsibility we bear to our fellow Christians throughout the world and in all the ages to act in the 'charity which is patient and willing to defer to the common mind'.[3]

ii

5.   The method we have adopted in our Report is to begin with a theological chapter of reflection on the Trinity and on the Church as communion, in which we set out our presuppositions. We explore the notion of God as Trinity, understood as a communion of persons joined in love. We see the Church as grounded in that divine life and itself called to a life of communion, with its 'order' constituted of relationships in which there is mutuality, and participation in a common life. Christ's gift of ministry to the Church is to nurture, maintain and enable the Church truly to be this fellowship.

6.   We go on to trace the story of the ways in which the ministry of oversight, or *episcope*, has fostered that communion, from its emergence in the New Testament. In outlining the New Testament account, and the story

[1]   *Deacons in the Ministry of the Church*, 1988.
[2]   Faith and Order Advisory Group, 1986.
[3]   Lambeth Conference, 1948.

which follows in the events of the first generation of the Church's life, we glimpse the development of structures of order which have helped to sustain communion in the Church through the ages. We describe the emergence of the threefold ministry of bishop, priest and deacon and outline the ways in which it has served communion for much of Christendom for most of the Church's life. We also look at the history of *episcope* in those Churches which, in the emergency situation of the sixteenth century, departed temporarily or until the present day from the threefold pattern of ministry; and which, in some cases, would still argue against a return to the traditional order. We have seen the function of all patterns of order in the Church as the maintaining of that unity in love which Scripture itself shows to be of the essence of the Church.

7.   Already in the New Testament, but more clearly in the immediate post-apostolic period, this essential task of maintaining the Church in unity can be seen as taking place on three planes: that which unites bishops and people in the local eucharistic community; the local and the universal which relates local communities to one another in the wider Church; and that of continuity through time - a concern which naturally came to be prominent only with the passing away of the first generation. It becomes a major theme of our Report - and indeed its organising principle - that these three planes have intersected in the person of the minister with special responsibility for oversight of the unity and common life of the people of God.

8.   In the history of the Church we see a community always stretched to encompass the greatness of its task, and sometimes, paradoxically, at odds with itself, so that the Gospel witness has been passed on and experienced in a fragmented way; with the result that different aspects of the tradition tend to be one-sidedly represented. Anglicans make no unique claim to possess the truth. We believe that sister-Churches must all find a convergence in the fullness of Christ. That has been our hope as, in the light of these theological and historical evidences, and what we are learning from the ecumenical convergence of our own time, we come to consider specific questions relating to the exercise of oversight facing Anglicans today.

2

The communion of the Trinity
and the life of the Church

i.   Communion unfolded in Scripture

9.   The Bible unfolds the story of the relationship of God to the world he has created. In the beginning God made men and women to live in a relationship of communion, with him and with one another. That is the message of the creation story in Genesis and of the history of the covenant people of the Old Testament. God established a covenant with the people: 'I will be your God, and you shall be my people' (Leviticus 26.12).

10.   Sin and its effects are the cause of the breakdown of communion: a breakdown between God and his people and between human beings; and of disintegration within the human personality. Adam and Eve hide from God; they put the blame on each other. Cain kills Abel because he believes that Abel has stolen God's favour. The Tower of Babel leads to dispersion and mutual incomprehension. And the long history of the Old Testament recounts the narrative of the people of Israel's infidelity to their side of the covenant promises, the subsequent breakdown of their relationship with God and the consequent disintegration of the life of the people of God.

11.   The New Testament tells the story of how God in Christ provides the means of restoring that which was, and is, lost by sin. The purpose of the work of Jesus Christ is the restoration of communion between humanity and God and between human beings; and of the individual's wholeness. Christ is lifted up from the earth to draw all to himself. He dies to gather into one the scattered children of God (John 12.32, 11.52). The restored relationship is offered to the Old Israel and to all people and nations. This restored creation is not only a return to the beginning but a new creation in Christ.

12.   The Church, the New Israel, is given by God in Christ as the place where the life of this new communion is offered, shared and lived out. The communion between Christians is brought into being in the sacrament of Baptism, and is maintained in the sharing of a common message and a

common eucharistic life; and that life is itself a communion with the Father and the Son in the fellowship of the Holy Spirit. 'That which we have seen and heard we proclaim also to you, so that you may have communion (*koinonia*) with us; and our communion (*koinonia*) is with the Father and with his Son Jesus Christ' (I John 1.3). It is God himself who calls men and women into communion with his Son Jesus Christ; and through our communion with Christ in the Spirit we enjoy communion both with the Father and with one another. 'God is faithful, by whom you were called into the communion (*koinonia*) of his Son, Jesus Christ our Lord (I Corinthians 1.9).

13.   The New Testament uses many images to describe the Church - it is the body of Christ, the temple, the vine, the bride, the new Israel. Underlying all these images is the idea of communion (*koinonia*).[1] *Koinonia* is more than simply human fellowship: it refers to the fact that we are drawn into the life of God the Holy Trinity and together experience something of that divine relationship. The Church, then, is that part of the world which has accepted the Gospel addressed to all people, which tries to live by it, and whose members are already drawn into communion with God the Holy Trinity and with one another in him.

14.   The New Testament shows the infant Church built up of those baptised into the life of the Holy Trinity, nurtured by Word and Sacrament, and living a common life. St. Paul sees Christians as a community, members of one body, who serve one another. It is within this community that the special ministry of service still nurtures the community and leads it in mission to the world.

15.   There is an intimate relation between the Church and the Kingdom. The Church is already the foretaste on earth of the Kingdom portrayed in the last two chapters of the Apocalypse (Revelation 21 and 22). The end of all things, according to St. John, is a community in which there will be no more temple, sacraments or ministry, for God himself will be immediate to his people. 'Behold, the dwelling place of God is with men. He will dwell with them, and they shall be his people; and God himself will be their God.' The Church is foretaste of that kingdom, first fruits of the kingdom and sign of the kingdom.

[1]   Cf. The Final Report of ARCIC, Introduction, 4.

16.   All this points to the fact that the Church is more than an institution; it is a way of 'being'. Its being is its grounding in the communion of God: Father, Son and Holy Spirit. The life of the Church partakes in the life of God the Holy Trinity. Our experience of life in the Church is confused, ragged, distorted, but there are moments of glory. That life is an incarnate foretaste of the eschatological life of the Kingdom and so it points ahead to the future consummation of the Kingdom. An understanding of communion and eschatology are thus necessary for understanding the nature of the Church and its ministry. The exercise of oversight in the Church must, equally necessarily, be related to the nurturing and maintenance of the communion of the Church and point to the vision of the Kingdom.

ii.   The communion of the Trinity

17.   If we are to understand this character of the being of the Church and the place and role of the ordained ministry within it we shall be helped by reflecting first on the vision of the Holy Trinity:

> We cannot have an ecclesiology until we have a proper Trinitarian doctrine, for we cannot expect of the Church anything less than a sign and a reflection of God's way of being in creation ... The Church must be conceived as the place where man can get a taste of his eternal eschatological destiny which is communion in God's very life.[2]

18.   The key to our human understanding of the divine order lies in the Person of Christ, in the incarnation of the eternal, only-begotten Son of God. Through him we know something of the life of the Trinity and the ordering of the relationships of the Persons within it. A right trinitarian theology must balance both the equality of the Persons of the Trinity and the distinction of the Persons. The Father is the Source, creating by his Word and in the power of the Holy Spirit; the Son, who is the eternal Word, became human by the power of the Holy Spirit and offered the sacrifice of his life to the Father; the Spirit nurtures God's people with life-giving power, enabling them to pray to the Father, in, with and through the Son. At the same time, the Persons are one in being and equal in their Godhead. If we are to keep before us an authentic vision of God, we must not lose sight of this balance.

19.   In this classic Christian perception of the Triune God, we are given some insight into God's way of being as that of Persons in a relation so profoundly reciprocal that they are one in being, so perfect in its mutuality that they will one will.   The interaction in love of Father, Son and Holy Spirit is a depth of participation in one another which makes the Trinity a unity.[3]   From the life of mutuality and fellowship of the Godhead love overflows into creation, sustaining the world in being and bringing it to its appointed end in glory.   The gift of God to the Church is the privilege of sharing here and now in the Divine life, and of extending the love of God in the world.   The Church's vocation is to live and witness as a fellowship, a communion which seeks to be one in its ecclesial being, and one in its will to serve its Lord; and in a mutual love which gives individuals, and local communities, and diverse Christian traditions, scope to be fully themselves and to participate equally in the common life.   To stress that the Church is communal is to emphasise relationships; the personal is thus prior to the institutional; the institutional exists to nurture and sustain the relations of human persons joined, as far as is possible for us as creatures, in a resemblance to that Trinitarian life.   This view of the Holy Trinity has profound implications for the Church and for the exercise of all forms of authority in the Church.

20.   In the differentiation of the Persons in the Trinity we glimpse the fundamental principle of order.   The Father begets the Son and the Holy Spirit proceeds, and that is a matter of eternal order in the Being of God, and it is an eternal distinction in relation.[4]

---

3   This unique relational character of the Persons of the Trinity is sometimes referred to as the 'social' Trinity, in which each person of the Trinity is perfectly open to the other and interdependent as in a relationship of mutual giving and receiving. This has led some recent theologians, most notably Jurgen Moltmann, to perceive God the Father through his intimate relationship with the Son, as mysteriously and paradoxically passible yet unchanging, sovereign yet vulnerable. The 1987 Report of the Doctrine Commission, *We Believe in God*, took up this theme:
'... the three Persons are as inseparable in their nature as they are in their creative and redemptive activity. If one suffers, then all suffer, or better, if God is in Christ suffering for our redemption, then this is the sign and guarantee of the Triune God's eternal involvement in human suffering and human destiny. For authentically Christian speech about God is always speech about the Holy Trinity ' (pp. 158-9).
Such reflection has been of immense importance in the thinking and spirituality of many Christians today. However, some fear that it posits a challenge to the sovereignty and impassibility of God; a view expressed in the debate in General Synod in July 1987.

4   Some would see in the Sonship of the second Person of the Trinity an exemplification of dependence on, and derivation from the Father, without any implication of inferiority, but as a proper relation of hierarchical order within the unity of the Holy Trinity.

21.   No human society can mirror the mystery of the divine life perfectly. But we may see in the diversity in which the Father is Creator, the Son Redeemer and the Holy Spirit Comforter and Sanctifier, ground for believing that, at our creaturely level, distinction of function and differentiation of relationship are proper and necessary in the ministerial order of the Church. Creation, Redemption and Sanctification belong to God, and are his gift to his people. The co-operative ministry of the Persons in the Godhead is to be reflected in the co-operative character of Christian ministry in the Church; and God's one will for the world's good is reflected in the ways in which the community is able to act as one through the representing and focusing function of the ordained ministry, and particularly through the episcopal ministry of oversight through the ages. The bishop is focus of unity in Christ and at the same time in the sparkling diversity offered by the gifts of the Spirit. The bishop is the *polupletheia* (the multitude) in his person, the many in the one.[5]

iii.   **The life of the Church**

22.   If the principles of relation and order in the life of the Trinity not only provide patterns for the life of the Church and its ministry, but are the very ground and being of the Church's life, we may take it as fundamental that the Church receives its identity from the God in whom it lives and has its being. Incorporation into the Divine life at Baptism is experienced in the life of prayer. The prayer and thanksgiving of the Church is a sharing in the priesthood of Christ, as his people offer themselves in, with and through Christ, in the power of the Holy Spirit, to the Father. We are counted worthy to stand in the presence of God, through Christ, by the Holy Spirit: we are prayed in by the Holy Spirit. In the Eucharist the Church experiences most fully that communion, in Christ the Father through the Spirit, in which the Kingdom is experienced here and now in the eschatological feast. Its institutional framework is an incarnational expression of that communion, and in this way too the Church is called to be an image of the Trinitarian God.

---

[5]   See V. Lossky, *Mystical Theology in the Eastern Church* (tr. London, 1957), and Appendix I on 'the corporate person'.

23.   As the Church participates more deeply in the life of the Holy Trinity, as it is drawn more deeply into the eternal divine fellowship so the human face of the Church will be conformed to the Triune God and bear God's image in the world. The Church will be an authentic sign only insofar as in and by the power of the Holy Spirit, it takes its identity from Christ, who is head of his body, the Church.

24.   The Church must be prepared to know in its incarnate life that pain and glory which were inseparable in the incarnation of the Son; to follow his example of unconditional, vulnerable, sacrificial love; it must be prepared to walk the way of the Cross, expecting and accepting pain as it accepts responsibilities others evade; and take risks for the sake of the Gospel it proclaims. The Church has to be open to follow Christ's example of *kenosis* and poverty, ready itself to become poor for the sake of the world, ready to bear in its body the marks of crucifixion. The Church cannot escape pain, both within its own life, and in its life in relation to the world. The Church will find its identity, not on the other side of pain and suffering, but in the very midst of it, where God meets us to heal and to restore and to give new life in the power of God's resurrection. The example of the sacrificial life and death of Jesus Christ is the pattern for the obedience of the Church, and for its ministry of service. Indeed it is Christ's ministry that is entrusted to the Church: his shepherding is our shepherding. All ministry is held from Christ in the Church.

25.   We have set out our understanding of the Church's *koinonia*, as a communion grounded in, and modelled upon, the relational and ordered and self-giving life of God the Holy Trinity and the sacrificial life of God the Son. We believe that it is within this broad understanding of the doctrinal context that the Church's ministry of oversight is best explored. That ministry is to be tested by the way it reflects the nature of God's Trinitarian life and love: by the way it images the divine life of perfect sharing, giving and receiving, receiving and giving; and by how far it is prepared to incarnate in its life the pattern of self-emptying in the incarnation of the second person of the Trinity. For guidance on the ways in which these broad principles are to be worked out in the life of the Church, we must turn to Scripture.

PART I: OUR HERITAGE

3

The New Testament

26.   We have not attempted to provide a comprehensive survey of the emergence and development of episcopacy and *episcope* from New Testament times until today. But we seek to give an outline of the story in what follows. We begin with Scripture, for all office in the Church is subordinate to the Word of God, and we hold to the traditional stance of Anglicans that Holy Scripture is the normative and primary witness.

Oversight

27.   The New Testament does not describe a precise form or single structure of ordained ministry which can be proved to have been there from the day of Pentecost, and can in the simplest sense be claimed as a direct and express institution by Jesus. Nevertheless, it clearly points to what have proved to be the consistent and essential elements in the episcopal office. The key concept of ministry within the New Testament is of the ministry of the whole people of God, in which particular and very varied ministries find their place as part of a coherent whole in the life and work of the one body. This 'people' of God seems already to have had a conscious sense of itself as 'gathered', a 'household' (I Peter 4.17, Hebrews 3.6), a people bound together although scattered in exile (Philippians 3.20) and looking in hope and expectation to life together in the city God has prepared for them (Hebrews 11.16).

i.   The role of the Apostles

28.   The story of oversight in the Church begins with Jesus' own calling and sending out of his disciples. In the first generation the primary ministry was that of the Apostles themselves. The Apostles were witnesses to the resurrection of the Lord and received from him a commission to preach the Gospel. In addition to giving historical testimony to the life, death and resurrection of Jesus they were also given the dominical commission to decide matters in dispute and to exercise discipline over those who sinned (the power of the keys). In respect of their first-hand historical testimony

to Christ they could have no successors. And yet they had certain responsibilities and powers which others in the community assumed after them. We have to look partly beyond the first century documents to see what forms of ministry the Church developed as and after the apostles passed from the scene, but the New Testament letters, the Pastoral Epistles in particular, provide a substantial body of evidence for the earlier stages of this development.

ii   The witness of Paul

29.   Paul understood himself to be called to be an apostle. He saw himself as commissioned by the risen Lord to preach the good news. It would be wrong to view Paul exclusively as a missionary; he continued to exercise pastoral concern for his congregations, using letters and emissaries. But it is clear that for Paul, the spread of the Gospel was fundamental to his role. He has received and is to pass on the tradition (*paradosis*). He understood himself to bear the solemn responsibility to 'guard, expound and teach the faith' as he had received it, and also to be a 'pioneer' in bringing it living and creative to the whole human community. He found 'words to address a wide variety of people', those who were already drawn to Christ and those 'outside the community of faith'.[1] Sometimes by sending representatives, sometimes by letter, Paul exercised 'oversight' over congregations he had established. He was the 'father in Christ' of those churches (I Corinthians 4.15; I Thessalonians 2.11) and also their 'nursing-mother' (I Thessalonians 2.7). Paul's oversight included concern to keep the congregation faithful to the truth of the Gospel, to guide the community in ethical matters, to care for the well-being of the people and to see that an offering was sent to the Church in Jerusalem (I Corinthians 16). So Paul believed his call also to involve the feeding and nurturing of the growing flock. He encourages, comforts, exhorts them to live a life worthy of God. The Apostle expected obedience from those whom he led and regarded himself as having authority to discipline (Philippians 2.12 and I Corinthians 16). In the event of a serious breach of moral discipline, the apostle could declare forgiveness to a penitent person, but only 'in the name of Christ' (II Corinthians 2.10).

30.   Paul seems to have exercised personal oversight only over those congregations he had himself founded. Others had different views on the matter, and Paul's opponents in the Galatian churches quite openly

---

[1]   *The Nature of Christian Belief*, House of Bishops (1986), 67-68.

interfered. When this happened Paul had no outside authority to appeal to; he appeals to past experience, and to the Gospel as the final authority.

31.   In Paul's letters the overwhelming emphasis lies upon the Spirit as the creator of both vitality and order in the Church (as in I Corinthians 12-14; order at Corinth being less evident than vitality). The *Didache*[2] shows how there was a natural tendency for local churches at first to value their resident bishops and deacons less than itinerant prophets and teachers, perhaps because they seemed less obviously charismatic. The chief controversy about this settled, domestic 'office' revealed in the Pauline epistles themselves concerns Paul's own standing as an Apostle. The Gentile churches he has founded are themselves the living vindication of the Lord's call to him to be Apostle to the Gentiles; and their membership and acceptance in the one universal Church, with its focus and touchstone of communion in the mother Church of Jerusalem (Galatians 2.1-10), depend chiefly upon the authenticity of his apostolate (I Corinthians 9.1-2). While Paul has much to say of the principles and nature of Christian authority (for example, that its function is to set free, not to enslave (II Corinthians 1.24; 10.8)), he has nothing to say about the practical provision of a formal constitutional structure for his missionary churches; for these he himself, through his letters and his helpers, such as Titus, is the personal focus of loyalty under Christ.

32.   Local leadership emerged in the Pauline Churches too. So Paul asks the faithful 'to respect those who labour *among* you and are *over* you in the Lord' (I Thessalonians 5.12). His letter to the Church at Philippi is to 'all the saints in Christ Jesus, with the bishops and deacons' (Philippians 1.1-2). A number of factors of very different sorts clearly contributed to the selection of these local leaders: God-given natural ability, charismatic gifts, social position, one-time leadership in the Jewish community, wealth and the possession of a suitable home for meetings. As yet there was no consistent use of the terms 'presbyter' and 'bishop'. There is no blue-print in the Pauline letters for any formal relation to each other of those with responsibility for oversight, not are there any details of regular synodical gatherings.   Nevertheless, there is indication that local Christian communities were kept in touch with each other through those who, like Paul, were founders of the communities.   These leaders continued to exercise oversight, to exchange greetings and news, to take collections for

---

2   This short treatise on ethics and Church order is dated by scholars to the first or early second century.

communities in need and to maintain a consistency in belief and practice between the scattered Christian Churches. The example of the Council of Jerusalem in Acts 15, moreover, points to a perceived need in the early Church for a synodical oversight, in which a common mind might be sought and expressed.

iii   The Pastoral Epistles

33.   There are clear indications of the ways in which a ministry of oversight at the local level came into being as the churches endeavoured to be missionary communities spreading the good news; and also at the same time strove to remain faithful to the gospel and to preserve internal coherence and order. Although Paul's letters provide evidence of some community organisation, particularly when his churches faced conflict and differences of opinion, it is the Pastoral Epistles which tell us most about concern for organisation. The emphasis in the Pastoral Epistles is on the task of *guarding* the teaching, of keeping the community faithful to the tradition (I Timothy 1.4). The main task of the overseer is to safeguard the truth of the Gospel. Oversight has to do with managing the affairs of the household of faith and ensuring that the Word is preached and taught in purity. The bishop is responsible both for teaching and for combating false teaching (Titus 1.9; I Timothy 3.2).

iv   Bishops and presbyters

34.   In the Epistle to the Philippians we have mention of the two-fold ministry of bishops and deacons and no mention of presbyters. The name 'bishop' may have been used interchangeably with 'presbyter'. Yet it seems that sometimes there was clearly defined leadership among the presbyter-bishops, especially in that a small nucleus of people amongst the presbyters who had special responsibility to preach and teach (I Timothy 5.17). The model for this was likely to have been the council of presbyters in Jewish communities with a nucleus of rulers at the head of the Jewish councils. The ruling presbyters may be identified with the *episkopoi* of the New Testament, where the overseers are within the presbyterate but have special additional functions. This evidence, together with that of the leading role of James in the Jerusalem Church, and of Timothy and Titus as apostolic delegates in the Pastoral Epistles, are clear indications of the development of an 'episcopal' ministry of oversight.

35.   During the first century some diversity in structure between different regions and local churches was natural. In some churches spiritual leadership was in the hands of a group of elders or 'presbyters', as at Ephesus (Acts 20.17), under the overall authority of the Apostle. On the other hand, the mother church at Jerusalem had a single head, in the person of James, the Lord's brother. This 'monarchical' and apparently earliest form of pastorate could easily be fused with a presbyteral council, in which it would be natural for one man to be held as first among equals if he possessed special charismatic powers or seniority in years and wisdom, or, like Stephanas at Corinth (I Corinthians 16.15-16), was the first convert who then devoted himself to forming a community round him.

36.   In the pastoral Epistles to Timothy and Titus, presbyters are generally plural, the bishop singular, suggesting the probable conclusion that already among the college of presbyters exercising *episcope* or pastoral oversight, one is the commonly accepted president. The likelihood is that in some local churches an initially single pastor subsequently became joined in authority by a council of presbyters, while in others the development went the opposite way; that is, among a group of equal 'presbyter-bishops', one became distinct as presiding bishop without losing the sense of fully sharing a common pastorate and liturgical duty with his presbyteral colleagues, sitting with them in common council much like the twenty-four elders of the Revelation of John of Patmos (Revelation 4.4). In a relationship of primacy among equals, it is likely enough that in some places the primacy was more apparent than the parity, and elsewhere the other way round. It is evident that at the least the presbyterate is a function, order and office in which bishops have a full share. The *Didache* mentions bishops, as does the epistle written by Clement in the name of the Church of Rome to the Church of Corinth about the end of the first century. But in the Rome of AD 100 the name 'bishop' may still be applied to church leaders who are also called 'presbyters'.

v.   The ministry of oversight: an outline of its character and functions in the New Testament

37.   An essential principle which remains constant from the start, through all the variations of form, is that the ministry of oversight is not a human invention but a gift of God to the Church. It is a gift of guardianship of faith and order, enabling the Church to carry on the ministry of Jesus and to become what God intends, in mission, unity and holiness. It is God's

creative act within the young Church to bring into being and to sustain a pastoral office in which an image of his own nature can be seen, and in which and by which he points to the nature of the Church itself.

38.   The New Testament material may be tantalisingly fragmentary about the role and function of those who exercised oversight, but the high calling of those so chosen is clear. They are to model their ministry of shepherding on the ministry of Christ the Shepherd, tending the flock as he tended the flock. I Timothy 3.1-7 has a portrait of a bishop:

> To aspire to leadership is an honourable ambition. Our leader, therefore,
> or bishop, must be above reproach, faithful to his one wife, sober,
> temperate, courteous, hospitable, and a good teacher; he must not be
> given to drink, or a brawler, but of a forbearing disposition, avoiding
> quarrels, and no lover of money. He must be one who manages his own
> household well and wins obedience from his children, and a man of the
> highest principles. If a man does not know how to control his own
> family, how can he look after a congregation of God's people? He must
> not be a convert newly baptised, for fear the sin of conceit should bring
> upon him a judgement contrived by the devil. He must moreover have a
> good reputation with the non-Christian public, so that he may not be
> exposed to scandal and get caught in the devil's snare.

More awesome even than this is the way in which both the Gospel of St. John and the life and witness of St. Paul show that those who are entrusted with oversight are to follow the example of the 'one who came not to be served but to serve and to give his life a ransom for many'. Paul knew what it was to bear in his own body the marks of the Lord Jesus. In his ministry we see something of the high and costly vocation of those called to a task of oversight modelled on the shepherding of Christ.

39.   Accordingly, the most characteristic feature of the New Testament ministry of oversight is that it is pastoral. In the first Epistle of Peter, addressed to the Gentile churches of Asia Minor, the 'presbyters' are instructed to be shepherds after the pattern of Christ who is the Chief Shepherd, and therefore to be living examples to their flock (I Peter 5.24). Those who exercise oversight express the increasing exercise of the pastoral oversight of the Good Shepherd himself in his care of the 'lambs' and the 'sheep' of his flock (John 21.25-7). In the summary of a bishop's principal duties in the prayer preserved in the *Apostolic Tradition* (c. 217), the first duty is 'to feed thy holy flock'.[3]

---

3   Much later, in the thirteenth century, Thomas Aquinas points to this shepherding as the
     highest calling of the bishop, and the only aspect of what had by then become an office of
     great honour and seniority, to which the Christian ought to aspire.

40.   The bishop is to set an example of holiness of life, as one who is himself a sinner, and who enters into the suffering of others. At the same time he is the representative of Christ. So he is both a reconciled and a reconciling person. Like Jeremiah, he is given an authority to speak and act (John 1.9-11) as one who shares his people's pain, and endures their troubles with them. This is an incarnational ministry, and a ministry of the Cross, which always stands under Christ's unique High Priesthood of sinless self-giving; it is the ministry celebrated in the 'Christ-hymn' of Philippians 2.5-11 which speaks of Christ the Servant, whose glory is his self-humbling. In this way the minister with oversight helps his people to grow spiritually into an ever closer likeness to their Lord and union with him.[4]

41.   The highest qualities are required of the bishop, and these are not only spiritual or supernatural but include natural qualities of leadership and common sense (I Timothy 3.3-7; Titus 1.6-9). The charism of the Spirit is able to work in this way through the orderly structures which secure the Church in the world by resident and reliable ministry in the local community. The inclination to serve which puts the bishop humbly at the disposal of the community's needs is, paradoxically, the very essence of the bishop's role as 'overseer'. But true pastoral leadership is always that of a servant, conformable to the example of Christ, in its humility, charity and care of the flock. St. Paul's letters are full of a sense of Jesus as self-giving Servant, and here they clearly echo the Gospels (Luke 22.41-2; John 6.38; 12.24, 26).

42.   The model of conjoined endeavour contains within it the sanction implicit in the idea of the shepherd as guide, and as shepherds the chief task of those who exercised oversight was to gather and keep the flock together, united with one another in their Lord. The ministry of oversight was thus first and foremost a ministry of unity and communion. In all the specific tasks of oversight (preaching, mission, teaching, administering the sacraments, setting an example of holiness), the pastor was maintaining, nurturing and strengthening the unity of the Church and the purity of its faithfulness to the Gospel and thus to Christ.

43.   The emphasis on the task of 'guarding' the teaching, of keeping the community faithful to the tradition (I Timothy 1.4), inseparable from the ministry of unity, implies continuity over time. The main task of the overseer on this view is to safeguard the truth of the Gospel and its purity.

4   Cf. Colossians 2-3; Ephesians 3.

When the Church was attacked, for whatever reason, when it was threatened by heresy and schism, the bishop was its guardian. So, in the conflict with Gnostic dualism,[5] perhaps the gravest crisis of the Church's early history, the Church found the focusing of the apostolic teaching, mission and authority in the bishop an invaluable safeguard against division, and corruption of the faith.

44. But because that responsibility was never to be exercised apart from the community, we see already in the New Testament the beginnings of a pattern of 'consultation with the whole people of God, and especially with their representatives', of listening, of education[6] (the meat which should follow the milk (Hebrews 5.12)). At the Council held in Jerusalem (Acts 15) the Churches came into a common mind on the first issue of practice which threatened to divide the Church. They did so by bringing together the appointed representatives of the congregations and putting the decision to the people. *Episcope* is seen here at the service of communion in preserving faithfulness to the Gospel, and also as a guardianship of order in the community.

45. By visits and letters and meetings of leaders, those who exercised the ministry of oversight in the first generation in New Testament times were already beginning to act as ministers of unity in the maintenance of a single Church of Christ and to carry a responsibility for the handing on of tradition to the future.

46. Because the New Testament material is fragmentary it is all too easy to read back into this picture familiar models of ministry and to see there an episcopacy like our own. The evidence of modern scholarship must make the Church of England now question the Preface to the Ordinal of the Book of Common Prayer which says that it is apparent 'unto all men diligently reading the Holy Scripture and ancient Authors, from the Apostles' time there have been these Orders of Ministers in Christ's Church: Bishops, Priests and Deacons'. But we can say confidently that a ministry of personal oversight clearly emerged as the young Church struggled to be missionary, spreading the good news, as well as to be faithful to the Gospel and to preserving internal coherence.

5   A movement which threatened to infiltrate early Christianity with a belief in a god of evil at war with the God who is good, and with him a pantheon of demigods together with numerous debased variants of points of the faith.

6   *The Nature of Christian Belief*, House of Bishops (1986), 64, 65, 73.

4

Three planes of the Church's life:
episcopal ministry in the post-Apostolic period

47.   In and after New Testament times, then, the bishop came to exercise the ministry of unity in relation first of all to his local community. That community might, in time, come to consist of several worshipping congregations in a 'diocese'. But in the episcopal Churches it has remained spiritually and structurally the 'local church'; there, in acting as a focus of the community's worship and life, and in protecting it as guardian of its faith and order, the bishop stands in a relationship to the community which makes it possible for him to act on its behalf.[1] That is his responsibility in *the first plane of the Church's life*.

48.   In *the second plane of the Church's life,* in keeping contact and communication with the leaders of other worshipping communities on his people's behalf, the bishop has, in every age, been the person who has held the local community together with other Christian communities. Through the episcopal office, by meetings; exchanges of letter; taking counsel together; visitations and prayer for one another, whole communities might remain constantly in touch with one another throughout the Church. So the bishop held in unity the local and the wider Church.

49.   *The third plane of the Church's life,* witnessed in the succession of bishops from generation to generation, signifies and sustains the unity of the Church through the years, marking a continuity in time from the Apostles. For already in the New Testament period it seems likely that there was some way of ensuring the succession of leadership (although authority to certify ministers appears also sometimes to lie within the local congregations, exercised by a council of presbyters).[2] But Timothy has the 'gift of God ... through the laying on of my hands' (II Timothy 1.6), says Paul (cf. Acts 14.23).

---

[1]   This was a notion which owed something to secular legal thinking. But ecclesiologically it was always something more. See Appendix I, *The Corporate Person*, and Chapters 10 and 15.

[2]   Paul and Barnabas were thus commissioned for their Ministry (Acts 13.3).

50.   In this chapter we set out in some detail the traditional episcopal tasks and responsibilities in each of these planes. We do so without seeking to imply that the ministry of oversight is primarily structural. In Acts 20.28ff. Paul, as he leaves for Jerusalem, exhorts the leaders of the community at Ephesus to 'keep watch' over the flock placed in their care as shepherds who will guard and protect and defend. The welfare of the people is uppermost in his mind. All formal aspects of order in the Church must seek to serve God's people in this way; they cannot be an end in themselves.

A.   The first plane: the pastoral ministry in the local community

51.   There are many stories in early centuries of individuals being forcibly ordained to a ministry of oversight. The community testified by its acclaim at his ordination its recognition and acceptance of the bishop's ministry.[3] Those who exercised leadership thus did not come to hold the office apart from the Church; nor did they exercise it in their own right over the Church. Their authority could be recognised to be derived from Christ within the Church: and to be from Christ the Head of the Church, only because it was entrusted to them through his people.

---

[3]   Richard Norris has described the election of bishops in the early Church thus:
From one point of view, the election of a bishop was a local affair, involving the clerics and the laity of the church in a particular town. Elections were conducted - if that is the correct word - in what by modern standards seems to have been a highly informal manner. There is no evidence of systematic balloting. The people's role was essentially to accept or reject a candidate, quite possibly by shouting. No doubt many elections proceeded decorously and smoothly; others, we know, were hotly contested, and a few were accompanied by rioting. In some instances - as for example that of Ambrose - the people turned from the candidates who had been contesting the election to a third party, who was elected by acclamation, in much the same way as Roman troops in the third century created emperors, or the people of a city 'persuaded' some local notable to accept the financial burdens of a year's magistracy. In any case, the process of selection, however disorderly, assured that no candidate whom the people did not on the whole see as appropriate, as one whom they could follow, would come to office. The importance of this fact is clear. The authority of bishops - who were, after all, unlike any civil magistrate, elected to serve for life - depended in part on the capacity of the people to acknowledge their bishop as one in whom they could, so to speak, see themselves as Christians. And the bishop remained accountable to his flock - as witness the nervous care with which Eusebius of Caesarea tried to explain to his people back home how the creed of Nicaea came about and why he had signed it. ('The Bishop in the Church of Late Antiquity', Papers of the Consultation, *Episcope in Relation to the Mission of the Church Today*, background for *The Niagara Report* (1987), 3.1.1, p. 24).

52.   As shepherds, the chief task of those who exercised oversight could be described as feeding and as keeping the flock together, united with one another in their Lord. The ministry of oversight was, therefore, first and foremost a ministry of unity and communion. While that oversight was expressed in preaching, teaching, administering the sacraments, leading in mission, setting an example of holiness, the fundamental duty of the episcopal office was always to maintain, nurture and strengthen the unity of the Church. When the Church was attacked, for whatever reason; when it was threatened by heresy or schism, the bishop was to be guardian of its integrity.

53.   We find in Ignatius of Antioch (c. 35-107) a description of the bonds of love which bind Christ and his people in the Church in microcosm within the local eucharistic community. Ignatius stressed the importance of the community's acting and thinking as one with its bishop.[4] This is a free co-operation of those who are of 'one mind' and share 'one hope'. The bishop stood, as Augustine of Hippo (354-430) was later to put it, 'with' and 'among' his people.[5] In exercising this pastoral ministry of unity in the local community the bishop had a number of special responsibilities.

i.   **The Ministry of the Word**

54.   The Apostles were witnesses to the resurrection of the Lord, and they received from the risen Lord a commission to preach the good news of the Gospel. This was and remained a missionary endeavour. But it is also apparent that the need to ensure the authoritativeness of the transmission of the message to new generations of Christians was closely related to the emergence of a settled official ministry. Irenaeus (c. 130-200) wrote of the bishop as a minister of unity in this sense - as the one who keeps the local church in the apostolic teaching. His conflict with the Gnostics led him to attach importance to the idea that the episcopal office, exercised normatively from a *cathedra*, or 'teaching chair', at the Eucharist, had a responsibility to keep the Church firmly upon its apostolic foundation in the faith. The Gnostics claimed to have a secret tradition handed down from their own teachers. Irenaeus replied that the apostolic tradition was open and public, based on the Scriptures and taught publicly and continuously in those churches which had been founded by the Apostles. Orthodox doctrine was

---

4   *To the Magnesians*, 7.
5   *Enarrationes* in Ps. 126.3, CCSL 40, 1858-9; quoted also in ORC, 39.

to be sought in a church which had a continuous succession of bishops teaching the same faith from its chair. Outward continuity in the consecration of bishops in succession was here a sign of inward continuity of teaching.

55.   So as to discharge his teaching office of guarding the faith and preaching, the bishop needed to give time to study. It was his responsibility to unfold the Scriptures to the people at the Sunday Eucharist, so as to bring the Bible to bear on the events of daily life, and to help the people grow in understanding and knowledge of the faith. In both the East and the West in the patristic period the bishop was theologian and homilist, expounding Scripture and putting the faith into words for his people. In the best of such leadership - exemplified in the West in Ambrose, Augustine of Hippo, Gregory the Great - spiritual discernment, intellectual powers and sound judgement went together.

56.   The early bishop exercised his office as teacher as the local church's principal catechist, presiding over the process of the instruction and discipline of converts. During certain seasons, preaching had the catechumens especially in mind. For example, Gregory of Nyssa's lenten series on The Song of Songs, preached towards the end of the fourth century, discusses the meaning of baptism.

Mission and proclamation

57.   The missionary role of the bishop as minister of the Word altered after the first generations, as his principal function came, on the whole, to be the service of the needs of the life of the existing community. Augustine of Canterbury was sent to England at the end of the sixth century, as a monk-missionary, by Pope Gregory the Great, and consecrated Archbishop of Canterbury at Arles only when the mission was well established. During the period of decline of the Roman Empire and the early mediaeval centuries Christianity spread throughout Western Europe partly by conquest and partly by private enterprise, on the part largely of monastic missionaries such as Boniface (680-754) and Willibrord (658-739). Willibrord was consecrated Archbishop of the Frisians by the Pope in 695, and thus became a 'missionary bishop' rather in the way Augustine had. In the later Middle Ages the emphasis was upon the winning back of Christians who had strayed into heresy, with fresh missionary endeavour a conscious second to that. Bernard of Clairvaux argued in the twelfth century that

Christendom ought to put its house in order before it sought to convert Moslems or Jews to the faith. Again, we see some individuals achieving conversions. But it cannot be said to have been seen as a major responsibility of the episcopate to foster, or indeed to lead, mission in a mediaeval world where every soul in the greater part of Europe was baptised and all could be deemed to come already within the Church's fold.

58. That did not mean that the need for renewal was obscured. Throughout the later Middle Ages preaching concentrates upon the missionary call to the people of God to turn again from their sins and respond to the gracious calling of their Lord with their whole hearts.

ii. The ministry of the Sacraments

Baptism and Confirmation

59. As leader of the worshipping community, the bishop was the proper person to baptise, though from the beginning it was accepted that in case of extraordinary need any ordained minister or even a baptised lay person might baptise. As the normal minister of Baptism, the bishop was the spiritual father of his flock, administering in person or by proxy the sacrament in which the individual was 'born' to a new life. Where he had not personally been the minister of Baptism it was felt appropriate that the baptised person should be welcomed by him to the local community. The principle of episcopal 'confirmation' of an existing baptism by the laying on of hands is to be found in the Spanish Council of Elvira (300-3),[6] where an individual baptised by someone else in a case of 'need' is brought to the bishop. Canon 9 (8) of the Council of Arles, 314, says that a candidate who asks to be admitted to the Catholic fold from, for example, the Donatist sect, must be asked whether he has been baptised in the name of the Trinity. If he answers in the affirmative, he is not re-baptised, for he is already baptised by Christ. However, the candidate receives the episcopal laying on of hands, so that he may receive the Holy Spirit, and is admitted into the community as he desires. The role of the bishop is crucial here, in sealing the membership of the local community and declaring by his action that the baptised person is of Christ's flock.

---

[6] *Patrologia Latina* 84.306, Canon 38.

The Eucharist

60.   The central act of the early Church's worship was always the Eucharist. ' The bread which we break, is it not a participation in the Body of Christ? Because there is one loaf, we who are many are one body, for we all partake of the same loaf' (I Corinthians 10.16-17). Paul is saying that sharing in one eucharistic bread is what makes individuals one in a single communion. They form one body because they participate in Christ. Unity is thus embodied within the community by a sharing in the sacramental bread and wine.

61.   It was early felt to be appropriate that the one who led the community, its pastor and the personal focus of its unity, should act focally and representatively in making possible the participation of the whole community in the celebration of the Eucharist. In presiding over the Eucharist the second century bishop was seen as someone whose authority had the sanction of the Holy Spirit within the continuous succession of the Spirit-filled community. There was direct relationship between things unseen and mystical and the visible and tangible. In Ignatius of Antioch's thought the bishop became the very image or icon of Christ and, as Christ drew believers into fellowship (*koinonia*) with God and with each other, so the bishop becomes the focus of unity for the local church. Ignatius writes:

> Where the bishop is present there let the congregation gather, just as where Jesus Christ is, there is the catholic Church.[7]

As Ignatius describes it, God the Father and the society of heaven are represented on earth by the bishop with his presbyters and the people.[8]

62.   Ignatius's vision of the Church was not an abstract ideal: it was the picture of an actual worshipping community gathered round a table at which a bishop presided. The bishop was not a remote figure but the one pastor, who Sunday by Sunday, broke the bread at the Eucharist, and it was natural to see him as Christ's representative. On the table was a loaf of bread and a cup of wine with which the people in union with their bishop 'made Eucharist'. In this tangible and visible occasion was signified the very life of heaven, and in its sacramental signs Christ himself was present and active in love. At this period, where a church and a diocese seem to have been co-

---

[7]   *To the Smyrnaeans*, viii.1-2; cf. ix.1.
[8]   *To the Trallians*, iii.

extensive and identical, the community remained a congregation, a physical gathering. So a church was, for Ignatius, essentially a eucharistic community. The *ecclesia* is the people of God called out of the world to be one in 'making Eucharist'. Ignatius urges:

> Be careful, then to observe a single Eucharist. For there is one flesh of our Lord, Jesus Christ, and one cup of his blood that makes us one, and one altar, just as there is one bishop along with the presbytery and the deacons, my fellow servants.[9]

63. The notion that all that a bishop was and did, for and with his people, was focused for them when he celebrated the Eucharist with them, was not peculiar to Ignatius. Irenaeus shared it, and it is a constant theme in later writings. In Cyprian, Bishop of Carthage (d. 258) too, the bishop was the normal eucharistic president, with all that that implied for Ignatius:

> The Church is the people united ... to its shepherd. From this you should know that the bishop is in the Church and the Church in the bishop.[10]

In the early part of the third century Hippolytus of Rome in his *Apostolic Tradition* gave a prayer for the consecration of a bishop which called him a 'high priest' whose task is to 'offer the gifts of thy holy church'.[11]

iii. Discipline and reconciliation

64. The bishop's disciplinary role as shepherd, and the ministry of reconciliation implicit in his leadership of the eucharistic community, came together in the exercise of 'the power of the keys'.[12] This 'power' was early understood to be a commission from Christ to decide points in dispute, as well as to give rulings concerning the position of erring individuals within the society of disciples. Gregory the Great in the sixth century described the bishop as a minister of healing, because he is responsible for the ministry of the Word, for leading the eucharistic worship of the community, and for declaring forgiveness to the penitent.[13] The 'power of the keys' was

---

9   *To the Philadelphians*, 4.
10   *Letter* lxvi.8.
11   It is noteworthy that the ordination prayer for a presbyter in the *Apostolic Tradition* does not mention the Eucharist but specifies duties of government and administration. It is only in the fourth century that the bishop becomes the administrator and the presbyter becomes the usual eucharistic minister in the now sub-divided diocese, where he has pastoral charge of one of the local worshipping congregations.
12   Matthew 18.18.
13   Cf. Gregory the Great, *Hom. in Ez.* 1.10.17, CCSL 142.152.

seen in the Reformation period as tied inseparably to the ministry of the Word, for it is through the Word that men and women are won to faith in Christ and receive forgiveness.

65.   It was in line with the understanding that the bishop admits to membership of the local community that in the serious instances where the baptised lapsed into sin - murder, adultery, apostasy - in the early Church, the bishop pronounced the sentence of 'excommunication' on behalf of the community precisely because it was an 'exclusion from communion'. The re-admission of penitents was also a public act of the whole community, symbolising a return not only to a state of forgiveness before God, but also to the community of the body of Christ. Cyprian said that the ultimate decision about the restoration of the excommunicated must be in the hands of the bishop, advised by his presbyters and the 'confessors', and acting before the face of the congregation.

66.   A clear picture of what the disciplinary role of the bishops entailed is already to be found in the *Didascalia Apostolorum*.[14] It was to bishops that the promise of the Lord was understood to have been addressed: 'that which ye shall bind on earth shall be bound in heaven' (Matthew 18.18). The bishop's awesome task was to remember that he also bears the sins of all the members of his flock and so must 'give answer for all'.[15] The text outlines the procedures the bishop was to follow in dealing with cases of sin after baptism, and enjoins upon him the importance of discernment, of sternness with sin, and of mercy in forgiving those who repent.

67.   This responsibility for the discipline of the community probably accounts for the development in late Roman society of the bishop's broader role as the local church's equivalent of a magistrate. In due course much of a bishop's time often came to be taken up in the arbitration and settlement of disputes. (Augustine of Hippo apparently sat every day to give judgement.) The *Didascalia* advises bishops to hear cases on Mondays, so that the parties to the dispute may have time to be reconciled before the Eucharist on the following Sunday. The reputation that bishops acquired for wise and even-handed justice, administered in accordance with the teaching of the Scriptures, led the first Christian Emperor, Constantine, to give their

14   This early Church order, probably composed in Syria in the first half of the third century, was presented as the teaching of the Apostles and of Christ's disciples.
15   This is not at variance with a traditional Evangelical emphasis upon 'binding and loosing' being understood in terms of the proclamation of the Gospel. See para. 64 above.

decisions, under certain circumstances, the effect of law. In the Church itself, however, this activity was clearly understood to be an extension of the role of the teacher.

68.   Mission, teaching, administering baptism and confirmation, presiding at the Eucharist, exercising discipline, were the main - and interdependent - tasks of the shepherding ministry of the bishop in the local community. In all these ways the local community was gathered and held together and welded into a single body through the ministry of unity of the bishop.

iv.   Delegation and sharing: the threefold ministry of bishop, priest and deacon

69.   Bishops and presbyters belong in the New Testament to what is fundamentally a single order of ministerial priesthood. The evolution of the relationship between a unitary *episcope* and a college of presbyters in each locality[16] needs to be seen in the context of the expansion of the Church, and the consequent need for a division of labour in the ordained ministry. The natural bond between pastor and flock was inevitably stretched by the success of the Christian mission, which so enlarged the size of local churches that at least in large cities it soon became impossible for the one bishop to know each of his sheep personally; in rural areas there was a multiplication of small communities. It then became common to assign suburban or rural parishes to one, or in Rome, two presbyters.

70.   This was a division for practical reasons of what was in all but its unitary oversight an identical ministry of bishop and priest which makes the bishop a *primus inter pares* among his presbyters. In the first Epistle of Clement and the *Didache* 'presbyter' and 'bishop' seem to be used as though synonymous. But it is clear in Hippolytus that it had become generally the custom for a local bishop to be consecrated by bishops from other churches, with presbyters being ordained by the local bishop, the presbyters present joining in the laying on of hands. The local bishop was thus maintaining a succession of commissioning in his own see. The bishop not only presided at ordinations but could suspend a delinquent presbyter. The parity lay in 'sacramental power' (in relation, for example, to Baptism and Eucharist)

16   The threefold ministry of bishop, presbyter and deacon, established in Syria and Asia Minor by about 100 AD and soon after found as a general pattern, continued throughout Christendom until the sixteenth century, and still continues in the Churches which preserve the historic episcopate.

rather than in jurisdiction and the responsibility for ordinations. It long remained a disputed question whether bishop and presbyter belong to altogether distinct orders. Jerome thought they did not.[17] Bede emphasises that there is a common *officium*[18] and his thinking was followed by Paul the Deacon (d. 799), Rabanus Maurus and Haymo of Auxerre among the Carolingians of the next generations, and by many mediaeval authors after them.[19]

71.   We have to allow here for a complex process of shifts in understanding and practice which are not now fully accessible to us. In the second century, Ignatius could distinguish clearly between presbyter and bishop. In the fourth, Jerome can ask, 'What does a bishop do that a presbyter does not, except ordain?' There is a case for saying that what took place in this crucial period was a movement from the sacramentally bestowed charismatic endowment of an 'order' to the juridically bestowed power of an 'office'. That would imply that the bishop and the presbyter share the divine commission which makes it possible for them to act locally and representatively in the leadership of the worshipping community, and to administer the sacraments; but not the further commission given within the wider community of the Church, and by its legislative sanction, to lead a local group of congregations and to act as minister of unity.[20]

72.   This interpretation of events, and of the underlying theology, would tend to support the view that the precise form of episcopal ministry is at least to some degree at the disposal of the Church, but that it must enshrine a ministry (which presbyters share) of God-given 'representativeness'. On the other hand, the local church with its bishop is not only a part, but also a microcosm of the universal Church, and the episcopal office rests on something mystically far more profound than 'juridical' foundations, as is strongly emphasised in Orthodox tradition.

17   *Letter* 96.1, and see Chapter 5, paras. 121, 139 ff. and Chapter 6, paras. 185 ff. on the continuing debate, also Chapter 9, Section on 'Personal or corporate *episcope*.

18   *Patrologia Latina* 94.223.

19   See, for example, G.E. Dolan, *The Distinction between the Episcopate and the Presbyterate according to the Thomistic Opinion* (Washington, 1950). The 1557 *Institution of a Christian Man* continues the tradition. A little later than the *Institution* Archbishop Whitgift speaks of 'an equality' of bishops and priests *quoad ministerium*, 'in their ministry' (Whitgift, *Works* III.535-6).

20   See G. Dix, *Jurisdiction in the Early Church* (*Laudate*, 1938, repr. London, 1975), pp. 17 ff., and T.J. Jalland, 'The Doctrine of the Parity of Ministers', in *The Apostolic Ministry*, ed. K.E. Kirk (London, 1946), pp. 309-26.

73.   This early shift in the regular procedure for commissioning for ministry, and the concomitant recognition of the local Church as fully the Church in each place, reflects the growing understanding that the Gospel pointed to a need for a personal episcopal office. There is henceforth to be a chief pastor, whether of a single large city church with a team of presbyters serving it, or of a group of churches in a larger geographical area where the presbyters are looking after smaller local worshipping congregations. This personal pastoral leadership in preaching the Gospel, safeguarding sound doctrine, teaching and governing the faithful, presiding at the Eucharist and admitting to or excluding from Communion, is fulfilled in Christ's name. The pastor 'presents in his own person a small-scale image of the ministry of Christ himself '; his ministry is incarnational in that it exemplifies the way in which God deals personally and individually with men and women through a chosen person who represents him, and in whom 'time and space are transcended'.[21]

74.   The distinction of order which grew up between bishop and priest nevertheless represented a much less fundamental distinction than that which is hinted at in Acts 6.1-6, between the Apostles, who were to devote themselves to prayer and the ministry of the Word, and the seven who were to 'serve tables', that is, to look after the practical affairs of the community.

75.   The earliest deacons were needed primarily for local administrative duties concerned with the care of the poor and helpless. Male deacons also acquired limited liturgical functions, especially of reading the Gospel. They never presided at the Eucharist but, in an extension of their New Testament function of practical service, they prepared the vessels and 'served' at the Lord's Table. As the office of the bishop changed and became more administrative, deacons might become senior administrative officials at diocesan level, on the bishop's personal staff. These senior 'career' deacons not infrequently succeeded to episcopal office themselves, as did Gregory the Great, once Deacon of Rome. This special relationship of the diaconate to the episcopate was somewhat obscured by the development of a three-tiered ordained ministry, in which bishop, priest and deacon came to be distinguished as successive grades.[22] These three grades came to be seen as corresponding with the three grades of Old Testament ministry, of high priest, priest and Levite. But the Old Testament typology did not create the

21   *Growing into Union*, ed. C.O. Buchanan, E.L. Mascall, J.I. Packer, G. Leonard (London, 1970), pp. 13, 75-6.
22   *Deacons in the Ministry of the Church*, pp. 4-6.

threefold Christian ministry. That is a structure which owes its origin to the second century Church's inheritance from the sub-apostolic generation, in which an originally two-tiered ministry of bishop-priest and deacon,[23] passed into the three-tiered ministry to meet practical needs; with the presiding bishops representing apostolicity.

B. The second plane: collegial oversight linking the local to the universal Church

76.   From an early date, neighbouring bishops came in person to lay hands on a local bishop at his ordination. By this act they signified assent[24] to the election. A newly elected bishop, chosen by his flock, was duly entrusted with the charism of episcopal office by other bishops, who represented universal recognition. When the Council of Nicaea in 325 decreed that a Bishop should be consecrated by the Metropolitan with, if possible, all the Bishops of the province or, if not all, a minimum of three, the Council understood its minimal three to be representing the wider fellowship. In time neighbouring bishops sometimes came to play an increasingly prominent role in the actual process of selection, again representing thereby the catholic Church, which in them gave its consent to, and demonstrated its fellowship with, the local bishop.

77.   Through their fellowship with one another, at first expressed in informal ways and without formalised patterns of conciliarity, the presiding clergy of local churches were a living embodiment of the sacred tradition about Jesus Christ. This shared ministerial responsibility for safeguarding what was taught in the churches also goes back to an early stage. In Paul's discourse to the presbyters of Ephesus (who are here called 'bishops': Acts 20. 24-28) these leaders of the church were warned to be guardians of the true tradition against the false doctrine that threatens the very existence of the Church of Christ's redemption.

---

23   Cf. Jeremy Taylor, *Episcopacy Asserted, Works*, V.20.

24   The meaning of this assent was practically spelled out in the participation of the local bishop in regional synods of his peers; and it meant that he embodied in his person two roles. Just as, in virtue of his election, he represented the Christian people of his own town for the universal Church; so in virtue of the assent of the larger Church, symbolised by the mode of his ordination, he represented, in and for his flock, the whole corpus of local churches that were knit together in the communion of Christ - the universal people of God. And this too, needless to say, was both a basis for his authority and a definition of his accountability. The bishop embodied in his office - and no doubt too in his person - the tension between locality and universality. R. Norris, *op. cit.*, pp. 24-5.

78.   The pastoral responsibility for teaching the faith through proclaiming and expounding the Word was thus early understood to be a collective responsibility of pastors acting together. It was exercised in councils of gathered bishops but also 'collegially' in the looser sense of being a perpetual responsibility of bishops together, even when they were not formally assembled in Council. Yet the mutual correction and corporate maintaining of the larger community in faith and in order by those exercising *episcope* was not altogether without its structures and more formal modes of proceeding from the beginning (Acts 15). Christians met to consult together, both in local areas and with the intention of bringing representatives from the whole Church together, when there were differences or when decisions needed to be made. It is apparent from the first that the dynamics of such meetings were such that they cannot be seen to stand on their own, either as making decisions independently, or as involving only the leaders of the community. At the first Council at Jerusalem Paul and Barnabas came from Antioch and met the leaders of the Jerusalem community for discussion. Their conclusions were evidently accepted by the Jerusalem community as a whole, the message which was sent back with Paul and Barnabas came from the Apostles and elders together with the whole Church (Acts 15.30). The letter was read in Antioch to the whole community (Acts 15.30).

79.   Already in the middle of the third century Cyprian, Bishop of Carthage, describes the bishops as a collective body which unites the various eucharistic communities and maintains them in the truth. As he sees it, it is the faith and experience of a local church which its bishop brings to a Council of bishops.[25] In Council the bishops represented communities which were complete in themselves. The catholic Church was not a superior level of church organisation; it existed already in the particular churches and they were never swallowed up in a collective identity.[26] Yet the churches bore a family likeness to each other in spite of their differing situations and outlooks. They met together to discover a common mind so that each might be strengthened in its catholicity, made more obedient to Christ, and better able to represent him in the world.

25   At the 1988 Lambeth Conference the bishops were spoken of as 'bringing their dioceses with them'.

26   See paras. 72-3.

80.   There were thus individual bishops, each of whom possesses the episcopate in its fullness, and also a single episcopate in which all are joined together in unity. This seems to be the meaning of Cyprian's well-known sentence:

> There is one episcopate, in which each individual bishop has a share in the whole.[27]

Cyprian argued that there is a plenitude of episcopal charism when a bishop joins his teaching with that of other bishops. This was not a matter of majority opinion, but of the forming of a common mind in consultation, and the seeking of unanimity. Together, and waiting on the will of God, the bishops assembled in synod, with Christ present in their midst and the Spirit in their hearts, were seen as seeking a truth which is in each mind, but in its fullness greater than any individual can grasp or state. Cyprian had some experience of Councils of bishops, and he knew that there would be insistent partisan views and recalcitrant minorities. But he did not want to see a mere overriding of such parties; rather he looked to patient seeking of a faith in which all could agree.

81.   It was a natural consequence of this linking of the communities that restrictions were imposed on what individual churches could do. Frequent contacts between churches acted as a check upon private idiosyncrasies in teaching, at the same time as they maintained order. A local church, like that at Corinth, could not simply get rid of its clergy without satisfying other churches in the universal fellowship that the deposed clergy had been unworthy of their office.

82.   With the development of conciliarity came the leadership which was given to certain prominent churches which looked back to foundation by one of the Apostles. The book of Acts shows the expanding Church looking to Jerusalem for leadership. The second century Church came to find in churches of apostolic foundation, and in the West especially Rome where St. Peter and St. Paul died, a touchstone of authentic communion.

83.   The conciliar functions of bishops were still clear after the fall of the Roman Empire, despite the practical difficulties in unsettled times of assembling many bishops in one place. In the West in the Carolingian period the emphasis came to fall upon local Councils or Synods, assemblies of bishops of the emerging 'national' Churches; and at that time there was

[27]   *On the Unity of the Catholic Church*, 5.

certainly no sense that conciliar government was in any way in conflict with acceptance of a Roman primacy. In the West the prime role of the See of Rome was to protect the local episcopate in national churches from being oppressed and exploited by the secular powers. From the late eleventh century in the West there was a vigorous assertion of a monarchical papal primacy, which took its rise from the conflict with the temporal authority of Emperor and kings, but which had the result of discouraging recognition of the need for conciliar consultation. Even then there were Lateran Councils (notably that of 1215), which enacted significant legislation in matters of faith and order. And, during the 'conciliar movement' of the fourteenth and fifteenth centuries, there was a reaction against extreme claims of the papal monarchists, and an attempt to make conciliar government the supreme organ of authority in the Church in the West. Although it was not easy either in the period of the dominance of a theory of papal plenitude of power, or during the conciliarist debates, to see the bishop of Rome as a focus of unity *among* his fellow bishops (that is, to see primatial and conciliar government as complementary), the two always in practice existed side by side.

84. There is also a real sense in which the collegial responsibility of bishops has always involved all the faithful. The declaration of faith in baptism, from its earliest forms, required the candidate to make an intellectual assent as well as a commitment, and to express his or her faith personally before the community, as well as to God. And there was always room for teachers who were not among those entrusted with oversight in the community. (This became especially important in the case of monastic theologians, such as Anselm of Bec, who was later to be Archbishop of Canterbury (d. 1109), and then with the beginning of the universities in the Middle Ages, and with them the academic or professional theologian who was, from time to time, asked to help Councils of bishops.)

85. The recognition of the community's right and sometimes duty to engage in critical discussion of decisions on faith and morals and order is thus very ancient. The role of those who were not ordained has, however, varied a good deal. In the fourth century higher education was not restricted to Christian clergy and Augustine of Hippo contended with articulate and sophisticated pagans who wanted to know why a Christian Empire had not been saved by the Christian God. But after the time of Gregory the Great at the end of the sixth century, when the Roman Empire was falling into ruins, and the West was in danger of losing its heritage of classical learning, a clerical monopoly emerged. Christian scholars became

the preservers and carriers of learning in a violent age. Charlemagne encouraged the giving of serious attention to the teaching given to cathedral clergy; and in monastic schools all over Europe the reading of Scripture and the Fathers was kept alive. For much of the Middle Ages the laity were largely illiterate, and questioning by those who could read, and studied Scripture for themselves, was not encouraged by a hierarchy which feared that they would go astray in their simplicity. This comparative repression of the voice of the people contributed to the explosive call of the dissenters in the late Middle Ages and sixteenth century for the Bible in their own language and the right to read it.

C.   The third plane: the link between the local and the universal Church over time

86.   The third plane of the Church's life was, in the nature of things, a post-apostolic development, coming into being as successors had to be found for the Apostles. Succession is an inseparable part of the Church's life, for it is the vehicle of continuity. The outward succession of persons in pastoral office in faithfulness to the Gospel is sign and assurance of continuity in one, true, apostolic faith. The early Church found that in practice, such a visible succession of bishops in the local churches was a means of safeguarding the authenticity of the preaching of the Gospel in each.[28] Irenaeus stresses the importance of being able to 'enumerate those who were established by the Apostles as bishops in the churches, and their successors down to our time' because they can be pointed to as having consistently taught the one faith.[29] He describes how the Apostles commissioned Linus, and how Clement of Rome received 'the episcopate' from him. 'He had seen the Apostles and associated with them, and still had their preaching ringing in his ears ... in the same order and succession the apostolic tradition of the Church and the preaching of the truth has come down to our time'.[30] Thus, the existence of a visible succession of the ministry instituted by Christ was of importance from the earliest period in establishing the Church's identity and preserving it from syncretism, or confusion with heretical sects. To the secular historian the development of episcopal government appears a potent factor in ensuring the survival of Christianity in the hostile Graeco-Roman world. Within the Church, then, the episcopal ministry both symbolised, and

---

[28]   A most valuable discussion on this theme is to be found in *Growing into Union*, ed. C.O. Buchanan, E.L. Mascall, J.I. Packer, G. Leonard (London, 1970), pp. 77 ff.

[29]   *Adversus Haereses* 3.3.1.

[30]   *Adversus Haereses* 3.3.3.

secured in an abiding form, the apostolic character of the Church's teaching and mission.

87.   The continuity of oversight was always inseparable from the ecclesial continuity of the whole community in sacramental life and in faith. The bishop was successor to the Apostles by virtue of his being head of a particular church, president of a local eucharistic assembly. Apostolic succession inheres, not in the person of the bishop alone, but in the Church as a whole. So when Irenaeus writes succession lists, he does not trace the successor through consecrations but through thrones or sees, that is through entire local communities from which the consecrating bishop comes. He is not interested in the individual bishop apart from his flock. Apostolic succession is not a succession of individuals on their own, but an unbroken continuity of communities: for there can be no true succession of persons that is not mediated through the community.

88.   Consecration by the laying on of hands was, from the New Testament onwards, the normal means of commissioning for pastoral ministry. However, the act of consecration by validly consecrated bishops was not sufficient alone. It was also required that the whole community recognised God's gift of the Spirit for oversight to a person and, again, that the one being consecrated was being consecrated for a local community. So Cyprian wrote:

> Novatian is not in the Church, nor can he be reckoned a bishop ... for he does not succeed to anybody.

89.   So, the complementary elements of the gift of the Spirit for oversight and the continuity of commissioning through the episcopate, with the acceptance of the pastor by the people, came together in ordination.

90.   A particular difficulty about unity and continuity arose in times of schism. When the Christian community was divided the separated parties did not agree where continuity was to be found. And a bishop could not be a sign of unity if he could not be recognised by the whole Church. During the Donatist schism in north Africa in the fourth century the earlier standard patristic view that outside the catholic Church there could be no authenticity of ecclesial life or of ministry was severely tested. Augustine argued that if valid baptism could be received outside catholic unity, orders ought also to be recognised as valid even if they had been administered in schismatic communities, provided that the schismatic community could trace its ordinations back to a bishop in apostolic succession. This put a

considerable weight on linear succession. Although the bishops who met at Nicaea in 325 would never have thought that a person consecrated by three bishops in any circumstances whatever had claims to catholic recognition, it became the custom in the mediaeval West to think of ordination by a bishop in apostolic succession as the exclusive and sole test of ministerial and ecclesial validity.

91.   The outline we have sketched here of the development of episcopal ministry in patristic and mediaeval centuries unavoidably omits much local variation in style and practice, and presents the changes which took place over time in only the most general terms. We have, however, found that both the emergence of the early theology of episcopacy in Ignatius, Irenaeus, Cyprian, Augustine and others; and the historical evidence, draw a picture of an emerging and continuing ministry of unity, exercised in the three planes of the Church's life, and acting as the natural point of intersection between them. Collegial government by *presbyter-episkopoi* in some of the earliest local churches seems largely to have given way to the 'monarchical' bishopric of the second and third centuries by an unforced process of development to meet pastoral need; and thereafter to have become normative until the divisions of the sixteenth century, which resulted in radical reorganisation of Church-government in some parts of Europe. It remains, of course, a question of crucial importance ecumenically whether a personal, as distinct from a 'collegial', ministry of oversight can claim the support of Scripture and of the practice of the earliest communities so securely that such a ministry ought now to be looked to by all in a future united Church. We take the view that these are not necessarily incompatible structures, and that a personal episcopal ministry complements and enables collegial ministry in the Church. It is to this issue in particular that we address ourselves in the next chapter, and we return to it throughout our Report.

5

Episcope and episcopacy in East and West

A. Bishops in the Orthodox and Oriental Orthodox Churches[1]

92. The Orthodox would claim to have maintained the episcopal office without a break in tradition, from the early patristic era. The role of the bishop has been invested with a great deal of theological significance in Orthodox thinking. Certain concepts stand out:

  i. the bishop as bearer of the Apostolic tradition
  ii. the bishop as head and president of the eucharistic community
  iii. the bishop as head and representative of a local community
  iv. the bishop as link between Christian communities

To these may be added a further area, concerning the perception of the bishop and the way in which he embodies his ministry.

i. The bishop as bearer of the apostolic tradition

93. The bishop is teacher and transmitter of the faith of the Apostles. The Orthodox emphasis in the matter of apostolic succession is primarily on the succession of communities in Orthodox faith. The tactile succession is regarded by the Orthodox as essential primarily because it serves this end, and provides a demonstrable link with the authority of the apostolic communities. But the early succession lists of (for example) Irenaeus and Hegisippus are more concerned to list the orderly succession of bishops in a see than the actual 'consecrators'.[2]

---

1   There are differences in the episcopal office in the Churches of the 'Byzantine' (those Churches in communion with Constantinople) and 'Oriental' (among them the Armenian, Syrian, Coptic, Ethiopian and Indian Churches) families. The separation of the non-Chalcedonian Churches from the fifth century has led to a certain amount of separate development. We speak here chiefly of the 'Byzantine' Orthodox tradition.

2   Cf. para. 87. Ware underlines the importance of this link of the succession with a local community very strongly:
'The act of consecration, even when correctly performed by other validly consecrated bishops, is not by itself sufficient; it is also required that the new bishop shall be consecrated for a specific local church. Unless he succeeds legitimately to a throne, he has

94.   As well as being part of an apostolic community, the bishop must be *teaching* the apostolic faith to be in the apostolic succession. Most Eastern episcopal consecration rites include an examination of the candidate's faith far more rigorous than that of the Anglican rites. There is a clear aim of preserving doctrinal purity. A bishop who departs from this will not only be recognised to have done so, but may be rejected by his people.

ii.   The bishop as head and president of the Eucharistic Community

95.   For the Orthodox, the bishop is the centre of the community and 'guarantees' its life and its sacraments. Membership of the Church depends on being in relation to the bishop - who, of course, in earlier centuries was not a remote but a familiar locally known figure. Liturgical expression of this survives today in Orthodoxy in the formal bow to the bishop's stall or throne by a presbyter before he begins to celebrate the Eucharist. He is mentioned by name in prayers and bowed to if present. The *fermentum* of the bishops of Rome - the practice whereby the Pope sent fragments of Bread from the Eucharist at which he presided to the presbyters presiding over the Eucharist at the other parish churches of the City of Rome - gave expression to the same understanding.[3]

96.   A further dimension of the concept of the bishop as the centre of the eucharistic community is that he is also its representative. Although it is true that some of the Eastern Churches have a long tradition of lay theologians and lay participation in decision-making, it still remains the case that ecclesiologically the Orthodox would answer the question 'who represents the laity?' by 'the bishop, of course'. The bishop is the local representative of the *laos* - the people of God. This must be appreciated in order to understand what sometimes seems to Western eyes a lack of enthusiasm among the Orthodox for lay representation and participation in synods. It is also relevant to the issue of the 'representation' of women in the episcopate. The principle is that the bishop is not simply exercising a

---

3

no true share in the grace of apostolic succession, but is merely a pseudo-bishop' (*Bishops: But What Kind?*, p. 13).

This link between the local Eucharist and the bishop has been largely lost in Anglicanism. The 1662 Book of Common Prayer does not mention the Diocesan Bishop by name in the Prayer for the Church Militant and until recently Confirmations - an occasion when parishes *did* see their bishop - were not held in a Eucharistic context. The provisions for the mention of the bishop's name in the ASB Rite A Eucharist has gone some way to rediscovering the link between bishop and parish Eucharist. Cf. ORC, Munich, 47.

function among the many as a personal 'right'; he focuses and represents the whole body of men and women among whom he serves.

97.   The impression must not be given, however, that the bishop can act in isolation. The classic images show him in a network of *relationships* - with deacons at his side, and surrounded by his presbyters and people. The modern Anglican concept of a synod (with three 'houses' which can veto each other's decisions) has not developed in Orthodoxy; but in many parts of the Orthodox diaspora there are assemblies with both clerical and lay representation. In addition, the Bishop's Council - a relatively small group of senior clergy and laity who advise the bishop - has manifested itself in various forms. In situations such as that which is found in modern Greece, the gathering of all the clergy of a diocese is not unknown. In Russia the Holy Synod - *Sobor* - has included laity and clergy since 1917. The *Sobor* for the celebration of the Millennium of the baptism of Russia in 1988 continued to exemplify this tradition. In June 1990, the *Sobor* which elected Patriarch Aleksi II was composed of all the diocesan bishops, the heads of the monastic houses, and one clerical and one lay representative elected from each diocese. Each had an equal vote in the secret ballots.

98.   The relationship between the laity and the bishop was strengthened, in many parts of the Orthodox and Oriental Orthodox world, by the *milet* system imposed by Arab and Turkish Muslim conquerors. Each non-Muslim ethnic or religious grouping was treated as a separate entity within the Muslim state, enjoying (within certain limits) the right to maintain its traditions and organise its internal affairs. With the disappearance of a Christian civil power at local and national level, the bishop became the head of the whole Christian community in relation to all aspects of its life. He was thus resorted to by senior lay leaders and looked up to by the whole Christian populace as their father and protector to whom they could come for help and advice. Something of the approachability and (in the right sense) dependence that this experience helped to foster, can still be found in many parts of the Orthodox world.

iii.   The bishop as head and representative of a local community

99.   Orthodoxy sees the bishop as part of the structure of a local expression of the universal Church and not the bearer of a *potestas* or even a charism *in vacuo*, as it were. Liturgically this is expressed in the consecrating of a man *for a named see*. He is the father of the community

and 'the one through whom all charismatic manifestations of the Church must pass, so that they may be manifestations not of individualism but of the *Koinonia* of the Spirit and of the community created by it'.[4] On such a view a bishop without a community is a nonsense.[5]

100.   This is in keeping with the fact that frequently - probably normally in the earliest centuries - a bishop was chosen from *within* the community that he was consecrated to serve and therefore already shared in its 'apostolic tradition'. He was chosen from and by the *laos* (clergy and laity together) - originally by election. In practice this ideal has been lost in most of Orthodoxy, and candidates for the episcopate are usually selected by the Governing Synod of the Church - itself usually made up exclusively of bishops. The Moscow Council of 1917-18 laid down that henceforth bishops in the Russian Church should be elected by the clergy and laity. Political conditions have hitherto made the application of this rule impossible within the Soviet Union and Diocesan Bishops are appointed directly by the Patriarchate.[6]   In the changing situation it is not impossible that the 1917/1918 regulations will soon be implemented.

iv.   **The Bishop as the link between the Christian communities**

101.   The bishop is the bond between the local Church and the Church Universal in a way that no other minister can ever be. The local Church does not have to find representation to meet with representatives from other Churches; the **bishop** is its representative.[7] Central to this idea is the concept of 'the charismatic equality of bishops'. *Each* bishop is the icon of Christ and the channel through which the plenitude of the Spirit's gifts flows into his community. In this respect there is no difference between a

---

4   J. Zizioulas, *Being as Communion* (London, 1985), p. 199.

5   The link between bishops and a named see seems weaker among the Oriental Orthodox (where there are some interesting parallels with early Celtic monastery-based bishops). Thus, in the modern Coptic Church there can be found a 'Bishop for Social and Public Affairs' and 'Bishops General' with no dioceses. In India until the last century there do not appear to have been any defined diocesan structures in the ancient Syrian community, even when there was more than one bishop in the country.

6   T. Ware, *The Orthodox Church* (London, 1963), p. 299.

7   'Collectively the shepherds of the Church, whether apostles or bishops, speak with an authority which none of them possess individually ... together the members of the episcopate become something more than they are as scattered individuals, and this "something more" is precisely the presence of Christ and the Holy Spirit in their midst ... the "common mind" which the assembled bishops reach under the Spirit's guidance is not merely their mind but Christ's', T. Ware, in *Bishops: But What Kind?*, p. 16.

patriarchal see and a small rural one. The historical fact of having been founded by an Apostle, or the size and dignity of a city, may afford honour and even a degree of jurisdiction to a particular see, but it does not make its bishop more a bishop than any other. 'In the Orthodox Church such sees ... have never been distinguished from the rest of the episcopal sees from the point of view of the essential apostolic continuity in which both the historical and the eschatological perspectives merge into a synthesis.'[8]

102.   Nevertheless, it is manifestly true that Orthodoxy does afford a particular role to certain sees, especially in relation to gatherings of bishops. The primatial role of the Patriarch is an important one: he can summon the bishops in a given area, and it is generally through him that the decisions of the gathering are expressed and executed. Historically such an office has been attached to certain sees for reasons already noted, and especially to Constantinople.

103.   The autocephalous metropolitan areas of Orthodoxy are one of its distinguishing features. Zizioulas begins a defence of regional authorities, in terms of the necessity to preserve (on an incarnational basis) cultural and historical diversity:

> Different cultures mean different ways of approaching the faith and expressing it. It also means differing creeds and liturgical customs. All this can be achieved and served through regional synods united with each other in a universal communion of Churches. These regional synods should have authority on all matters, including doctrine, for it is mainly in matters of doctrine that expression of cultural diversity is evident and necessary. As in the early Church, baptismal creeds can be local. The movement towards ecumenical expressions of the faith in the early church has been mistaken as a tendency to subject the local level to the universal level of Church unity, whereas the proper way of understanding it is that of mutual sharing of the churches' experiences and problems so that by common consent they might remain different without betraying the fundamental principles of faith.[9]

The existence of the patriarchates does not obscure the fact that Orthodox bishops attend local Synods or 'international' Councils as the heads of their communities - a fact reflected in the ruling that classically only *diocesan* bishops may vote. The decisions which they articulate must be in line with the faith of those communities and must be *received* by those communities in order to have any lasting authority.

8   Zizioulas, *Being as Communion*, pp. 203 ff.
9   Zizioulas, 'The Institution of Episcopal Conferences: An Orthodox Reflection', in *The Jurist* 48 (1988): 1.

104.   It is thus incumbent on bishops to listen to the bishops of the rest of the Universal Church. 'Keeping in line' is not a stifling restriction, but is designed to enable the whole Church to speak and advance together, and therefore with authority. A bishop who finds himself 'out on a limb' should question his own position before the collective mind of the episcopate.[10] This sense of group solidarity, at least within each autocephalous Church, is much stronger in the Orthodox Churches than in the more individualistic West. Nevertheless, it has the same roots as the Western understanding of episcopal collegiality in the Roman Catholic Church and the developing sense of the solidarity of the House of Bishops within the Church of England.

v.   The perception of a bishop

105.   An important aspect of the Orthodox perception of a bishop in countries where the Orthodox Church is deeply rooted is his physical appearance. Beards and, increasingly, dress are simply matters of personal taste or fashion in the West. Not so in the East. The bishop has a *persona*. He is a *patriarch*, or image of the Father and the incarnate Son and has a beard as an expression (with strong significance for the Orthodox), of the masculinity that goes with the concepts. Flowing robes, hat, veil, staff, all contribute to an overall image and create a kind of 'otherness' which does not necessarily mean distance or unapproachability in a Western sense. Indeed, traditionally, Eastern bishops are very approachable, holding court for all to present their pleas, as Ambrose of Milan did at the end of the fourth century in the West.[11]

106.   Connected with the image of the bishop as Father or Patriarch is that of him as a Holy Man.[12] This is an elusive concept, but an important one. From the sixth century both Byzantine and Oriental bishops were chosen

---

10   At the same time the possibility of not reaching an agreement is faced by Fathers such as Cyprian - who 'considers that in the event of disagreement no compulsion should be brought to bear upon the dissident bishop or bishops. The Church, while still preserving unity, will be obliged to live for a time with the fact of this disagreement' (T. Ware, in *Bishops: But What Kind?*, p. 17). Cyprian's immediate context (*Letter 55*) is a discussion of the possibility of restoring the lapsed after a period of persecution. Cyprian would not have argued for toleration of diversity in all aspects of Christian belief and practice.

11   But this has to be kept within bounds. Bernard of Clairvaux wrote the *De Consideratione* for Pope Eugenius III (1145-53) to encourage him to make himself rather less approachable, so that he might have time for prayer.

12   *Bishops: But What Kind?*, p. 168.

from monks and marked out by special head-gear. Archdeacons do the administration; bishops are praying, liturgical figures. Again this does not necessarily mean that they are remote; on the contrary, they are to be an image of the 'Holy One in your midst'. (In recent times both the Church of Ethiopia and the Coptic Church have elevated a monk directly to the Patriarchate.)

B. The Background to the Reformation in the West

i. The local community

107. Some changes of emphasis during the Middle Ages in the West altered the perceived relationship of the bishop to the local community. What had begun in the early Church as a pastoral office exercised within a small local community, with a close interdependence between the bishop and his people, the shepherd and his flock, became increasingly a public office in a wider world. Some bishops of wealth and high family became important imperial officials in the late Roman Empire, with concomitant administrative and judicial responsibilities.[13] As the Empire disintegrated into barbarian kingdoms, bishops in general became important in their cities as sustainers of order. When the Empire fell, the ancient pattern of city dioceses gave way to a new pattern of division by tribal boundaries, and later by feudally determined regions, so that it became a practical impossibility for the bishop to preside at more than a few of the Eucharists in his widespread diocese. At the same time, under the new systems of land-tenure, medieval bishops were unavoidably powerful as feudal lords and magnates. Although the mediaeval period had many holy and dedicated bishops - England's Archbishop Anselm (c.1033-1109) notable among them - numerous (and sometimes justified) criticisms were made in the later Middle Ages against prelates who flouted their wealth before the poor and behaved without humility. By no means all English bishops at the Reformation were guilty of lordliness and neglect of their pastoral duties. Many of Cardinal Wolsey's colleagues were assiduous, even before Henry VIII put his reforms in hand, in overhauling diocesan administration, improving standards among their clergy and taking their pastoral responsibilities to the laity seriously. But there appears to have been sufficient resentment in Europe at large against 'proud prelates' to create a sense that the ancient function of the bishop as leader of 'the Church in each place' was no longer being carried out as it should be. To some of the Continental reformers this seemed to

---

13   For example, Basil the Great (c.330-79).

have created an emergency situation in which order in the Church no longer stood under the Gospel.

Leadership

108.   Underlying these very broad changes of perception were several changes of practice which contributed in time, and in various ways, to the diminution of the bishop's role as local pastor. The growth of the notion of grades[14] of ordained minister - deacon, priest, bishop - in a 'ladder of honour' like a civil service, began to create a sense that there was a barrier of intermediaries between the laity and their diocesan family head.   In the medieval period bishops' palaces increasingly tended to spawn officials such as chancellors and chaplains. In these centuries, the archdeacon often saw to tasks which the bishop no longer performed in person, such as visitations, the administration of justice in ecclesiastical courts and appointments to ecclesiastical offices.   This proliferation of officers and subordinates meant that it was no longer obvious to the people that 'the whole cure of the diocese is in the bishop', as Jeremy Taylor was to put it in the seventeenth century.[15]   Further: it was not uncommon for a bishop (who might spend long periods away from his diocese) to leave his pastoral tasks to an assistant or suffragan bishop, so that even the strictly episcopal functions his officials could not discharge (they could not, for example, conduct confirmations) were thus delegated.[16] In mediaeval England such assistants were frequently Irish diocesans who preferred to live in England, or abbots given titular 'dioceses' in parts of the world which were not under Christian rule, and where, therefore, they could not reside as bishops themselves.   So they, too, presented an anomaly in relation to the pastoral cure to which they had nominally been consecrated.

The Eucharist

109.   Certain   liturgical changes had taken place in the pattern of celebration of the Eucharist   since ancient times, and although these do not relate exclusively to the bishop's role as eucharistic president in the local community, they have some relevance to the process by

---

14   With the addition of a series of minor orders such as sub-deacon and acolyte.
15   *Episcopacy Asserted, Works*, V.156.
16   On suffragans, see Chapter 11.

which the bishop ceased to be seen by his people as their natural and proper celebrant. The bishop's seat or *cathedra*, from which he expounded the Scriptures, became separated from the altar. As the celebrant began to stand with his back to the community, with the table placed at the end of the church and not in the middle, a sense of separation between bishop or priest and community, was created. The words of consecration began to be said in a whisper and eventually in silence. Masses were sometimes said by the celebrant without a congregation present, so that the sense of the essentially community character of the Eucharist was easily lost. The symbolic, if largely inadvertent, shutting out of the people had the effect of tending to separate bishop or priest from his community in other ways.

Discipline

110. Another change in emphasis in the role of a bishop gradually came about in relation to discipline. In the early Church the bishop was not only the one who normally admitted converts to the community in Baptism; he was also the officer who excommunicated sinners and re-admitted penitents on behalf of the community. In the mediaeval period this ancient episcopal role was still important in the case of serious offences. In penitential canons of 963, for example, we find the instruction that every bishop shall be in his episcopal chair on Ash Wednesday to hear penitents. But as the bishop's integral relation with the community was weakened, so the function of penance as a way of convincing the community of a person's sincerity and change of life was obscured. As a result, it came sometimes to be seen rather as a means of giving satisfaction to an angry and punishing God. Coupled with this went the development of a strong view of the personal power of the bishop to bind and loose - a power which was seen as supremely vested in the Bishop of Rome as Peter's successor. Whether exercised by the Pope or by some other bishop, it came often to be experienced as a claim to jurisdiction far beyond the scope of the power of the keys when it was used to bring recalcitrant princes to heel, and was therefore a political and civil as well as spiritual penalty; and when it was threatened as a sanction where taxes were not paid as due to the Church, and could thus be used to strike fear into ordinary people. Beneath these developments, however, the theological understanding that the bishop has a responsibility to act, in justice and in mercy, as the disciplinary officer of the community, remained intact.

Private penance

111.   A further change in this area was the result of the move to a general
system of 'private penance'.[17]   The shift to infant baptism in the West from
the end of the fourth century meant that it became unlikely that anyone
would go through life without committing some relatively serious sin after
baptism, or at the least a great many venial ones, which cumulatively
weighed heavily on the soul.   The provision for dealing with penitents was
gradually modified to meet the need for a repeated repentance throughout
the community.   By Carolingian times this pastoral need was being met by
private confession to a priest, who imposed a penance according to a scale
laid down in canons published in the area so that everyone might be treated
equally.   The penitential canons were often ratified by kings, but in intention
they were the provisions of bishops.   Bishops were thus continuing to
oversee the system juridically, even though what passed between penitent
and confessor was not a public but a private matter, and pressure of demand
made it impossible for the bishop to hear all penitents himself or to
pronounce absolution personally in every case.

ii.   Councils

112.   The conciliar functions of bishops, and also their collegial
relationship, fell somewhat into abeyance during the mediaeval period,
partly as a result of great practical difficulties in assembling many bishops
in one place in the unsettled society of the period after the fall of the Roman
Empire in the West.   Local Councils did meet, particularly in the
Carolingian period, as assemblies of Bishops of what may loosely be called
'national' churches; and at that time there was certainly no sense in the West
that this was in any way in conflict with acceptance of a Roman primacy.
From the late eleventh century, vigorous assertion of papal plenitude of
power tended to diminish the role of Western conciliar government in the
Church.   Nevertheless, the series of Lateran Councils called from 1123, and
successive Councils in the thirteenth and early fourteenth centuries,
maintained the custom of conciliar meetings, and in the 'conciliar
movement' of the fourteenth and fifteenth centuries conciliarity[18] was put

---

17   Compare *The Priesthood of the Ordained Ministry*, Faith and Order Advisory Group (1986),
        64.
18   With the proviso that others besides bishops had voting rights at times, so that this high
        doctrine of conciliarity coexisted with a limited doctrine of episcopal collegiality.

forward as a challenge to what had by then come to seem to some a 'papal monarchy'. The idea that a Council could be used to maintain a 'balance of power' in the Church and to redress grievances and initiate reforms was cherished by several of the sixteenth century reformers, and the calling of the Council of Trent was in part a response to their pressure.

iii.   Continuity

113.   Continuity of the Church's life through time went on uninterrupted in the ministerial succession of bishops in the mediaeval West, and also in the East, after the schism of 1054, which was deemed by neither side to have interrupted that succession.   But there were significant challenges from as early as the twelfth century, from the groups which criticised the wealth and lordly behaviour of the higher clergy, and some of which argued that the traditional pastoral ministry ought to be abolished.   By the late fourteenth and early fifteenth centuries, Lollards were proposing a form of voluntary association, with democratic government in the Church, as a way of escaping 'clerical tyranny'.   It was a movement in Bohemia which led to the first decisive break of the Reformation period in the orderly succession of a mutually recognised ministry.   The Bohemians had pressed for the giving of communion in both kinds to the laity, which had for some generations ceased to be the custom.   As a result of the ensuing row, they had been left without a bishop.   They could get priests only by sending ordinands to Italy, where the ordinands had to forswear their beliefs before they could receive episcopal ordination, and then returned to break their oath and administer wine to the laity.   When the Bohemians consulted Luther, he told them to proceed as the Apostles had done in the New Testament: to pray for the guidance of the Holy Spirit, individually and together, then to meet and to elect those who seemed suitable.   The leaders of the community were then to lay hands on them and commend them to the people.   The theologians of the Council of Trent reacted against such claims to an exclusively 'popular' making of ministers, by asserting the view that the power to ordain lay with bishops alone.   Both sides thus tended to lose sight of the three-point balance of the doctrine that ordination requires the calling and gift of the Spirit; acceptance by the community; and a link with the order of the Church universal.[19]

19   See paras. 174 ff.

C.   The Roman Catholic Church since the sixteenth century

i.   From the counter-Reformation to Vatican I

114.   Although the Counter-Reformation produced new models of episcopacy in such exemplary figures as St. Charles Borromeo (Archbishop of Milan from 1560 to 1584) and St. François de Sales (Bishop of Geneva from 1602 to 1622), it did little to advance or clarify the theology of episcopacy or to resolve theological uncertainties inherited from the later Middle Ages such as those concerned with the relationship between the Pope and other bishops; and the precise nature of episcopal consecration. The First Vatican Council of 1869-1870 was an interrupted Council with an unfinished agenda, although its definition in the Constitution *Pastor Aeternus* of the primacy, universal jurisdiction and infallibility of the Pope led many to believe that, in future, General Councils of the universal episcopate would be judged unnecessary and so discontinued. *Pastor Aeternus* was originally planned to be part of a much larger scheme, *De Ecclesia;* taken out of this wider context it could hardly avoid being one-sided in its treatment of the relationship between the Pope and the rest of the episcopate, even though it was stressed that the 'power of the Supreme Pontiff is far from standing in the way of the power of ordinary and immediate episcopal jurisdiction by which the bishops ... feed and rule, as the shepherds, the particular flock assigned to them', and argued that the jurisdiction of the bishops is 'asserted, confirmed and indicated by this supreme and universal shepherd'.[20]

ii.   Vatican I completed by Vatican II

115.   It was this one-sidedness that Vatican II sought to redress by its own balanced treatment of the whole field of ecclesiology, in what is beyond doubt its key document, the Dogmatic Constitution on the Church (*De Ecclesia*), entitled *Lumen Gentium*, promulgated in 1964. The theology of episcopacy which was presented in *Lumen Gentium* and confirmed in other conciliar decrees (such as that on the Pastoral Office of Bishops in the Church, *Christus Dominus*, of 1965) is briefly summarised here in the

[20]   *Pastor Aeternus*, III.

following paragraphs:

116.　While Vatican I is in no sense denied, the ecclesiological context is rather differently envisaged in *Lumen Gentium*. The controlling model of the Church is now that of the pilgrim People of God, and the statement that the Church of Christ '*subsists* in the Catholic Church' (*L.G.*I, 8) is an amendment of an earlier version which simply said that the Church of Christ *is* the Catholic Church, an amendment designed to give Roman Catholics the possibility of recognizing the Church of Christ in other ecclesial communities.

iii.　The local Church

117.　Special emphasis is placed on the diocese, upon local or 'particular churches, which are constituted after the model of the universal Church; it is in these and formed out of them that the one and unique Catholic Church exists' (*L.G.*III, 23). This affirmation endorses a theology of the Church as communion in which 'the total community which constitutes the Church is not made by adding together the local communities (meaning the dioceses), for each community, however small, represents the Church in her entirety'.[21] Such a theology of the Church as communion undergirds the continuing work of the Anglican-Roman Catholic International Commission.[22] Its effect is a revision of the 'pyramidal' theology of the Church. The fullness of the Church is already found in the local, diocesan Church.[23] But that local Church cannot stand in isolation; it is to be in communion with the other local churches through its bishop.

iv.　The bishop in his diocese

118.　It is also declared in *Lumen Gentium* that others within the dioceses are called to share in the mission of the bishop, especially the priests who are associated with their bishops as 'prudent co-operators of the episcopal college ... and constitute, together with their bishop, a unique sacerdotal college' (*presbyterium*) (*L.G.*III, 28). A whole chapter (*L.G.*IV) follows on the subject of the laity, who are clearly understood to 'share the priestly,

---

21　J. Hamer, *L'Église est une communion*, Paris, 1962, as quoted in J.M.R. Tillard, *The Bishop of Rome* (London, 1983), p. 150.
22　Cf. *Final Report*, Introduction.
23　Cf. *Christus Dominus*, II.i.11, and paras. 99 ff., 309, and Chapter 15.

prophetic and kingly office of Christ' and whose 'dignity and responsibility', it is stressed, should be recognised and promoted by the Church's pastors.[24] *Christus Dominus* stresses the corporate identity of the people of the diocese as 'a section of the people of God' who constitute 'one particular Church in which the one, holy, catholic and apostolic Church of Christ is truly present and active' (II.i.11).

v. Collegiality

119.   A major achievement of Vatican II in the theology of episcopacy is the fuller articulation of the doctrine of episcopal collegiality. Bishop Christopher Butler has acknowledged that, 'the Council expresses itself very cautiously about the immediate sub-apostolic period', affirming only 'an historical and theological continuity between New Testament times and that later, clearer period and its belief that this continuity is due to an apostolic intention'.[25] In this sense there is in the contemporary Church a succession from the original college of the Twelve, 'with Peter at its head', to the apostolic college of the bishops 'in communion with one another and with the Roman Pontiff in a bond of unity, charity and peace'. Though this college has no authority unless united with the successor of Peter, 'whose primatial authority ... remains in its integrity', it is nevertheless affirmed that 'together with their head, the Supreme Pontiff and never apart from him, they (i.e. the order of bishops) have supreme and full authority over the Universal Church, ... exercised in a solemn way in an ecumenical Council' or by such form of corporate action, approved by the head of the college, which will allow 'a truly collegiate act' to result. Individual bishops are set out over particular dioceses but 'as they are members of the episcopal college ... each is bound to have such care and solicitude for the whole Church which, though it be not exercised by any act of jurisdiction does for all that rebound in an eminent degree to the advantage of the Universal Church'. Though such language is cautious and guarded it has the revolutionary effect of restoring to the college of bishops its universal role. In the ultramontane theology which seemed to dominate Vatican I, diocesan bishops were seen as little more than local delegates of the Pope and of the Roman Curia. *Lumen Gentium*, however, rejects the view that bishops are

---

24   A particular emphasis is placed upon the bishops' duty to proclaim the Gospel, pastorally and in mission, and to be spiritual guides of their flocks (*Christus Dominus*, II).

25   B.C. Butler, *The Theology of Vatican II* (London, 1967), p. 86. All other quotations in this section are from *Lumen Gentium*, in the edition of Flannery, *Vatican Council II: The Conciliar and Post-Conciliar Documents* (Leominster, 1981).

to be regarded as 'vicars of the Roman Pontiff'; on the contrary they are 'vicars and legates of Christ' and 'exercise the power which they possess in their own right' (*L.G.*III, 27).

vi.   Episcopal Conferences

120.   The principle of collegiality, which in the strictest sense refers to the Universal Church, has implications for the life of particular Churches within nations or cultural regions. It is first of all declared that 'it has come about through divine providence that, in the course of time, different Churches set up in various places ... have their own discipline, enjoy their own liturgical usage and inherit a theological and spiritual patrimony'.[26] This section of *Lumen Gentium* (III, 23) not only upholds the traditions of 'the ancient patriarchal Churches' but also commends contemporary Episcopal Conferences, which are judged to be 'in a position to contribute ... to the concrete realisation of the collegiate spirit (*collegialis affectus*)'.

vii.   The distinctiveness of the episcopate

121.   The second most important achievement of Vatican II in its reflection on the nature of episcopacy is the clear and unequivocal statement, that 'the fullness of the sacrament of orders is conferred by episcopal consecration'.[27] For centuries theologians had debated whether the episcopate was really a separate or distinct order from the presbyterate. In the sixteenth century the view adopted by many of the Reformers, that the presbyter was already in the fullness of orders, could claim some precedent.[28] However, since the liturgical reforms of Paul VI, this consecration is now called episcopal 'ordination' in order to make it clearer that the distinction between bishop and presbyter is of a sacramental character and not merely of a jurisdictional nature. It is seen as conferring on bishops a threefold gift; the *munus docendi* (the gift of teaching), of the *munus sanctificandi* (the gift of the office of sanctifying), and of the *munus regendi* (the gift of ruling or governing); this corresponds to the threefold office of him whom they represent and in whose person they act, Christ himself, who is Priest (*Pontifex*), Teacher (*Magister*), and Shepherd (*Pastor*). This clarification

---

26   Cf. Article 34 of the Anglican 39 Articles on 'rites and ceremonies'.
27   *Episcopali consecratione.*
28   See paras. 70, 139, 185 and discussion in Chapter 9, section on 'Personal or corporate *episcope*', para. 307 ff.

has now made possible a more balanced view of the three gifts and the development of a theology of the ministry of teaching which can affirm that 'among the most important duties of bishops that of preaching the Gospel has pride of place' (*L.G.*III, 25). It takes two things to constitute a man 'a member of the episcopal body'; episcopal consecration must be accompanied by 'hierarchical communion with the head and members of the college' (*L.G.*III, 21, 22).

viii. Developments since Vatican II

122.   The Second Vatican Council was important not only for the filling out it brought to the rather one-sided ecclesiology of Vatican I, but also for the new avenues it opened up for further exploration: a process upon which the Roman Catholic Church has been engaged since the end of the Council in 1965. It has often been a painful and contradictory process; marked by hope but also by tension, controversy and frustration.   Profoundly important matters are still being clarified: the relationship between the Bishop of Rome and the other bishops in communion with him; the precise theological status and authority of such instruments of the *collegialis affectus* as the International Synod of Bishops or the National Episcopal Conferences; the proper application of collegiality within the structures of each particular diocese (with regard both to the presbyterate and to other members of the People of God).

123.   Perhaps the most important practical area of growth since the Council has been the development of the Episcopal Conference, described by Canon 447 of the 1983 Code of Canon Law, as a 'permanent institution' and as 'the assembly of the bishops of a country or of a certain territory, exercising together certain pastoral offices for Christ's faithful of that territory'. According to Canon 450 of the new Code of Canon Law, 'all diocesan bishops and those equivalent to them in law, all coadjutor bishops, auxiliary bishops and other titular bishops[29] who exercise in the territory a special office assigned to them by the Apostolic See or by the Episcopal Conference', are members by right of an Episcopal Conference while 'ordinaries of another rite may be invited, but have only a consultative vote, unless the statutes of the Episcopal Conference decree otherwise'. Other

29   In the Roman Catholic Church, the term 'suffragan bishop' is not used in the same way as it is among Anglicans, that is, to describe 'auxiliaries'. It retains the original meaning it had in the Church of England with reference to the relation between an Archbishop and his 'suffragans', i.e. the bishops of dioceses within his Province.

titular bishops and the Nuncio or Apostolic Delegate are not members by law. Recent efforts to clarify the role of Episcopal Conferences include discussion at the Synod of Bishops in 1969 and in 1985 and a draft document of the Vatican Congregation for Bishops which has been circulated to all the Conferences; an international colloquium on the nature and future of Episcopal Conferences, organised by a number of Catholic universities in response to the call of the 1985 Synod for more theological study was held at Salamanca in 1988.[30]

124. Controversy within the Roman Catholic Church has been focused in recent years upon two sensitive areas which are of interest to all episcopally ordered Churches. The first concerns the authority of a primate among his fellow-bishops. A case which arose in the late 1980s in the United States of America has raised the delicate question of the rights of the Pope (whether acting in his capacity as Patriarch of the West, or as Universal Primate) to discipline a diocesan bishop either by removing him from office or by suspending him from the exercise of some of the authority which inheres in his office.

125. The second area concerns the appointment of bishops. A number of recent papal episcopal appointments, notably in Germany and Austria, have been made in the teeth of the opposition of cathedral chapters. These have raised the equally delicate question of the rights of the Papacy to set aside or modify the rights of a local church to exercise through its cathedral chapter a significant role in the choice of its own bishop. In fact, capitular election, though once the rule, is now an exception limited almost exclusively to German-speaking countries.[31] These rules do not govern the appointment of bishops in the Eastern Churches in communion with Rome.

126. The Second Vatican Council, like other Councils in the history of the Church, has perhaps opened up almost as many problems as it has solved. The often painful search for the right solution to such questions continues; it continues in the context of the Roman Catholic Church's commitment to and involvement in ecumenical dialogues, both bilateral and multilateral, which themselves have been wrestling with difficult questions of ministry and

---

30   For the papers of this colloquium see *The Jurist* (Studies in Church Law and Ministry: Catholic University of America, Washington, D.C., XLVIII (1988), 1.

31   The present rules governing episcopal appointments in the Latin rite will be found in the memorandum provided by Dr. Brian Ferme and printed as an Appended Note. See Appendix II on The Normal Procedure in the Roman Catholic Church of the Latin Rite for the Appointment of Bishops.

authority. We note these difficulties here as examples of the processes of development at work under the Holy Spirit in episcopal as in non-episcopal Churches in our own time, and as affording some valuable comparisons with problems of autonomy, interdependence, and episcopal collegiality at present confronting the Anglican Communion.

D.   The Old Catholic Churches

127.   The Old Catholic Churches of the Union of Utrecht are small, but their distinctive witness is indissolubly linked to a certain vision and theology of the local church and of the episcopate. They do not trace their ecclesial identity to the Reformation. The origin of the Old Catholic Church in the Netherlands is to be found in the early eighteenth century protest of the members of the Cathedral Chapter of Utrecht against what they considered to be the intolerably high-handed and unjust treatment of their Archbishop by Rome, which was guilty in their view of scandalously disregarding the rights not only of Cathedral Chapters but, more importantly, of local churches and their bishops. In a recent paper the present Archbishop of Utrecht underlines the fact that the Pope continued to be prayed for by name in the Canon of the Mass until early in the present century; commenting on this practice, he remarks: 'By this I want to make clear that the primacy of the Pope was not the problem for the Church of Utrecht, but rather it was the way in which he exercised authority, and that, especially, the rights of the local church were not respected by Rome, which assumes the right of the appointment of bishops to be its own'.[32] The origin of the Old Catholic Churches in most other countries is to be found in the conscientious refusal of a number of Roman Catholics, particularly in Germany and Switzerland, to accept the definition by the First Vatican Council in 1870 of the infallibility and universal jurisdiction of the Roman Pontiff; a refusal largely grounded in the conviction that this definition did violence to the historic Catholic understanding of episcopacy.

128.   The Old Catholic Churches have therefore a very high doctrine of the rights and dignity of the local church (by which they understand the diocese). In principle bishops are always elected by the clergy and representative laity of their own diocese, although in some countries (notably in Poland) the diocese makes a list of three candidates from which the Prime Bishop makes his choice. The idea of auxiliary or non-diocesan

[32]   Antonius Glazemaker, 'Communion and Episcopacy: An Old Catholic Perspective, in Communion and Episcopacy', ed. Jonathan Draper (Cuddesdon, 1988).

bishops is not looked upon with favour; but where they exist, they have a voice but no vote in the International Bishops' Conference.

129.   In principle again, each diocese has its own diocesan synod (with representation of the laity as well as of the clergy) and in some countries (as in the Netherlands) there is also a general, or national, synod.   There is some variation between the different national Churches as to the precise status and the constitutional rights and powers of such synods; but however high the degree of authority accorded to them it has to respect what is considered to be the inherently and properly 'episcopal' authority of the bishop in his own diocese, and of the bishops acting collegially in questions of faith and morals.

130.   At another level, the IBC (International Bishops' Conference of the Union of Utrecht) does exercise a real, if limited, authority.   It exists to maintain and strengthen communion between the bishops who are its members and the Churches they represent and it possesses the powers necessary for the effective exercise of this duty.   Its doctrinal basis is the 1889 Utrecht Declaration of Faith, and it alone can admit bishops to membership of the Union, having first recognized the validity and canonical regularity of their consecration.   Although the Conference claims 'no independent jurisdiction in the single churches of the Union', it does claim competence 'for all questions which touch the maintenance of fellowship between the Old Catholic Churches as well as the relations with other Churches' and it imposes on each bishop the obligation 'to carry through the resolutions of the IBC in his area of jurisdiction'.   It is moreover 'authorized to express its opinion on questions of faith and morals, which are in dispute; to make declarations of faith and basic matters for the community of the Old Catholic Churches over against other churches; as well as to make agreements, if occasion arises, with other Churches concerning mutual church relations.'[33]

131.   The Old Catholic bishops are well aware of the limited nature of their authority in a divided Church.   In 1970 they called for a new ecumenical Council to restore the broken unity of the universal Church, and made the following appeal:

> We ask all Christians and especially all bishops and responsible leaders of
> the Church to become more and more conscious of their joint

[33]   The quotations are from articles of the International Bishops' Conference, agreed on 12th September 1974.

responsibility for the possibility of a new truly universal Council which
can speak and take decisions for all Christians[34]

Nevertheless, since this was written, the German Old Catholic Synod,
meeting in May 1989, has made a decision in principle to open all three
orders of the threefold ministry to women. This may be thought to call into
question the clear picture given above of the institutional structures of
authority in the Old Catholic Churches. It remains to be seen how the other
Churches of the Union of Utrecht will react to this decision, and also how
the German Church would react to any attempt on their part to prevent this
decision from being implemented.

E. *Episcope* in the Churches of the Reformation and their heirs

132.   Since the sixteenth century, a variety of polities has been proposed by
way of alternative or modification to the episcopal structure.[35] Even
amongst those which originated in the most extreme conviction that ministry
could only legitimately be derived from the local congregation of 'gathered
believers' (acting at the direct prompting of the Holy Spirit and free, under
the same Spirit, to change their ministers at any time), there has in almost
every case come to be some supra-congregational authority. At the risk of
generalising fine differences, we sketch here the main traditions of the
'Reformation' Churches and their heirs. The Church of England, which has
always regarded itself as 'Catholic and Reformed', is considered in the next
chapter.[36]

133.   Four principal themes have run through the debates:

---

[34]   Cf. J. Visser, *Episcopacy Today: An Old Catholic View*, in *Bishops: But What Kind?*, p. 50.

[35]   The phrase 'non-episcopal Churches' is unsatisfactory, and although we have not avoided it altogether, we would point out that *episcope* is exercised in the Churches we describe in the following sections, and that many of them would regard their ordained ministers as corresponding with the *episkopoi* of the early Church.

[36]   'Some would regard the ministry of the Church as solely derived from and subject to the will of the Church, the Spirit-bearing Body, while others regard it as the original gift of Christ to his Church, to be preserved in unbroken succession', said the Archbishop of Canterbury in a sermon of 1946. 'These are not,' he added, 'necessarily contradictory views'. Printed in *Church Relations in England* (Conversations between representatives of the Archbishop of Canterbury and representatives of the Evangelical Free Churches in England) (London, 1950) p. 6.

(i)   the manner of God's gift of ministry to the Church and the extent to which the detailed arrangements of ecclesiastical polity are legitimately at human disposal.

(ii) the question whether there is only one 'order' of ministry or more.

(iii) the relationship of the elements of 'order' and 'office' in the commissioning of the ministry.

(iv) the balance of corporate and personal in the higher structures of Church-government.

Broadly, the tasks of governing in the Church are seen to be:

(a)   the organisation of common effort in mission and to meet social need, such as that of the poor.

(b)   the maintenance of discipline justly and evenly throughout the wider community.

(c)   the enacting of legislation binding on the participating congregations and with their consent (at least by representation).

(d)   the making of administrative arrangements (for example, in the setting up of boards, agencies, committees with specific responsibilities, and answerable to the Churches).[37]

(e)   to oversee the calling and commissioning of ministers so that it may be possible to ensure their 'regular calling' and allow for the possibility of their moving, as ministers, to serve new congregations.

i   The Charismatics and the Baptists

134. Among the Churches most resistant to the idea of supra-congregational *episcope* in the sixteenth century were the Anabaptists and those other radical communities whose emphasis was supremely upon the return to what were believed to be the most important New Testament principles of Church order, and above all upon the freedom to be Spirit-led. The 'holiness' and 'pentecostalist' Churches which are the heirs of the latter have in very many cases formed associations, as have the Independent and Baptist Churches which are in part the descendants of the former. It remains the general view among these communities that the local congregation or community of believers is the basic ecclesial unit, 'having, under God, the power to govern and administer its own life and activities

---

[37]   We might add by way of illustration: in-service training, pensions, trusteeship of property, ministerial grants, building loans and grants, arbitration in disputes, and much else.

and owning no outside human authority with power to control its actions'.[38] The essence of the idea of the Church Meeting is that Christ is the only Head of the Church and that he is present as risen Lord when his people meet in his name. The purpose of the meeting is to share in worship, prayer, discussion and reflection with the aim of discerning together by the guidance of the Holy Spirit the mind of Christ. The Declaration of Principle which forms the basis of the Baptist Union states:

> That our Lord and Saviour Jesus Christ, God manifest in the flesh, is the sole and absolute authority in all matters pertaining to faith and practice, as revealed in the Holy Scriptures, and that each Church has liberty, under the guidance of the Holy Spirit, to interpret and administer His laws.

The local congregation chooses its pastors at the leading of the Holy Spirit, but does not regard them as having received a permanent commission or 'order' which is indelible. They remain answerable to the community as its officers.[39]

135. In such 'congregational' structures, as they have gradually associated together for certain purposes of Church government, a balance has had to be achieved between respect for the rights of self-government of the congregation and the organisational and 'oversight' role of any associations they may form, and of their chairmen or presidents. Although in principle self-governing congregations may delegate certain responsibilities to a central association and its instruments and give them authority to take action on their behalf, it is not always a straightforward matter to maintain an agreed balance of authority.[40] Nevertheless, it has proved generally necessary, especially in the matter of mutual ecclesial recognition and the

---

38   F. Bacon, *Church Administration: A Guide for Baptist Ministers and Church Officers* (Bristol, 1981), p. 32.

39   In the Pentecostalist-Roman Catholic Conversations, in which Anglican charismatics took part, there was relatively little comment on ministry. It was, however, agreed that there is 'unity ... between the formal structure [of the eucharistic celebration] and the spontaneity of the charismatic gifts' (34, *Growth*, p. 428).

40   Northern Baptists in the USA, for example, found that there was a tendency for conventions in each state and their secretaries to acquire too much power, and a study by the American Institute of Management in 1961 suggested that the General Council and General Secretary should be given more authority, with co-operating societies and boards as programme agencies of the Convention. The Southern Baptists discovered a tension between an 'aristocratic' government by state representation on boards and standing committees and the 'democratic' government by the 'messengers', from each Baptist Church co-operating with the Convention, who make up the Convention itself. A.C. Piepkorn, *Profiles in Belief* (New York, 1978), II.398.

mutual recognition of ministries[41] to form some kind of association with wider authority than that of the congregation.[42] The principle which governs the Church Meeting governs decisions of the Association and Union. Their decisions are reached by the same theological approach and will then be considered in local churches. Their authority will then be confirmed as of Christ if the local church so decides.

136. British Baptists have always laid great stress on the local gathered community of believers as the visible expression of the Catholic Church in that place. At the same time they have also emphasised the importance of association. The Church is wider than the local congregation. So from the beginning they formed Associations for mutual support, prayer, encouragement, shared mission, etc. Through meetings of Messengers appointed by the churches they drew up Confessions of Faith, issued prayer calls, wrote pastoral letters and so on. When churches called pastors they frequently consulted with churches and leaders with whom they were in regular association. Among early Baptist documents and confessions of faith there are references to their belief that a duly constituted Assembly, Association, Union had ecclesial significance, even though it did not have authority to over-ride the authority of the local church. Out of this concept grew the development of the national Baptist Union with some supra-congregational authority, but it has to be recognised that it is a derived authority and cannot be imposed against their will on the congregations from which it is derived. Many Church Trusts provide for the Union to arbitrate in disputes between pastors and churches, or between members and leaders, or between church and Association, etc., and lay down that the decision of the Union shall be binding on both parties. This is significantly different from the concept of derived authority. At the same time the wording of the Trust usually makes it quite clear that in normal life the authority of the Union in no way takes away the authority of the Church Meeting.

---

41   See further, the section on 'Mutual recognition and reconciliation of ministries' in the chapter on *Ecumenical Progress.*

42   Among the General Association of Baptists, Article (11) of the 'Separate' Duck River Association says that 'No person has the right to administer the ordinance of the Gospel (i.e. the sacraments) unless he is legally called and qualified'; the National Primitive Baptists' Convention of the USA insist that ministers must 'come under the imposition of a presbytery by the majority of the Church of Christ', that is, that they must be commissioned by a supra-congregational ministerial meeting. Piepkorn, II.443, 448.

137.   Churches of these traditions characteristically recognise 'deacon' and 'elder'. Nevertheless, there is considerable variation in the understanding of the ministerial functions and standing of the two. In present-day English Baptist churches, for example, there may be deacons and elders; only elders; or only deacons, in a particular congregation. These are in principle appointed by the congregation. They are responsible for 'managing the affairs of the church from day to day and ... guiding and leading the church in its decisions'.[43] These are not, however, ordained ministers, for it is understood that such ministers must be overseen in their training and appointment by the General Superintendent of each Area (who may be a woman).[44] Reformed Mennonites in the USA retain a strongly congre-gationalist system while admitting bishops as officers as well as the 'deacons' and 'elders', who in these churches are the pastoral ministers.[45] There is thus no consistent pattern in this ecclesiology, in the number of types of officer, or in their appointment by the local community or a wider authority; nor is it agreed in any regular way in churches of these traditions as a whole whether ministerial office is in any sense to be regarded as an 'order'.[46]   Some would want to deny even that it is an office. The Society of Friends stress that elders and overseers do not receive 'elevation to an office but rather recognition by the Meeting that certain friends have or may develop a special capacity to be used in serving the spiritual and temporal needs of members of the

---

43   Bacon, p. 33.
44   *Ibid.*, pp. 12-15.
45   Piepkorn, II, pp. 376-7.
46   The Report's discussion of Ministry is widely felt to reflect an underlying doctrine of the Church not easily reconcilable with Baptist convictions as to the centrality of the local congregation of gathered believers and the place of the ordained Ministry in relation thereto. It is not found reassuring to be confronted with the affirmation that the ordained Ministry 'is constitutive for the life and witness of the Church' (II.A.8) - even when the situation is partly retrieved by a later recognition that the ordained Ministry 'has no existence apart from the community' (II.A.12). Baptist concern in this general area has widely been expressed in relation to the issue of lay presidency at the Lord's table. It is of course importantly true that the Report does not absolutely confine such presidency to the ordained Ministry (Commentary 13, 14). Yet the directive thrust of II.A.13, 14 is heard as an affirmation of a basic distinction between 'ordained' and 'lay' that raises questioning. It is not that Baptists in general deny the calling and gifting of different people for different functions within the Church of Christ. If a lay person presides at the Supper it is by commission of the Church, so authorising him or her for this 'ministry'. The differentia is that it is the *local* church that so commissions on (so it is believed) the authority of Christ entrusted to it. It should be clear that important questions about both the nature of ordination and the centrality and authority of the local church are here posed. *A Supplement to the Baptist Union Council's Response to Baptism, Eucharist and Ministry*, prepared by The Advisory Committee for Church Relations, p. 5.

Meeting'.[47] Yet a responsible function repeatedly and regularly accepted and exercised by the same person looks indistinguishable from an office, even if it is not so designated.

138. The ecclesiological stress in Baptist Churches[48] is strongly upon the first plane of the Church's life, that of the local community or congregation with its pastor and his assistants.[49] Nevertheless, the General Superintendent is appointed by the Baptist Union Council after a process of selection and nomination in which local churches in the Area and the representatives appointed by the Associations within the Area participate. This exemplifies, in principle and in practice, a view of *episcope* as both corporate and personal. The Superintendent holds an office not an order. Nevertheless, the Superintendent is described as an agent of the Union. It is not questioned that his or her task is to be 'pastor of pastors' (*pastor pastorum*). He or she is also charged with the task of providing pastoral oversight for the churches, encouraging and advising them in their mission. Part of his or her task is to provide leadership in the Area in taking initiatives for the furtherance of Christian witness and education. He or she is there to facilitate ministerial settlements and also to represent the Baptist Union at the appropriate level in ecumenical discussion and action.

47   *Church Government*, London Yearly Meeting of the Religious Society of Friends, (London, 1968) p. 856.

48   There are many Baptist Churches not in the Baptist Union, nor in any other Unions such as the Strict and Particular Baptist Union, the Old Baptist Union, and Grace Baptists. So it cannot be assumed that every local Baptist Church stands where British Baptists generally stand. The Baptist Union of Scotland has quite a different ethos from the Baptist Union of Great Britain, as instanced by radically different approaches to the Inter-Church Process. Again the Baptist Union of Wales, though affiliated with the Baptist Union of Great Britain as the Scots are, has a distinctive Welsh culture and a strong independency stress. The Baptist Union of Ireland is now separate.

49   Bernard Green, General Secretary of the Baptist Union of Great Britain, comments on the implications of this emphasis for the participation of Baptists in ecumenical activity:
' There are two major levels of ecumenical activity - national and local. We now have a clear mandate for national involvement. What happens locally is for the local church to decide. We cannot force or commit local churches; but then which denomination can whatever its view of episcopacy? In practice many will follow the lead given by the Union. Some will not. Some have publicly dissociated themselves from the decision while positively staying in full and active membership of the Union. A small number of churches has left the Union because they are strongly anti-Roman Catholic and do not wish to be guilty by association. They will thus become independent.'

ii.   The Reformed and the Presbyterians[50]

139. The means of supra-congregational liaison in Reformed and Presbyterian churches have from an early date shown greater consistency than those used by Churches deriving (broadly speaking) from the 'radical' Reformation. The emphasis on the local congregation is a characteristic of Independency. Presbyterians put the presbytery in place of monepiscopacy and congregationalists the local congregation. The two approaches began to coalesce in England only after the Act of Uniformity of 1662 drove out the presbyterians (whom the Declaration of Breda had hoped to comprehend) as well as the Independents. By the Presbyterians, the presbytery or council of presbyteries was seen as the form of permanent Church government established in the primitive Church, under the general assembly at Jerusalem, while the apostolate was regarded as an extraordinary commission, expiring with the deaths of the Apostles themselves and handing on no (episcopal) succession. It was pointed out that the Apostles themselves sat in the Jerusalem assembly as elders, and no more, and that the 'moderator' or president of that assembly was James, who was not an apostle. Presbyters were all 'pastors' and 'bishops'; and the higher ministry they exercised was corporate, not vested in an individual. In that way, a supra-congregational ministry might be provided for without compromising the principle of the parity of all ministers[51] or that of the local congregation being the fundamental unit. There could also be continuity in the ministry, with those who had previously been admitted to office trying and ordaining new ministers, but always at the will and with the consent of the people. Calvin, who held a high doctrine of the Church, proposed in the draft Ecclesiastical Ordinances for Geneva (1541) that a candidate for ministerial office should be presented to the Council of Presbyters, who, if they accepted him, had authority to give him certification which he could show to the people to whom he was to preach. In that way he could be seen to be 'received by the common consent of the company of the faithful'. Calvin also stressed the importance of regular meeting of presbyters for fraternal discipline, so as to maintain standards.

---

50   We group Presbyterian and Congregational polities rather loosely together here. They share one Christian World Communion by the Act of Union of 1970, but the World Alliance of Reformed Churches is a consultative body only, and not part of the polity (certainly not an authoritative part) of its member Churches. See *Nairobi, 1970*, Proceedings of the Uniting General Council (Geneva, 1970).

51   Cf. paras. 70-2, 121, 185 and Chapter 9, section on 'Personal and corporate *episcope*.

140. It was not in dispute that there ought to be rulership in the Church. In fact, Calvin pointed to I Timothy 5:17 as warrant for distinguishing between 'teaching' and 'ruling' elders. In many Reformed and Presbyterian polities a central legislative and judicial body has emerged, made up of equal numbers of 'ruling' (pastors) and 'teaching' elders, which exercises oversight over all congregations in its geographical jurisdiction, serves as an appeal court for individual congregations unable to resolve their difficulties internally, and transmits initiatives to provincial or national assemblies. Presbyteries have Chairmen or Moderators, but holding office only for a time. Here again, it is the first plane of the Church's life which is supremely important, with the wider relationship of communities serving the needs of the Church's local life. There is not deemed to be a place for a governmental structure of a sort requiring permanent officers in a lasting relationship to the wider community. Partly as a result of modern media pressure, there is, however, a recognition of the need for the Moderator to be a 'spokesman', who can speak for the community much as a bishop does in other traditions; there would seem to be some return here to the ancient episcopal role at least in this respect.

141. The reason for Reformed and Presbyterian refusal to accept any such office lay in sixteenth century determination to resist claims to personal power held by bishops in their own right and neither answerable to the community nor limitable by the community.[52] Accordingly, we still find fighting talk of liberty for local congregations today.[53] The association of a 'personal' higher authority with concomitant restrictions upon the autonomy of the local congregation is still a potent force in the resistance of Churches of these traditions to 'episcopacy', even where a corporate *episcope* is accepted as a practical aid to efficient Church government (on the strict understanding that those who share in it do so as presbyters and have no

---

[52] The existence of 'bishops' within a presbyterian system in the Church of Scotland from 1560 to 1690 should be weighed carefully here. At issue in that period was whether the episcopate could be justified as a separate order, and the broader question of answerability seen, in the political circumstances of the day, as a threat to royal authority. (Hence James I's remark, 'No Bishop, no King'.)

[53] For example, the United Church of Christ (USA) in responding to BEM, comments that 'The move from Christ the servant who is our Liberator to notions of dependency and submission mediated by the clergy, who do not preside at, but over, the sacraments, is hardly a matter of neutral semantics. It is a move, likely not intended, that raises anew the suspicion that hierarchy is nearby when the threefold pattern of ministry is present'. This with much appreciative comment on the ministry text of BEM as a whole. M. Thurian, *Churches Respond to BEM*, II, WCC, Geneva, 1986, p. 333. Cf. para. 313.

permanent tenure of any office of oversight other than the pastorate of the congregation to which they are inducted).

142.   In the last decade, the United Reformed Church in our own land (which now includes the Churches of Christ (Disciples)) has achieved a merging of two groups of churches, the 'congregational', which place oversight in any local fellowship which covenants together to be God's Church in a particular place; and the 'presbyterian', which lodge oversight in a general assembly of such churches. This has been done by creating a common District Council which resembles the Presbyterian 'presbytery' and has a measure of authority. Oversight is here essentially conciliar.[54] The District Council has as its first function 'the oversight of the ministry'. It does not have oversight of the churches as such, though another of its functions is 'to care for all the churches of the District Council and to visit them by deputies at regular intervals for consultation concerning their life and work'. There are twelve Provincial Synods, with representatives from the churches; these have authority to appoint Departments and Committees. There is a General Assembly of Representatives from the Districts, which appoints Departments and Committees and the Moderators of Provincial Synods, who are responsible to it and paid out of central funds. A Moderator in the URC holds an office distinct from the pastorate to which he is inducted. His context is conciliar. He (or she) presides over the meetings of the Synod and exercises a pastoral office towards the ministers and churches within the Province; presides, or appoints a deputy to preside, at all ordinations and inductions of ministers within the Province. There is also a Moderator of the General Assembly. The term 'oversight' is used in the context of the District Council: 'The Moderator shall participate with each District Council in the Province, being a member of each such Council in the discharge of its responsibilities and in particular in the oversight of local churches and ministers'. 'Oversight' is also used of Provincial Synods and the General Assembly, which has as its primary function 'to oversee the total work of the Church'.

iii.   The Lutheran Churches

143.   The early Lutherans - as the negotiations at Augsburg (1530) show - wished to retain the historic structures of the Church and remain under the authority of the existing bishops. But this was not everywhere possible. In

---

[54]   'The oversight of the United Reformed Church shall be the concern both of the local church and wider representative councils' (*Structure*, para. 3).

Sweden there was no interruption in the historic succession. In Denmark and Norway the office of bishop was deliberately retained, although through presbyteral succession and without consecration to a separate order. In other areas, such as the independent German states and free cities, Lutheran secular rulers often accepted the title *summus episcopus* (thus acting in some respects as 'emergency bishops'), whilst delegating strictly ecclesiastical and spiritual matters to a consistory or synod.[55]

144. As a result, while the practice of episcopacy in some of the Scandinavian Churches is in some ways closer to that of the Roman Catholics, Anglicans and Orthodox, a fundamentally 'congregationalist' or 'presbyterian', and an 'episcopal' pattern, existing side by side in some areas, raise the question whether the 'basic unit in the Lutheran Church is the local parish, and the minister of the parish is not a representative of the bishop, but ... himself directly and independently a bearer of the ministry'.[56] In Finnish Lutheran Churches canon law confers something very like episcopal authority on the rector of a parish. But the bishop remains the *pastor pastorum*, making visitations of the parishes.[57] The Finnish Evangelical Lutheran Church has recently voted in favour of women bishops.

145. In this century the title of 'bishop' has been very largely restored amongst those Lutheran Churches which abandoned it at the time of the Reformation. In the Lutheran Churches in Germany new forms of episcopal ministry began to emerge during the period of the Kirchenkampf - the struggle of the Church under the Nazis - from 1933-45. Today the 'office of bishop' is used in all Lutheran Churches in both East and West Germany. It is now also found in an increasing number of Churches deriving from German Lutheran Missions in Africa, Asia and Oceania. In the USA it has been increasingly adopted by all but the Missouri Synod and is found in the newly united Evangelical Lutheran Church in America, with which the Episcopal Church in the USA has an agreement of 'Interim Eucharistic Sharing'. Moreover, Churches in the developing world deriving from Scandinavia have retained the forms of episcopacy of their mission

---

55   For a survey of the reasons for local variation in Lutheran response to the question of the historic episcopate at the time when each of the Lutheran Churches came into being, see *Episcopacy in the Lutheran Church*, ed. I. Asheim and V.R. Gold (Philadelphia, 1970).

56   F. Cleve, 'Scandinavian Lutheran Bishops', in *Bishops, but what kind?*, p. 80.

57   *Ibid.*, pp. 81-2.

Churches. Thus episcopal ministry and the episcopal office are in a significant phase of development within Lutheranism.

146. In all this, Lutheran Churches have generally shown a preference for an episcopal polity in which there is personal as well as corporate leadership. In German Lutheran Churches the Landesbischof shares authority with a presbyteral synod which elects him and can remove him from office (and of which he is not a member),[58] but he has functions which go beyond those of the Moderator of a Reformed or Presbyterian assembly. He has duties of visitation and ordination; he issues pastoral letters; he has responsibility for the maintenance and teaching of Biblically sound doctrine. The Leitender (leading) Bischof chairs a Bishops' Conference of 'assistant' or 'suffragan' bishops in the great Landeskirchen, in some of which (because of their size) there are subdivisions into districts further subdivided into deaneries, thus creating an additional level of hierarchical organisation.[59] In the Lutheran Churches which are recovering an episcopal office, a vigorous debate continues over the relation between bishop and synod. The bishop is bound in many ways by the synod's decisions but he retains a personal spiritual authority. The precise limitations of the personal authority of a Lutheran Bishop are still largely understood in the terms set out by Melanchthon in the sixteenth century.[60] In principle, all bishops are equal in office.[61] They have the authority to make regulations for the government of the Church and for worship, and congregations and their clergy who are under the bishop's oversight are bound in charity to obey such regulations. But the bishop may not declare that salvation depends on the observance of any regulations he makes.

147. The bishop may be elected for life, or for a term of years, after which he reverts to being a simple pastor. Some Churches - especially the

---

[58]   *Bishops, but what kind?*, p. 96.

[59]   *Niagara*, Appendix IV.

[60]   Cf. Melanchthon, *Apologia* for the *Confessio Augustana*, tr. G. Tappert, *The Book of Concord* (Philadelphia, 1959), XIV.1, 5.

[61]   Andreas Aarflot, Bishop of Oslo, comments:
       'Seeing the office of the ordained ministry essentially as one, the Lutheran Church does not see the office of bishop as qualitatively distinguished from the office of the pastor or priest. Rather it conceives of the episcopal office as an extension of the one office of ordained ministry into a wider field of responsibility ... In short, the concept of ministry and episcopacy as it is developed in the Lutheran Reformation does not provide for a difference in substance between the office of an ordained minister and that of a bishop. It is not a distinction of quality but of responsibility.' *The Collegiality of Bishops: A Lutheran Perspective*, in The Nature and Future of Episcopal Conferences, *The Jurist* (Studies in Church Law and Ministry, Catholic University of America, Washington, D.C., vol. XLVIII, 1988, 1).

German regional Churches - have only one bishop. In such Churches the bishop shares his episcopal office with superintendents or area deans who perform such duties as ordinations and visitations in sub-regions of the regional Church. In other Churches - especially in Scandinavia - a familiar pattern of diocesan episcopacy (and even primacy) is to be found. In the USA the two patterns are found respectively in bishops who preside over regional synods; and in the office of a presiding bishop.

148.   Some Lutheran Church constitutions specifically speak of the work of the bishop under the heading 'the activity of the chief shepherd'. The bishop's office is increasingly seen to be not limited to one congregation:

> According to the evangelical conception every pastor is the regular shepherd of his congregation.[62]

149.   As a natural consequence of the return to episcopacy, forms of episcopal collegiality are now also developing. In the United Evangelical Lutheran Church in Germany (VELKD) Church laws are passed by the concurrent vote of the General Synod and the Conference of Bishops. Among the Nordic Churches an International Conference of Bishops has a co-ordinating and consultative role. The function of the 'house of bishops' within the Nordic countries varies but there are special corporate responsibilities for the bishops - especially in relation to discipline, worship and doctrine.

150.   The development of episcopal ministry within Lutheranism has not been influenced only by internal pastoral and theological considerations. Ecumenical dialogue between Lutherans and other Christians has an increasingly important role to play in the development of Lutheran thinking - and practice - about episcopacy. The Baptism, Eucharist and Ministry text of the World Council of Churches (the Lima text), has been very significant and is regarded by many Lutherans as expressing an acceptable understanding of episcopacy. Lutheran discussion with Anglicans and with Roman Catholics has also had considerable influence on Lutheran thinking - both in Europe and in North America.

151.   The doctrinal position of the Lutheran Church is still given authoritative expression in the *Confessio Augustana*, the Augsburg

---

62   W. Maurer: *Das synodal evangelische Bischofsamt seit* 1918, Fuldaer Heft, Vol. X, Berlin 1955, as quoted in *Episcopacy in the Lutheran Church?*, ed. Asheim & Gold (Philadelphia, 1970) p. 86. Cf. LRC, *The Ministry in the Church*, 45-49.

Confession of 1530, where Article 28 describes the office of bishop in strong terms:

> The episcopal office is, according to God's laws, to preach the Gospel, forgive sins, judge the teaching of the Church, condemn teachings opposed to the Bible, and expel godless people (whose character is notorious) from the Christian congregation - all this without the secular power, but only through God's Word.[63]

152. A variety of polities in Lutheranism have in common the intention of ensuring that ministerial office is not confused with indelible order: and that it is understood that arrangements for the higher government of the Church are of human devising and not of divine institution.[64] Polity is seen as 'indifferent'.[65] It falls broadly into the category of 'rites and ceremonies' (cf. Article 20 of the Thirty-Nine Articles, which refers to this sixteenth century controversy). It is thus at the disposal of particular Churches to determine its framework. On the other hand, local leadership is regarded as being of divine institution; with the distinction of the 'orders' of priest and bishop regarded as post-apostolic, and of human not divine origin.

153. Though episcopal ministry is entrusted among Lutherans to people whose titles, duties, manner of choice, and appointment may differ considerably, such diversity has never been regarded as destructive of communion. Lutherans do not regard a uniform structure of Church order as absolutely necessary for communion.[66] In particular they would continue to reject the absolute theological necessity of the historic succession of bishops for the maintenance of the apostolic succession of the faith of the Church. Nevertheless, Lutherans in ecumenical dialogue have been especially open to understanding the historic episcopate as a sign - but not the sole guarantee - of apostolic succession, and to the restoration of the historic episcopate where it has been lost.[67]

154. Although the bishop is not deemed to be the successor of the Apostles in holding a higher order than a presbyter, he can be seen as their successor in carrying the responsibility for government in the Church. The Pullach

63 Cf. Anglican-Lutheran Conversations, Pullach Report, 1972, 79, *Growth*, p. 24.
64 Cf. J.C. Brauer in *Episcopacy in the Lutheran Church*, ed. Asheim and Gold, p. 197.
65 Cf. Anglican-Lutheran Conversations, Pullach Report, 1972, 89, *Growth*, p. 26.
66 Cf. *Confessio Augustana*, Art. 7.
67 Cf. *Lutheran Understanding of Episcopal Office*, Lutheran World Fellowship (Geneva, 1985), 10 and 11. Cf., too, Chapter 14, section on 'The Anglican-Lutheran proposals'.

Report of the Anglican-Lutheran Conversations of 1973 recognised 'that all who have been called or ordained to the ministry of Word and Sacrament in obedience to the apostolic faith stand together in apostolic succession of office' (para. 77). There is, then, a limited sense in which continuity over time is seen as a function of oversight in Lutheran communities, but it is regarded as a succession of function rather than a succession of order. That notwithstanding, there would still seem to be a case for at least saying that a succession of office is a succession of order.[68]

155. Within the general pastoral office, with its fundamental task of proclaiming the Gospel and administering the Sacraments, contemporary Lutheranism has most recently described the functions of episcopal ministry (whether the name 'bishop' is used or not, and whether or not bishops are seen as standing within the historical succession) in the following way:

- advising and supporting the congregations in their life of worship, witness and service, by visiting them, listening to their needs, responding to their questions and helping to solve their problems;
- enabling Christian faith to grow in the Church and in the life of all its members;
- assuring that the teaching of the Church is in harmony with the Gospel as interpreted in the confessions of the Church and to warn against false teaching and help people in their struggle against it;
- to speak out and express the mind of the Church in matters of public concern like justice and peace;
- planning and soliciting support for mission outreaching both in the Church and in the world;
- ordaining pastors or by authorizing others to ordain, and serving pastors as a pastor;
- being involved in approving, training, calling and placing of pastors, and in concern for the situation and tasks of other church workers;
- exercising discipline according to the Church's requirement, correcting what is amiss in the life of congregations and the life of pastors;
- carrying out the decisions of the Church as its constitutions prescribe and thereby assuming certain administrative tasks;
- advising and supporting institutions that are providing public and diaconal services in the name of the Church;
- expressing and serving the unity of the Church in relating to other churches and to confessional and ecumenical organizations;
- representing the Church in the public sector.[69]

---

68 See Chapter 9 on *Ecumenical Convergence*, 'Remaining areas of difficulty', on the question of succession.

69 *Loc. cit.*, note 67.

156. Thus despite differences between Anglicans and Lutherans upon the necessity of the historic episcopate for unity[70], there are large areas of agreement with Lutherans over the nature and exercise of episcopacy. Above all bishops are jointly seen to serve the unity of the Church. 'They represent the larger Church to congregations committed to their charge. They represent the communion of those congregations within and to the larger Church.'[71]

iv. The bishops of the *Unitas Fratrum* (Moravian Church)

157. The immediate origins of the Moravian Church lie in the Community of Herrnhut in Saxony, formed under the leadership of Count Nikolaus Ludwig von Zinzendorf (1700-1760). The first settlers were Moravian descendants of the Church of the Bohemian Brethren, founded in 1457 by a section of the movement initiated by the Czech reformer Jan Hus (1369-1415). This *Unitas Fratrum* (Unity of the Brethren), whose orders, name and traditions the Moravian Church inherited, can thus claim to be the oldest surviving protestant church north of the Alps, while Zinzendorf has been hailed as a pioneer of ecumenism. In the 1730s the Moravians sent out some of the earliest protestant missionaries, so that the *Unitas Fratrum* became the first international protestant church. Today it has half a million members in twenty autonomous provinces spreading over five continents.

158. If a distinction is drawn between an understanding of a bishop as someone consecrated for life to a distinct order of ministry, and an understanding which makes 'bishop' a title for the presiding minister of a church for a period only, then Moravian bishops belong in the former group. A Moravian bishop's episcopacy is not ended when he retires from full-time ministry; indeed bishops have sometimes been consecrated on retirement. The office of bishop is not restricted to the ministry of ordination, nor is it merely titular, nor merely an honour for distinguished ministers.

159. The bishop, consecrated by other bishops, maintains the Moravian episcopal succession. 'A bishop alone has the right to ordain, or to consecrate to the various orders of ministry.' As well as maintaining the personal succession, bishops are guardians of the Christian tradition, and

---

70   See, too, the chapter on *Ecumenical Progress*, section on 'Mutual recognition and reconciliation of ministries'.

71   *Loc. cit.*, note 67.

particular Moravian traditions, within the Moravian Church. They have an especial concern for the maintenance of orthodox teaching.

160.   A Moravian bishop is a bishop of the whole Unity and not just of the province in which he lives, although the rule is that 'where possible, at least one bishop should be resident in each province.' As well as maintaining the unity of the tradition over time, he has a concern for the unity of the world-wide Moravian provinces. One link is the presence of bishops from other provinces at episcopal consecrations. But the bishop also has a particular duty to pray for the entire Unity, as indeed for the Church of Christ as a whole. The Moravian Church has always maintained a strong concern for Christian Unity, and bishops are prominent in the ecumenical relations of the Moravian Church.

161.   From the beginnings of the renewed Moravian Church in Herrnhut, it has distinguished between spiritual and administrative leadership. The provincial and Unity synods elect boards to administer the affairs of the Province or the Unity. A bishop with administrative gifts may be elected a member or chairman of the board, as a board member with spiritual and pastoral gifts may be elected and consecrated a bishop. When the General Conference (as it was then called) was established in 1741, both of the bishops then in Europe were among the twelve members, one as chairman. Today bishops are board members or chairmen in several provinces, including the British Province. In some provinces the bishop is an *ex officio* member, but in most cases the two offices remain separate, and are more commonly held by different people, with the bishop an essentially non-authoritarian figure.

162.   Bishops are *ex officio* members for life of the synods of the Province in which they were elected. Boards are required to consult bishops, as spiritual leaders, 'in all matters concerning the work of the Province or District which fall within (the bishop's) sphere of responsibility'. In matters of doctrine and practice, the opinions of bishops, as guardians of the tradition and orthodox teaching, are normally to be sought 'and given due consideration and weight'.

163.   As spiritual leader, the bishop is expected to visit congregations 'for the deepening of their spiritual life'. He has a particular pastoral responsibility for the ministers as *pastor pastorum*. A bishop who is not in an administrative position (and even more so, one who has retired from full-time ministry) is felt to be particularly well-placed to perform this

function. Bishops share in the decisions about selection of candidates for the ministry and maintain a special relationship with them throughout their training. The bishop has the right to ordain only when commissioned to do so by a provincial board or synod, but retains the right to decline to ordain a particular candidate.

164. Moravian bishops are addressed as 'brother', and do not have any distinctive dress, although the title Right Reverend (and sometimes, the purple stock) are used in areas where Anglican influence is strong and these are therefore thought customary for bishops.

165. Moravian bishops stand in an unbroken succession which reaches back beyond the establishment of the renewed Moravian Church in the eighteenth century to bishops of the Church of the Bohemian Brethren in the mid-sixteenth century. That Church had had bishops since 1467, but it is now known that there was no direct succession from bishops of the Catholic Church. However it was believed for most of its existence that the *Unitas Fratrum*'s bishops did stand in such a direct succession, and it was partly in order to secure Anglican recognition for Moravian ministers working in the English colonies that the renewed Moravian Church obtained the consecration of its first bishop at the early date of 1735 from one of the last bishops of the old *Unitas Fratrum*.

166. In recent years, Anglican bishops have joined in the consecration of Moravian bishops on several occasions, in areas as far apart as Britain, Tanzania and Alaska. Moravian episcopacy has long been attractive to Anglicans. Speaking in the House of Lords in 1748 John Thomas, Bishop of Lincoln, argued that true bishops did not have to be like those of the English and Irish established churches. His example was the bishops of the *Unitas Fratrum*, who were not lords, had no involvement in public affairs and no revenues, indeed sometimes worked with their hands like the Apostles.

167. The style of Moravian episcopacy has a distinctive contribution to make to today's ecumenical understanding of episcopacy. Bishops freed from administrative work to concentrate on spiritual leadership, and an episcopate which is non-hierarchical and non-authoritarian are concepts of particular value as reminders of the need to keep the tasks of bishops in a proper balance.[72]

[72]   All quotations are from the *Unity Church Order* (Oxford, 1960).

v. Methodism

168. Methodist polity developed along lines indicated by Wesley, but it was not until after his death that certain crucial decisions of policy were taken. At first he himself had seen the Methodist societies as remaining within the Church, *ecclesiolae in ecclesia*, working for revival in the Church of England. By 1747 he had abandoned doctrines of the divine institution of the episcopate and of apostolic succession and was of the opinion that the New Testament shows that continuity of succession in the ministry has been maintained through the presbyterate. He took the view that a bishop exercises oversight for which he must be answerable. After his death in 1791 nine senior preachers sent out the 'Halifax Circular'. 'There appear to us to be but two ways,' they argued: 'either to appoint another King in Israel, or to be governed by the Conference Plan, by forming ourselves into committees.' There was a conscious sense of the need to balance the episcopal with the presbyteral system and to ensure that 'the preachers' do not 'rule without consulting the people'.[73] A theology of 'corporate pastorate' emerged in the doctrine that the Conference has a supreme authority from God endorsed by the consent of those involved. It proved, nevertheless, not always easy to make the Conference responsive to local needs, and it was suggested that 'provincial' conferences should meet regularly. The move to a Conference in which lay people and ministers met together altered the principle of the 'corporate pastorate', however, and in today's British Methodism the Conference divides in such a way that only the members who are ministers have responsibility for overseeing the appointment and discipline of ministers.[74]

169. While Wesley's English Methodists remained members of the Church of England until after his death, the American ones were independent ecclesially from the beginning. They therefore faced sooner the tension between the ideal of democratic self-government and the acceptance of the authority of a 'bishop' or 'superintendent'. Wesley himself chose Coke as superintendent and he wanted him to choose Asbury as another. Both were confirmed in their office by the Baltimore Christmas Conference of 1784. Central to the early Methodist system was the principle of itineracy, with oversight by the annual conference of travelling preachers to maintain discipline and send out preachers for the next year. These new

---

73   Cf. the Kilhamite protest.
74   J.C. Bowmer, *Pastor and People* (London 1975), pp. 37 ff.

appointments were given out by the bishop or superintendent. During the course of the nineteenth century the system settled down into a pattern of 'stationed' ministry, which reinforced the division into geographical areas of jurisdiction. The bishop in the United Methodist Church of the USA, formed in 1968 when the Methodist Church (itself brought into being by the Uniting Conferences of 1939) united with the Evangelical United Brethren Church, is the holder of what in some sense is certainly a personal pastorate. At the 1968 uniting service, two of the bishops clasped hands as they and the 10,000 delegates declared themselves united in the Lord and in the United Methodist Church.[75] Nevertheless, the bishop remains an elder. There is no separate episcopal order of ministry. The bishop is elected to the jurisdiction of a certain area by the local Conference and entrusted with certain executive functions and powers. He is empowered to ordain deacons and elders, though only after their election by the annual conference. The bishops arrange the pattern of districts, appoint the district superintendent and announce the appointment of travelling ministers to their posts, as the first Methodist bishop did. But the Council of Bishops, meeting annually, exercises a corporate pastorate of superintendency of the whole Church.

170.   In the English Methodist Church (which united in 1932 the Wesleyan Methodist, the Primitive Methodist and the United Methodist communities), the Conference is supreme in the exercise of oversight, making and revising legislation as the governing body of the Methodist Church. It is made up of equal numbers of ministers and laymen, although the President is always a minister, and acceptance of candidates is the responsibility of the Ministerial Session.[76] The Full Representative Session of the Conference can accept candidates for ministry (men or women) and deal with ministerial discipline and doctrinal issues in dispute, and all matters of 'pastoral efficiency'. 'Stationing', that is, the appointment of ministers to circuits also belongs to the Full Representative Session.[77]

---

[75]   Piepkorn, II, p. 585.

[76]   The committees which interview them and make recommendations include lay people.

[77]   See, further, the essay by J.S. Kent, 'Episcopacy in Church and Society', in *Anglican-Methodist Relations: Some Institutional Factors*, ed. W.S.F. Pickering (London, 1961) (Papers presented to the Study Commission on Faith and Order of the World Council of Churches), pp. 83 ff.

vi.   Towards a common doctrine of oversight

171.   From the point in the sixteenth century when the pattern of episcopal ministry was decisively altered in the Churches of the Reformation, certain issues of principle and matters of practice have remained divisive. We have seen the concept of the diocesan 'local Church' challenged by Christians for whom the local congregation of 'gathered believers' is paramount. We have seen the rejection of the notion that bishops belong to an 'order' of ministry which permanently distinguishes them from priests. We have seen a 'corporate' or 'collegial' presbyterate sometimes replacing a personal and collegial episcopate in the oversight of a group of congregations. But we have also seen the rediscovery of some of the elements of the traditional episcopal ministry, not only among Lutherans and Methodists, but more widely in non-episcopal Churches; and at the same time, a deeper appreciation in Churches which have retained the historic episcopate, of the value of many of the reforms of the sixteenth century and after. We have, in short, much better mutual understanding and the beginnings of a movement towards, if not a common structure in the Church, at least a mutually acceptable doctrine of oversight.

6

The Church of England since the Reformation:

the theology

I.   The fundamentals

172.   We have had to deal in broad strokes with profoundly complex events in order to set the scene for the sixteenth century and subsequent developments in the Church of England, as they concern bishops.   But we have thought it important to give an account of the common history we share with the Orthodox Church until the schism of 1054, and with the Roman Catholic Church until the sixteenth century; and of the views of *episcope* held in the Churches of the Reformation among whom the Church of England has also numbered herself as 'Catholic and Reformed'.

Continuity

173.   There was no intention in the Henrician, Edwardine or Elizabethan legislation to make any fundamental change in the understanding of the nature of episcopal ministry, or to allow any interruption in the succession, for the English Reformers believed they saw a clear Scriptural warrant for episcopal ministry.[1] Henry VIII retained the three-fold ministry of bishops, priests and deacons.   The episcopate continued to be regarded, as it had generally been in the Middle Ages, as the perfecting and highest fulfilment of a priesthood which, although it must in practice be bestowed on the individual before he becomes a bishop, remained in essence a deputed office under that of bishop.   The present Canons of the Church of England enshrine what has always been its teaching and practice when in Canon C.1.2 it is affirmed: 'No person who has been admitted to the order of bishop, priest or deacon can ever be divested of the character of his order'.   The

---

[1]   They believed that the New Testament evidence for the three-fold ministry was more unequivocal than modern scholarship suggests.   Cf. here the emphasis of the Liturgical Commission of the General Synod upon the Archbishop's declaration that 'a bishop is consecrated within the historic succession of the Church's ministry, as the Church of England has received it' (*Report* (1977), p. 29).

intention here is to affirm the irrevocable nature of Christian response to the calling of the Holy Spirit and Christ's faithfulness.

a.   The making of a bishop: the roles of the Holy Spirit and of the Church[2]

174.   The gift of the Spirit is attested by the simple invocation (*epiklesis*) which commits to the kneeling priest under the hands of the archbishop and other bishops present, the responsibilities of the office and work of a bishop in the Church of God.

175.   This was not wholly an uncontroversial element in the sixteenth century liturgy.   There was an implication to some reformers' minds that the imposition of hands by bishops together with an *epiklesis* constituted a claim to an episcopal power which was independent of the community and held by bishops from God as an exclusive, personal possession.   In the light of this anxiety Whitgift (Archbishop of Canterbury from 1583) comments:

> To use these words, 'Receive the Holy Spirit', in ordering of ministers, which Christ himself used in appointing his apostles, is no more ridiculous and blasphemous than it is to use the words that he used in the supper ... The bishop by speaking these words doth not take upon him to give the Holy Ghost, no more than he doth to remit sins, when he pronounceth the remission of sins; but by speaking these words of Christ, 'Receive the Holy Ghost; whose sins so ever ye remit, they are remitted, etc.,' he doth shew the principal duty of a minister, and assureth him of the assistance of God's Holy Spirit if he labour in the same accordingly'.[3]

The words are, in short, a prayer; they ask God to act.   The laying on of hands and the invocation of the Holy Spirit in ordination is properly seen as the action of Christ's representative or representatives in the community. The Liturgical Commission of the General Synod said in 1977 that the 'essential form and matter of ordination is prayer with the laying-on of hands, preceded by the assent and prayer of the people'.[4]

176.   The work of the spirit is inseparable from the action of the Church, both the whole people of God and their episcopal representatives, whose own commission includes the authority to ordain.   Cranmer's paper on the doctrine and discipline of the Church of 1538 is quite clear that Scripture

2   See also Chapter 12 on the Appointment of Bishops.
3   Whitgift, *Works*, Parker Society I.489.
4   *Ordination Services, Series 3*, by the Liturgical Commission of the General Synod (1977), p. 5.

gives a divine institution for orders,[5] and Becon (c. 1513-67) emphasises that it is also necessary for the candidate for ordination to 'submit himself to the judgement of the congregation, either to be admitted or to be refused'.[6] In the rite of ordination of 1662 text of *The Book of Common Prayer* of the Church of England, candidates are presented to the people and provision is made for the bishop to ask the people if they know of any 'impediment or notable crime' in the candidate. Each candidate is asked if he believes himself to be 'truly called' by the Holy Spirit. At an ordination to the priesthood, the priests present join the bishop in the laying on of hands to signify that the commission entrusted to them is shared; the people present signify their assent; and the bishop on behalf of the community prays God to grant the gift of the Holy Spirit to the candidate for a specific purpose. At the consecration of a bishop, the archbishop lays hands on the candidate, together with his fellow-bishops taking part in the consecration, with the declared intention of ordaining him to the episcopate: 'Receive the Holy Ghost for the office and work of a bishop in the Church of God, now committed unto thee by the imposition of our hands'. The laying on of hands occurs within a context which defines its purpose. That is to say, it would be ineffective in isolation; it does not have an automatic character, as some of the Reformers feared was being claimed for it in the sixteenth century. The bishop or archbishop acts within 'the Church of God', that is, the universal Church. There is a conscious bringing together of human and divine, personal and corporate authorising. The prayer and the laying on of hands takes place in the context of the Eucharist precisely because ordination is an act in which the whole Church is involved.

b.   The liturgy of consecration

The sixteenth century and 1662

177.   The fundamental Anglican understanding of the nature and function of the episcopal office can be inferred from the sixteenth century Ordinal and its 1662 revision. The Form of Ordaining, or Consecrating,[7] of an Archbishop or Bishop, places its primary emphasis on the teaching office of the bishop in a pastoral setting, and his duty to maintain the faith:[8]

---

5   Cranmer, *Remains*, Parker Society, p. 484.
6   Becon, *Catechism*, Parker Society, p. 319.
7   The double technical term contrives to leave open in some degree the question whether the episcopate constitutes a separate order from the presbyterate. See para. 185.
8   Cf. the Epistle from Acts 20, the post-consecration instruction and Collect.

- the Collect asks for grace that the bishop 'may diligently preach the Word, and duly administer the godly discipline thereof '.
- three questions are addressed to the bishop-elect concerning the faith of the Church, the teaching office of the bishop and the exercise of discipline in relation to false doctrine.
- the prayer that precedes the laying on of hands asks in the first instance for grace that the bishop-elect 'may evermore be ready to spread abroad thy Gospel'.
- at the presentation of the Bible, the bishop is charged first to 'Give heed to reading, exhortation and doctrine'.
- the first function to which specific reference is made in the post-communion Collect is to 'preaching the Word'.

This emphasis reflects sixteenth century anxiety to redress the imbalance which had arisen in the late Middle Ages between the ministry of the Word and the ministry of the Sacraments.

178.   There is also a strong emphasis in the service on the bishop's disciplinary responsibility. He is required to 'correct and punish' within his diocese all who are 'unquiet, disobedient and criminous'. He is enjoined to 'minister discipline'. He is encouraged 'to reprove, beseech, and rebuke with all patience and doctrine'. The bishop's exercise of discipline is explicitly related to his responsibility as a guardian of the faith.[9] It is asked that he might 'admonish the godly discipline of the Word of God'. He is required to affirm his willingness 'to banish and drive away all erroneous and strange doctrine contrary to God's Word'.

179.   There is a third emphasis on the life of holiness to which the bishop is called. He is to be adorned with 'innocency of life'; 'deny all ungodliness and worldly lusts and live soberly, righteously, and godly'; be a 'wholesome example, in word, in conversation, in love, in faith, in chastity, and in purity'. All these requirements seek to meet the demands of Scripture and are clear in the two passages that are provided at the service as the readings for the Epistle. The bishop's vocation to holiness is set within the Scriptural context in which he has a primary responsibility to act on behalf of the community as teacher, interpreter and defender.

The Alternative Service Book

180.   The publication of *The Alternative Service Book* (1980) makes no departure from the understanding of a bishop's office in *The Book of*

9   On guardianship of the faith, see further Chapter 10.

Common Prayer. A clear emphasis in the modern liturgy is upon the bishop's role in the universal Church. The notes stipulate, in the tradition laid down by the Council of Nicaea, that at least three bishops must take part in the consecration of a bishop. From the opening prayer of preparation and throughout there is an emphasis upon the interdependence of the ministry of bishop and people. In the reading of the Preface to the Declaration of Assent and in what follows, the bishop is to affirm and declare his loyalty to the inheritance of the faith of the Church 'uniquely revealed' in Scripture, 'set forth' in the Creeds and 'proclaimed afresh' by the Church in each generation.

181.   The Declaration that is read by the Archbishop sets out more fully than the 1662 text the multiplicity of tasks that are laid upon a bishop.

> A bishop is called to lead in serving and caring for the people of God and to work with them in the oversight of the church. As a chief pastor he shares with his fellow bishops a special responsibility to maintain and further the unity of the church, to uphold its discipline, and to guard its faith. He is to promote its mission throughout the world. It is his duty to watch over and pray for all those committed to his charge, and to teach and govern them after the example of the Apostles, speaking in the name of God and interpreting the gospel of Christ. He is to know his people and be known by them. He is to ordain and to send new ministers, guiding those who serve with him and enabling them to fulfil their ministry. He is to baptise and confirm, to preside at the holy communion, and to lead the offering of prayer and praise. He is to be merciful, but with firmness, and to minister discipline, but with mercy. He is to have a special care for the outcast and needy; and to those who turn to God he is to declare the forgiveness of sins.

This statement endorses the primitive emphasis on the bishop's liturgical or sacramental role. Its concerns are further underlined in the prayer of the Archbishop which follows immediately after the consecration. This prayer refers to the functions of leadership in proclaiming the gospel; renewing the Church's ministry; uniting the Church's members; feeding the flock; teaching; guarding its faith and sacraments; presiding at worship; exercising authority.

182.   A primary emphasis in the ASB service is on 'leadership', for a number of stated purposes:
*   the opening words of the Declaration remind the congregation that, 'a bishop is called to lead in serving and caring for the people of God and to work with them in the oversight of the church'.
*   the final question that is asked of the bishop-elect concerns his willingness to 'lead your people to obey our Saviour's command to

make disciples of all nations'.

- the prayer that follows immediately upon the laying on of hands asks for grace and power that the bishop 'may lead those committed to his charge in proclaiming the gospel of salvation'.
- the post-communion Collect has at its heart the petition that the bishop 'may lead the people committed to his charge'.

c. Controversies

183. Episcopal order in all its fullness, then, continued in the Church of England at the Reformation, and was, as the Ordinal shows, understood as being in continuity with that of the ancient Church. Nevertheless debates on the theology of the episcopal office in the centuries that followed were hard-hitting and sometimes bitter. It is often forgotten how radical were the challenges to Anglican understanding of episcopacy in the centuries that followed.[10]

i.   *An ordinary not an extraordinary ministry*

184. The notion that bishops in particular might have been an extraordinary and temporary provision, needed only in the apostolic and sub-apostolic age, but having no place in the modern Church, was canvassed from the late Middle Ages; and the question was raised in sixteenth century England too. Whitgift reflects on the argument that the Apostles were in a unique position to witness to the words and deeds of Jesus and to his resurrection, and that no later successor could bear their eye-witness. 'I think,' he says, 'the apostolic function was extraordinary, in respect that it had for the time certain especial properties, as to bear witness of the resurrection of Christ, and of his ascension, which they did see with their eyes; also to plant and to found churches, likewise to go throughout the whole world. These, I say, were temporal and extraordinary; and so was the apostleship in this respect, but yet ordinary in respect of their chief function, which was to preach the gospel and govern the churches which they had planted'.[11] 'Whatsoever was extra-ordinary, as immediate mission, unlimited jurisdiction, and miraculous operations, that was not necessary to the perpetual regiment of the Church', argues Jeremy Taylor (1613-67), for if it had been, the Church could not have continued without them. Christ 'promised his perpetual assistance' in the 'ordinary office' of 'preaching,

---

10   See, for example, the summary in O. O'Donovan, *On the Thirty-Nine Articles* (Exeter, 1986), pp. 108 ff.

11   Whitgift, *Works*, Parker Society I.471.

baptising, consecration, ordaining and governing. For these were necessary for the perpetuation of a Church'.[12] A generation later, opposing the views of the Latitudinarian bishop Benjamin Hoadly, Wright preached an ordination sermon on 'The Rights of Christian Priesthood' in which he says, 'It will be granted that the Persons ... immediately commissioned by our Saviour to preach the Gospel, and exercise the other parts of the Apostolic Office, acted by Divine Authority; it must be said therefore that either they had Authority from Christ to commission others successively to ordain to the same offices, or else that the Power of exercising that Authority dy'd with them'.[13] Thus the dispute had the positive effect of helping to clarify what are the tasks of a continuing 'ordinary' apostolic office, that is, one which is an integral part of the Church's order.

ii.   Parity of ministry [14]

185.   Behind this debate lay another, on which we have already touched, as to whether Scripture, and what we know of the early Church's pattern of domestic life, warrant the distinction between the presbyteral and episcopal orders which was being made throughout the Church until the Reformation.[15]   Pressure from Presbyterians was strong in the later sixteenth century and throughout the seventeenth. They advocated the view that the presbyteral office was indivisible, and that it alone could claim divine sanction; they pressed for a corporate exercise of oversight by the presbyterate above the congregational level.   James Ussher (1581-1656), Archbishop of Armagh, was able to establish the authenticity of the seven genuine letters of Ignatius of Antioch, and these provided important evidence that there were true bishops in the immediate post-apostolic Church, and thus that episcopacy could be regarded as a direct legacy of the

---

12   Jeremy Taylor, *Episcopacy Asserted, Works*, V.19-20.
13   Wright, *The Rights of Christian Priesthood* (London, 1717), p. 4.
14   On this topic, cf. paras. 70, 121, 139.
15   The Council of Trent in the sixteenth century found it difficult to agree on the long-standing issue of 'parity of ministry' between priest and bishop, except to insist that bishops have 'superiority' in their power to confirm and ordain by divine warrant, and that this is something more than an 'office'. It took the view that, although jurisdiction may be entrusted by the human authority of the Church here and now, even that is ultimately a divine gift, for the Church cannot legitimately bestow an authority which is not Christ's gift too. Jurisdiction is authority for a purpose, limited by its function (ARCIC AII.16-22). The technical term 'jurisdiction' cannot be avoided, although we acknowledge that its associations still carry a baggage of difficulties.

Apostles and of divine institution.[16] The Church of England never adopted the view that 'presbyter' and 'bishop' remained interchangeable terms after the New Testament period. Indeed, some revisions in the wording of the Ordinal were made between the sixteenth century and the 1662 versions to emphasise the point. The 1550 Ordinal, for example, speaks of 'ordering' in relation to the diaconate and presbyterate, but 'consecrating' for the episcopate. Within the rite for the episcopate itself 'ordain' and 'order' are not used, and even 'office' occurs only once, but 'consecrate', 'work', and 'ministry of a bishop' are found instead. In 1662 'ordaining or' were inserted before 'consecrating' in the title of the rite for the episcopate; and 'ordained and' was inserted before 'consecrated' in the words used at the presentation of the candidate.[17] In *The Perpetual Government of Christ's Church*, Richard Hooker proposes the view that:

> The Bishop is a Minister of God, unto whom with permanent continuance, there is given not only power of administering Word and Sacraments, which power other presbyters have; but also a further power to ordain Ecclesiastical persons, and a power of Chiefty in Government over Presbyters as well as Law men, a power to be by way of jurisdiction a Pastor even to Pastors themselves.[18]

iii.   'Esse', 'bene esse' and 'plene esse'

186.   A question of great importance ecumenically is whether, if bishops can be seen as having at least a very early place in the tradition of the Church's life, they are to be regarded as essential to its being as the Church (of the *esse*), or merely as valuable to its fullness of life (of the *bene esse* or *plene esse*).[19] In the period prior to 1662 it was generally assumed by Anglicans[20] that the Reformed Churches of Continental Europe, though not episcopally ordered, were certainly truly Churches. Indeed, there were cases of ministers who had not been episcopally ordained being accepted without reordination into the Church of England from such Churches. Partly for political reasons, that was unacceptable in the case of the

---

16   See C.M. Ady, 'From the Restoration to the Present Day', in *Apostolic Ministry*, ed. K.E. Kirk (London, 1946), p. 434 on the shift to a new confidence in the later seventeenth century. King James I, robustly placing the Church of England in the right in contrast to both 'puritans' and 'papists', had already asserted 'That Bishops ought to be in the Church, I ever maintained it as an apostolic institution and so the ordinance of God'. *A Premonition*, in *Works*, ed. J. Montague (1616), p. 301.

17   P.F. Bradshaw, *The Anglican Ordinal* (London, 1971), p. 149.

18   *Of the Laws of Ecclesiastical Polity*, VII, ii.3.

19   See on this theme, *The Historic Episcopate*, ed. K.M. Carey (London, 1954), p. 105 ff.

20   With notable exceptions such as Jeremy Taylor and Thorndike.

Presbyterians in England and Scotland. The first Scottish bishops in the reign of James VI of Scotland and I of England were consecrated directly. Those appointed in 1661 who had not been episcopally ordained deacon or priest were ordained to those orders privately before being consecrated publicly in Westminster Abbey. In 1662, the Act of Uniformity excluded clergy who had not been episcopally ordained, and from that point episcopal ordination has been required for all Anglican clergy.

187.   In the controversy surrounding the Non-jurors, a further significant shift of concern began to take place. After 1688, nine bishops (and some four hundred priests) refused to take the Oath of Allegiance to the new monarch. They were deprived of their benefices and sees[21] and new bishops consecrated. Non-jurors continued to regard the original bishops as the lawful holders of office, and some of them consecrated successors secretly to preserve what they regarded as the true episcopal succession. One of the issues thus sharpened was whether succession in ministerial order through the episcopate is constitutive for the continuing life of the Church, and unbreakable by any outside authority (especially that of the State). The 'High Church' view that this is so was pressed by many in reaction against the trends towards a more secular and politicised view of the role of the episcopate during the eighteenth century, and it had strong advocacy in the Oxford Movement from the eighteen thirties. It coloured the insistence of the Chicago-Lambeth Quadrilateral of 1886-8 upon the 'historic episcopate' as one of the fundamentals of faith and order upon which the Church must stand foursquare.[22]

188.   Nevertheless, the Church of England as a whole has never committed itself to the view that the episcopate is of the *esse* of the Church. Universality and unity are of the *esse* of the Church. As the ecumenical movement gathered momentum at the end of the nineteenth century and the beginning of the twentieth, some Anglican apologists were anxious to stress that in speaking of the 'historic episcopate' they were upholding a reality which, though it might belong to the fulness of catholicity, did not require a theology which would exclude from acceptance as true Churches those ecclesial bodies which had no episcopate.[23]

---

21   Although, of course, they remained bishops. The King had powers only to deprive them of benefices or sees.

22   On this article of the Quadrilateral, see several of the essays in *Quadrilateral at One Hundred*, ed. J. Robert Wright (Ohio, London and Oxford, 1988). See, further, paras. 289 ff.

23   See, further, the chapters on *Ecumenical Convergence* and *Ecumenical Progress*.

II.   The three planes of the Church's life

a.   The ministry of unity in the local community

i.   *Leadership, oversight and pastoral care*

189.   It has been consistently the Anglican way to view the diocese as the fundamental normal unit of Church administration.[24] The diocesan 'local church' has its centre and focus in a personal leader, who is its pastor. As Jeremy Taylor in the seventeenth century put it:

> The cure of the diocese is in the bishop; he cannot exonerate himself of it, for it is a burden of Christ's imposing, or it is not imposed at all; therefore this taking of presbyters into part of the regiment and care does not divest him of his own power or any part of it, nor yet ease him of his care, but he must still *episkopein*, 'visit' and 'see to' his diocese, so that 'he hath authority still in all parts of his diocese'.[25]

On this view, the bishop has the 'whole power' of the ministry of Word and Sacraments in the diocese and the presbyters may not exercise any ordinary ministration without licence from the bishop.

190.   'They had power and capacity by their order to preach, to minister, to offer, to reconcile, and to baptise; they were indeed acts of order but they might not by the law of the church exercise any of these acts without licence from the bishop', that is a matter of 'jurisdiction, and shows the superiority of the bishop over his presbyters by the practice of christendom'.[26] The relation between the bishop and his presbyters makes him pastor of those with whom he shares his pastoral ministry. He is also pastor to his deacons, as well as to all his people. Thus the bishop is the chief minister in his diocese, with responsibility in canon law for giving authority to exercise priestly, diaconal and lay ministries there. The diocese remains in principle a single eucharistic community in Anglican polity, and the bishop remains the minister who supports, and endorses by his presence, the many varied activities of the living community of the Church in the diocese.

---

[24]   With the exception of the colonial period in America, where parishes were the basic unit and episcopal oversight was for a time exercised from England (see Chapter 8).

[25]   Jeremy Taylor, *Episcopacy Asserted, Works*, V.156.

[26]   Jeremy Taylor, *Episcopacy Asserted, Works*, V.152.

191. Oversight and pastoral care can never be separated. Nevertheless, it has not infrequently been the case in the history of the Church of England, as in the wider Church, that the coupling of leadership with 'serving and caring for the people of God' has been obscured to some degree by contemporary expectations about leadership, which have given the 'Lord Bishop' a 'lordly' role. The pastoral service which puts the bishop at the disposal of the community should, paradoxically, be the essence of his role as 'overseer or superintendent'. A bishop is to be 'the servant, not the lord of souls' and 'conformable to the example of Christ, by humility, charity and care of his flock'.[27]

ii. The ministry of the Word

192. The New Testament principle that the bishop has a special responsibility for the ministry of the Word and the maintenance of the community in the truth of faith, is endorsed in the sixteenth century Ordinal by the presenting of a Bible to the new bishop, with the words, 'Give heed unto reading, exhortation and doctrine. Think upon the things contained in this book. Be diligent in them, that the increase coming thereby may be manifest unto all men'.[28] There is a direct link here with the bishop's early role as leader of the single local worshipping community, which was brought out by sixteenth century reformers as they sought to redress the imbalance which had arisen in the later Middle Ages between the ministry of the Word and the ministry of the Sacraments. They emphasised the saving power of the Word; the ministry of the Word is seen as central to the ministry of reconciliation because Scripture brings people to Christ. The rite of ordination of a bishop in *The Alternative Service Book* continues to require the bishop-elect to make a promise in answer to the Archbishop's question, 'Will you be diligent in prayer, in reading Holy Scripture, and in all studies that will deepen your faith and fit you to uphold the truth of the Gospel against error?'

193. In the last two hundred years a willingness to treat the Bible for academic purposes like any other ancient text, to apply to it the criteria of the historian and the scientist, has sometimes produced crises of popular

---

27   Thomas Wilson, *Sacra Privata, Works*, V (Oxford, 1860), pp. 64-5.
28   The priest is given a Bible with the words, 'Take thou authority to preach the Word of God, and to minister the holy Sacraments in the Congregation, where thou shalt be lawfully appointed thereto'. The deacon is given a New Testament with the words, 'Take thou authority to read the Gospel in the Church of God, and to preach the same, if thou be thereto licensed by the Bishop himself '.

confidence. And in recent decades the availability of modern media of communication has meant that the bishop does not any longer speak in such crises only to his own local congregations. It is the bishop's task here to seek, with his fellow bishops, to help the community to see the importance of the continuing story of the Bible's preservation, and of the unfolding of its teaching in each generation. It is an important aspect of the feeding of his sheep that the bishop should seek to preserve from any anxiety which may seem to threaten their faith, those who have no means of assessing what sometimes may appear to be negative implications of what scholarship may seem to be saying about the fundamentals of Christian belief.[29]

iii.   The ministry of the Sacraments

194.   The Declaration read by the Archbishop in *The Alternative Service Book* declares that 'the bishop is to baptise and confirm, to preside at the holy communion, and to lead the offering of prayer and praise'.

195.   No change of principle or practice was made in England in the sixteenth century in the pastoral understanding of the bishop's role as in principle still the eucharistic head of the local diocesan community, the regular minister of Confirmation,[30] and ultimately responsible for discipline, as for the ministry of absolution. Anglican practice retains, from before the separation from Rome in the sixteenth century, the ancient distinction between Baptism and Confirmation. The bishop alone may confirm the candidate with the laying on of hands with prayer (and sometimes chrismation). These actions effectively signify that the candidate is a member not merely of a local congregation, nor indeed of one particular denomination or ecclesial body, but of a universal body in which the bishop is the visible sign of continuity. In Confirmation the bishop acts (as he does in Ordination), as the one who symbolises the unity of the local church, the spatial unity and the temporal unity and continuity of the church: that is, as the person in whom the three planes intersect. It is for this reason that Anglicans have been unwilling to give up the principle of episcopal Confirmation, in spite of the enormous pressures this places upon

---

29   See, further, Chapter 15.

30   Anglican practice is if anything more rigorous here than that of the Roman Catholic Churches, where in certain exceptional circumstances a priest may occasionally confirm; and that of the Orthodox Church, where a priest is the normal minister of the single, unbroken rite of initiation. It must be remembered, however, that in both these cases the candidates are anointed with chrism, which must always be consecrated by the bishop.

the bishop of a large diocese. Confirmations are a time at which the people have a strong sense of their relationship with the bishop, and, through the bishop, with the wider church.

196. The belief that the bishop is in principle eucharistic president of the local diocesan community has not in itself been the subject of serious controversy in the Church of England. It has been taken as part of the bedrock understanding of the bishop's role from the sixteenth century, as it was before that date in England and elsewhere. It has, however, been clearly evident in practice only recently; the bishop today often presides at the Eucharist in the parishes he visits. In the notes to the service of Holy Communion in *The Alternative Service Book* it is stipulated that when the bishop is present, it is appropriate that he should act as president. He may also delegate sections of the service (32-49) to a priest; but he retains the role of absolving and blessing the assembly.

iv. Moral authority and discipline

197. Both *The Book of Common Prayer* and *The Alternative Service Book* put an emphasis upon the importance of the bishop's setting an example of 'innocency of life', living 'soberly, righteous and godly', as a 'wholesome example, in word, in conversation, in love, in faith, in chastity and in purity'. The exercise of discipline in the community is intimately related to the quality of the bishop's own life. It is in 'imitation of Christ' that the bishop exercises a Christ-like discipline 'with all patience and doctrine', merciful at the same time as just.

198. *The Book of Common Prayer* includes an emphasis upon the 'comforting of the terrified conscience', as Lutheran tradition characteristically described it. This is found in the exhortation to be given when the minister announces the day of a forthcoming celebration of Holy Communion:

> If any of you ... cannot quiet his own conscience, but requireth further comfort or counsel, let him come to me, or to some other discreet and learned Minister of God's Word, and open his grief; that by the ministry of God's holy Word he may receive the benefit of absolution, together with ghostly counsel and advice.

Here the sacramental ministry is seen in the Lutheran way as inseparable from the ministry of the Word; but it is of importance that the comfort of the conscience is linked here with the ancient ministry of absolution, the declaration of God's forgiveness, which was and has continued to be confined to priests and bishops.

199.   The bishop must 'correct and punish' those in his pastoral care who are 'unquiet, disobedient and criminous' (to use the sixteenth century language). He does so as chief minister of the diocese. This is a personal authority in the sense that it is exercised by an individual to whom it is entrusted. But it is also corporate and communal, for the bishop derives his authority in matters of discipline from the acceptance of his people as well as from Christ their Head.   Obedience to one entrusted with the responsibility of oversight is thus an expression of loyalty to the fellowship. The bishop acts not in dominion, but in the interests of an order which can be described as 'love in regulative operation'.[31] This is all part of the Church's life as a community which seeks to submit to Christ, and whose members ought to live with respect for one another's needs. The bishop's power to require compliance acts for the sake of peace and mutual love and the maintenance of the truth.

200.   The sixteenth century Church of England retained a Canon Law whose origins are far older than the refinements (and corruptions) of the penitential system to which the reformers objected in the practice of the late mediaeval Church. Although the *equipage* of the penitential system was partly discarded in sixteenth century England, the Canons settled on in 1604 provided comprehensive legal sanctions in moral matters. Something had to be done to make up for one's offences. It was intended that 'notorious crimes: adultery, whoredom, incest, drunkenness, swearing, ribaldry, usury or any other uncleanness and wickedness of life' should be 'punished by the severity of the laws'.[32] The very exemplary character of the moral authority which bishops and other clergy ought to exercise is enshrined in law, and sanctions provided for it. Ministers, 'having always in mind, that they ought to excel others in purity of life, and should be examples to the people who live well and Christianly, do so under pain of ecclesiastical censures, to be inflicted with severity, according to the qualities of their offences'.[33]

---

31   AR, 82.
32   *Canons of 1604*, Cardwell, *Synodalia*, xcii ff.
33   *Canons of 1604*, lxxv.

201.   There was no question in the minds of the framers of these canons but that the community, through its officers, ought to exercise authority in moral matters, and an authority in which there is not only the attractiveness of example, but the element of discipline for offenders, too.[34]   Nor was it questioned that the community, through its officers, ought to exclude from the Eucharist those who were guilty of persistent and public offences: 'Notorious offenders ... openly known to live in sin notorious, without repentance', or who have offended against the law of charity which binds the community together ('who have maliciously and openly contended with their neighbours, until they shall be reconciled').[35]   The same exclusion applies, *ipso facto*, to schismatics.[36] *Mutatis mutandis*, and with due concern to distinguish private counsel and absolution from public discipline by Church Courts and legal remission of legal penalty, the underlying principles here were consciously those of the early Church, where the whole business of penance was a public matter.[37] But it cannot be said that the English reformers intended to restrict authority in moral matters to a community action, either through exclusion from Holy Communion or through the courts. There is recognition in *The Book of Common Prayer* that a priest, and *a fortiori* a bishop, is entrusted with authority to declare absolution. In the ordination of a priest in the 1662 service we have, 'Whose sins thou dost forgive, they are forgiven; and whose sins thou dost retain, they are retained'.[38] An absolution follows the General Confession at morning and evening prayer, as well as in the service of Holy Communion.

202.   In present-day understanding the bishop is servant of the community as he exercises discipline. This authority is defined in modern English Canon Law in terms of the bishop's 'jurisdiction as ordinary'. This ordinary inherent jurisdiction still requires him to 'correct and punish all such as be unquiet, disobedient, or criminous'. Church of England Canon Law says that the 'inferior clergy who have received authority to minister in any diocese' owe 'canonical obedience ... to the bishop of the same'. Further, this ordinary, inherent jurisdiction gives the bishop the right of summoning all diocesan synods and conferences and of presiding at them. Moreover, 'no resolution in any ... synod or diocesan conference shall have

---

34   Not of course to be exercised without mercy.
35   *Canons of 1604*, xxvi.
36   *Canons of 1604*, xxvii.
37   See B. Poschmann, *Penance and the Anointing of the Sick* (im Breisgau, 1950, repr. Frieburg, 1967), tr. F. Courtenay.
38   In the ASB service this quotation from John 20 occurs only in the Gospel.

effect without the sanction of the bishop', although that sanction 'is not lightly nor without grave cause to be withheld' (Canon C18.5).

203.   Thus in pastoral care, the ministry of the Word and Sacraments, and the exercise of discipline, the bishop carries out his ministry of oversight in the local community.   His ministry is never to be understood apart from those with whom he shares his oversight, in delegating to them various tasks which belong in the first instance to himself.   (The position of suffragan bishops who share in a special and uniquely close way the ministry of oversight of a bishop in the 'local church', the diocese, is discussed in another chapter (see Chapter 11).)   Nor can the bishop's ministry be separated from the ministry of the whole people of God in the diocese: bishop, presbyters and people belong together.   Amongst his people the bishop is the personal focus of their unity, and principal agent in maintaining and strengthening that unity.

b.   The corporate pastorate

204.   In the formal, synodical exercise of episcopal collegiality in England, the House of Bishops has had a changing role.   It has always exercised a 'moral authority' less easily definable than its constitutional powers, but inseparable from them as giving corporate episcopal authority its continuing character of a leadership to which the Christian community has naturally looked.

205.   The constitutional powers have always in England been to some degree defined and, in part at least, controlled by secular government. Mediaeval kings never settled the precise limits of the powers of ecclesiastical Councils, but they took a keen interest in their fiscal role, and recognised them as legislatures, capable of making canons binding on persons holding ecclesiastical office and - within the penitential system - upon all the faithful when they sinned.   The structural parallel with Parliament was strong enough already in the thirteenth century for a House of Clergy to sit below the House of Bishops in the Convocations of the two provinces of Canterbury and York.

206.   At diocesan level the synodical structure from the Middle Ages was fundamentally different in consisting of a single bishop acting as president, with a 'college' of presbyters.   This difference is important; it was insisted upon, to the extent of making a suffragan bishop 'count' as a member of the

clergy in order to preserve the principle of single-person episcopal presidency (preserved today in part by the diocesan bishop's power of veto).[39] A mediaeval bishop promulgated statutes which ran in his own diocese; he did so in principle 'in synod', but in practice often by his own fiat.[40]

207. At the Reformation, the two provincial Convocations, but not the diocesan synods, were recognised as having power to make canons with a force comparable in certain respects with secular legislation. They required Royal Assent, like laws made in Parliament. They were to be obeyed throughout the Province whose Convocation made them. They could not, however, contradict secular law or bind the secular authorities. The parallel between the Upper and Lower Houses of Parliament and the Upper and Lower Houses of the Convocations was recognised, and the diocesan bishops who sat in the House of Lords constituted a living bridge between the two systems.[41] A strategic device of some brilliance enshrined the pragmatic compromise that although Councils must be called by 'princes', and Convocations ought therefore to be summoned by the monarch who also summons Parliament, the Archbishop was nevertheless also in some sense the convener.[42] Convocations were deemed to be dissolved with (but not by) Parliament.

208. Sixteenth century thinkers brought a number of assumptions about the nature of conciliar government to the framing of the formularies of the Church of England. Article 21 of the Thirty-Nine Articles speaks only of General Councils. Its preoccupation is with their summoning ('General Councils may not be gathered together without the commandment and will of Princes'), with their potential for error ('they may err') and with their authority ('things ordained by them as necessary to salvation have neither strength nor authority, unless it be declared that they be taken out of Holy Scripture').[43] These concerns arose directly out of topics of heated

39   E. Garth Moore, *An Introduction to English Canon Law* (Oxford, 1967), p. 23. Cf. Synodical Government Measure (1969) Sch. 3, 28 (e). A suffragan bishop is not now a member of the House of Clergy.

40   C. Cheney, 'The Earliest English Diocesan Statutes', *English Historical Review*, 75 (1960), 1-29; and 'A Group of Related Synodal Statutes of the thirteenth century', *Mediaeval Studies presented to Aubrey Gwynn, S.J.*, ed. J.A. Watt *et al* (Dublin, 1961), 114-32.

41   Cf. the mediaeval emphasis on the *pontifex* as 'bridge-maker'.

42   See E. Gibson, *Synodus Anglicana* (London, 1702, repr. Farnborough, 1967) pp. 15-17, 'The summons upon [the] intimation of the Royal Pleasure, being still issued in his Grace's Name, and under the Archiepiscopal Seal'.

43   Cf. *Reformatio Legum Ecclesiasticarum*, 14, ed. Cardwell, *Synodalia*, p. 6.

contemporary debate among reformers, and, like much else in the sixteenth century discussion of problems of authority, the debate here suffered from a tendency to divide up the issues into *theses* or 'articles' suitable for treatment in formal disputation. The same polemical preoccupations recurred again and again in the writings of the sixteenth century divines, and made it difficult for anyone to develop a positive, balanced and comprehensive conciliar theory. The first Anglicans had - and knew they had - an imperfect knowledge of the early Councils and later ones alike;[44] they were aware that they were working with faulty texts.[45] But they thought they had stressed the key points.

209 . In the circumstances of the time[46] it was of importance for the Anglican reformers to emphasise the normality of a secular sovereign summoning a Council and ratifying its decrees. It was argued that, apart from the Councils of the primitive Church, this had historically been the pattern.[47] In any case, it was protested, a Council called by a Pope could not be 'free'.[48] The bishops who come to it will be the Pope's men and must vote as he directs.[49]

i.   Membership of Councils and Synods

210. The membership of Councils was widely discussed in the sixteenth century. Three points commonly arose here: whether it is important that the Council should consist of 'good men';[50] whether a larger number carries more weight than a smaller number; whether a Council must be 'representative' of the whole Church. These two last points are interrelated. Latimer says that a larger number is not necessarily better; it is not a matter of a majority decision.[51] There was some awareness here of a patristic sense that a Council should have the widest possible base, but apparently no strong feeling in favour of the universality for which Cyprian and Celestine I had

---

[44]   This is admitted by a number of reformers. See Greenslade, S.L., 'The English Reformers and the Councils of the Church', *Oecumenica* (1967), pp. 96-7.

[45]   Jewel, *Works*, Parker Society, I.341.

[46]   That is, not only the English situation, where the King had Royal Supremacy, but also in parallel with provisions in reformed Churches on the Continent, where princes and magistrates also often convened meetings of the Churches.

[47]   Rogers, *Works*, Parker Society, p. 205.

[48]   Greenslade, *op. cit.*, pp. 101, 104, 106.

[49]   Jewel, *Works*, III.205.

[50]   Latimer, *Works*, Parker Society, I.288.

[51]   *Ibid.*, cf. Greenslade, p. 101.

pressed.[52] 'Representativeness' is a much more complex matter in sixteenth century eyes. Ignatius of Antioch had argued at the turn of the first century that the whole Church entrusted to a bishop is present in his person. This sense seems less strong in the sixteenth century debates.[53]

ii. The force of conciliar decrees

211. At issue in all this, in the sixteenth century debates and after, was whether a Council's decrees could have any force at all if it was not properly summoned, or its work not properly ratified, or its membership in some way lacking. The question of the guidance of the Holy Spirit was raised, but the notion of Christ's presence where two or three are gathered in his name, and the concomitant principle that Christ must be the president of any true Council seemed more important[54] against the background of revolt against 'papalism'. Here the reformers' concern was to prevent any usurpation of Christ's Headship of the Church. The suspicion was that a Council was liable to act like a 'human' institution and, without divine guidance, to behave as though its decrees could add to Scripture or even outweigh or contradict its teaching. It was for this reason that there was so much talk of 'error' in conciliar decision,[55] and so much underlining of the importance of consonance with Scripture as the test of all conciliar decrees. It seemed obvious to those who framed the Thirty-Nine Articles that some Councils have erred; that their definitions even sometimes contradict one another. They argued that that must mean that no-one's faith is 'bound' by a Council unless what it has said can be confirmed out of Scripture.[56] Councils cannot make a rule of faith, says Jewel.[57] Tyndale, Cranmer, Whitaker, and a host of others agree that Scripture is the guide and judge of all that Councils do.[58] But even if there was some suspicion in England of the record of Councils, the principle of equality of episcopal brotherhood in

---

52   H. Chadwick, 'The Status of Ecumenical Councils in Anglican Thought', *Orientalia Christiana Analecta*, 195 (1973), 373 and 394, cites Cyprian, Ep. 55.6, and Celestine, Ep. 18.1.

53   *Ibid.*, p. 393, citing Ignatius, *Ad. Eph.* 1; *Ad Magn.* 2, *Ad Thrall.* 1. Luther reviles the whole idea of such a form of representativeness.

54   E.g. Jewel, *Works*, Parker Society II.995.

55   Chadwick, 'The Status', p. 395.

56   *Ibid.*, p. 401 and Cardwell, *Synodalia*, p. 6.

57   Jewel, Parker Society, II.996.

58   Tyndale, Parker Society, III.99 *et al*. For a recent bibliography, see B. Gogan, *The Common Corps of Christendom* (Leiden, 1982).

guardianship of the faith was affirmed by the sixteenth century settlement.[59]

212. In his Conference with Fisher the Jesuit, William Laud in the seventeenth century set out a case for the view that 'the Church being as large as the world, Christ thought it fitter to govern it aristocratically', that is, by a multiple episcopate. I have carefully examined this for the first six-hundred years,' he says, 'even to within the time of St. Gregory the Great.'[60] As Laud saw it, it is the duty of bishops to provide a system of checks and balances in mutual correction. What was done amiss by a bishop, he says, was corrigible by a synod of bishops.[61] Thus, as Newman was later to put it, 'bishops everywhere ... are the elementary centre of unity', and bishop is superior to bishop only in rank (for example as archbishop or metropolitan.[62]

iii. General and local Councils

213. In 1606, Richard Field published a treatise *Of the Church*, in which he reflected at some length on the purposes Councils served when something went wrong with the normal system of checks and balances. General Councils, he thought, were called for three reasons, 'the suppressing of new heresies, formerly not condemned'; 'a general and uniform reformation of abuses crept into the Church'; and 'the taking away of schisms grown into patriarchal Churches, about the election of their pastors'.[63] Field was also interested in representativeness. He comments that those with 'authority to teach, define, prescribe, and to direct' have the 'deciding and defining voices', but that laymen may be present too, 'to hear, set forward, and consent unto that which is there to be done'.[64] He insists upon the importance of openness. There must be no 'secret' meeting[65] (a point with which Dean Stanley of Westminster agreed in 1867, and which he criticised in the conduct of the first Lambeth Conference). Field thought that 'patriarchs' ought to preside in Councils 'as having an honourable pre-

---

59 Cf. *Articuli Cleri*, 1558, Cardwell, *Synodalia*, II.493. Some unfinished business remained, however.
60 Laud, *Works* (Oxford, 1849), II.222.
61 Laud, *Conference with Fisher*, IX.ic.26.
62 John Henry Newman, 'The Catholicity of the Anglican Church', *Essays Critical and Historical* (London, 1890), II.20, 23.
63 Richard Field, *Of the Church*, 1606 (ed. Cambridge, 1854), V.48. The reference is to the first four Ecumenical Councils.
64 *Ibid.*, V.49, p. 15.
65 *Ibid.*,

eminence above and before other bishops, in such assemblies'.[66] He acknowledged that the Holy Spirit did not guide Councils in such a way that they were guaranteed to be free from error; Councils may err and sometimes have.   That is clear from the fact that they proceed by 'mediation, study and search' and do not expect 'immediate revelation'.[67] There are hints here of the picture of a central and pivotal, but qualified and limited role for bishops in conciliar government; but the sixteenth century preoccupations are still dominant.

214.   William Laud's Conference with Fisher the Jesuit in 1622 represents a new departure because Laud gave serious thought to the question of the powers of independent action of provincial or national synods representing only part of the universal Church. 'The making of canons, which must bind all particular Christians and Churches, cannot be concluded and established.' he said, except in a General Council.   When a situation arises - as it had done in the sixteenth century - when there is an emergency with which only a General Council can deal, but it is not possible to hold one,[68] the Church must pray for such a Council and either wait for it, 'or else reform itself *per partes*, by means of national or provincial synods'.   He says that that is not an idea which ought to surprise us;[69] it is 'as lawful for a particular Church' ... 'to reform what is amiss in doctrine or manners' as it is for it to 'publish or promulgate' the catholic faith.[70]   It is surely better to do that than to wait?[71]   He cites Jean Gerson as his authority for saying that a Church may be reformed *per partes*.[72]   This is not envisaged by Laud as a licence for independent local action in everything, but as an emergency measure only.

iv.   Upper and Lower Houses

215.   In 1606, John Overall, Bishop of Norwich, compiled his 'Convocation Book', in which a series of canons set out the principles of relations between Church and State.[73]   The King refused to let Convocation

---

66   *Ibid.*, V.20, pp. 16-17.
67   *Ibid.*, V.51, p. 48.
68   A debate on the holding of a General Council went through several stages among the Lutherans and caught the imagination of sixteenth century Anglican divines.
69   Laud, *Works*, II.235.
70   *Ibid.*, p. 167.
71   *Ibid.*, p. 169.
72   Jean Gerson, *De Concilio Generali*, I.
73   See, further, Chapter 12.

accept it, because its teaching on 'the Divine Right of Kings' seemed to justify revolution in certain circumstances. The book was not published until 1690, when it contributed to a controversy over the right of princes to call synods, the rights of archbishops to prorogue them, and the rights of the Lower House of Convocation over against the House of Bishops. This came at a time when the issue of parity of ministry was also much debated, and some saw in the Lower House's assertion of its independence an incipient presbyterianism, with presbyters claiming for themselves 'the most important act of Church government, the judging in points of doctrine', as Gilbert Burnet put it.[74] The Lower House was in fact asserting only a right to be on the same footing in relation to the Upper House as the Commons to the Lords in Parliament; that is, to have power to adjourn by its own authority. The Upper House took the view that it was of ancient usage for the Archbishop, as President, to adjourn both at once.

216. The difficulties raised were real enough, for while the Bishops were sitting in the House of Lords they could not meet in Convocation, and therefore, if the two Houses must always meet simultaneously, a good deal of Lower House working time was lost while the Upper House was otherwise engaged. But, as is the way with such disputes, the controversy roused old bitternesses and stirred up questions about fundamentals. The Upper House said that it could make no concession without injury to the Church's very constitution as an episcopal Church. The Lower House said that it was not challenging the superiority of bishops to presbyters as of divine ordinance and apostolic institution, but wanted only what was necessary for it to function efficiently as the Lower House of Convocation. Yet loud murmurs were heard to the effect that the Church had not in reality decided whether bishops were superior to presbyters by divine appointment or only by the ordinances and practice of the Church. In 1717 the squabbling Convocation was prorogued by Royal Writ. The Convocation of Canterbury did not meet again until 1852, that of York until 1861.[75]

217. The tone of the Victorian Convocations was very different. The Lower House recognised its place in 'humble petitions'. In the February Sessions of 1859, for example, the Lower House thus addressed the Upper: 'Your petitioners observe with thankfulness the progress which continues to

74   Gilbert Burnet, ii.283.
75   T. Lathbury, *A History of the Convocation of the Church of England* (London, 1842, 2nd ed., 1853), pp. 336 ff. See, further, Chapter 12, 'Church and State', section on 'The Seventeenth and Eighteenth Centuries'.

be made towards the restoration of synodical action in the Church of England ... Your petitioners have seen with satisfaction the appointment of a committee of the Lower House in May, 1857, to consider the best means of securing the united counsel and co-operation of the clergy and laity of the Church'.[76] In a discussion of procedure we see it agreed that the Prolocutor of the Lower House may present its views to the President of the Upper House, or individual members may go through a bishop to address the Archbishop. But, as Randall Davidson, later Archbishop of Canterbury, put it, 'The President knows nothing of the other house but through the Prolocutor'.[77]

218.   In all this, even during the controversy at the turn of the eighteenth century, it is assumed that the House of Bishops not only has seniority, but constitutes the Church in Council, with assistance from the presbyters as and when their Lordships choose to accept it. The presbyters in the House of Clergy constitute a body, with a corporate personality which can speak through the Prolocutor (cf. Appendix I). But it is a corporate identity of a different order from that which the bishops possess. Its corporate identity exists to enable it to speak with a single voice in matters of decision-making on behalf of priests in the province and not as a means of linking together the local diocesan Churches. Nor does it, like the House of Bishops, have a special responsibility of oversight in the maintenance of the faith and its guardianship.

v.   Bishops, clergy and laity

219.   In 1920 a wholly new structure was brought into being, alongside the ancient Convocations but having membership in common with them as regards bishops and clergy. The National Assembly of the Church of England consisted of thirty-eight bishops, two hundred and fifty-one clergy and three hundred and fifty-seven laity, including forty women. Davidson, the Archbishop of Canterbury, as its Chairman, told the members that they were meeting:

> ... no longer as members of a voluntary Church Council, however important, a Church Council without actual powers or legal status, but as a formal, legally constituted body, part of the constitution of the Church and Realm, possessing well defined powers.[78]

76   Chronicle of Convocation, p. 27.
77   Chronicle of Convocation, p. 34.
78   *Proceedings*, p. 5.

220. The Convocations expressed some concern about the new arrangements, although they conferred unprecedented legislative powers, for fear that the Convocations would 'cease to exist or retire into the shade'.[79] Various ecclesiological points of view were put. Dr. B.J. Kidd argued that 'such authority as the National Assembly had, it had more or less in respect of the representative principle, whereas in Convocation the authority was not derived from below, from the Church as a whole, but was derived from above. The members of the Lower House sat in Convocation for the purpose of consultation by the bishops. The bishops themselves derived their authority from their predecessors, and ultimately from the Apostles and from our Lord Himself'.[80] Canon E.C. Baldwin and the Rev. H.P. Burdett saw the new Assembly as the Church by representation 'acting through its bishops and elected clergy and laity' as the 'governing body of the Church'.[81] If it were the Church, 'it must possess the authority of the Church', so it might be argued that the authority of the Convocations had in fact passed to the Assembly.[82] On the other view, that Convocation remained the senior body, it seemed to the Archdeacon of Winchester that we must say that Convocation has the guidance of the Spirit but the Assembly does not.[83]

221. The constitutional questions were more easily settled. Yet the old and the new existed a little uneasily side by side. In the Chronicle of Convocation (Canterbury) for 1923-4 we have an account, for example, of the making of the Prolocutor of the Lower House, where the Prolocutor-elect is still presented to the Archbishop for his election to be confirmed, after he has been elected 'with the unanimous consent of the clergy', and the Archbishop instructs him in Latin that he must defend the honour of the Convocation, and so on (p. 9). This was consistent with Dr. Kidd's view of the authority of the Lower House as derived from above. On the other hand, in the Constitution of the Church Assembly it is provided that matters of doctrine, rite or ceremony must be debated and voted by separate Houses before being put to the Assembly for acceptance or rejection, apparently thus giving the laity as a body equal status with the bishops as a body and the clergy as a body. The equality of the Houses in this is tempered only by the requirement that the Measure must be put finally 'in a form proposed by the House of Bishops'.

---

79   Canterbury, Convocation Chronicle, 1921-2, p. 154.
80   Kidd, *ibid.*, p. 458.
81   Baldwin, *ibid.*, p. 460.
82   Burdett, *ibid.*, p. 461.
83   *Ibid.*, p. 461.

vi. The General Synod

222. By the Synodical Government Measure of 1969, which brought into being the present General Synod, the Church Assembly came to an end and was replaced by a new structure, freshly constituted from the two Convocations. The Queen's declaration stated that 'The Convocations of Canterbury and York, duly called together in obedience to our Royal Writs, are on this day joined together in accordance with the Synodical Government Measure, 1969, and the House of Laity added to them in accordance with that Measure, so as to constitute the General Synod of the Church of England'.[84] The Church Assembly surrendered its functions in favour of the new body with a series of speeches which recognise the difference between the two. The Chairman of the House of Laity, Sir Kenneth Grubb, said, 'we have made a real effort, helpfully, and when possible, promptly, to reply to the requests sent over from the Convocations for the opinions of the Laity'.[85] From now on there was to be 'partnership in discussion and decision', as the Archbishop of Canterbury put it.[86] The Archbishop of York said the same at the opening of the General Synod itself. The laity, he pointed out, were to 'take their place alongside the clergy in the Councils of the Church'.[87]

223. Constitutionally, however, there is still some significant continuity with previous practice. The Convocations of the two provinces continue, and at each the Archbishop of the province has the 'right' of 'presiding' (Canon C 17.4). The Lower House of Convocation still speaks through a Prolocutor (Canon G 3)). At Diocesan level, although the Synod is designed to be democratically representative, it is provided that 'nothing ... shall prevent the bishop from summoning a conference of persons *appearing to him* to be representative of the clergy and laity of the diocese on such occasions and for such purposes as he thinks fit'.[88] A bishop will normally preside at a diocesan Synod although clerical or lay vice-presidents may also sometimes do so at the bishop's invitation (Schedule 3 (43[10])). Episcopal leadership is still strongly marked. The Houses of Bishops and Clergy of the General Synod still have the same membership as those of the Convocations, with the Archbishops of Canterbury and York as joint

84   *Proceedings*, 1970, p. 3.
85   *Proceedings*, 1970, p. 458.
86   *Proceedings*, 1970, p. 55.
87   *Proceedings*, 1970, p. 6.
88   Synodical Government Measure, 1969, Schedule 4 (7).

presidents of the Synod.[89] It remains the case that in 'a provision touching doctrinal formulae or the services or ceremonies of the Church of England or the administration of the Sacraments or sacred rites thereof shall, before it is finally approved by the General Synod, be referred to the House of Bishops, and shall be submitted for such final approval in terms proposed by the House of Bishops and not otherwise'.[90] The House of Bishops, then, retains a significant measure of seniority in authority in constitutional terms, despite the equality between the Houses in debate and voting which is also enshrined in the present constitution. This reflects its continuing 'moral authority' as the House of ministers entrusted with oversight and with guardianship of faith and order.

224.   In recent years within the Church of England, there have been signs that Bishops are being called upon to play a larger role as a corporate pastorate. The General Synod has asked the House of Bishops to respond on matters where guidance in the face of the Church's uncertainty has been called for.   In the last decade the Bishops' Report on *The Nature of Christian Belief* and their two Reports on the Ordination of Women to the Priesthood have been a response to this call for corporate episcopal leadership.

225.   The House of Bishops has a formally recognised function in Synodical Government in the area of legislation and decision-making; a function which it shares with the House of Clergy and the House of Laity; and a function in which the Crown in Parliament is also involved, although the Synod has its independence. The Parliamentary model on which our national Synodical Government is largely based has both advantages and disadvantages. We may complain about the cost and the time involved, the confrontational and party political style that can mar its work, a pattern of meeting that effectively rules out the participation of many of the laity. But we suspect that any pattern of representative Church Government is liable to faults of this kind.

226.   An electoral system produces 'representatives' in the other Houses on a different basis from that on which members of the House of Bishops represent their people, and that can result in a confusing impression of a Parliamentary-style democracy working alongside a sacramental system. For bishops have no electing constituency. The bishop at his ordination is

---

89   Schedule 2, Articles 2 and 4.
90   *Ibid.*, 2, Article 7.

called to be a chief pastor sharing with his fellow bishops a special responsibility. That responsibility is not answerable to the other Houses by the counting of votes, but it is in mutual charity, and for the common good, that the bishops must seek to express the common mind.

227. Two further developments in the last century have given importance to the unitive role of the bishop's ministry in relation to the 'second plane' of unity. The establishment of the Lambeth Conference and the other world-wide Anglican structures of the Anglican Consultative Council and the Primates' Meeting, alongside the ancient Primacy of Canterbury, have helped to integrate the local Church into the wider fellowship. The emphasis on each diocesan bishop 'taking his diocese' with him to the Lambeth Conference in 1988 expressed in action this further possibility of uniting local to universal in the person of the bishop. (These developments within the Anglican Communion are discussed in greater detail in Chapter 8.)

228. A second and more recent development is the result of the ecumenical movement. At a diocesan level bishops and others who bear oversight in the churches often have regular meetings and in this way forms of 'ecumenical oversight' develop. Sponsoring bodies and the establishment of regional ecumenical Councils (as in Merseyside and Milton Keynes) open up possibilities for experiencing and symbolising a wider unity of Christians in the joining together of those who exercise oversight. (This is discussed more fully in Chapter 14 on *Ecumenical Progress*.)

c. Continuity in time

229. Church of England thinkers have consistently taken the view that bishops are the normal officers in whose persons the continuity of the Church is directly visible. Although, in Anglican eyes, there was no break, in fact or in intention, with the apostolic succession of ministry at the time of the Reformation, that succession must be seen in the context of a theology of apostolicity understood as the faithfulness of the whole living community to the Gospel.

230. The claim to sixteenth century continuity in Anglican Orders was soon challenged by Roman Catholic authors. It was suggested that Matthew Parker's consecration as Elizabeth I's Archbishop of Canterbury was invalid, or that Bishop Barlow, who was the chief consecrator of Parker,

had not himself been validly consecrated, and that there was therefore a break in the line which invalidated all subsequent Anglican ordinations. There were, too, assertions that the form of ordination, which left out the giving of the 'instruments' of office (in the case of priests, the paten and chalice), made the rite incomplete and ordinations conducted by it null and void. Also the Ordinal had omitted the words 'for the office and work of a priest' (or 'bishop') from the service, and it was therefore contended that the specific intention to make a priest or a bishop was not present.

231. The historic fact of the consecration of Matthew Parker is not now seriously challenged. It has since come to be realised that the 'giving of the instruments' had been a mediaeval addition to the liturgy and could not therefore be regarded as essential.[91] The words 'for the office and work of a priest' (or 'bishop') were added to the Ordinal in 1662, so as to underline the distinction between priest and bishop which was being challenged by the Presbyterians. This had the result, in addition, of making the intention quite clear; but there is no real question of an earlier defect of intention. There was, beyond question, no intention in the sixteenth century Church of England to make a break in theology or practice in the episcopal succession. At no time since then has the consecration of bishops in the Church of England involved less than three bishops in that succession. Thus in his person the bishop truly and effectively symbolises the relation of himself, and all those with whom he is bound in his diocese, with the Church through the ages back to the time of the early Church.

232. But it is of primary importance that such a succession should stand in the continuity of apostolic faith and the life of the community. The consecrating bishops do not act alone but under the Holy Spirit and with their people. Apostolic succession is a function of the apostolicity of the whole Church. In the recognition that this is so lies hope for the future reconciliation of ministries between episcopal and non-episcopal Churches, and between episcopal Churches themselves, where estrangement has broken or damaged communion.[92]

---

91   Several bishops at the Council of Trent did not think the ceremony essential. In 1947 Pius XII in the Constitution *Sacramentum ordinis* gave an authoritative ruling that the 'matter' of the Sacrament of Order was the imposition of hands alone and that 'at least in future' the *traditio instrumentorum* 'was not necessary for validity'(cf. *The Christian Faith in the Doctrinal Documents of the Christian Church*, ed. J. Neuner and J. Dupuis (4th ed., London, 1982), pp. 506-7).

92   See, further, Chapters 9 and 14.

233. We feel able to assert with confidence, then, that through the vicissitudes of the Reformation and the crises of succeeding centuries the Church of England has maintained an episcopate in which the continuities are clear and strong and the preservation of the principles and practice of the early Church has always been important.

7

The Church of England since the Reformation:

the practicalities

234. It is a bishop's task to live out the ideals of his calling and commissioning in a busy and demanding daily life. In the letters and diaries and sermons of English bishops through the centuries, the realities of doing the job are plain, and we have thought it helpful to sketch both the commonplaces of episcopal experience and some of the changes of emphasis over the centuries in a few examples of bishops at work. In early and mediaeval centuries it was thought important that a bishop should not seek the office out of ambition for worldly success. In a wry acknowledgement of this, we see Edmund Grindal, Bishop of London from 1559-1570, and later Archbishop of York and then of Canterbury, writing to his friend the Reformer Peter Martyr on the Continent to say that he has felt it right to accept the bishopric of London only because it would be irresponsible to let it fall into the wrong hands. He found being a bishop a high-profile business. He had to defend his people against racketeering landlords and air pollution (the London smog) and deal with public order offences in an age when a bishop was not always concerned with social welfare. It fell to him, as an Ecclesiastical Commissioner, to enforce regulations to prevent the entry of slanderous and seditious literature into the Port of London. He wrote 'familiar' letters, man-to-man, to Sir Robert Cecil, one of the chief ministers of Elizabeth's reign, on points of ecclesiastical concern in the Government's behaviour. He had to watch the destruction by bonfire at Cheapside of copes, crosses, censers, altar-cloths, bells, books and banners, as a result of Puritan purges of all things 'Romish' after Mary's reign. Moderately Puritan in his own sympathies, he refused to act against Puritans in London. He had to accommodate in the pulpits of the city a range of preachers from the fashionable to the popular. Among his episcopal contemporaries, Thomas Bentham of Coventry and Lichfield is to be observed trying to master the finer points of local finance and politics, while John Parkhurst of Norwich seems to have been at times almost overcome by the administrative demands made on him. All these Elizabethan bishops found their pastoral responsibilities interpreted for them by circumstances in ways dictated by contemporary demands; they were thrust into public

life, where they had to try to keep a balance in the use of their time and influence.

235. Henry Compton, another Bishop of London (from 1674-1713), had lived through the period of exile which had sent many Anglican divines to the Continent during Cromwell's supremacy; he had seen the Restoration Settlement which restored the Church of England to its legal footing as the Established Church; and he was acutely conscious of the difficulty of now arriving at a working position in relation to the Presbyterian challenge to the very existence of episcopacy on the one hand, and what he saw as the danger of persecution if the King's Roman Catholic sympathies put English Protestants in the position of the French Huguenots. He did his best as Bishop to meet his clergy's need for guidance and a chance to air their anxieties, by holding 'Conferences' at which he would give an address, and then throw the meeting open for general discussion. Particularly popular were themes arising out of the country-wide controversy over the perceived differences of theology and practice between Anglicans and Roman Catholics. Compton was no theologian, but he seems to have had a good, clear mind. His accounts of these discussions, and what we know of his sermons from contemporaries, show him to have been full of common sense but without style or eloquence, responsive to contemporary religious and constitutional problems, but at bottom straightforwardly convinced that all rests on the authority of Scripture as interpreted by the Creeds and the Thirty-Nine Articles.

236.   His great strength as a diocesan bishop was his practicality. He made the existing machinery of the Church's life work. He encouraged his clergy to make rotas for preaching; to discourage private christenings at home (in which he was notably successful); to bring back regular catechising on Sunday afternoons; to meet with the bishop every month to consult with him about their parish problems and the parishioners in their care. He wanted his clergy to get to know their people, to be conscientious in visiting the sick, holding services in which the liturgy was carefully and seriously enacted, preaching so as to instruct their people 'on the whole mind of God as far as relates to things necessary for salvation', adapting what they say for the simple or the more sophisticated.[1] He retained, at the same time as carrying out his local diocesan duties with exemplary care, that sense of his

---

[1]   Eleventh *Conference*, p. 23.

responsibilities in the wider world which involved him in Restoration politics.

237. He had, as Bishop of London, a loosely-defined jurisdiction over the American Colonists in Virginia, resting on the precedent of custom.[2] He put a great deal of effort into correspondence with the 'Plantations', trying his best to establish the Church of England in America, and including in his pastoral care white settlers, native Indians and African slaves alike. In later years his work was assisted by the Society for the Propagation of the Gospel, which was approved by Convocation in 1701 and given a Royal Charter in 1702, with the Archbishop of Canterbury as its president and Compton as its Vice-President. The work of the Society did not intrude on the Bishop of London's legal jurisdiction in the Plantations, but it did, with his co-operation, greatly forward his missionary work there.

238. From 1709 Compton took up the causes of the Episcopal Church in Scotland, where the episcopal clergy were suffering persecution at the hands of the Presbyterians; and of French protestant refugees, whom he had come to know well and to respect during his exile in France during the Commonwealth period. That led him in time into an interest in achieving union between the continental protestant Churches, especially the Reformed communities of Switzerland, and the Church of England.

239. We see Henry Compton, then, a man of his time in his prejudices and political affiliations, not, it was thought, a promising bishop when he was first appointed, developing into a bishop who understood very well the priority which the pastoral care of his diocese should have, and at the same time discharging the missionary tasks of a bishop and his responsibilities to the wider Church with uncommon zeal. The demands placed upon him as an administrator are in many respects strikingly similar to the burden of administration placed upon our modern bishops.

240. William Wake (1657-1737) had charge of the Diocese of Lincoln from 1705-1716. Wake was particularly conscientious in examining candidates for the ministry, in an age when young men of good family were often put forward for livings who had neither vocation nor gifts for ministry. We have a glimpse of him meeting a mature candidate for ordination, a Dr. William Stukeley, medical man and antiquary, who

---

2   Charles I gave the Bishop of London jurisdiction over all Anglican congregations outside the British Isles at a time when William Laud was Bishop of London and the Archbishop of Canterbury under something of a cloud.

offered himself for the ministry at the age of forty-one. He did his best to cope with the difficulty that bishops were required to reside in London for a good part of the year so as to sit in the House of Lords or attend at Court. He would catch up on his visitations and confirmation duties when he was in his diocese, whenever the weather did not make travelling impossible. He criticised his clergy for not attending to their duty to instruct the people, whom Wake found distressingly ignorant about the faith. He tried to curb plurality in the holding of benefices and to help those of his clergy at the other end of the income scale who were in serious poverty.

241. At the age of twenty-seven, Joseph Butler was appointed preacher at the Rolls Chapel in London, where he delivered a series of sermons on moral themes, which were to be a strong influence on Jane Austen in their published form. He was also a philosopher in the fashion of the day, publishing the influential *Analogy of Religion* in 1736, in an attempt to prove the truths of the Christian faith on the principle of their analogy with scientifically ascertainable laws. Queen Caroline, who cultivated philosophers and had heard his Rolls Sermons spoken well of, made him her Clerk of the Closet in 1736. Thus Butler won further patronage. After the Queen's death in 1738, he was offered the bishopric of Bristol. He thought it a mean offer, because it was the poorest See in England, and he accepted it only on condition that he might retain the income from a benefice at Stanhope.

242. Though he was himself a pluralist, Butler showed remarkable independence for his time under the pressure to act corruptly in matters of money. He impressed contemporaries with his personal frugality. When he was offered the See of Durham in 1750, he refused to accept the condition that he should make certain appointments. 'The bishops as well as the inferior clergy take the oath against simony', he reminded the Duke of Newcastle.

243. He shared the widespread contemporary pessimism about the 'decay' of religion in England. He had refused the Archbishopric of Canterbury when it was offered to him in 1747, on the grounds that he did not have the spirit to undertake 'to support a falling Church'. Yet in an age when only the scientific and rationally demonstrable was intellectually respectable, and many ordinary people believed that science had debunked Christianity and stopped going to Church, he endeavoured to do his duties in his diocese conscientiously, to be generous with whatever wealth came to him, to set in his own person an example of holiness and asceticism of life, and to keep

things going in the Church at grassroots level in honest faithfulness.

244. Horace Walpole said of him that he 'had been wafted' to his See 'in a cloud of metaphysics and remained absorbed in it'. But as Bishop, he, like others, experienced the problem of having too many demands placed upon him, and of finding it difficult to maintain a balance in the discharge of his duties. His duties in his parishes and his charitable projects and ambitious building schemes seem to have silenced the philosopher, and almost the preacher in him, except for sermons on public occasions.

245. Samuel Wilberforce, Bishop of Oxford, then of Winchester (1869-73) began to see, perhaps more clearly than many had done before him, the importance of the Church's mission in a wider world. Yet, like Compton, he was far from neglecting his domestic responsibilities. In his letters[3] he responds to a vicar who is sending him four candidates for Confirmation but is anxious to know what to teach them about Confession; he balances justice and mercy in a letter to an incumbent charged by his Churchwardens with various scandals; he inspects the plans for the restoration of a church and points out practical disadvantages (the pulpit is too high and there is nowhere for the children to sit); he makes a grant to a poor clergyman, on condition he can be sure that it is 'to meet real family needs'; he writes to *The Guardian* about the Missionary Bishops Bill and Church Bills in Parliament (1853) and with firm courtesy to Sir James Stephen, who seems likely to wreck a valuable piece of legislation. He became well-known for the seriousness with which he took his pastoral responsibilities and for his reforms in the diocese.

246. But at the same time he was looking outward. 'I think it is impossible to overvalue the benefit to the Church at home of the return, from time to time, of such men as my right reverend brethren', he says of missionary bishops, 'to tell us what is being done in distant lands ... What did the Apostles do, after going on a missionary journey in distant Phrygia, but come back to narrate to the Church at a central home, what it had pleased God to do by their hands',[4] he asks. He saw difficulties. 'The question is ... how there shall be maintained a real, living unity between two branches of a Church, the one of them being Established and the other not Established'.[5] But he also saw great benefits to the Church in England from its

---

3   *The Letter-Books of Samuel Wilberforce, 1843-68*, ed. R.K. Pugh (Oxford, 1970).
4   *Ibid.*, p. 280.
5   *Ibid.*, p. 257.

participation in mission. 'There has been a manifest growth in the estimate of the Church people of England, of what the home Episcopate is, since we have sent forth the Colonial Episcopate. Instead of regarding the Bishop as a sort of embossed ornament, to stand at the top of the banister, and to be seen on going up and down the stairs, people had at last come to understand that, if he was worth his salt, he must be ... the hardest working man in his diocese - a man who was for ever devising schemes for spreading truth and binding hearts together'.[6]

247.   Charles Thomas Longley was Bishop of Ripon and then of Durham, before becoming Archbishop of York in 1856 and then of Canterbury in 1862. He worked hard at Ripon among the mining communities and the remote villages of his diocese. He could be firm on points of clergy discipline. He established a Diocesan Church Extension Fund to encourage the building of schools and churches. He began to encourage what he was later to call 'opportunities of mutual conference', in the form of ruridecanal chapters at Ripon and Durham. At York he would have liked to establish diocesan synods, but he saw that they would cause bad feeling and strife among those who opposed the idea. But he summoned the Convocation of the Northern Province to meet in 1861, in the belief that 'members of the Convocation should have periodical opportunities of meeting together, of counselling in common for the advancement of the interests of the Church and of religion in this country'.[7] This strong sense of the importance of practical collegiality, at presbyteral and at episcopal level, strongly foreshadowed his great work as Archbishop of Canterbury in overseeing the birth of the Lambeth Conferences.

248.   The Colenso affair, which indirectly brought about the first Lambeth Conference,[8] reflected widespread contemporary controversy over the issue of the place of critical scholarship alongside private judgement on the one hand, and the Church's authoritative interpretation of Scripture on the other. Longley did his best to provide judicious and balanced and sensible guidance for his diocesan clergy to help them find their way through the thickets of the debates.

249.   He was aware at Canterbury of the great recent extension of the responsibilities of the Archbishopric. 'The present state of the Church, at

---

6   *Ibid.*, p. 280.
7   Charge addressed to the Clergy, 1861, p. 8.
8   See the next chapter, paras. 264 and 272-8, also note to para. 272.

home and abroad, the multiplication of the Colonial Episcopate, and the great uncertainty as to the legal *status* of several of the Colonial Sees, must entail upon me an amount of labour and anxiety which has not fallen to the lot of my predecessors within the last century and a half', he commented. He saw equally clearly the continuing priority of the claims of his own diocese of Canterbury upon his pastoral care as their own diocesan bishop, of 'those engagements which bring me into communion with yourselves, enabling me to support and encourage you in the discharge of your parochial duties', he said to his clergy.[9]

250. In a bishop of the mid-twentieth century we see the combination of energy and commitment with diffident holiness. Nugent Hicks, Bishop of Lincoln (1933-41) after a period as Bishop of Gibraltar where he made lasting links with Orthodox Christians, came home to many tasks: 'First the lay-readers ... the whole machinery must be overhauled from top to bottom; secondly, there is the matter of religious provision in the new housing areas; thirdly, clerical stipends, especially in some country parishes'. 'I am not sure that I am strong enough', he confessed. But others saw his 'sincere kindliness of heart and the inner happiness which radiated his whole being' and knew that 'he was never too tired or too busy to attend to high or low, rich or poor, in any kind of need or trouble. People came to him'.[10] James Inskip, Suffragan Bishop of Barking, wrote his own reminiscences,[11] in which he recollects all sorts of activities, in supporting women's suffrage, in presiding at a protest meeting over unemployment where 'the audience did not appear to have much connection with the Churches', in dealing with the human toll of bombing during the Second World War. 'It was expected of suffragans', he said wryly, 'that they should run and not be weary, and that they should walk and not faint, but woe betide them if they should attempt to mount up with wings as eagles'.[12]

251. William Temple, son of a previous Archbishop of Canterbury, and himself to become in due course Primate of York and then of Canterbury, was a man of the twentieth century in his social concern. As Rector of St. James's, Piccadilly, from 1916, he became involved in the Christian Social Union and the Life and Liberty Movement, as he had earlier, as a schoolmaster, supported the Workers' Educational Association. The Life and Liberty Movement was to be a national mission to overcome the apathy

---

9   Charge intended for Delivery to the Clergy of the Diocese of Canterbury, 1868, p. 3.
10   M. Headlam, *Bishop and Friend* (London, 1944), p. 115.
11   *A Man's Job* (London, 1948).
12   *Ibid.*, p. 177.

of ordinary English people in their response to Christianity, and especially in their commitment to the Church of England. Temple wanted to see reforms designed to free the Church of England from the dead hand of its dependence upon Parliament, and he campaigned for the plan for a Church Assembly in which the Church could debate and legislate upon its own affairs. By 1921 he had been consecrated Bishop of Manchester.

252.   As a bishop he faced the administrative load conscientiously if without enthusiasm. He kept the diocese's finances in good order, divided off Blackburn, so that two sensible areas of jurisdiction were formed. His strength did not lie in the personal side of pastoral work, that is, in work with individuals,[13] but in preaching he was outstanding, clear and cogent without rhetorical flourish. He would preach on the sands to the Bank Holiday crowds in Knox's Blackpool Mission every year. He seems to have been generally beloved in the Diocese for the personal qualities of shining happiness, serenity, beaming goodwill, on which many remarked.

253.   At the same time he continued both to write theology and to work for social causes in the wider arena. He became chairman of the *Collegium*, a small group of ecumenically minded friends, meeting in London, which prompted the Conference on Politics, Economics and Citizenship in Birmingham in 1924 and the ecumenical Conference on Life and Work. The Birmingham Conference drew fifteen hundred members, more than half of them from Europe and Asia. The result was a lasting boost to ecumenical concern for the common social witness and shared mission of the Church. Temple pressed the view that by working together Churches come to pray and to appropriate together their common faith. He was to take a lead in the Life and Work Movement and in the 1938 Edinburgh Conference on Faith and Order.

254.   He exemplifies in this period of his Manchester bishopric a bishop confronted with the dilemma as to whether or not the Church should intervene in politics. It was Temple's view, expressed in *The Times*, and in private correspondence that Christian leaders 'acting for goodwill' should do anything in their power to bring peace in industrial disputes such as the General Strike of 1926, for example. And where it was necessary to resist interference by the State in Church affairs, he spoke out, as he did in the case of Parliament's rejection of the *1928 Prayer Book*.

---

[13]   Although those who knew him say that no-one left his presence without feeling blest.

255. We could multiply examples. But perhaps these are enough to illustrate the striking modernity of some of the dilemmas of the Church of England's earlier bishops, and the classic and enduring character of some of the problems faced today. Real life in a broken world is always a struggle to realise an ideal which remains beyond the reach of fallen man. Our bishops kept before them the ideals of the theology of *episcope* we have been outlining and on the whole they succeeded very well in setting an example of holiness to their people in their stewardship of the things of God.

256. Like their predecessors, our modern bishops have to cope with the pressures of administration within their dioceses, to seek to keep in as close contact as possible with their clergy and people, to resolve the dilemma of the extent to which they should become involved in political issues and yet to strive to find time for theological reflection so as to discharge their teaching role.

257. Both the strength and the weaknesses of the episcopal system have been most transparently evident in the lives and 'episcopal styles' of individuals. The early and mediaeval bishop was, at his best, a loving pastor; at his worst in the late Middle Ages, a rich and powerful figure in a society ordered to meet the needs of the few who occupied its higher echelons rather than of the whole people of God. It was to the behaviour of individuals that the reformers reacted, in the sixteenth century revolution and its mediaeval antecedents in the twelfth and fourteenth and fifteenth centuries, as much as against what they understood to be a theology of episcopacy which seemed to make abuses possible.

258. No separation ought to be made between what a bishop is asked to do and what he is called to be. For in the manner in which he carries out those episcopal functions, in a life of holiness, he points those in his charge to the life of God in Christ. The bishop is to be an example in holiness to his flock.[14] Consistently through the years the demanding picture of the high

---

14 Six Reformation or Post-Reformation Anglican bishops figure among the *Lesser Festivals and Commemorations* of the ASB. Of these, two - Thomas Cranmer in the sixteenth and James Hannington in the nineteenth century - are included as martyrs; leaving three seventeenth century bishops - Lancelot Andrewes, Jeremy Taylor and Thomas Ken - and one more recent bishop, Edward King, Bishop of Lincoln from 1885 to 1910. Of these, only the last seems to have enjoyed a genuine popular cultus. As a Methodist scholar comments, 'on 24th May 1935, the Church of England came as near to a deliberate canonization of one of her sons as at any time since the Reformation', cf. John A. Newton: *Search for a Saint: Edward King* (Epworth Press, London, 1977), p. 10; and cf. *The Commemoration of Saints and Heroes of the Faith in the Anglican Communion* (Report of a Commission appointed by the Archbishop of Canterbury, SPCK, London, 1957), p. 40.

calling of bishops there in the New Testament has been repeated, as it is in the ordination service of every bishop.

259.   In every age, personal holiness has been compelling. But it has not always worn the same face. Half-jesting, John Henry Newman wrote a letter in August 1832 in which he remarked, 'I mean by the episcopal air, gravity, decision, self-possession, a certain dryness of manner, a reserved courteousness'.[15] That can be compared with the story told of a more recent American bishop who, asked how he saw his episcopal duty, answered that he tried to say to his people, 'Come on, let's go'.[16]

15   John Henry Newman, *Letters and Diaries*, III, 82.
16   See *Bishops: But What Kind?*, p. 161.

8

Episcopacy in the Anglican Communion

The story in outline

260. The expansion of Anglicanism outside the British Isles began as a result of the commercial enterprises which took members of the Church of England abroad to live. In America, the Colony in Virginia, for example, had royal patronage and Anglican members. In the seventeenth century chaplaincies were set up in European ports and spread further afield with the formation of the East India Company, which had chaplains in India from 1614. These members of the Church of England abroad were regarded as being under the jurisdiction of the Bishop of London.[1] The foundation of the first Anglican missionary societies, and the expansion of their work in the eighteenth century, provided a further impetus to Anglican expansion and resulted in new conversions to Anglicanism.

261. Although many missions were committed to establishing an indigenous clergy (the first African priest was ordained in 1765) England retained control. An Act of Parliament was required to create a new bishopric and new bishops had to be consecrated in London under royal mandate. In 1783 Samuel Seabury was elected by the clergy of Connecticut in America to be their bishop. But this was after the Declaration of Independence; he could not take the Oath of Allegiance to King George III as part of the consecration service; so he could not be consecrated by English bishops. Seabury was consecrated by bishops of the Episcopal Church in Scotland in 1784. This created a precedent unwelcome in England, and led to the 1786 Act which allowed the Archbishop of Canterbury to consecrate those who were not subjects of the British Crown. In 1788 two further bishops were consecrated for America. By 1836 bishops for Nova Scotia, Quebec, Calcutta, the West Indies and Australia had also been consecrated. In 1864 the first African bishop was consecrated in Nigeria.

262. At an early date it became clear that both legally and practically the

---

[1] See Chapter 7, para. 237.

Churches in the colonies were to become separate and distinct self-governing entities. Prior to 1866 the Crown granted Letters Patent creating dioceses and appointing bishops with ecclesiastical jurisdiction wherever it was considered desirable to do so. However, this practice ceased after the Privy Council expressed the opinion that the Crown could not confer ecclesiastical jurisdiction upon such a new bishop, in a colony which had an independent legislature.[2] The individual Churches thereafter organised themselves on a synodical basis and it was their own national legislatures which gave many of them statutory recognition and powers.

263.   The various Churches within the Anglican Communion are regarded in law as voluntary bodies organised on a basis of consensus. The essence of the Anglican Communion is that it is a fellowship of Churches historically associated with the British Isles. It embraces all those Churches and dioceses which are in communion with the See of Canterbury and recognise the Archbishop of Canterbury as the focus of unity.

264.   The desire to come together for 'common counsels and united worship'[3] has led the bishops of the Anglican Communion to meet periodically at Lambeth since 1867 under the presidency of the Archbishop of Canterbury (see paras. 272-8). The Lambeth Conference is, however, a voluntary gathering with no legislative powers and no basis in canon, ecclesiastical, civil or common law. Nevertheless, where Resolutions passed by the Conference have been received with general acceptance by the Churches represented they have thereby attained what may be regarded as, in strictly non-legal terms, an 'authoritative' character.

265.   The relationship between the Church in the Colonies and the 'mother' Church in England was complicated by the fact that the relationship of Church to State in England[4] could not be extended outside the British Isles. This was by virtue of a declaration by order in Council in the time of Charles I and made necessary the beginning of local synodical government, first in New Zealand in 1844; and the eventual granting of independent constitutions, to New Zealand in 1857, South Africa in 1876, the West Indies in 1883, for example.

266.   The development of episcopacy in this wider Anglican world was,

2   Re: Lord Bishop of Natal (1865), 3 Moo. P.C.C. N.S. 115.
3   Introduction to 1867 Lambeth Conference.
4   On which see Chapter 12.

and still continues to be, influenced by the local cultural context and local styles of leadership and structures of authority. Nevertheless, the reports of successive Lambeth Conferences from the first in 1867, show that a coherent understanding of the nature and function of episcopacy is shared by the various parts of the Anglican Church. The understanding fundamental to the different local expressions of episcopacy remains consonant with that which we have traced through the centuries.

A.   The bishop in the local church

267.   The earlier Lambeth Conferences were concerned to lay down guidelines for the maintenance of an episcopal system in a Communion which was still growing in the mission fields and in what was still conceived of as a 'colonial' framework. The Conferences emphasised repeatedly the fundamental character of the relationship between a bishop and his diocese and upheld the principle of one bishop in one diocese. In 1867 it was allowed there might be 'peculiar cases' of race or language, but 1920 maintained that difficulties should not be allowed to interfere with the principle that there can be 'but one Church and one Authority'.[5] In 1930 there was a clear statement of 'the ancient Catholic principle that the fundamental unity of Church organisation is the territorial Diocese under the jurisdiction of one Bishop', with an assertion of the ecclesial completeness and autonomy of such a local church. 'A duly organised Diocese under its Bishop has the right, subject always to its duty to the whole fellowship of the Church, to decide and act for itself in its own affairs.'

268.   A significant test of the 'one bishop, one diocese' principle, and of the rule that a diocese is a territorial unit, has been the demand for 'ethnic' bishoprics, with what might be called 'cultural' rather than geographically defined areas of jurisdiction. These may coincide, but they need not necessarily always do so, as in the case of the Diocese of Aotearoa in New Zealand, the Order of Ethiopia in Southern Africa, the Navajoland Area Mission in the United States of America.

269.   The principle that the territorial diocese is the fundamental unit of church organisation was underlined by early Lambeth Conferences in the repeated insistence that clergy going from one diocese to another should

5   Committee on Development of Provinces, Lambeth Conference, 1920.

carry Letters Testimonial from their own bishop, without which the bishop of their new diocese would not grant a licence to minister among his priests. An especially difficult problem[6] was the relationship of religious communities to their diocesan. A Committee of the 1897 Conference recommended that every priest ministering to a religious community should be licensed for that purpose by the Diocesan Bishop: it stressed that care should be taken that the Community should not interfere with the canonical obedience which each clergyman owes to the Bishop of the diocese in which he ministers. It was this same principle of safeguarding the relationship between diocesan and his people that lay behind Resolution 72 of the 1988 Lambeth Conference. This Conference:

1. Re-affirms its unity in the historical position of respect for diocesan boundaries and the authority of bishops within those boundaries; and in the light of the above.
2. Affirms that it is deemed inappropriate behaviour for any bishop or priest of this Communion to exercise episcopal or pastoral ministry within another diocese without first obtaining the permission and invitation of the ecclesial authority thereof.

270.   Thus there has been a careful insistence in a time of overseas expansion on maintaining the relationship between bishop and diocese and taking a stand against parallel jurisdictions. The tasks in which the bishop exercises his oversight in his diocese have been set out in some detail by the Lambeth Conferences of 1968, 1978 and 1988, with a notable emphasis on mission:

Within the wider context of the mission and ministry of the whole Church, the diocese is often seen as basic to the life and unity of the local Church. This unity is personified and symbolised in the office of the bishop. Under God, the bishop leads the local church in its mission to the world. Among other things, the bishop is:
(a)   a symbol of the Unity of the Church in its mission;
(b)   a teacher and defender of the faith;
(c)   a pastor of the pastors and of the laity;
(d)   an enabler in the preaching of the Word, and in the administration of the Sacraments;
(e)   a leader in mission and an initiator of outreach to the world surrounding the community of the faithful;
(f)   a shepherd who nurtures and cares for the flock of God;
(g)   a physician to whom are brought the wounds of society;
(h)   a voice of conscience within the society in which the local Church is placed;
(i)   a prophet who proclaims the justice of God in the context of the Gospel of loving redemption;

---

[6]   As it has been from the beginning of Western monastic communities in late patristic times.

(j)   a head of the family in its wholeness, its misery and its joy. The bishop is the family's centre of life and love.[7]

B.   Linking the Churches

a.   The establishment of Provinces

271. The function of bishops as ministers of unity was underlined by the Lambeth Conference of 1920.[8] Its Committee on Development of Provinces endorsed the view that this ministry of unity should normally be discharged collegially by the gathering together of local dioceses into Provinces. This was already the case in the British Isles: the Church in Ireland was brought into a new relationship with the State by the Irish Parliament of 1560. Struggles between Presbyterians and Episcopalians in Scotland resulted in a presbyterian organisation for the Church of Scotland. An Episcopal Church in Scotland survived, however, among those who kept to episcopacy at the Revolution Settlement of 1690. Scotland is now a province in full communion with the Church of England. The Welsh Church became a separate province when it was disestablished in 1920. With the consecration of Samuel Seabury in 1784, and three years later two further American bishops, an episcopate derived from the Church of England was constituted, and the first Anglican Province outside the British Isles and independent of the Church of England was formed. The first Lambeth Conference expressed the view that 'The association or federation of Dioceses within certain territorial limits, commonly called the Ecclesiastical Provinces, is not only in accordance with the ancient laws and usages of the Christian Church, but is essential to its complete organisation'.[9] It is seen as the best means by which discipline may be maintained, the election of bishops confirmed and the Church enabled 'to adapt its laws to the circumstances of the countries in which it is planted'. The 1867 Conference also stated a belief that the relationship of diocese to province should be governed 'on the one hand by the subordination of the bishops of the Province to a Metropolitan, and on the other by the association of the Dioceses in Provincial action'.

---

7   *The Truth Shall Make You Free, Report* of the Lambeth Conference 1988 (London, 1988, p. 61.
8   Resolution 9, vii.
9   Committee D, 1867.

b.   The emergence of world-wide Anglican collegiality

i.   The Lambeth Conference

272.   The development of the wider episcopal fellowship in the collegial gathering of Lambeth Conferences came naturally within Anglicanism, and was consonant with the Church of England's view that it continued the ministry of the universal church at the Reformation. In the 1860s, there came from Canada a suggestion that there should be a 'National Synod of the bishops of the Anglican Church at home and abroad'.[10] This they saw as a 'means ... by which the members of our Anglican Communion in all quarters of the world should have a share in the deliberations for her welfare, and be permitted to have a representation in a General Council of her members gathered from every land'.[11] The Canadians envisaged this as an essentially conciliar gathering, the next best thing to 'the assembling of a General Council of the whole Catholic Church'.

273.   The Canadian proposal was heatedly discussed in both the Lower and the Upper House of Convocation in England. Different views were expressed on the implication of bishops coming together in such a way. Some thought that it would enable those who held authority from God in the Church to say what is 'the faith of the Church from the beginning'. The bishops in Council would 'maintain to the end that given faith'.[12] Others thought it a much simpler matter: 'to bring them to a better understanding of the common wants of the Church' and 'to give them heart and courage to undertake their several duties'.[13] The Dean of Westminster made the point that the history of Councils had not been encouraging - 'the general course of their steps has been marked by crime and sin'.[14] The question of the 'bindingness' of such Councils was also at issue. Canon Seymour contributed the view that 'it was a received axiom in the Catholic Church that ... articles of faith were not binding upon the whole Church until the

---

10   Printed in R.T. Davidson, *Origin and History of the Lambeth Conferences, 1867 and 1878* (London, 1888), p. 32. The suggestion was prompted by an incipient crisis over jurisdiction in South Africa. The 'Colenso Affair' in 1863, in which John Colenso, Bishop of Natal, appealed to the Judicial Committee of the Privy Council against a ruling of his own Metropolitan (deposing him because of his views on Scripture), led to the questioning of the existing arrangements between the Provinces and the mother Church in such matters of jurisdiction.

11   *Ibid.*, pp. 34-5.

12   The *Chronicle of Convocation*, Feb. 13, 1876, p. 724.

13   *Ibid.*, p. 729.

14   *Ibid.*, pp. 731-2.

Church had received them ... laymen giving their assent in the ancient church'.[15] Some had a vision that once Anglicans met in Council, they might unite first with the Greek Church, and afterwards with other Churches. On the question of bindingness the Bishop of Oxford commented, 'that which is not a Council of the Churches cannot pretend to do that which it belongs to a Council to do - i.e. to lay down any declarations of faith', ... 'such declarations are binding when laid down by a properly constituted council or Synod because such bodies have a right to claim the inspiration and overruling presence of him who guides the Church to a right decision'.[16] All this shows how uncertain members of the Church of England were about the best pattern of conciliarity to adopt for their growing Communion of Churches, and in those Churches themselves similar reservations were expressed.[17]

274. Nevertheless, the First Lambeth Conference met in 1867. The Archbishop in his opening speech said:

It has never been contemplated[18] that we should assume the functions of a general synod of all the Churches in full communion with the Church of England, and take upon ourselves to enact canons that should be binding upon those here represented. We merely propose to discuss matters of practical interest and pronounce what we deem expedient in resolutions which may serve as safe guides to future action. We have no direct precedent to guide us.[19]

275. Lambeth Conferences are thus not (and cannot be) legislative bodies for the whole Anglican Communion; their Resolutions are not binding upon the Provinces and cannot be enforced. Nevertheless, because of the view of episcopacy to which Anglicans are committed, expressed in Ordinals and in the statements of the Lambeth Conferences, the Resolutions of a Lambeth Conference count for a good deal. When all those charged by their local Church, within the ministry of the Universal Church in its Anglican expression, are gathered together to seek a common mind, then that counsel

---

15   *Ibid.*, p. 778, Feb. 14.

16   *Ibid.*, p. 804. On the questions of 'reception' and 'bindingness', see further Chapters 10 and 13.

17   'Historically, it was in England itself that the sharpest challenge to the authority of the Lambeth Conference and therefore to the wider primacy of the Archbishop of Canterbury was first expressed in 1867 and it was, in fact, the particular relationship of the Established Church of England with the Crown that was largely responsible for preventing an earlier movement from independence to interdependence.', R. Greenacre, *Lost in the Fog?* (London, 1989), p. 8.

18   This does not, of course, quite accurately reflect what the Canadians had in fact asked for at first.

19   Davidson, p. 10.

of assembled bishops must be, and is, taken very seriously indeed by those on whose behalf they give guidance.

276. While the meeting together of all the bishops of the Anglican Communion has clearly filled a need, and made it possible to experience and express the communion that exists amongst Anglicans, the question of the authority of the Lambeth Conference has always been a sensitive matter. Lambeth 1920 remained clearly of the opinion that its authority was a moral one:

> The Lambeth Conference ... does not claim to exercise any powers of control or command. It stands for the far more spiritual and more Christian principle of loyalty to the fellowship. The Churches represented in it are indeed independent, but independent with the Christian freedom which recognises the restraints of truth and love. They are not free to deny the truth. They are not free to ignore the fellowship ... the Conference is a fellowship in the Spirit.

277. The question of the authority of the Lambeth Conference has been raised recently increasingly sharply owing to the need for provinces, free to act autonomously, to consider the case for restraint when they come to take decisions in matters that affect the life of the whole Communion: matters concerning an Anglican response to international bilateral and multilateral dialogues and the development of the ordained ministry, particularly the opening of the episcopate to include women (see Chapter 13).

278. Anglicans have consistently been aware of the anomaly of holding such a conference in a divided Christendom. And statements of Lambeth Conferences have shown the bishops aware of the incompleteness of their Communion when there is a division in the universal Church. They have continued to look forward to a greater unity and to the possibility of holding a genuinely Ecumenical Council, and have correspondingly affirmed the provisionality of Anglicanism.[20] Both the ecumenical agendas of Lambeth Conferences, and the presence of ecumenical observers (from episcopal and non-episcopal churches) testify to the felt need of Anglicans for a fully universal Church. The welcoming of all of the bishops of the United Churches of the Indian sub-continent into the fellowship of the 1988 Lambeth Conference was a sign of a move towards this greater wholeness.[21]

[20]   On 'provisionality', see further our discussion under that heading in Chapter 13 on *Women in the Episcopate.*

[21]   'If the 1968 Lambeth Conference was able to declare that episcopal collegiality is an apostolic heritage given to the whole body or college of bishops, the context showed clearly that this body was not thought to be limited to the bishops of the Anglican Communion. It must nevertheless be admitted that we find less clarity in the language of the 1978

ii. The Anglican Consultative Council

279. From the end of the last century the need has been felt for some organ or organs of 'higher authority' for the Anglican Communion. But just as the Communion has stopped short of turning the Lambeth Conference, or any other body, into an organ with 'teeth' and with jurisdiction (and indeed that is a constitutional impossibility), so other organs of higher authority have restricted powers. In the debates surrounding the establishment of a Lambeth Conference questions of representativeness were often raised. After a lengthy discussion of possibilities in previous Lambeth Conferences, the Lambeth Conference of 1968 recommended the establishment of the **Anglican Consultative Council** with representatives from the Anglican Churches. (This discharges responsibilities previously carried out by earlier bodies - The Lambeth Consultative Body; the Advisory Council on Missionary Strategy). Its notable feature is that it brings together bishops, clergy and laity under the presidency of the Archbishop of Canterbury. The ACC thus provides a forum for episcopal, clergy and lay participation at a Communion-wide level. It meets every three years. Its functions have been clearly set out and agreed to by the Provinces. But questions remain unresolved about the kind of body the ACC is and the nature of its authority, in what sense it is 'synodical' and what is its relationship to the form of collegial oversight which has been a part of the life of the Church since early times. These points were debated at the 1988 Lambeth Conference and there was a consensus in favour of retaining the seniority of the Lambeth Conference as a forum of those who exercise episcopal oversight.

iii. The Primates' Meeting

280. The Meeting of Primates was established at the Lambeth Conference in 1978. The advantage of this smaller episcopal meeting is that it can gather more frequently and help the Archbishop of Canterbury take major decisions about Lambeth Conferences, or about any matter affecting the whole Communion. The minutes of the 1979 meeting comment:

Conference where Resolution 13 could speak of the collegial responsibility of the whole episcopate in a context which apparently did not look beyond the episcopate of the Anglican Communion', R. Greenacre, 'An Anglican Response', *The Nature and Future of Episcopal Conferences, The Jurist*, XLVIII (1988), p. 394.

The role of a **Primates' Meeting** could not be, and was not desired as, a higher synod in that sense. Rather it was a clearing house for ideas and experience through free expression, the fruits of which Primates might convey to their Churches.[22]

The Primates' Meeting concerned itself with initiating and leading a discussion in the early eighties on authority in the Anglican Communion and in 1987 produced a background report for the Lambeth Conference on *Women and the Episcopate*. More recently it has, amongst other things, produced a report, *Communion, Women and the Episcopate*, passing it to the Provinces for debate. Resolution 18 of the 1988 Lambeth Conference wanted to see 'a developing collegial role for the Primates' Meeting under the presidency of the Archbishop of Canterbury, so that the Primates' Meeting is able to exercise an enhanced responsibility in offering guidance on doctrinal, moral and pastoral matters'.[23]

iv.   The development of Primacy [24]

281. The break with Rome and the establishment of Royal Supremacy inevitably raised questions over the position of the Archbishop of Canterbury. In the sixteenth century there were those, like Cartwright, who believed that Archbishopric is an innovation, a 'new ministry'. Others followed Whitgift in maintaining that the Council of Nicaea 'doth not only allow of the name but also the office of Metropolitan, archbishop' and that 'mention is made of a patriarch', so that such higher episcopal oversight has ancient precedent. His view was that, in the ancient church, Primates, 'first bishops', Patriarchs, Metropolitans, 'Bishops of the mother city', and Archbishops, were all one. Generally, Anglican Apologists maintained that there was room for Patriarchs in the West, but not for universal primacy. That is to say, they stopped short of allowing a universal bishopric, but held that Metropolitans in their provinces had the right to make bishops and the duty to care for them. Anglicans accepted the standing of the ancient Orthodox patriarchates and in England recognised the seniority of Canterbury's position over that of York, reflected in the title of the Archbishop of Canterbury as 'Primate of All England'.[25]

22   Minutes of the Primates' Meeting, 1979, p. 4.
23   *The Truth Shall Make You Free, Report* of the 1988 Lambeth Conference, p. 216.
24   Cf. paras. 83, 102, 124-5, 127, 147, 321 ff.
25   It should be noted that some Anglicans from at least the seventeenth century were open to the idea of a universal primacy located in Rome. See 'Primacy and Collegiality: an Anglican View', *Lambeth Essays on Unity* (SPCK, London, 1969), p. 16 *et al.*

282.   In practice, medieval tradition made it plain what an archbishop ought to do.   In 1571 it was possible to list the duties of an archbishop thus: all that pertains to bishops also pertains to archbishops, but over and above his ordinary episcopal duties the archbishop has a responsibility to know how things are going throughout his province, and he ought, if he can to visit the whole province at least once.   If a see is vacant, he must fulfil the duties of its bishop until he is replaced.   If his bishops need discipline, he must give them fatherly counsel and warning.   He hears and judges appeals to his archiepiscopal Courts, and he convokes provincial synods, this last at Royal command.   It is his responsibility to install the bishops of his province once they have been chosen and elected.   Hence the Archbishop of Canterbury was never simply a symbol of unity of the Church of England with moral authority and no jurisdiction.   There was, through the Church courts, always a legal and jurisdictional component to his primacy.

283.   With the growth of the Communion and the establishment of fresh Provinces, new 'metropolitans' have come into being as Primates or Presiding Bishops in the Anglican Communion.   Not all of these primacies are attached to 'fixed' sees,[26] and it is not everywhere the case that the Primate has a see of his own.   In the Episcopal Church in the United States (ECUSA) and now in Canada the Presiding Bishop or Primate has been 'freed' from diocesan responsibilities to be a 'chief executive'.   Both these variants raise certain questions about the relationship of *episcope* and pastoral ministry.

284.   The Lambeth Conferences have been cautious about the concept of a single primacy of the Anglican Communion, and have not gone far towards defining its authority.   The 1908 Lambeth Conference said that 'no supremacy of the See of Canterbury over Primatial or Metropolitan Sees outside England is either practical or desirable'.[27]   Nevertheless, the 1908 Conference wished to bear witness to the universal recognition in the Anglican Communion of the ancient precedence of the See of Canterbury. The 1930 Conference contrasted as two 'types of ecclesiastical organisation' a 'centralised government' and a 'regional' authority 'within one fellowship'.[28]   The 1948 Conference commented that 'former Lambeth Conferences have wisely rejected proposals for a formal primacy of

26   E.g. Wales and Scotland.
27   Lambeth, 1980, p. 418.
28   Lambeth, 1930, Committee Report on the Anglican Communion.

Canterbury'.[29] Lambeth 1968 described the role of the Archbishop of
Canterbury in greater detail:

> Within the college of bishops it is evident that there must be a president.
> In the Anglican Communion this position is at present held by the
> occupant of the historic See of Canterbury, who enjoys a primacy of
> honour, not of jurisdiction. This primacy is found to involve, in a
> particular way, that care of all the churches which is shared by all the
> bishops.[30]

There has thus been a strong sense of the reality of a Canterbury primacy.
Lambeth 1978 added that the fellowship of the Anglican Communion is
grounded in loyalty to the Archbishop of Canterbury as 'the focus of unity',
and that loyalty was warmly evident at the 1988 Conference. Underlying
the Anglican understanding of the role of the primate is the theology of the
ministry of oversight which makes the bishop representative and focus of
the life of the community. This is thoroughly in line with the development
of ministry in the early Church in which primacy, exercised in collegiality
and conciliarity, was regarded and experienced as a symbolic primacy,
caring for the unity and well-being of the Church, rather than a 'primacy of
jurisdiction'. This was the character of the universal primacy envisaged by
the Archbishop of Canterbury when he spoke of the future in a united
Church during his visit to Rome in 1989.

285. It is, however, clear that in spite of the desire that the primacy of the
Archbishop of Canterbury should be supremely one of focusing unity; and a
primacy of honour rather than jurisdiction, certain functions have accrued
to the office. The Archbishop of Canterbury has always invited bishops to
the Lambeth Conference. He is president of the Lambeth Conference and
the Anglican Consultative Council, a 'permanent link' between the two
bodies; as president of both he exercises metropolitan authority over isolated
dioceses, which are not yet within provinces; in 1988 it was the Archbishop
of Canterbury and not the Primates' Meeting that was asked in the first
Resolution of the Conference to convene a Commission to consider the
implications of a woman being consecrated a bishop.[31]

286.   We ought not to leave the subject of primacy without noting that
there remains a tension, and an increasing one, between the responsibilities
of the Archbishop of Canterbury within the Church of England, and his

---

29   Without defining fully what such 'formality' would entail (Lambeth, 1948, p. 84).
30   Lambeth, 1968, p. 137.
31   The Eames Commission. See Chapter 13.

primatial functions in relation to the Anglican Communion as a whole. This is partly a matter of division of time and energy; and partly of loyalty, where (as in principle may be the case) Provinces make independent legislative decisions which test the bonds of common faith and order.

C.   Continuity through time

287.   The Lambeth Conferences have upheld the view that the episcopate is the ministry of continuity. Lambeth 1958 describes its role here:

> In ordination ... the individual must affirm that he believes himself to be called of God to the ministry, and the Church must be satisfied of . . . . . his call and his fitness for the work. Then the Church also calls and the body of the faithful assents to the ordination. Ordination must be performed by those who have received and are acknowledged to have received, authority to exercise *episcope* in the Body, and to admit others to share in that ministry. This acknowledgement by the Body of the authority of the ordaining member means that his own ordination to the ministry of *episcope* must be recognised and accepted. From this arises the principle of continuity by succession, which appears to be indispensable, at least from the human point of view.[32]

288.   It is of importance ecumenically that the same Conference notes: 'This is not to say that God cannot dispense with the succession if he wishes, as indeed he did when the Aaronic priesthood was superseded by the appointment of the High Priest of our Confession' (Hebrews 7: 11-28).[33] The 1958 Conference sums up the Anglican position economically: 'The Anglican tradition has always regarded episcopacy as an extension of the apostolic office and function both in time and space, and, moreover, we regard the transmission of apostolic power and responsibility as an activity of the college of bishops and never as a result of isolated action by any individual bishop'.

289.   Something needs to be said here about 'the historic episcopate locally adapted in the methods of its administration to the varying needs of the nations and peoples called of God into the unity of this Church' (Lambeth Quadrilateral, 1888).[34] This is the fourth article of the Chicago-Lambeth Quadrilateral, in the form of words adopted by the Lambeth Conference of 1888. Dr. Vincent, assistant bishop of Southern Ohio, was anxious in the

[32]   Lambeth, 1958, pp. 2, 88 and 137.
[33]   (1958, 2.88) There are points here of relevance to the search for mutual recognition of ministry between episcopal and non-episcopal Churches.
[34]   See, too, para. 187.

debates of the 1880s to make it clear that the phrase 'the historic episcopate' 'was deliberately chosen as declaring not a doctrine but a fact, and as being general enough to include all variants'.[35] The intention was to make the Anglican doctrine of episcopacy as capacious as possible within the limits set by the realities of what episcopacy had been in the history of the Church; and at the same time to emphasise the importance of a history which contains tradition. As the Report of the Joint Commission on Approaches to Unity to the American General Convention of 1949 put it, episcopacy is 'a fact accompanied by its historical meaning'.[36] It is what might be described as a fact of revelation, and thus a fact carrying doctrinal implications.

290.   Those doctrinal implications we have sought to draw out from the history in our earlier chapters. But one or two further points ought to be made here. In 1920, the Lambeth Conference addressed the difficulty that the episcopate has not seemed the natural instrument of unity to those Churches which have, since the sixteenth century, rejected episcopacy. The Conference stressed that there was no question of denying 'the spiritual reality of the ministries of those communions which do not possess the episcopate'. But it held that the episcopate is nevertheless 'the best instrument for maintaining the unity and continuity of the Church'. With the same proviso, the 1958 Conference spoke more strongly of the belief 'that a ministry acknowledged by every part of the Church can only be attained through the historic episcopate'. The role, not only of episcopacy as a particular form of *episcope*, but of the 'historic episcopate', that is, the actual episcopate as it has existed in the Church and exists today, remains of crucial importance.

291.   It is also of importance for unity that we should see our way clearly on the subject of what does and what does not constitute an admissible 'local adaptation' to different cultural contexts.[37] A test here must be whether the 'local adaptation' allows the episcopate to continue to act collegially with full interchangeability of ministries and a shared sacramental life under a single episcopate. For example, in African dioceses the leadership role of the bishop may have about it something of the tribal chief, head of an extended family, settling squabbles in the congregation in a fatherly way.[38] In the

35   *Quadrilateral at One Hundred*, ed. J. Robert Wright (Ohio, London and Oxford, 1988), pp. 118-9.

36   *Ibid.*

37   A striking case in point is the consecration of women bishops in some parts of the Communion. See Chapter 10.

38   *Bishops: But What Kind?*, pp. 140-1.

developed world the bishop can seem chiefly administrator and public figure. In Brazil he may be doing a secular job as well as being a bishop. The spiritual role of the bishop may seem in African, Asian or Latin American cultures to make him a 'holy man' in all the different ways that idea has been understood in these different parts of the world. In Asia and parts of Africa the missionary role of the bishop may predominate. None of these 'local adaptations' is divisive; on the contrary, they enrich the corporate pastorate of the episcopate of the whole Communion. And none is incompatible with the profound continuity of the Church through the ages as the one Body of Christ.

292.   By way of brief summary, we may perhaps underline again the consistent adherence of Anglican theology and practice, in this world-wide arena of a growing and diversifying Communion, to a view of episcopacy derived from Scripture and earliest Christian tradition; and in which the intersection of the three planes of the Church's life in the person of the bishop makes him the focus and minister of unity.

9

Ecumenical convergence

293. The consistent pairing of Faith and Order testifies to the fact that from the beginning of the Ecumenical movement of this century, theological dialogue between the Churches has had to give serious attention to issues raised by the structures of ordained ministry, and not least to the question of *episcope* and episcopacy. The first stage of such dialogue was one of apologetic; the Churches which had retained (or claimed to have retained) what came to be called the 'historic episcopate', tried to explain and justify that retention and to commend episcopacy to the non-episcopal Churches, while the non-episcopal Churches in their turn tried to explain and justify their abandonment of this ministry. In response, the episcopal Churches gradually began to treat more critically some of the weaknesses in their own traditional theologies and the abuses and contradictions in their own praxis. They began to realise the extent to which such inconsistencies militated against the credibility of their apologetic for episcopacy. The Churches which had not retained the historic episcopate began a similar self-examination, and began to ask to what extent what then seemed the impossibility of maintaining it in the sixteenth century had caused them to make a positive principle out of what was originally perceived as a necessity. A new stage has now been arrived at (although not all Christians or all Churches have yet reached it), through a degree of convergence which has allowed theologians of all traditions to get behind the traditional debate about episcopacy, and to affirm that a ministry of *episcope* is one of the gifts necessary to express and safeguard the unity of the body of Christ.[1] This affirmation gives freedom to recognise that *episcope* can take a number of different forms. It also gives room for the Churches to agree on the vital necessity and urgency of searching together for renewed embodiment of the traditional order of episcopate, presbyterate and diaconate.[2] That search is already beginning to be successful. A striking convergence in the life of the Churches is taking place hand in hand with growing consciousness of agreement in faith.

---

1   BEM: Ministry III, A, 23.
2   *Ibid.*, A, 24.

294. It must not be imagined that the only pressures for change have been consciously and directly ecumenical; but it can at least be said that pressures for reform internal to each Church and related to its own particular problems have received powerful stimulus from the ecumenical dialogue. So we begin with the ecumenical conversations.

a. Ecumenical conversations

295. A number of texts emerging from multilateral and bilateral dialogues which discuss episcopacy and *episcope*, witness to growing convergence in the understanding of oversight as it is exercised personally, collegially and communally; and to the recognition on all sides that, for visible unity, there must be consensus on oversight. The Anglican Communion has responded to several of these in the Resolutions of the 1988 Lambeth Conference.[3] It has seemed important to see the Anglican response as part of an endeavour which is involving many other Churches in their conversations with one another, and so we refer here to a number of bilateral reports, not all involving Anglicans.

Baptism, Eucharist and Ministry (the Lima Text)

296. The World Council of Churches' Faith and Order Commission's (Lima) text on *Baptism, Eucharist and Ministry*, published in 1982, has a special place because it brings together the reflections of the most broadly-based ecumenical group in Christendom. It is a fruit of the multilateral dialogue begun in Lausanne in 1927. The importance of this 'Lima' text can be seen in the way in which many of the bilateral texts quote the *Lima Text* and build upon it.[4]

---

3   Resolution 3 is on the Baptism, Eucharist and Ministry text of the World Council of Churches (The Lima Text); 4 on Anglican-Lutheran Relations; 5 on Anglican-Orthodox Relations; 6 on Anglican-Orthodox Relations; 7 on Anglican-Reformed Dialogue; 8 on the first Anglican-Roman Catholic International Commission's Final Report; 9 on relations with the Methodist Church; 10 on the Baptist World Alliance; 11 on Pentecostal Churches; 12 on United Churches in Full Communion.

4   A special mention ought also to be made of the work of the Group of Les Dombes. The Group is not an official dialogue commission but a group of French-speaking theologians from the Roman Catholic, Reformed and Lutheran traditions which meets regularly at the Abbaye des Dombes in France. On episcopacy the Group published in 1975 *Towards a Reconciliation of Ministries* and in 1976 *The Episcopal Ministry*, both of which were influential upon the convergences reached in *Baptism, Eucharist and Ministry*. In particular the connection that was expressed there between apostolic succession in life and mission and the fullness of the sign in the orderly succession of episcopal ministry, owes much to the work of the Group.

297.   The following dialogues are of particular significance in connection with *episcope* and episcopacy.

Anglican-Lutheran Conversations

Pullach Report, 1972
Niagara Report, 1987   (Niagara)

Anglican-Orthodox Conversations

Moscow Statement, 1976
Athens Statement, 1978
Llandaff Statement, 1980

Anglican-Roman Catholic Conversations

Final Report, 1981   (ARCIC)

Anglican-Reformed Conversations

God's Reign and our Unity, 1984   (AR)

Baptist-Reformed Conversations

Report, 1977   (BR)

Lutheran-Roman Catholic Conversations

The Ministry in the Church, 1981   (LRC)

Methodist-Roman Catholic Conversations

Denver Report, 1971   (MRC, Denver)
Dublin Report, 1976   (MRC, Dublin)

Old Catholic-Orthodox Conversations

The Nature and Marks of the Church, Chambésy, 1977
The Unity of the Church and the Local Churches, Bonn, 1979
Ecclesiology, Zagorsk, 1981

Reformed-Roman Catholic Conversations, 1977 (RRC)

The Episcopal Ministry has paragraphs on the importance and role of the bishop which complement what is said in the *Niagara Report*. The bishop, 'in union with his community is to ensure and signify the Church's dependence on Christ, a source of its mission and foundation of its unity ... It is in this relationship with Christ the Chief Shepherd, which is experienced within the Church, that the presence of the *episcope* is a reminder to all of the divine initiative'. The text speaks of bishops as the 'pre-eminent signs' of the bond linking the past and the future. They inherit whatever could be handed on from the Apostles and 'in the present and for the future, they guarantee the continuity of the Church's advance in her pilgrimage to the Kingdom' (Quotations taken from the text published in English in *One in Christ*, 14 (1978), 271-83). A further text of 1985 on *Le ministère de communion dans l'Église universelle (The Ministry of Communion in the Universal Church)* has not yet been published in English.

Roman Catholic-Orthodox Conversations   (ORC)

The Sacrament of Order in the Sacramental
Structure of the Church, New Valamo, 1988

World Council of Churches

Baptism, Eucharist and Ministry   (BEM)[5]

298. In considering the results of ecumenical conversations so far, we look first to the growing consensus and secondly, to the remaining areas of difficulty over the nature and exercise of *episcope* in the Church.

b.   Areas of Ecumenical Agreement

299. *A shared understanding of the nature and functions of a pastoral leadership* in the three planes of the Church's life. The BEM text outlines a theology of episcopal ministry in three 'planes', in which the concept of a pastoral ministry is central.

> Bishops preach the Word, preside at the sacraments, and administer discipline in such a way as to be representative pastoral ministers of oversight, continuity and unity in the Church. They have pastoral oversight of the area to which they are called. They serve the apostolicity and unity of the Church's teaching, worship and sacramental life. They have responsibility for leadership in the Church's mission. They relate the Christian community in their area to the wider Church, and the universal Church to their community. They, in communion with the presbyters and deacons and the whole community, are responsible for the orderly transfer of ministerial authority in the Church (BEM, M29).

300. This theology of a ministry in the Church in which the three planes of its life intersect is paralleled in the ARCIC text on Ministry, too. There the threefold role of the bishop in relation to the local Church (understood as the diocese), in uniting the local church to the communion of churches, and the local church to the historical continuity of the apostolic Church, is central. 'The communion of the churches in mission, faith and holiness through time and space, is ... symbolised and maintained in the bishop.' (ARCIC M16)

301. In the Reports and Agreed Statements, bilateral and multilateral, both those in which Anglicans have taken part, and others, there is consensus that the ordained ministry is a pastoral office. That is everywhere seen to imply

5   The bulk of these texts are printed in *Growth*.

leadership of the community. For episcopal Churches, 'pastoral authority in the Church belongs primarily to the bishop, who is responsible for preserving and promoting the integrity of the *koinonia* in order to further the Church's response to the Lordship of Christ and its commitment to mission' (ARCIC, AI, 5). For all Churches, the pastor is minister of unity, 'gathering' the community, and entrusted in general with the responsibilities we have been outlining in earlier chapters, although for some the emphasis is upon the local 'gathering'. Baptist and Reformed speak of:

> particular ministries, whose function it is to gather the Christian fellowship together through the preaching and teaching of the word, to build up the Church, to lead and train for service. Also related to this function is the presidency at the celebration of the Lord's Supper and at the observance of baptism (BR, 31)

302. This pastoral ministry of unity is agreed to require 'regular' commissioning. To give two examples: Anglicans and Reformed are able to say together that:

> The one ... ordained is called to be a focus of unity for the whole body. Ordination is the act which constitutes and acknowledges this special ministry of representation and leadership within the life of the Church locally and universally (AR, 80)

Methodists and Roman Catholics agree that the:

> 'connectional' character of the ministry ... whereby everyone who is authentically called by the Holy Spirit is both authorized by that same Spirit through duly recognized persons in the community of faith and assigned a place of service in that community (MRC Denver, 94)

A personal, collegial and communal ministry

303. There is no dispute that the ordained, pastoral ministry should be 'exercised in a personal, collegial and communal way'. The BEM text explains something of what has come to be meant by these three interdependent terms:

> It should be *personal* because the presence of Christ among his people can most effectively be pointed to by the person ordained to proclaim the Gospel and to call the community to serve the Lord in unity of life and witness. It should also be *collegial*, for there is need for a college of ordained ministers sharing in the common task of representing the concerns of the community. Finally, the intimate relationship between the ordained ministry and the community should find expression in the *communal* dimension where the exercise of the ordained ministry is rooted in the life of the community [and] requires the community's effective

participation in the discovery of God's will and the guidance of the Spirit.

> The ordained ministry needs to be constitutionally or canonically ordered and exercised in the Church in such a way that each of these three dimensions can find adequate expression. At the level of the local eucharistic community there is need for an ordained minister acting within a collegial body. Strong emphasis should be placed on the active participation of all members in the life and the decision-making of the community. At the regional level there is again need for an ordained minister exercising a service of unity. The collegial and communal dimensions will find expression in regular representative synodal gatherings. (BEM, M26, 27)

We refer the reader to our earlier chapters for our fuller account of these principles. Though entirely in harmony with it, they are not, of course, the equivalent of the notion of three 'planes' of the Church's life, but a further expression of the threefold character of the relationship of the ordained ministry to the local and wider community it serves.

304. It is the question of oversight of a number of congregations which is crucial. It is generally accepted, even in non-episcopal Churches, that pastors with responsibility for congregations share with one another a ministerial collegiality:

> We agree that the basic structure of the Church and its ministry is collegial. When one is consecrated to the special ministry, one accepts the discipline of being introduced into a collegial function which includes being subject to others in the Lord and drawing on the comfort and admonition of fellow ministers.

Methodists and Roman Catholics agree that: 'the collegial and individual aspects of the ordained ministry are closely related' (MRC, Dublin, 89). The balance of 'personal' and 'corporate' is not, however, everywhere the same. 'Collegiality' is expressed on the Reformed side by the synodical polity, and, on the Roman Catholic side, by the episcopal college ... In the Reformed polity, the synod functions as a corporate episcopacy, exercising oversight of pastors and congregations (RRC, 102).

c.   **Personal, collegial, communal**

305. The suspicion is sometimes still voiced that personal pastorate, however acceptable at congregational level, can easily become at diocesan level an unacceptable personal 'power' over the people.[6] The safeguard

6   See Chapter 5, especially paras. 139 ff. and Chapter 10.

here ought to be that the commission for oversight entrusts exactly the authority needed to exercise pastoral office and no more,[7] and must always be at the service of the community because the pastor has no authority apart from the community. This is what is meant by saying that pastoral ministry is both personal and communal. And it is for this reason that for the good of the *koinonia*, the communion of the fellowship, it is right that everyone in the community should respect its authority. The relationship of collegiality binds the community together further.[8] It is essentially a relationship of equals, traditionally described as 'brotherly'. Within it, pastors meet as representatives of their communities for mutual support and encouragement, as well as for consultation about matters which are their particular responsibility. It extends to the relationships the pastor shares with those ordained to work with him in the pastorate, and with all his people, as they work together in the community, but here there is not equal responsibility, and the term 'collegiality' is not strictly accurate. The pastor is answerable to God for his people. All this can be said equally of the congregational as of the episcopal system. The difference lies in the permanence of the relationship in which the episcopal pastor is placed not only to his own people, but to the universal Church.

d. Remaining areas of difficulty

306. It would be wrong not to acknowledge that for many Christian communities the profound concerns about order with which we have been dealing seem comparatively unimportant when they are set beside the urgent needs of suffering humanity and the simple Gospel imperative to follow Christ which transcends all divisions.[9] It was out of the mission-fields that the call to unity first and most strongly came a century ago, because the old mutual hostilities of the Western Churches were incomprehensible, and indeed a stumbling-block, to new Christians in the wider world. Nevertheless, it remains the case that unless we can resolve our differences there can be no visible manifestation of that unity to which Christ calls all his people in the community of the Kingdom; and in which, in a redeemed order, he calls the Church to serve the urgent needs of the world. So we concentrate here on the progress which is being made in mending our disagreements over church government; for that is what, substantially, they

---

7 Cf. ARCIC AI, 5 and II, 17.
8 See, too, Chapter 11, C.ii I and iv and section D.
9 'The real divisions are not the traditional ones of faith and order, but the divisions on issues of justice and peace' (AR, 16).

remain in relation to the episcopate and *episcope*. We look here to a visible unity in which the Church may be one so that the world may believe.

a.   **Personal or corporate** *episcope* **(differences of polity)**

307.   The Anglican-Reformed conversations sought to pinpoint a difference of understanding of the pastoral office which remains perhaps the most serious unresolved issue between episcopal and non-episcopal Churches.

> There remains as a point of real difference the importance given to the bishop as the one who, in a more than functional sense, stands as a personal symbol of the catholicity and apostolicity of the Church. Reformed Churchmanship has not developed anything exactly comparable to this, and perhaps it is at this point that one of the deepest emotional barriers to union lies (AR, 9).

This structural, and at the same time mystical, difference remains of great importance.   Churches which have retained a presbyteral or corporate *episcope* since the Reformation[10] have developed a theology of oversight which is in some cases opposed in principle to a personal exercise of *episcope*, if that is seen as entrusted by ordination, and not as a mere office,[11] to the president of the collegial and conciliar meeting of the pastors of local worshipping communities in a particular area.[12] That is to say, we can make only an approximation to equivalence by bringing together bishops and moderators and chairmen and presidents in a sharing of oversight in local ecumenical schemes. The underlying theology is not yet a matter of common faith held in common order.

308.   When the Baptist-Reformed conversations of 1977 said that 'the local congregation is not a sub-department of the one Church of Christ, but manifests and represents it', they were echoing the Second Vatican Council's *Lumen Gentium*, 26, 'The Church of Christ is truly present in all local gatherings' and speaking the language of Orthodox tradition.[13] The difficulty, and the historic difference, has lain in the understanding of the relationship of local interest to universal insofar as that is articulated through the linking together of the ordained ministries which represent their local communities to one another. The Baptist-Reformed conversations are clear that 'in itself' the local Church 'is not the universal Church of

10   See Chapter 5.
11   See later in this chapter under 'Order and office and function'.
12   See, too, paras. 70, 121, 139, 185 on 'parity of ministry'.
13   Cf. Anglican-Orthodox Conversations, Dublin Report, 1984, 13.

Christ'.[14] 'Church "happens" not only where Christians gather as a congregation, but also where congregations meet as such or through their appointed representatives. There also the one Lord builds his one Church'.[15]

309. There is a mystery here which has to do with the manner in which the Church in each place is one and complete, and yet only the universal Church can be fully the Church. Local communities are linked with the universal Church as 'local manifestations of the full reality of the Catholic Church'.[16] They are not mere parts of a whole but wholes in the whole. That is made structurally possible in the episcopal Churches by the unity of the episcopate.[17] But in a divided Church, and a Church in which not all member Churches retain the historic episcopate, that is not in practice universally the case, and therefore the episcopate is not recognised by all to be a sign and instrument for the realisation of this mystery.

310. In Churches which have wholly or partially rejected episcopacy from the sixteenth century, the model for oversight has normally been some form of association of representatives of congregations, commonly of ministers (and sometimes other leaders sharing ministry with them in the congregations), forming what is again seen as a corporate pastorate, but on a rather different basis. Because the basic unit of Church organisation here is the congregation, and that of an episcopally ordered Church is the diocese, there is a sense in which the bishop of a Roman Catholic, Anglican or Orthodox diocese corresponds to the pastor in a congregational structure. That is to say, the level of organisation at which a personal pastoral office properly becomes corporate is that at which whatever is understood to be the 'local church' joins with other local churches in common action.

311. The authority of the president, chairman or moderator of such an assembly to act personally (with or without reference to the assembly as a whole), varies with the understanding of the personal character of the pastoral office, and that in its turn depends upon what is understood to be the basic unit of community life. In English (non-episcopal) Methodism, for instance, functions fall to a corporate pastorate which Lutheran bishops

---

14   BR, 38.
15   BR, 39.
16   Lesslie Newbigin, in *Bishops: But What Kind?*, p. 152.
17   Cf. Cyprian, *On the Unity of the Church* 5, PL 4.516-81. See, too, paras. 99 ff., 117 and Chapter 15.

may, in some cases, perform personally.[18]

312.   It remains the case, however, that among the non-episcopal Churches, and within the episcopal systems of, for example, certain Lutheran Churches, questions of the relationship of order, office and function remain at issue.[19] At the level of the 'first plane' of the Church's life, these matters still constitute perhaps the principal area of difficulty in arriving at consensus on the nature and purpose of the episcopal office. It is here that pluriformity is now most evident.

313.   Even here it is difficult to generalise. In 1970, the Uniting General Council of the Alliance of the Reformed Churches throughout the world holding the Presbyterian Order; and the International Congregational Council, agreed a Constitution which would enable them 'to manifest more fully their essential oneness ... in order to further the mission and unity of the Church catholic.[20] This was a joining of Churches in common action, with a Council of delegates of member Churches empowered to 'make and administer policies, plans and programmes, in accordance with the purpose of the Alliance'. But the stipulation is made that 'none of these provisions shall limit the autonomy of any member Church'.[21]

314.   As in the first plane, difficulties of order remain over the permanence of the relationship of the ministry of oversight to the community, so in the second plane of the Church's life we may perhaps see the persistent unresolved difficulty in terms of the continuing tension between autonomy and interdependence in mutual love.[22]

b.   Succession[23]

315.   There is no dispute that essentially the Church is the historically continuing presence in the world of the incarnate Word of God. A key difficulty here lies in the Churches' understanding of the place of the bishop in the apostolic and historic succession of faith and order from apostolic times:

---

18   See, too, Chapter 5, sections on Lutheranism and Methodism.
19   See further, later section on 'Order and office and function' in this chapter.
20   *Nairobi, 1970*, Proceedings of the Uniting General Council (Geneva, 1970), p. 39.
21   *Ibid.*, p. 41.
22   See, too, paras. 76 ff. and Chapter 10.
23   See further, Chapter 15 on this theme.

Reformed and Roman Catholic both believe that there is an apostolic
succession essential to the life of the Church (RRC, 100)

There is no longer any doubt in most Christian minds that the third plane of
the Church's life, the apostolic succession of its continuity in the faith over
time, is essential to its being. The difficulty arises over the understanding of
the relationship of episcopal succession to this apostolic succession.[24]
Although apostolic succession of faithfulness to truth is carried in the whole
community, it is widely seen as also depending in part upon continuity in a
God-given ministry of leadership. The concept of a sacred tradition of
teaching antedates the concept of an apostolic succession of pastors, but the
second became necessary to safeguard the first.

316.   This is felt by the ancient episcopal Churches to be of central
importance.[25] Since the Roman Catholic Church and the Eastern Orthodox
Churches have such a high degree of common tradition and common
understanding, concerning not only ordination but the sacramentality of the
Church (a subject first explored by the Joint International Commission in
the Munich Declaration of 1982), they are able to read their shared history
of episcopacy in a way that cannot be matched in any other bilateral
dialogue. They are able to point to 'a common doctrine and practice' and to
'the traditional doctrine in East and West'. Apostolic succession in its fullest
sense is a succession of the whole community; it is also a succession of local
churches. It is firmly within this ecclesiological context that the claim is
made that 'the episcopate appears as' a 'central point of the apostolic
succession' (ORC, 45).

317.   It cannot be overemphasized that this does not mean that the visible
succession of ordinations is the only factor to be considered. In the course
of history the Church has observed groups of bishops and individual bishops
whose juridical succession could hardly be faulted. Yet they have not been
reckoned to share in the apostolic succession because they have not been seen
to share in the tradition of Catholic teaching and in the universal
communion of the local churches. Teaching and communion are not less
significant than the visible manifestation by which legitimation is put beyond
controversy.

---

24   'It is the role which the succession of bishops plays within this wider concept of
        apostolicity which is one of the main controversial points' (Anglican-Lutheran
        Conversations, Pullach Report, 56, *Growth*, p. 21).
25   Here the subtitle of the Valamo Declaration is of great significance - 'with particular
        reference to the importance of apostolic succession for the sanctification and unity of the
        people of God'.

318.   Ministerial succession within the apostolic succession of the whole community is also seen to be central in other dialogues:

> Lutheran-Roman Catholic dialogue notes that the apostles ... had a responsibility for building up and leading the first communities, a ministry that later had to be continued ... such a special ministry proved to be necessary for the sake of leadership in the community. (LRC, *The Ministry in the Church*, 1981, p. 17)[26]

Anglican-Reformed conversations see ministerial succession as normal and normative as the appointed means of assuring the continuing apostolicity of the Church's life:

> Historic continuity of office-holders is, in fact, the normal way by which the continuity of any corporate body is secured and signified (AR, 89)

> The succession of public episcopal ministry could be appealed to [in the early Church] as a ground of assurance that what was being taught was the authentic message of Jesus and the apostles (AR, 88)

319.   There is, then, some degree of consensus that episcopal ministry is normally integral to the community's continuity in apostolic succession of life and faith. BEM's language on apostolic continuity is not of guarantee. It is not said that bishops 'guarantee' the fidelity of the Church to apostolic teaching and mission but rather that they serve, symbolise and guard the continuity of apostolic faith and communion.[27] We would affirm here that the bishop is a sign of assurance, but no individual bishop on his own can provide a cast-iron guarantee of maintenance in the truth of the apostolic tradition.

---

26   Cf. A-L, 79-82 (Pullach Report, 1972), *Growth*, pp. 24-5, and *The Niagara Report* (1987). Baptist and Reformed reject 'the historic form of the episcopate' as 'of the *esse* of the Church' (BR 31).

27   *Churches Respond to BEM*, vol. VI, p. 33. It is perhaps worth noting that the Roman Catholic Church in responding to the *Lima Text* makes use of the controversial term 'guarantee', though only after an eirenic exploration of its implications:

  Thus his (the bishop's) ministry is a sacramental sign of integration and a focus of communion. Through the episcopal succession, the bishop embodies and actualises both catholicity in time, i.e. the continuity of the church across the generations, as well as the communion lived in each generation. The actual community is thus linked up through a personal sign with the apostolic origins, its teaching and way of living.

  In that perspective, episcopal succession can rightly be called a *guarantee* of the continuity and unity of the church, if one recognises in it the expression of Christ's faithfulness to the church to the end of time. At the same time it lays upon each individual office bearer the responsibility to be a faithful and diligent guarantor.

320. This emphasis upon an *episcope* inseparable from the community it serves is undoubtedly helpful in getting over one of the strongest objections of non-episcopal Churches in the past: to a personal episcopal office handed on in linear succession by the imposition of hands in a manner which might seem to make it independent of the community and capable of being the personal possession of the bishop. It should not, however, in our view, be taken to diminish the importance of a continuity of commissioning in this way within the community. It has always been of importance in the Anglican tradition that there was no break in episcopal succession in the sixteenth century. We would suggest that further study is needed of the relationship of episcopal to apostolic succession in all Churches, with a view to discovering means by which the episcopal sign and assurance of apostolicity may be fully recovered in the one Church of the future.

c. Primacy[28]

321. Little discussion has so far taken place ecumenically of the role of primacy in a future united Church, but it is not in dispute that it needs to be set in the context of an ordained ministry exercised in a personal, collegial and communal way.[29] We quote here from the most substantial published treatment in the existing ecumenical Reports, with particular reference to the episcopal ministry of a Primate among his fellow bishops:

> If primacy is to be a genuine expression of *episcope* it will foster the *koinonia* by helping the bishops in their task of apostolic leadership both in their local church and in the Church universal. Primacy fulfils its purpose by helping the churches to listen to one another, to grow in love and unity, and to strive together towards the fullness of Christian life and witness; it respects and promotes Christian freedom and spontaneity; it does not seek uniformity where diversity is legitimate, or centralize administration to the detriment of local churches.

> A primate exercises his ministry not in isolation but in collegial association with his brother bishops. His intervention in the affairs of a local church should not be made in such a way as to usurp the responsibility of its bishop.[30]

---

28   Cf. paras. 83, 102, 124-5, 127, 147, 281 ff. See, too, the pre-Vatican II exploration of K. Rahner and J. Ratzinger, *The Episcopate and the Primacy* (tr. Edinburgh/London, 1962).

29   Cf. BEM, Ministry, 26, 27, *Growth*, p. 489.

30   ARCIC, AI, 21. See, too, the Explanatory Note to Resolution 8 of the 1988 Lambeth Conference, *The Truth Shall Make You Free*, p. 212. An exploration of the problems of maintaining a right balance between primary and collegial episcopal ministry was attempted in preparation for the Second Vatican Council by K. Rahner and H. Ratzinger, *The Episcopate and the Primacy* (tr. Edinburgh/London, 1962). Some of the key issues were consciously in play much earlier.

322.   As we have seen, Anglican tradition has found a primacy of Canterbury valuable, and has chosen primates or presiding bishops for Anglican Provinces[31]. Ecumenically both the style and character of a primacy in a future united Church, and the particular questions of the role of the bishop of Rome, are seen as matters on which we have yet to come to a common mind. In the tradition of the Churches a primate is a bishop writ large. That is to say, he is himself (in most cases)[32] bishop of a diocese, and the equal and brother of his fellow bishops. He must respect their rights of jurisdiction in their own dioceses. But at the same time, by virtue of his office, he can under certain circumstances act on behalf of his fellow bishops in the wider Church. It is our view that an episcopal and diocesan structure in which the balance of personal, collegial and communal is carefully maintained, lends itself best to the development and safeguarding of such a primacy.

323.   We have noted that, because of the separation from Rome in the sixteenth century, Anglican thinking on primacy has welcomed regional primacy of patriarchs, metropolitans or archbishops but been suspicious of the case for a universal primacy.[33] The progress of the ecumenical movement lends a new urgency to the question of the value of a universal primacy. We should like to encourage further study of the theology of primacy and of the implications for the Church of England of the acceptance of a primacy in a future united Church.

d.   Jurisdiction

324.   The question of episcopal jurisdiction remains a difficulty ecumenically, and once more it is the case that it has not yet been

---

'The Pope cannot arrogate to himself the episcopal rights, nor substitute his power for that of the bishops.
The episcopal jurisdiction has not been absorbed in the papal jurisdiction.
The Pope was not given the entire fullness of the bishops' powers by the decree of the [First] Vatican Council.
He has not virtually taken the place of each individual bishop.
The bishops have not become instruments of the Pope.
Collective Statement of the German Episcopate Concerning the Circular of the German Imperial Chancellor in respect of the coming Papal Election, endorsed by Pope Pius IX, printed in O. Rouseau, 'La vraie valeur de l'Episcopat dans l'Église d'après d'importants documents de 1875', *Irénikon*, 29 (1956), 121-50 and translated in K. Rahner and J. Ratzinger, *The Episcopate and the Primacy* (tr. Edinburgh/London, 1962).

31   Paras. 281 ff.
32   ECUSA and Canada, for example, are exceptions.
33   Specifically in relation to the jurisdiction such a Primate would have. See paras. 324 ff.

comprehensively discussed in bilateral or multilateral conversations. Again, the work of ARCIC is particularly important here in emphasising the concept of 'limitation of office'. We quote:

> 16. Jurisdiction in the Church may be defined as the authority or power (*potestas*) necessary for the exercise of an office. In both our communions it is given for the effective fulfilment of office and this fact determines its exercise and limits. It varies according to the specific functions of the *episcope* concerned. The jurisdictions associated with different levels of *episcope* (e.g. of primates, metropolitans and diocesan bishops) are not in all respects identical.

325. The Report goes on to emphasise that 'jurisdiction' has different scope and reference in application to diocesan or metropolitan bishops, or to a universal primate.

> The use of the same juridical terms does not mean that exactly the same authority is attributed to all those exercising *episcope* at different levels. Where a metropolitan has jurisdiction in his province this jurisdiction is not merely the exercise in a broader context of that exercised by a bishop in his diocese: it is determined by the specific functions which he is required to discharge in relation to his fellow bishops.

326. The difference reflects the different positions in which the diocesan and metropolitan bishops stand in the respective responsibilities of their offices to serve the *koinonia* or fellowship of the wider Church. Correspondingly, their authority, too, is a reflection of their duty of service to diocese, province and universal Church.

> 17. Each bishop is entrusted with the pastoral authority needed for the exercise of his *episcope*. This authority is both required and limited by the bishop's task of teaching the faith through the proclamation and explanation of the Word of God, of providing for the administration of the sacraments in his diocese and of maintaining his Church in holiness and truth (cf. Authority I, para. 5). Hence decisions taken by the bishop in performing his task have an authority which the faithful in his diocese have a duty to accept. This authority of the bishop, usually called jurisdiction, involves the responsibility for making and implementing the decisions that are required by his office for the sake of the *koinonia*. It is not the arbitrary power of one man over the freedom of others, but a necessity if the bishop is to serve his flock as its shepherd (cf. Authority Elucidation, para. 5).

327. The ARCIC text moves on to consider the special question of the jurisdiction of a universal primate:

> So too, within the universal *koinonia* and the collegiality of the bishops, the universal primate exercises the jurisdiction necessary for the fulfilment

of his functions, the chief of which is to serve the faith and unity of the whole Church.

328.   Here the issue of the jurisdiction of the Bishop of Rome is of especial concern to Anglicans because of their sixteenth century heritage:

> 18. Difficulties have arisen from the attribution of universal, ordinary and immediate jurisdiction to the bishop of Rome by the First Vatican Council. Misunderstanding of these technical terms has aggravated the difficulties. The jurisdiction of the bishop of Rome as universal primate is called ordinary and immediate (i.e. not mediated) because it is inherent in his office; it is called universal simply because it must enable him to serve the unity and harmony of the *koinonia* as a whole and in each of its parts.
>
> The attribution of such jurisdiction to the bishop of Rome is a source of anxiety to Anglicans (Authority I, para. 24*d*) who fear, for example, that he could usurp the rights of a metropolitan in his province or of a bishop in his diocese; that a centralized authority might not always understand local conditions or respect legitimate cultural diversity; that rightful freedom of conscience, thought and action, could be imperilled. (ARCIC, AII, 18-18)

These lingering anxieties set before us a programme of work ecumenically in connection with both the theology and the practical exercise of primatial jurisdiction.

e.   Order and office and function

329.   We have seen[34] that almost all Christian communities have come to recognise the need for oversight, with a wider responsibility than for a single congregation; for a system of Church government to ensure that ministers are chosen and trained and commissioned in an orderly way, and that faith and order, holiness and truth, are maintained, so as to enable Christians to act effectively together in mission and in care for the needs of the world. The relationship of that *episcope* to the community varies not only in the balance of personal and corporate in its exercise but also in the elements of the ministry of oversight which are seen as restricted to those holding a commission for ministerial leadership. Some functions go with the office, some with ordination; some can be delegated, some not.

330.   But it is not simply a matter of distribution of functions. Some things are perhaps best done by a bishop acting alone, and others certainly ought to be decided by full discussion in a synod; but in both cases the integrity of the local congregation and the wishes of the people must also be respected.

34   See Chapter 5.

There are dangers[35] that the bishop may become an autocrat, or, at the other extreme, that he may become a cardboard figure behind whom parties in the Council manoeuvre for the real power. The difficulty, then, is not only to state in a formal way how best the personal and corporate elements in Church government should be deployed, but to preserve the delicate balances which enable bishop and council and committee to function in the way which best serves the people of God.

331. The distribution of functions must answer the community's needs as the body of Christ. The bishop must always carry the special responsibility of the leadership which unites, and certain functions would seem to follow from that. He will have the primary responsibility for the ministry of teaching the faith, especially the preaching of the Word; for the proclamation to the world of the Evangel, the good news; for leading the local community in worship, especially administering the sacraments; for the interdependent ministries of discipline and reconciliation. All these may, with his permission, be delegated to other ordained ministers serving in his diocese, and the ministry of teaching and leading the community in worship[36] may be shared with lay people too.[37]

332. Where, as in the case of the bishop, commissioning for pastoral care also entrusts ultimate responsibility for the local community, it carries the administrative load of initiating and maintaining all the work of the diocese.[38] In addition it carries authority to commission new ministers. In an episcopal system that is exemplified in the bishop's ordination of priests to serve in his diocese (though on the understanding that they are to be

---

35   See, too, 'United Churches' in the chapter on *Ecumenical Progress*.

36   Readers have a special role here. Lay people may also, in emergency, baptise. See para. 59.

37   Although the regular ministry of the Word normally takes place within a worshipping community, it is also the ministry of mission and outreach and so it goes before the Church's coming to a particular place. Thus, it has always had a role, even where there is not as yet a regular worshipping community with its need for a sacramental life and for a pastor with continuing responsibility for the people. It is for that reason that it can be exercised by those not regularly commissioned for pastoral leadership and the ministry of the sacraments and of discipline and reconciliation. Nevertheless, it is proper and customary for lay preachers to be licensed by the bishop, and to be invited to preach by the local pastoral minister. These have been traditional safeguards of orthodoxy.

38   This continuing domestic administrative load, which is a large part of 'Church government', is certainly 'ordinary' rather than 'extra-ordinary' ministry (see Chapter 6, para. 184) and the necessity of this function is a major argument against the view that the apostolic office was for one generation only.

ministers 'in the Church of God').[39]   There is no exact counterpart in a
congregational system, because there is no delegation of the pastoral
responsibility for a group of the pastor's people, such as takes place when a
priest is given pastoral charge of a parish.   So the pastor cannot ordain
personally in a congregational church.   The exercise of authority to
commission new ministers is, in congregational systems, always an act of the
corporate pastorate, acting as a 'presbytery' on behalf of the wider
community.   The equivalent in the episcopal system is the corporate act of at
least three bishops in the consecration of a new bishop, again acting on
behalf of the wider community.

333.   There are implications here for the relationship of 'office' to
'orders'.   Most communities would agree that some offices can be held and
some functions discharged only by those commissioned for pastoral
ministry, though not all would agree fully which these are, some arguing
that that is for 'human' deciding, not of divine institution.   The Church of
England bishop, the Roman Catholic bishop and the Orthodox bishop will be
bishops for life.   These bishops will, however, hold the 'office' of their
particular pastoral charges only until they resign or retire.   The moderator
or chairman of Reformed or Methodist or other groups of 'non-episcopal'
local congregations will hold office for a period only.[40]   The Church of
England has always maintained that a bishop is not simply a presbyter
entrusted for a time with responsibility for oversight.[41]

334.   It is not in question that oversight can be and is exercised in the
Church by officers who are not bishops, such as moderators, or presidents,
or chairmen of meetings of local pastors.   We are therefore faced with the
question why the Church of England should seek to maintain the historic
episcopate in its midst, and to uphold its value in today's movement towards
a future united Church.   In our own Church, as we have seen before and
after the Reformation, episcopal consecration entrusts to the bishop
additional responsibilities as minister of unity, responsibilities to the wider
Church which are not directly shared by presbyters, and which do not all
come to an end with his retirement from his pastoral office or depend upon
his being a diocesan bishop.

---

[39]   The priests do not discharge all the functions of the pastorate because they stand in a
different relationship from their bishop to the community which forms the basic (diocesan)
unit of the Church's organisation which is the local church.

[40]   To help in making comparisons, it should be noted that Anglican bishops are now holding
office on average for about twelve to fifteen years, although of course they remain bishops
after retirement.

[41]   Cf., on 'parity of ministry', paras. 70, 121, 139, 185.

335.   In Anglican, Roman Catholic and Orthodox polities, it is understood that some functions can still be discharged, with the permission of the pastor, by those who no longer hold pastoral office but who have been ordained.   At the request of one who has pastoral charge, a retired bishop may still confirm or ordain, and he and a retired priest may still administer the sacraments or give absolution.   But the majority of 'governmental' powers are relinquished with office, and among them, all those jurisdictional functions which are exercised above the level of the 'personal' pastorate of the local church.[42]   Some paradoxes remain.   Office may be corporate, as in the case of a Reformed presbytery.   Orders must always be given to an individual.   But it is of the essence of ordination that it is (at least in intention) universal, that is, to a ministry 'in the Church of God'.   It stands for ever mysteriously at the heart of the unity which makes the 'Church in each place' one with the Church universal.   (We speak of that as a 'Kingdom' truth not yet visibly realised.)

f.   Women in the Episcopate

336.   The question of women in the episcopate discussed in our later chapter[43] is, of course, itself a substantial remaining area of difficulty ecumenically.   We refer our reader to our comments there, and note here only that the theme continues to receive attention in ecumenical conversations.   In a specifically ecumenical context, the question of the ordination of women is not in general divisive between Anglicans and the non-episcopal Churches, many, if not most of whom, already welcome women into their ordained or specially-commissioned ministries.   By the same token, women are widely entrusted with oversight in these Churches. The Orthodox Churches remain firmly opposed to the ordination of women to priesthood or episcopate, and there could at present be no possibility of mutual recognition or reconciliation of ministry between Anglicans and Orthodox where Anglicans include women among their ordained ministers. Much the same is true of rapprochement between Anglicans and the Roman Catholic Church,[44] although here the question is the subject of continuing

42   An archbishop, metropolitan or primate (including a pope), has no powers beyond those of a bishop when he retires from office.

43   Chapter 13.

44   From the Letter of His Holiness Pope John Paul II to the Archbishop of Canterbury, 8 December, 1988:
       'In responding to your communication, I would first of all acknowledge the signs of openness to fuller communion with the Catholic Church which were evident at several points in the Conference, not least in your opening address and in the resolutions on the Final Report of ARCIC-1.   At the same time, I must express my concern in respect of those developments at Lambeth which seem to have placed new obstacles in the way of

active discussion, and stands on the agenda of the Second Anglican-Roman Catholic International Commission.

Conclusion to Part I

337. With these unresolved issues, in which there are nevertheless lively signs and good hope of future agreement we come, perhaps appropriately, to the end of Part I of our Report. We turn in Part II to the way forward for the future. Many of the issues discussed there are painfully divisive among Christians at present; but it will be clear that there is also much that is encouraging and that a great deal of progress is being made. Our Group has seen many matters begin to fall into place as we have discussed these problems in the light of the conclusions we have been able to draw from the reflections of Part I. We set out these conclusions in outline in our next chapter, as a preliminary to Part II.

---

reconciliation between Catholics and Anglicans. The Lambeth Conference's treatment of the question of women's ordination has created a new and perplexing situation for the members of the Second Anglican/Roman Catholic International Commission to whom, in 1982, we gave the mandate of studying 'all that hinders the mutual recognition of the ministries of our Communions'. The ordination of women to the priesthood in some provinces of the Anglican Communion, together with the recognition of the right of individual provinces to proceed with the ordination of women to the episcopacy, appears to pre-empt this study and effectively block the path to the mutual recognition of ministries.

The Catholic Church, like the Orthodox Church and the Ancient Oriental Churches, is firmly opposed to this development, viewing it as a break with Tradition of a kind we have no competence to authorize. It would seem that the discussion of women's ordination in the Anglican Communion has not taken sufficiently into account the ecumenical and ecclesiological dimensions of the question. Since the Anglican Communion is in dialogue with the Catholic Churches - it is urgent that this aspect be given much greater attention in order to prevent a serious erosion of the degree of communion between us.'

PART II: LOOKING FORWARD

10

The emerging theology

338.   The theology of *episcope* and episcopacy is embedded in the long and complex story which we have been telling in outline in our earlier chapters. This chapter seeks to draw the threads together.   We begin with the connection between a Trinitarian theology of relationship and order in the Church (Chapter 2) and the principle of the intersection of the three planes of the Church's life which we have explored in Chapters 3 - 9.   We try to draw out here the main theological themes from the history so that it may be clear how they have guided our considerations in the following chapters where we discuss contemporary issues in the Church of England; and developments within the Anglican Communion and in our relationships with other Churches.

339.   The two great themes of the story we have been telling are interdependent.   It is within the context of our Trinitarian faith that we are able to speak of the Church as fellowship or communion (*koinonia*).   Within our understanding of God as a Trinity of Persons we discern the principles of order and relation which we judge to be important in the life of the Church, and in the Father's sending of the Son the ground and pattern of the Church's mission.

340.   We can speak about the Trinity only as a mystery which we receive in faith.   But, at the same time, the truth about God is something that we apprehend and test in the light of experience.   That is where we discover its truth for ourselves.   It has to be true within our own personal and local experience; it has to be tested against the experience of our generation; and it has to relate to and be tested by the deposit of truth which is the inheritance of faith conveyed by the Church down the centuries.

341.   It is only as personal and local insights are tested against wider insights in contemporary society, and as these in turn are tested against the insights of the Church down the ages and looking to eternity, that we may dare to believe that we are glimpsing the eternal truth.

342.   These three dimensions of human experience in the apprehension of the truth about God - the personal and local; the contemporary and

157

universal; the historical and apostolic - are fundamental to the Church's life. Indeed, they are the three planes of the Church's life which intersect and must be seen to intersect within the office of the bishop if he is to be the focal point of the unity and witnessing of the Church and of her life in Word and Sacrament, and the guardian and interpreter of her teaching.

i. The story of God's gift of a ministry of oversight

343.   God gives to the Church many gifts to sustain, guard and nurture its fellowship. One of the primary gifts is the gift of a ministry of oversight. Through this pastoral office an image of Christ's own ministry is seen, and in it and through it God points to aspects of the nature of the Church itself.

344.   The Church is constituted by the participation of its members through baptism in the communion of God's own life and love. Joined to Christ, by the power of the Holy Spirit, Christians enjoy communion both with God the Father and with one another in that divine life. All is to be caught up at last in the fullness and perfection of the communion of God's Kingdom. The Church already enjoys a foretaste of that life, and is its first fruits. The vocation of the Church is to be a living sign of that Kingdom which is God's purpose for the whole world. Hence its vocation is twofold, that of itself living the life of the Kingdom in faithfulness and joy, and of calling all people to share in that life under God. This basic understanding of the mystery of the Church, as grounded in the life of God himself, is fundamental for understanding the nature and purpose of the ministry of oversight.

345.   A ministry of oversight emerged from New Testament times. The Epistles, as well as the record of apostolic preaching in the Acts of the Apostles, illustrate how apostolic *episcope* served the unity of the Church by its ministry in the local church, and in holding the local churches together in a wider communion of faith and sacramental life. From the New Testament beginnings of a ministry of oversight in the Church, we have seen a relatively settled and consistent system of threefold ministry emerge in the patristic centuries. That system was characterised above all by the continuance from the New Testament of the understanding that episcopal ministry must at the heart of its many tasks serve the unity of the community. The service to which the gathered people of God is called, which the bishop must oversee and inspire, is only truly reflective of the triune God if it is a service of unity. This unity is the only proper context

of God-centred relationships within which the Church offers its praise to its Lord and its service and calling to the world.

346. The same theological principles lived on in the changing circumstances of the early Christian centuries, giving rise in time to personal episcopal ministry, and a settled and consistent pattern of threefold ministry, in which a single bishop shared his ministry of oversight with presbyters and deacons. The ministry of oversight was exercised in a variety of functions. The emphasis was not always upon the same ones; the pattern shifted according to the particular needs of individual communities. Differences in cultural contexts meant that East and West shared a basic pattern but not all the functions or the style of exercise of episcopacy developed in the same way. Nor have they remained the same everywhere. Cultural, political and social circumstances did, and still do, affect the exercise of oversight, and the working model changes.

347. Nevertheless, the service of mission and unity has involved an *episcope* in the local Church which has remained a constant throughout the history of the Church. In the local community the minister with oversight has always exercised leadership in mission; in the ministry of the Word and the Sacraments; in worship, prayer and praise; in guardianship of the faith; in the declaration of the forgiveness of sins to those who turn to God; in discipline; and he has had special responsibilities in commissioning for ministry in the Church on behalf of the community.

348. Until the Reformation, broadly speaking, what we have called the second and third 'planes' of the Church's life were linked in the ministry of oversight. It was clear that the bishop was the minister in whom the unity of all local Churches at one time were visibly connected, and also of the whole Church through the ages.[1] The responsibility for commissioning for ministry in the Church was shared by those who exercised oversight,[2] in such a way that it was possible for existing ordained ministers to be 'recognized' by other Churches. That meant that a priest or deacon could move to another diocese, with his bishop's permission, and his recommendation to his new bishop.

---

[1] With, of course, division separating the non-Chalcedonian Churches from the fifth century and Eastern and Western Churches from the schism of 1054, but in neither case with loss of the historic episcopate.

[2] As Article 23 of the Thirty-Nine Articles puts it, by those 'who have public authority given to them in the congregation'.

349. The great historic schisms between the Chalcedonian and non-Chalcedonian Churches and, later, between the Greek East and the Latin West, which prevented those, recognized on both sides as being bishops, from acting as a single episcopate; and to an even greater extent, the later divisions of the Reformation, in which even the mutual recognition of ministry was lost, severely damaged unity and communion within the Church. Even though there is today a growing acknowledgement of a kinship between the exercise of *episcope* in the episcopal and in the non-episcopal churches, the lack of a reconciled ministry of oversight remains a stumbling block; this damages God's gift of unity to the Church which is given to the Church as a sign of the Kingdom.

350. That is not to say that episcopacy must be regarded as a single invariable form of ministry. But at the Reformation a divisive pluriformity came into being, as reformers sought to return in their different ways to what they variously understood to be an apostolic Church order.[3] Only in our own century has there begun to be convergence once more, starting from a common recognition of *episcope* as a gift of Christ to the Church in which all may be one.[4]

ii.   The bishop as sign and focus of unity and communion

351. The emphasis in our preceding chapters upon the three planes of episcopal ministry was unavoidably schematic. But we suggest that it will have served to say something of fundamental significance about the nature of the historic episcopate, theologically speaking. It demonstrates how, through the office of a bishop, the Church is maintained and strengthened in unity in its service of God and its witness to the world. In the local church the bishop focuses and nurtures the unity of his people; in his sharing in the collegiality of bishops the local church is bound together with other local churches; and, through the succession of bishops the local community is related to the Church through the ages. Thus the bishop in his own person in his diocese; and in his collegial relations in the wider church; and through his place in the succession of bishops in their communities in faithfulness to the Gospel, is a sign and focus of the unity of the Church.

---

3   We have sketched the resulting varieties of system in Chapter 5.
4   We have outlined some of the main developments here in our chapters on *Ecumenical Convergence* (9) and *Ecumenical Progress* (14).

352. Insofar as we understand and see the working of the providence of God, we believe it to point to such an episcopate renewed in a future united Church. That is why, we argue, the loss of a common episcopate, the resulting existence of parallel episcopates and divisively diverse forms of oversight ministries, diminishes the sign of unity and continuity. Parallel ministries of oversight reflect an imperfect, restricted, or impaired communion. A divided ministry damages the catholicity of the Church and limits eucharistic communion. A local church which is not related through a ministry of oversight to all other Christians through the world fails to reflect the catholic fullness of baptismal unity. The seriousness of this is not for the Church's life only, but in the impairing of its work in mission, in calling the world to the joy of belonging together to the one family of God through Jesus Christ his Son. A single fellowship, served by a reconciled ministry, enables the Church to interpret and hand on the one Gospel in all its fullness.[5]

iii. Mission and proclamation

353. If we look at the ten key elements most recently identified in the Anglican Communion as pertaining to the office of bishop,[6] four are directly concerned with *episcope* exercised in mission to the world beyond the Church. The bishop's task is not simply that of tending the flock of God and uniting it in faith. It is also to serve God's whole world and all who dwell in it, proclaiming by word and deed the good news of God's healing and setting right; and to engage with the very souls of those who make up society, revealing to them, and winning their assent to, God's mysterious purpose of good.

354. That inward and spiritual unity within the Church which it is the bishop's duty to serve can never be fully manifest, will always be impaired, till the fractures of the wider world which are also experienced in the Church, are healed in the love of God. Hence the absolute demand on the episcopate to spearhead the missionary task of the Church for the reality of reconciliation *within* the Church has its place within God's great purpose of the world's reconciliation: the

---

5   This is why, in the chapter on *Ecumenical Progress*, we give prominence to the search for the recognition, reconciliation and re-integration of ministries in the ecumenical search for visible unity.

6   See Mission and Ministry section of the Report of the Lambeth Conference (1988), p. 61. The list is given at the beginning of Section II of Chapter 13 on *Women in the Episcopate*.

work of God's healing and binding which it is the Church's task to proclaim in the world. That is why bishops must give priority to leading their people in mission both locally and nationally, for mission is the context in which the Church's life is lived.

a.   Relationship, order and mission: The first plane of the Church's life

355.   The two inseparable themes of relationship and order in the Church run through all that we have said. Relationships must always be between persons, and it is essential, in talking of structures in matters of order, never to lose sight of the minister with oversight as a person. That is to say, he holds a personal office in which it is of the first importance that he should set an example as an individual, which helps to bring his Lord to his people. The modern bishop's 'Come on, let's go'[7] has its counterpart in Mark's Gospel: 'Arise, let us go now' (14:42). Jesus said those words as he was about to go willingly to his arrest, conviction and death. The leadership which is service has always been at its best the ministry of the suffering servant, a leadership which accompanies God's people as they follow Jesus along the way of the Cross, which follows the leadership of Jesus himself in a way which others find of comfort and help as they seek to do the same.[8]

356.   But relationships in the ministerial order of the Church also have a formal and structural character, in which we speak of a 'personal' ministry in a rather different sense. Here the bishop is a 'corporate person'.[9] Christ's ministry is entrusted to the whole people of God, to all the baptised; the episcopal ministry is called by the Holy Spirit from within that community and with the consent of that community; it is a ministry exercised in relation to the community and with the support of the community. There is a mutuality of relation between bishop and people; he gives to his people but also receives from them. In the same way the people receive from their bishop but also give to him. This fundamental relational character implies that the bishop must know and be known by the people in the midst of whom he administers the sacraments. And in guarding the faith the bishop has the task of listening to his people, receiving their insights and discerning the mind of the whole people committed to his charge. The

---

7   See para. 259.
8   This modern equivalent and its parallel are referred to by Lesslie Newbigin in *Bishops: But What Kind?*, p. 161.
9   See Appendix I.

bishop is to be with and among his people: they are to act and think together.[10]

357.   The pastoral character of the episcopal office is most clearly seen as the bishop fulfils the commission of the Good Shepherd; 'feed my sheep'.[11] Accordingly, in the local church the bishop has the special responsibility of ensuring the continuing fidelity of the Church: to the message transmitted from the Apostles; to the right ordering of the Sacraments; to the maintaining of the due order of the Church; and of seeing that the apostolic mission is continued.   It is of the nature of the bishop's office that he leads a local church by his presiding over the sacramental eucharistic celebration of Crucifixion and Resurrection which makes the Church.   His ministry is focused in the Eucharist where he presides in the midst of his people and ministers Word and Sacrament, and, in a different way, in the local synod when the bishop gathers with his priests and people.   His authority in all this is in no sense a personal *possession;* nor is it to be exercised according to the world's ideas of power or status.   He feeds his sheep as the servant of Christ and servant of the servants of God.

358.   The relational character of the episcopal ministry is seen also in the delegation of certain episcopal functions to presbyters, deacons and the non-ordained ministers whose ministry meets particular needs and changing circumstances.   The ordering of ministry in relation to the bishop gives stability and harmony to the community in a way reflecting what we glimpse of the order and harmony in the relationship of the persons of the Trinity.

359.   The bishop thus bears a special responsibility in relationships with his people, with ministers he ordains and accredits.   And he bears a special responsibility for maintaining the relationship between God and the community, especially through his ministry of the Word and in the sacramental life of the community.

360.   So in his person the bishop focuses the life of the diocesan community he serves.   That is to say, he becomes the focus of the community's corporate action, helping the people to act as one body: both in their sacramental life, and in everything else they do.   He is made by his ordination God's representative to his people; and also his people's representative, as their leader and the one who acts on their behalf in the

10   Cf. para. 53.
11   John 21.17.

wider community. At the same time, he serves within and among the people whose pastor he is, remaining himself a member of the people of God (the *laos* or laity),[12] and having no authority apart from the community,[13] and exercised within it. That is the essence of what it means to speak of the bishop as both 'priest' and 'pastor'.[14]

361. To say that the bishop is his people's representative may be no more than to say that he is the person who has been chosen to represent them;[15] to say that he is also God's representative to his people is to speak of a divine initiative in his commissioning. All Christian communities recognise the special relationship of pastoral ministry to the enabling of the Spirit. Not all have accepted that there is a deeper mystery in the way the Holy Spirit makes the minister his instrument than can be accounted for on the view that his continuance in ministry remains at the disposal of the congregation or other competent authority in the Church which commissioned him. This special relationship of the pastoral ministry to the giving of the Spirit is recognised in episcopal Churches in the ministry of confirmation when the bishop invokes the Holy Spirit upon the candidates ('Let your Holy Spirit rest upon them', ASB), and at ordination, for example when the bishop lays his hands on the head of the candidate and says, 'Send down the Holy Spirit upon your servant N for the office and work of a priest in the Church' (ASB).

b.   Relationship, order and mission: The Second Plane of the Church's Life

362. A further aspect of the relational ministry of the bishop is the sharing

---

12   And remaining, too, of course, both priest and deacon.
13   See *The Priesthood of the Ordained Ministry*, Faith and Order Advisory Group, (1986), and Para. 53 on Augustine's thoughts here.
14   At and after the Reformation, many Churches have refused to use the title 'priest' for the ministers, because of its association with a theology of ministry which some reforme = believed to imply that human priests were claiming an authority which belongs only to Christ, our one High Priest. The title 'pastor' has, on the other hand, been generally very widely acceptable to Churches of the Reformation, and their heirs. Yet it seemed to Augustine of Hippo that it was a claim of at least equal arrogance to call oneself 'pastor', when Christ is the one Shepherd of his people. That would be so if Christ himself had not commissioned the apostles to feed his sheep (John 21.17). (Cf., too, Norris, 'The Bishop in the Church of Late Antiquity', *loc. cit.*, p. 25.) The principle which must not be lost sight of is that the minister has no authority but that of Christ in his body the Church.
15   With, of course, all the provisos to which we point in our discussion of the appointment of bishops in Chapter 12 on *Church and State*.

of oversight in collegiality with the other bishops. And increasingly in an ecumenical age oversight is being extended in relation both to those who bear oversight in other ecclesial communities and to the members of those other communities.

363. Communion cannot be separated from unity, and unity in Christ makes all Christians one in his Body. We have worked throughout in our discussions, and in writing this Report, in recognition of the imperative to serve that unity, which itself serves the Church's mission to the world. We consider here the main implications for the theology and practice of episcopal ministry in the wider Church. 'The bishop in his official capacity represents the whole Church in and to his diocese, and his diocese in and to the councils of the Church. He is thus a living representative of the unity and universality of the Church'.[16]

364. What is symbolized when bishops come together, even in the Lambeth Conferences, which are by definition not 'Councils',[17] is that wider corporate role, the brotherhood or collegiality of the ministry of oversight. It was clearly felt at the 1988 Lambeth Conference that the Anglican Consultative Council, representative though it is in a sense of laity and clergy as well as bishops, could not serve either symbolically or functionally as could the Lambeth Conference itself, or the Primates' Meeting, which are meetings of bishops.

365. In our treatment of the historical theology we have chiefly spoken of episcopal collegiality as in principle a seamless garment. But there remain for Anglicans a number of sharply pressing questions about the ecclesial status of the autonomous Provinces, that is, whether they are to deem themselves 'Churches' of the Communion, and how far such a sense of identity can square with interdependence in a single Anglican Communion. Problems of 'relationship' arise at many levels, as do issues of common order.

366. In a divided Church, the bishop's linking role must often in practice at present be confined to the diocesan churches of his own Communion. But it is still true that the bishop takes his people with him in spirit when he goes as representative of his Church to meet the representatives of other Churches for brotherly counsel in synods or councils. He may take clergy

16   Cf. *Anglican-Methodist Conversations*, Interim Report (1958), pp. 25-6.
17   See paras. 264 and 272-8.

and laity with him in person in modern synodical structures, but it is the meeting of those with a ministry of oversight which is central to conciliar government. At this level the personal pastorate becomes corporate. 'Acting as a body' becomes possible in a further way.

c.   Relationship, order and mission: The Third Plane of the Church's Life

367.   The 'sign' of ordination, and the ordered succession of bishops within the succession of the faith and life of the Christian Community, are among those elements which are in an episcopal Church constitutive for the fullness of the apostolic continuity in that Church.   That is to say, episcopal succession is not to be divorced from the continuity of life, witness and mission of the whole Church.   Bishops do not guarantee the Church's fidelity to the apostolic witness and mission.   Apostolicity belongs to the whole Church and that is why it belongs to the ministry within the Church. Nevertheless, the bishop has the special task of safeguarding the continuing fidelity of the Church to the message received and transmitted by the Apostles, maintaining the right order of the Church and the continuation of the apostolic mission.   The orderly succession of bishops within an episcopal Church is intended to be a sign to the community that that Church is teaching and acting as it has always taught and acted.   The episcopal ministry thus symbolises and helps to secure in an abiding form the apostolic character of the Church's teaching, its sacramental life and mission.   So succession, properly understood, is not so much a succession of individuals as an unbroken continuity of communities (which are themselves made up of persons in relation).[18]

368.   Recognition of this crucial vocation of the bishop to preserve and maintain unity in matters of faith and order must have particular significance in a divided Christendom.   Not only are the bishops to keep their ecclesial community in unity when it is threatened by party rivalries and schism from within; but they should bear a particular responsibility for exercising leadership in the healing of divisions between the churches; thus exercising their ministry of unity in the service of the universal Church through time as they discharge their responsibility for the maintenance of faith and order.   'Schisms arise in the Church of God when the leaders of

18   See paras 86 ff. and 315 ff.

God's people disagree.'[19] Such healing of divisions is essential to the wider reconciliation through Christ of a fragmented and deeply divided world.

The bishop as guardian of faith and order

369. The 1922 Doctrine Commission suggested that since 'the authority of the Church in the realm of doctrine arises from its commission to preach the Gospel to all the world', we may rely on 'the promises, accompanying that commission, that the Lord would always be with his disciples, and that the Holy Spirit would guide them into all the truth'.[20] In answer to the question, 'Why, then, does the Holy Spirit allow imperfect consensus, periods of learning from our mistakes, and so slow a growth in understanding?' we must answer that in God's undergirding of our decisions our human needs and failings are accepted and allowed for, and the mode of our learning together is in tune with the enabling of our growth in holiness through living together in the faith. If God never forces his people's consent it must follow that the Spirit's guidance is not irresistible and that the Church in history, humanly sinful and fallible, has not necessarily at all points been perfectly responsive to its infallible guide.

370. The recognition of the need for reception is not new. In the case of the admission of the Gentiles to the Church and the matter of circumcision, Paul's actions in one part of the expanding Church were in advance of the decision of the whole Church. Before this was determined to be right it had to be agreed by the 'Apostles, Elders and the whole Church' (Acts 15). Similarly, in the process of formal definition and statement of orthodox teaching it took centuries before the mind of the whole Church was formally expressed in the formulation of the Creeds and by Ecumenical Councils. Nearer our own time is the example of the process of reception of the insights of Vatican II, or of the fruits of ecumenical dialogues like BEM and ARCIC, which are going on in our midst. These examples illustrate something of the diversity of means by which reception proceeds. The present issue of the reception of women's place in the ordained ministry is a part of this complex and continuing process.

371. The process of reception can and normally does involve, under the power of the Spirit, the discerning of the mind of the people of God and the

---

19   Rabanus Maurus in the ninth century. See L. Saltet, *Les réordinations* (Paris, 1907), p. 111.
20   *Report* of the Doctrine Commission (1922), (London, 1938), p. 35.

articulating of the mind of the people through synodical decisions. We have noted chapter by chapter that in the process bishops, both individually and collegially, have a special responsibility as guardians of the faith. They are the 'form' or 'vessel' which ensures that the 'matter' or 'content' of the faith is held safe. It is their responsibility to listen to, discern and guide the forming of the mind of their people, the synodical process and the reception of the decisions of Councils. Beyond that must always lie an embodying of the decision in the life of the community. As Councils have sometimes erred,[21] the reception process is necessarily 'open'. That is to say, it is possible for a conciliar decision subsequently to be supplemented or corrected. But if, in the course of time, the Church as a whole receives a synodical decision this would be an additional sign that it may be judged to be in accordance with God's will for the Church.[22] Yet it remains for the 'consent of the faithful' in every age to continue actively to receive it as in harmony with apostolic truth.

372.   At times in the process of discovery of the fullness of truth in which we are still engaged, there have been major crises: for example over the Arians in the fourth century. We face one now in the realm of order.[23] In such circumstances there has proved to be a special place for the ministry of oversight. The fundamental process of decision-making by judgement and 'embracing' goes on in the community as a whole. But those with a ministry of oversight have a responsibility for dealing with crises and taking emergency action when fundamentals are in question.[24] This is a special exercise of the underlying and continuing responsibility for the guardianship of the faith, borne by the universal Church and focused as a matter of order in the leaders of the community. If this is right, and the office of oversight is as we have described it, the implication would seem to be that when fundamental matters of faith and perhaps also of order are in question, the Church can make judgements, consonant with Scripture, which are authoritative, and that in such emergency conditions these will normally need to be made by those with a responsibility for oversight for practical

---

21   Cf. Article 21 of the Thirty-Nine Articles.
22   *Final Report of ARCIC, Authority I*, para 6; *Elucidation* para 3; *Authority II*, para 25). Cf. Reception is a long range and far reaching process in which the whole Church seeks to recognise and affirm confidently the one faith ... and confidently to lay hold of the new life which that faith promises. (*Gathered for Life: The Official Report of the Vancouver Assembly*, WCC, 1983).
23   See Chapter 13 on *Women in the Episcopate*.
24   The Reformed theologian Wollebius, who published a *Compendium* of Christian theology in 1626, sees the twofold pattern thus. See further our discussion of 'Decision-making and reception' in Chapter 13 and Appendix IV.

reasons of urgency and rapid communicability, and also as carrying an immediate and binding though provisional authority.

373. We need to be clear what this means. Such a judgement must satisfy rigorous conditions. It must be consonant with Scripture. It must share the characteristic of all right decisions in matters of faith, in clarifying the truth, not seeking to add to it. It must be made with the intention that it be a statement of the whole fellowship. That means that such a pronouncement is made focally and representatively for the whole community, and remains ultimately to be received by the whole community. It must be made without duress (for example, political pressure), with the intention of issuing a decision on a matter of faith or morals which the mind of the Church will be able to recognise. These are all indications that it is being made under the guidance of the Holy Spirit.

374. When all these conditions are fulfilled (and this will sometimes become clear only over time), the truth expressed in the definition or the decision on a matter of order may be taken to be authoritative for the Church and to have been arrived at under the guidance of the Holy Spirit. That does not mean that the definition cannot be perfected or made complete; or that it cannot be subsequently reinterpreted or redefined or corrected. It is of its essence an emergency statement, and as such has force as what we may call a 'working consensus'. But because it carries the ordinary inherent authority of those to whom the ministry of oversight has been entrusted, it is decisive for the emergency situation.[25] We may see 'obedience' as a committing of the community to the truth thus expressed, on the understanding that it may come to be more fully grasped and more exactly expressed, or modified, as a result of its receiving by the whole people of God. That is the manner in which it is immediate and binding, and at the same time provisional, as expressing a truth free from error in the most exact language which can be framed at the time.

---

[25] Melanchthon suggested during the Lutheran debates of the first half of the sixteenth century that obedience is due in the same way to a decision arrived at through the Church's structures of decision-making rightly used in this way, as to any right understanding of Scripture. 'When a pronouncement is made according to a right understanding of the Word of God, it is necessary for everyone to observe it, just as certain holy Councils have pronounced on various controversies' (Melanchthon on the Colloquy of Ratisbon, 1541, *Corpus Reformatorum*, 4.352). William Laud, too, speaks of 'obedience' in such a context (Laud, *Conference with Mr. Fisher the Jesuit, Works*, pp. 62-3).

375. The full operation of these processes clearly requires a united Church. In the present divided state of the universal Church they can proceed only imperfectly. Further division, which would further hamper their working, is still sometimes threatened under pressure of controversy. There is an imperative need to arrive at a means of provisional decision-making in the separated Communions which will both strengthen their internal unity, and foster the cause of unity in the universal Church.

376. This brings us to the notion of 'confessional identity' and the related question of what a Communion or a Province may do or decide on its own account in the present divided Church, without further prejudice to the unity of the body of Christ.[26] The sixteenth century Articles of the Church of England endorse the view that such 'traditions' as rites and ceremonies are at the disposal of the Church in different places to decree as appropriate to local needs.[27] The Article says that these must meet two tests. The first is conformity with Scripture, and the second that they should be established locally by common authority (*publica auctoritas*). The Articles argue that such rulings ought to be obeyed in these circumstances in deference to that authority, and so as to avoid troubling the consciences of weaker brethren. They are obeyed, in other words, for the preservation of order, conceived of in terms of obedience and mutual respect. Bishops carry special responsibilities of guardianship in all this, both as forming the College of bishops in a province or nation and as regards their collegial fellowship with one another in the wider Church. It is important that these two collegial 'corporate identities' be kept in balance, so that proper local needs are met and at the same time provincial or national Churches do not become inward looking. The matter is further compounded by the legitimate existence both of traditions which are 'customs of the Church produced by the frequent and long-continued usage of the great part of the community' and which are rightly precious to that group of Christians; and also of traditions of the Church universal, that is, of the whole community over time. So long as it is without prejudice to theological consensus, there must be room for variety in practice.

377. The right to vary 'rites and ceremonies' was not, even in the sixteenth century, a straightforward matter of variation in the forms of services. Liturgy is also theology.[28] The difficulty is to define the limits of that

---

26   See Appendix IV.
27   Article 34 of the Thirty-Nine Articles.
28   The debate about 'rites' was set on foot by the reformers because they believed that the Church was teaching the people theological errors through its rites (especially in the penitential system and in encouraging the veneration of images, for example). The claim to

variation which must operate if there is not to be a consequent division in matters of faith and order.[29]

378. It is a fact of history that in the Anglican tradition legislative decisions can be taken only at Provincial level.[30] We believe that the Provincial right to make legislative decisions, binding on Anglicans who live and worship within that Province, is complementary to two higher laws. The first of these is the law of mutual charity, by which Christians learn to see themselves as members of one body of Christ, and to act for the common good. The second is the law of humble receptiveness to the working of the Holy Spirit, which means that all formal decision-making in the Church must have a provisional character,[31] and remain subject to the forming of the truly unanimous common mind which alone can be a sure indication that the Church has heard and understood the voice of the Spirit. Both these laws, of course, operate on both sides of the debate with which we are here concerned.

379. These are laws of a different kind from those which can be passed by a synod. As we have argued, they are articulated in part through synodical debate and decision-making, but they also involve the active participation of all the people of God in a less formal process of decision-making to which we have referred. In both, bishops have a particular part to play by virtue of their office. Traditionally, they have guided and overseen the synodical process in its legislative task; and as guardians of the faith it has been their responsibility to assist the people of God in their shared work of listening to the Holy Spirit and forming a common mind.

380. We do not pretend that the responsibilities of the bishops over time to act in their communities as guardians of apostolic faith and order are easily defined. But we suggest that they are inseparable from the responsibility to

---

vary rites and ceremonies locally was thus also in some measure a claim to authority locally in deciding matters of faith and larger questions of order. William Beveridge (1637-1708) picks out 'two things' as belonging in some such autonomously determinable way to a Church's authority: 'the decreeing of ceremonies' and 'the determining of controversies'. *Ecclesia Anglicana*, p. 118.

29   T.I. Ball summed up the problem neatly in 1877. Both matters of 'practice' and matters of 'doctrine' as 'received in the Church' have been drawn out of 'the Church's written *depositum*, the Holy Scriptures'. But the extent of the Church's 'power over rites and ceremonies is very large indeed. The extent of the authority of the Church in controversies of faith ... is confined within very narrow limits'.

30   See Chapter 8.

31   On 'provisionality', see further, the section on 'provisionality' in Chapter 13.

balance ecclesial autonomy in province or nation with a sense of the interdependence which is *koinonia*.

---

381. Mathematically speaking, three planes must intersect at a point. It is in the belief that we are speaking of something more than an analogy, and are indeed describing a visible expression of a spiritual reality, that we have argued that in an episcopal Church the three dimensions of the Church's life, appropriately, though not of course exclusively, meet in an episcopal Church in the person of the bishop.

382. We face today a great challenge in the renewal of order in the Church to make possible the full realisation of the communion to which we are called in the Kingdom. In meeting that challenge the episcopal ministry has a leading part to play, as it has always had in the guardianship of faith and order. The challenge must be met with the largeness of vision which takes account of the need of all humanity for a common life in Christ in which all are fully represented, and which seeks to reflect in the communion of the Church, as far as that may be possible for created beings, the mutual love of the Persons of the Trinity.

11

Episcopacy in the Church of England:

i. delegation and sharing

A. The Burden of Office

383. A bishop in the Church of England today faces the great central difficulty of the office to which Gregory the Great in the sixth century, Bernard of Clairvaux in the twelfth, and many others have pointed through the centuries. He is to be the still centre of the spiritual life of his diocese, setting a personal example of holiness. He needs time for prayer and study. But his people require him to be always available and to sustain a workload which would be construed as onerous by even the most energetic in secular employment. In what follows we speak chiefly about the practicalities of his task, because it is there that something can usefully be said about priorities and means of enabling him to do his job in the way which best serves his people. But all this must be understood in the context of the imperative to find a place for the spiritual refreshment of converse with God, and for the reading and reflection which are indispensable if he is to be a strong and capable guardian and interpreter of the faith and of the ministry of the Word.[1]

384. In some respects, a bishop's tasks have become even more numerous and complex in the modern world. Modern bishops have become more accessible, less the princely representatives of an ecclesiastical establishment of the sixteenth century, than men of God among their people. The bishop today, as in earlier ages, works in the community as a public figure. His symbolic and focal role is important, and he is widely regarded as speaking and acting for 'the Church'. It is plain that the office of the bishop still means much to society beyond the diocese and that the wider community welcomes and looks for episcopal involvement. Many 'secular' groups or organisations greatly value the interest, patronage, support - or even criticism - of the Church through the bishop's attendance at their meeting or his association with an organisation. The personal and focal ministry of the

---

[1] See *The Nature of Christian Belief*, House of Bishops (1986), 78.

bishop thus extends beyond the immediate pastoral care of his own flock into a mission to the world, to which the world is open in many and sometimes surprising ways. The personal and pastoral role has to be carried with the wider public role. The public role has enlarged with the expansion of the media, which means that a bishop has to be available to the press; and today's ease of travel makes it possible to expect bishops to take on commitments within the national structures of the Church, ecumenically and in the wider Anglican Communion, in addition to fulfilling increasingly demanding expectations within their dioceses. The Council of Churches for Britain and Ireland and Churches Together in England promise a positive ecumenical future and offer wider opportunities for Christians to work together in this Decade of Evangelism; but this is bound to create further demands on the bishop for more consultation and for joint decision-making, often of a sensitive character requiring time and a clear head.

385. Bishops must give a strong lead in mission, both locally and nationally, not as something extra to their primary commitment to their care of the Church, but as an essential element in that care. For it is the bishop's task to help his fellow Christians in the diocese to work for the reconciling of the world, for the proclamation of God's power to heal the broken, overcome sin and bring forgiveness in people's lives. Without this bonding together in God's love in Christ Jesus of the fractured and divided world, no unity in the Church, even the longed-for ecumenical coming together, can be complete; or even a worthy offering to God. It is the bishop's task to help his people bear this truth in their hearts and live by it.

386. The passing of new legislation, much of which brings in the direct approval of the bishop as a necessary part of the legal process, makes its own demands. Some approvals are formal; but others require detailed thought and attention.[2] Contemporary bishops are engaged not only in their traditional task of preaching but also in much public speaking. If a bishop is to be an effective preacher, he must spend time in preparation. If he is to be a competent public speaker he must be well-informed. Chaplains and others can assist; but much of his preparation has to be his own. Add to this a stream of correspondence, and days filled with interviews, and it is hard to see how bishops are easily to have the necessary time for prayer or spiritual development, or for the theological reflection; which are both essential if

---

2   The Benefices Measure, for example, while bringing a number of advantages in procedures for parochial appointments, itself adds to the episcopal work-load.

they are to speak with spiritual or moral authority and knowledge about any issue.

387.   The chief dangers in all this would appear to be, first, that the bishop may become mentally and physically exhausted in striving conscientiously to discharge his responsibilities within what might be called the domestic routine of Church life, in dealing with the smaller human demands, the mass of paper and the numerous committees; and be at risk of losing the higher vision of his calling.   A second danger is that if the bishop always accepts invitations he may, arguably, inadvertently diminish the ministry of his clergy and of the people of God whom he serves.   Priests in the parishes need to be seen and felt to lead their own people; the bishop shares his *episcope* with them, and with others who are involved in various capacities in his exercise of oversight in the diocese, by affirming them in the discharge of their roles.   Some review of episcopal priorities may be valuable here, with a view to freeing bishops for the work which properly falls to them alone, and at the same time enabling and enlarging other ministries in the Church.

We turn now to the question of the ways in which *episcope* may and should be shared.

B.   Delegation and sharing

388.   A bishop is the person in whom the three planes of the Church's life intersect.   He is a 'corporate person'.[3]   That is to say, he holds an office which is personal, but also collegial and communal.[4]   His is therefore of its essence a shared ministry.   The solutions to the problem of over-burdening the bishop must ultimately lie in the proper understanding and regulation both of the tasks which fall uniquely to the bishop, and of the sharing of *episcope*.

389.   A diocesan bishop is the symbol and representative of the Christian family which constitutes the diocese.   We have argued that nothing ought to call in question this role of the bishop of a diocese.   Even those who would stress very strongly the 'shared' character of episcopal office are clear that the diocesan has a special role, that teamwork does not diminish the function of leadership.   The question is whether there is any contradiction between

3   See Appendix I.
4   See, too, 'Personal, Collegial, Communal', in Chapter 9, section c; and section D of this chapter on the strict sense of the term 'collegiality'.

the 'personal' *episcope* in which the bishop remains in some sense 'chief' (*primus*), and an *episcope* exercised in some respects 'with' all other officers in the diocesan community, and beyond that with the community as a whole. We see no paradox in the view that this supremely personal episcopal ministry at the same time belongs to the whole community. We suggest that it is of the essence of the matter that the authority of a bishop, which is given to him by the community of the Church, is returned by him to the community in the exercise of his ministry. As the 1988 Lambeth Conference put it, bishop and diocese are 'mutually accountable to each other for their ministries'.[5] The full relation of bishop and priests within the diocese extends in a different way to the people as a whole; for bishops, priests and deacons remain members of the *laos*. This is strikingly apparent in the growing sense of self-awareness of today's Church as a community in worship and in mission, sharing in their common baptism a commission for ministry.

390. It is on that basis that we set out here our view of the ways in which the episcopal office may be delegated or shared. We recognise from the outset that in every English diocese there is a clear understanding expressed in Canon Law[6] that there is a single episcopal head. The diocesan bishop is the chief pastor and has jurisdiction within and over his diocese. But in all but a very few English dioceses there are suffragan or area bishops and that single episcopal head may exercise many of his episcopal functions through them or through assistant bishops. Their role presents particular theological and practical difficulties and we consider these issues separately later in this chapter.

391. Although they are interdependent, and indeed overlap, a distinction has to be drawn between the direct exercise of episcopal pastoral ministry; the provision of local pastoral care; and the discharge of administrative duties. The episcopal ministry is discharged by sharing, first and most directly (within the diocese), with the priests who themselves take pastoral care of the parishes. Thus episcopal ministry is discharged at a local level by those to whom the bishop has given authority to minister.[7] In the case of a parish priest, at his Institution to a benefice the bishop says 'Receive this charge, which is both yours and mine'. This reflects the fact that the bishop

5   *The Truth Shall Make You Free*, Lambeth Conference, 1988, Mission and Ministry Section, p. 157.
6   Canon C 18.
7   See J. Ramsbotham, 'Suffragan Bishops' in *Bishops*, ed. G. Simon (London, 1961), pp. 91-2.

is committing to the incumbent part of his pastoral responsibility, the parish being part of his diocese. The new incumbent has under the bishop full responsibility for the cure of souls, although that responsibility in turn may be shared in a team ministry between a Rector and Team Vicars. The community therefore experiences the bishop's own ministry through the ministry of priests.[8]

392. The bishop's personal care within the community is exercised not only in the general cure of souls entrusted to the parish priest but also to some degree through the diaconate. Deacons often have special skills which may be used in the discharge of their ministry - administrative, educational and pastoral. There is also the possibility of deacons (at present especially women deacons) being placed 'in charge' of parishes. This raises questions about the relationship in which the diaconate stands to the bishop in his ministry of oversight.[9] But all this reflects both the fact that the ministries of priests and deacons are an extension of the bishop's own ministry; and the sharing by which priests and deacons are given authority, freedom and responsibility in their work. The underlying process here is one of delegation, for delegation is simply a way of expressing the sharing of ministry. Delegation leaves the ultimate pastoral responsibility in the hands of the bishop.

393. The bishop has an important pastoral responsibility as 'pastor of pastors'.[10] In carrying out this responsibility he can rely upon his archdeacons. The archdeacon discharges an ancient diaconal role as the bishop's administrative and executive officer.[11] He has statutory jurisdiction next after the bishop over a portion of a diocese. Archdeacons are required to assist him in his pastoral care and office[12] as are his rural deans, who must report any case of serious illness or other form of distress amongst the

---

8   But see next paragraph for the position with regard to deacons.

9   *Deacons in the Ministry of the Church*, 339-44. The diaconate is, for many, a step on the way to the priesthood. But it need not be so. The distinctive or permanent diaconate is at present a *de facto* feature of our Church's life; women deacons cannot at present be ordained priest; and some deacons of both sexes may have a vocation to the diaconate for life. We should like to see pastoral awareness of their special needs further developed, some provision made for a 'career-structure', and continuing consideration given to the conclusions of the Report on *Deacons in the Ministry of the Church* (1988).

10   'It is almost as though it was a case of he in them and they in him. All the bishop's pastoral care of his clergy has this coinherence as its very foundation. Canonical obedience is necessitated by it. A great deal of diocesan administration is the corollary to it', J. Ramsbotham, 'Suffragan Bishops', *ibid*, p. 94.

11   See *Deacons in the Ministry of the Church*, paras. 8 ff. and 21.

12   Canon C 22.

clergy.[13] Today's bishops also take a personal interest in their clergy and visit them in their homes, invite them to come and talk about their ministry and its problems once a year, or as often as possible, invite them to come together for discussion, make pastoral addresses, show them hospitality informally as well as formally, and strive in every way that time and energies allow to affirm and 'enable' their ministry. Yet there is clearly a felt need on both sides for good provision for episcopal care and encouragement of the clergy in their ministry and that may mean the bishop's entrusting some of this work to other officers.

394.   This primary delegation and sharing is only one of the means by which the bishop exercises a corporate office. At present in England bishops usually share their *episcope* further by delegation of particular tasks to diocesan officers.[14] This different form of delegation is essential if the bishop is to have assistance in the important practical tasks of administration within his diocese. Hence diocesan officers are employed to be a resource for the bishop and to service the life of the diocese.

395.   Because the cathedral is the seat of the bishop and a centre for worship and mission,[15] cathedral chapters, and in particular the dean or provost, have a special role within the diocese. The historic tradition of independence which Anglican cathedrals enjoy does not diminish the responsibility which the dean or provost carries in the cathedral in relation to the bishop, the diocese, and the wider community. Diocesan bishops make a point of worshipping regularly in the cathedral apart from official occasions.

396.   When it is successfully managed, such sharing of oversight allows the delegated 'personal' ministry of the bishop to use individual talents, interest and experience in others so that they may reach out in a 'personal' intimacy which pressure of numbers makes it impossible for the bishop to share in his own person.[16]

---

13   Canon C 23.
14   In a modern version of the *familia* with which a bishop surrounded himself in a mediaeval
        cathedral.
15   See the new Care of Cathedrals Measure, Clause 1.
16   We see it as important that officers in the diocese should be entrusted with responsibilities
        which make use of their talents and experience. It is clear that this is a high priority with
        diocesan bishops already; but we would note that it requires a flexibility in diocesan
        deployment of resources. The Church is considerably less wealthy than is sometimes
        imagined; and a diocese is understandably suspicious of its own central diocesan expenditure
        when that is extended at increasing cost to the parishes. A bishop is expected to handle and
        respond to the calls made upon him with the often extremely limited resources that are
        usually available to him. We should like to see this kept critically under review.

397. Bishops are always taking counsel with their clergy and laity in formal and informal ways which reflect the Augustinian principle that a bishop is always 'with' and 'among' his people as well as being their leader. The best bishops have always found means of enabling clergy and laity alike to participate in diocesan policy-making and decision-making. Synodical government involving the laity, routinely, as full decision-making members, is a comparatively recent innovation,[17] and it is still developing. The structures exist in the form of Diocesan[18] and Deanery Synods, Bishop's Council, and a range of Diocesan Committees. But there are difficulties in encouraging parish initiatives in policy-making, in helping the local community and the parish church to realise that the synods are theirs, and all the structures and committees which serve the bishop also serve them. There is also the practical difficulty that by creating a system in which there must be constant consultation over policy and decisions, episcopal initiatives to be implemented by Diocesan Committees, committee initiatives to which the bishop has to respond, both bishop and people have been placed under a time-consuming burden.

398. There remain deeper questions concerning the balance between episcopal and synodical authority which have not yet been resolved in our theology or our practice. These have to do not only with the pragmatic allocation of tasks and responsibilities, but also with the theological character of the relationship of personal and corporate in episcopal ministry; with the need for a bishop to be both approachable and known as a friend among his fellow-Christians, and a figure who keeps some distance in the dignity of his office and who has, by virtue of that office, a certain authority. It is important here to be clear about two different senses of 'election'. The bishop is 'elected' in the sense of being chosen by God and the community to fulfil an episcopal ministry, and the bulk of the members of the Synod are 'elected' by a modern democratic process.

399. Some further issues arise in connection with the deployment of resources and the sharing of the burden of episcopal ministry at provincial

---

17   That is, dating from 1970 as regards the constitution of the General Synod, but having precedent in the Church Assembly for most of this century. See paras. 219 ff.

18   At a formal level, the modern bishop is not occasionally but regularly a Bishop-in-Synod. The bishop will generally chair the Bishop's Council which (as the Standing Committee) is responsible for the business of the Diocesan Synod and prepares its agenda, and will thus be at the centre of the process which initiates business.

and national level. These have particular reference to what we have been calling the 'second plane' of the Church's life. There already tends to be some division of episcopal labour at national level.[19] Bishops develop special areas of interest, either through using the earlier expertise with which they come to the episcopate; or through their experience as bishops. We should like to see this continue, with sustained effort to ensure that the corporate episcopate provides a shared oversight in England in which gifts are efficiently used for the good of the community.

400. It is likely that in future the collegial role of the House of Bishops will have a higher profile as the Church of England seeks to bear its witness in the increasing complexities of a pluralistic society. In our view, this makes it all the more important that bishops should number among their ranks some gifted theologians; and that as bishops together they should engage seriously and often in theological reflection. It also raises the question of the place of suffragans in this collegial activity. Although it may be impractical to envisage a House of Bishops including all suffragans, we believe there is a case for seeking to ensure that they are properly involved in the more general process of episcopal theological reflection, for that is an inalienable part of their role as bishops (see further the following section on suffragan bishops).

C.   Suffragan bishops

401. There is always a tension in the Church's life between developed theological principle and the meeting of practical needs which sometimes seems to run on ahead of the theology, and has to be explained and justified *ex post facto*. This is the case with the present system of suffragan bishops in the Church of England and their equivalents in other episcopal churches. On the whole, it works, although often on an *ad hoc* basis. But it does not fit in precisely either with the historical precedents on which it claims to rest, or with a theology of episcopacy which sees the three planes of the Church's life as intersecting in the person of the bishop. In the twentieth century suffragans have greatly grown in number in the Church of England. At the time of writing there are already sixty-four and the provinces of Canterbury and York are alone within the Anglican Communion in having

---

[19]   We believe that Chairmanship of Central Boards need not necessarily fall to bishops, although we should like to see a continuing episcopal Presidency. Such Chairmanship can be so consuming of time and energy as to make it impossible for the bishop who holds it to perform his full range of episcopal duties.

more suffragans than diocesans.[20] This is a clear case of response to a felt and expressed pastoral need. But it has taken place without a consolidated review of the ways in which a bishop's duties ought to be shared or delegated.

402. We seek here, (i) to give an account of the evolution of the concept and practice of 'suffragan' bishopric in the Church; and, (ii) to present the views of the Group on the ways in which we should like to see suffragan bishopric understood and suffragan bishops exercising their ministry in the dioceses of the Church of England today.

a. The first 'Suffragans'

403. The term 'suffragan' originally had a different sense from that in which Anglicans now use it. It referred in the Middle Ages to the bishops who 'assisted' the Metropolitan, that is, the diocesan bishops.[21] This usage reflected the ancient custom of dividing large dioceses into smaller ones, with a natural headship remaining with the bishop of the important city, where what had now become what we should today call a 'province', had a diocesan centre. That centre remained a diocese in its own right, of which the Metropolitan was bishop. The *chorepiscopos* (literally country-bishop), is still quite widespread, among the Syrian and Coptic Churches in particular. Originally *chorepiscopoi* were, as their name suggests, bishops of villages or country areas who ministered on behalf of the Metropolitan (whose own 'city' would of course be very small by modern standards). The *chorepiscopoi* are a legacy of a stage when it was unclear whether the expanding local community could best be served by priests as a team of assistants to the diocesan bishop, or by dividing the area into further dioceses, each with its own bishop. At present, in both the Oriental Orthodox and Eastern Catholic Churches, the *chorepiscopoi* are prelates but in priests' orders.

404. The Orthodox Churches have a long tradition of bishops without sees. The office of titular bishop seems to have received reinforcement (if not its actual beginning) by the eviction from their dioceses of bishops from the Eastern Provinces of the Byzantine Empire by the Turks. When these died,

---

20   GS 551, 12. See, too, the figures at the conclusion of Section b following.
21   Its literal meaning is those whose 'vote', or loyalty he could count on. This usage continued in the sixteenth century alongside a sense closer to the modern one. See section b following.

successors were consecrated in the hope that they would be able to return to the occupied sees. As time passed and the eastern provinces were not reclaimed, such bishops proved useful in furnishing a patriarchal court, acting as diplomats and ambassadors. The titular bishop is, at least in principle, a diocesan bishop, temporarily unable to serve in his diocese.

405. *Chorepiscopoi* were appointed in the West from the mid-eighth century, under the pressure of a successful mission in German lands which was creating a pastoral need which could not be met by existing diocesan bishops. They caused some controversy over their authority to ordain, even with the consent of the diocesan.[22] The provision of 'suffragan' bishops in the West in our modern sense, appointed to help the diocesan bishop, is allowed for in the Canons of the Fourth Lateran Council (1215), as a matter of 'urgent necessity'. The suffragan must be locally acceptable, and the particular need envisaged is for a suffragan who can speak the local language, where the diocesan does not (Canon 9). It is stressed that there should not be two heads in one church, and that the vicar is to be obedient to the bishop in everything. In Canon 10, the Council covers problems arising where the bishop is too heavily loaded with work, is ill or old, or where there is an emergency such as might arise in time of war. Then the 'episcopal vicar' has charge of the people and acts as *coadjutor* and *cooperator* with the bishop. This type of suffragan is the deputy for the diocesan.

406. This permission was exploited in England from the thirteenth century, where suffragan bishops were appointed to carry on the spiritual work in dioceses in the absence of the diocesan. In the days when a bishop had no ready means of contact with his diocese whilst absent on weighty affairs of Church or Crown, it can readily be seen that expediency warranted an arrangement whereby the bishop had another bishop to deputize for him. That was the position in England, such assistant bishops having titular sees nominally located in non-Christian places (*in partibus infidelium*), or being 'absentee' bishops of Irish dioceses. The principal functions of suffragans were conferring of orders and confirming. Their status was that of subordinate bishops. They were consecrated for the purpose of assisting the diocesan bishops, who exercised an inherent power in delegating to them some of their episcopal functions. Such a suffragan was an episcopal deputy in respect of those spiritual ministrations which are

---

22   See P. Hinschius, *System des Katholischen Kirchenrechts mit besonderer Rücksicht auf Deutschland* (Berlin, 1878), II.161 and L. Saltet, *Les réordinations* (Paris, 1907), p. 109 ff.

performed by a bishop by virtue of his orders. So far as the temporalities were concerned, they were put under the management of a *coadjutor* whenever a bishop was too infirm in body or mind to carry out his episcopal duties. There remained a clear distinction between the episcopal functions which could be performed only by someone in episcopal orders and matters such as collating to benefices, granting institutions, dispensations and the like, for which it was not necessary that the *coadjutor* should be episcopally ordained.

b   **Suffragan bishops in England from the Reformation**

407.   The expediency of the arrangement received statutory recognition in the Suffragan Bishops Act of 1534, which recorded that no provision by Act of Parliament had previously been made for Suffragans:

> which have been accustomed to be had within this realm, for the more speedy administration of the sacraments and other good wholesome and devout things and laudable ceremonies, to the increase of God's honour and for the commodity of good and devout people.

The Act proceeded to name towns to be 'taken and accepted for sees of bishops Suffragans to be made in this realm ... and the bishops of such sees shall be called Suffragans of this realm'. Tudor reform of the ecclesiastical laws stressed that a diocesan is not to be absent except on Church business or for grave national emergency, and retained the principle that the appointment of a suffragan ought to be an exceptional and short-term provision; a sick or elderly bishop who could no longer carry out his duties might also have a suffragan.[23] The diocesan's personal authority remained, but was exercised through his suffragan, so that there was no problem of 'two-headedness'.

408.   The appointment of the suffragan was no longer to be a matter solely for the diocesan bishop. Every archbishop and bishop 'being disposed to have any suffragan' was required to present two names to the King who had:

> full power and authority to give to one of those two ... the style title and name of a bishop of such of the two sees aforesaid as to his Majesty shall be thought most convenient and expedient.

---

23   During the sixteenth century Suffragans were appointed for Ipswich, Thetford, Colchester (2), Berwick, Penrith, Shrewsbury, Marlborough, Dover (3), Bedford, Bristol, Taunton, Hull, Shaftsbury, Nottingham.

Having conferred such title upon him the King was to present the chosen person to the Archbishop of the Province requiring the Archbishop to consecrate him.

409.　It should be noted that whilst the King was from 1534 onwards to have the authority and sole right to confer a title on the suffragan, the powers of the suffragan were limited by the terms of the commission given to him by the bishop in the same way as they had been prior to the passing of the Act.　The Suffragan Bishops Act 1534 followed naturally after the Appointment of Bishops Act 1533 had prescribed the procedure for election of archbishops and bishops.　It was designed to affirm the Royal Supremacy in relation to all bishops which was already established in relation to diocesans.

410.　Section 2, which remained in force until repealed by Section 15 of the Dioceses Measure 1978, provided that the suffragan bishop

> shall have such capacity, power and authority, honour, pre-eminence, and reputation in as large and ample manner in and concerning the execution of such commission as by any of the said archbishops or bishops, within their diocese shall be given to the said Suffragans, as to Suffragans of this realm heretofore has been used and accustomed.

The words 'heretofore has been used and accustomed' raise the question of what the previous practice had been, but there is assurance from Bishop Gibson that persons received to be suffragan bishops in England before the Act were confined to the exercise of such powers only as they had commission for from time to time.[24]　So there was no alteration of the relationship between the bishop and his suffragan; the extent to which the bishop was willing to delegate his episcopal functions being left to his discretion.

411.　Anglican writers of the sixteenth century had mixed opinions about the use of suffragans.　Ridley and Tyndale were opposed to them, on the grounds that they were signs of the overweening pride of bishops in the late medieval Church.　Parker took them for granted.　Bullinger, not an Anglican but highly influential in the Elizabethan Church, had some of Ridley's and Latimer's reservations about late medieval practice, but he approved the principle which he saw as put into practice in the early Church, of appointing *chorepiscopoi* as 'vicars and suffragans', who might

---

[24]　Gibson's Codex, p. 135 referred to in *Phillimore's Ecclesiastical Law*, 2nd edition, 1.78, 79.

execute the office of the bishop throughout that part of the country, where 'the country or region was larger than that the care and oversight of the bishop placed over the city would suffice'. Latimer identified a precedent in Samuel's choice of 'two suffragans, two coadjutors, two co-helpers ... to help him discharge his office' when he was old.[25]

412. The Canons of 1604 recognised the existence of suffragans,[26] although from the end of the sixteenth century the practice of appointing suffragans lapsed.[27] Nevertheless, Jeremy Taylor (1613-67) tried to provide a fuller theological underpinning in his *Episcopacy Asserted*.[28] He began, not from the problem of over-large dioceses and over-busy bishops, but from that of the unavoidable involvement of bishops in public affairs which would from time to time take them away from their dioceses. It is not unlawful, he says, for bishops to have some secular employment. The Apostle Paul was a tent-maker. Bishops should not seek to involve themselves in secular affairs, but they ought to do what they can for the good of the community. He finds ample precedent for the right of bishops to delegate. In the early Church bishops 'delegated to presbyters so many parts of the bishop's charge as there are parishes in his diocese', at first as common assistants, and later with parish cures of their own. Those functions which only a bishop can perform were not so delegated. But it was possible for a bishop to make 'express delegation of the power of jurisdiction', as Paul did to Tychicus. Epaphroditus 'although he was then bishop of Philippi' spent time with Paul and was then 'certainly non-resident', so that 'one in substitution' would have been needed. In the post-apostolic period Jeremy Taylor finds various examples. Cyprian, for instance, had at some time two suffragans and two priests.

413. The guiding general rule in all these Western medieval and post-medieval provisions up to this point had been that where a diocese was simply too big, the proper course of action was to subdivide it. A suffragan bishop was appointed in case of short-term emergency need, so that the

---

25   Ridley, *Works*, Parker Society, p. 55; 112; 175; Tyndale, Parker Society, I.274.

26   By Canon 35 any bishop or suffragan who admitted any person to sacred orders who was not duly qualified was suspended from ordaining for two years. By Canon 60 every bishop or his suffragan was required to observe the custom of confirmation in his visitation every third year.

27   See P. Collinson, 'Episcopacy and Reform in England in the later sixteenth century', in *Godly People*, ed. P. Collinson (London, 1983), pp. 155-89, on contemporary discussion of the provision of diocesan 'superintendents' and other projected solutions to the problem of busy bishops and over-large dioceses.

28   Jeremy Taylor, *Works*, ed. C.P. Eden (London, 1849), V.

pastoral care of the diocese might not suffer. It is not until the later seventeenth century in England that the implications of the Henrician statute were more clearly seen to be the emergence of a new permanent suffragan, who worked with and answered to his bishop in some manner which must not result in the diocese becoming a monster with two heads. In Charles II's declaration touching ecclesiastical affairs immediately before his Restoration, we find:

> Because the dioceses, especially some of them, are thought to be of too large extent, we will appoint such number of suffragan bishops in every diocese as shall be sufficient for the due performance of their work.[29]

414.   This was not acted upon for two centuries. It was late in the nineteenth century that practical need seems to have prompted the fuller implementation of the laws already in existence. In 1870, suffragans were consecrated for Nottingham and Dover, which were two of the towns listed in the Suffragan Bishops Act of 1534.

415.   The Suffragans Nomination Act 1888 heralded the new era of rapid growth in the number of suffragan sees. The preamble states that 'it is desirable to add to the number of towns for the purposes of the (1534) Act' and the Act empowered the Queen to add other towns for sees of bishops suffragans as if they had been included in the 1534 Act. Such towns were duly added and suffragans appointed for them and for towns named in the 1534 Act. The tendency to increase the number of suffragans has continued.[30] In 1901 there were nine. By 1921 there were 21; by 1941 there were 38; by 1961 there were 44; by 1966 there were 49; by 1974 there were 59 suffragans. That is, during the first 73 years of this century, the Church created on an average a new suffragan see every eighteen months. Today, as we have noted, there are well over sixty.

416.   There were those who thought that this system, which had grown up almost casually but by necessity, was an unwarranted innovation in the system of the Church's ministry. Instead of keeping the same number of dioceses and multiplying the suffragan bishops, they argued, it would be

---

29   Gibson's Codex *loc. cit.*, p. 134.

30   The Dioceses Commission in their *Report* on *Episcopacy and the Role of the Suffragan Bishop* (GS 551) underlined the problem of the continuing rapid increase in the number of suffragan bishops in the Church of England.

more in keeping with the primitive Church, and probably better as a way of pastoral care, if the dioceses were multiplied.[31]

c   Current law[32]

417.   Some clarification and tidying up of these areas of difficulty was achieved by the provisions of the Dioceses Measure of 1978. This Measure sets out two methods of delegating or subdividing episcopal jurisdiction. These are contained in Sections 10 and 11 and are introduced by the words 'Provisions with respect to the discharge of episcopal functions'.

418.   Section 10 is entitled 'Temporary delegation by instrument of certain functions to suffragan bishops' and Section 11 is entitled 'Permanent provision by scheme with respect to discharge of episcopal functions'. In Section 10 two functions only are mentioned specifically: the administration of the rite of confirmation and the holding of ordinations. The bishop may make an instrument delegating these functions to the suffragan without obtaining the consent of the diocesan synod. He has therefore the freedom to do by way of instrument what his predecessors were able to do by way of commission[33] both before and subsequent to the Suffragan Bishops Act of 1534. The instrument is personal to the suffragan and will be temporary in the popular sense of the word only if a particular period of time is specified in the instrument. Otherwise it will continue during the time that the suffragan holds office under his diocesan bishop. Each then knows where he stands.

419.   To deal with the possibility of the diocesan bishop ceasing to hold office first, the section enables the suffragan to continue to act under his instrument[34] until two months after a new diocesan bishop has taken office. Whilst no doubt intended to preserve some continuity, the provision automatically places the new diocesan bishop in a potentially difficult

---

31   In March 1964 a report by five diocesan bishops under the chairmanship of the Bishop of London, recommended that there ought to be a hundred or more dioceses, and that these dioceses should be grouped in a larger number of provinces and therefore with an increased number of archbishops. Archbishop Ramsey showed no sign whatever of being attracted to this idea, and it has not won general acceptance in the Church of England.

32   *The Dioceses Measure, 1978, A Review:* Report by the Dioceses Commission (GS 925) is before the General Synod as this *Report* goes to press, and may result in some amendments to the Dioceses Measure, 1978 at a later date.

33   The power to give a commission was abolished by Section 15, Dioceses Measure, 1978.

34   Save in relation to collation to a vacant benefice (section 14).

situation in relation to the suffragan. He may either renew the instrument in the same terms as were used by his predecessor so as to maintain the continuity of practice, or he may extend the scope of the delegation of functions. If he were to reduce the number of functions delegated to the suffragan it could damage their personal relationship and also the status of the suffragan.[35]

420.   It is for the diocesan bishop to decide what functions he wishes to delegate to his suffragan and the conditions to be attached to such delegation before he submits the instrument for the consent of the diocesan synod. The absence of any identification in the section of the functions which should be delegated to a suffragan undoubtedly gives flexibility to the diocesan, but at the same time it means that there is no uniformity of practice within the dioceses. It also follows that a new suffragan can have no clear picture of functions he will be expected to perform by virtue of his office.

421.   Section 10 has implications in relation to the functions of the diocesan bishop and in recognition of this the section provides that the making of an instrument delegating functions to a suffragan shall not be taken as divesting the bishop of the diocese of any of his functions.[36] However, the practical reality of the situation is that with the consent of the diocesan synod the diocesan bishop delegates functions to another bishop, who then discharges them. There is then a sharing of episcopal responsibility and oversight within the diocese between two or more bishops, depending upon the number of suffragans in the diocese.

422.   In contrast to Section 10 which is described as temporary but in practice creates a permanent state of delegation of functions, Section 11 is designed to be permanent in dividing a diocese into areas and binding not only the bishop of the diocese at the time when the scheme is made, but also his successors in that office (S.11 (6)). A diocese is a geographical area which forms a circuit of jurisdiction. Dividing it into areas divides up the circuit. The Scheme must specify the bishop who is to have, or the bishops who are to share, the episcopal oversight of an area. The Scheme must

---

35   The Dioceses Commission has pointed out that: There is evidence that some at least of the parochial clergy, and very many of the laity regard a Suffragan Bishop as a sort of inferior substitute for their 'real' Bishop, the Diocesan, even in matters which have been agreed between him and the Diocesan to be his sole responsibility. Episcopacy and the Role of the Suffragan Bishop: A Second Report by the Dioceses Commission, GS 697.

36   There is, of course, a sense in which there is no need to enact by statute a power of 'extension' already inherent in the office of the bishop.

provide that he 'shall discharge such of the functions of the bishop of the diocese as may be specified in the Scheme'. The section provides that the making of a Scheme shall not be taken as divesting the bishop of the diocese to which the Scheme relates of any of his functions (S.11 (7)). Here again the Measure has introduced a lawful sharing of episcopal oversight within the diocese. The diocesan bishop may chose to retain a geographical area of his own[37] alongside the geographical areas assigned to the area bishops. It may appear that he has merely a residual position when the Scheme has provided for the suffragans to discharge many of his functions. Yet, because the area bishops have a clear demarcation of responsibility, the diocesan bishop is given an opportunity to develop a special role as the unifying force within the whole diocese.

d   Suffragan bishops in today's Church of England: the practice and the theology

423.   The mediaeval Western provision for suffragan bishops, who were for all practical purposes, episcopal vicars, which the sixteenth century and subsequent legislation of the Church of England continues (with modifications), has, in modern practice, undergone a change of purpose. The fundamental difficulty today is not that bishops have to be away from their dioceses for long periods on Church or State business, although they may in fact have to travel a good deal outside their dioceses. Nor is it the continuance in office of bishops unfitted by age or infirmity to remain in charge of a diocese. It is, we have argued, that diocesan bishops (especially in large dioceses with substantial populations) are simply expected to do more than it is possible for a single individual to accomplish, and that some of what they do is not uniquely their responsibility. The presenting practical problem in episcopal Churches[38] has come to be the manner in

---

37   The Dioceses Commission's recommendation that he should do so was not accepted by the Synod (see GS 697, 3). Cf. GS 551, 14 on the distinction between formal and informal Area Schemes and GS 551, 15 on specific areas of responsibility. See, further, our discussion in what follows.

38   The problem is addressed in all episcopal Churches today. In the Roman Catholic Church there are both titular and auxiliary bishops. Certain auxiliary bishops may be designated 'coadjutors'. Such bishops have the right of succession to the diocesan. An auxiliary will assist the diocesan bishop and takes his title from a see now no longer in existence (usually from classical Asia Minor or North Africa), though English auxiliaries have used defunct Anglo-Saxon titles such as 'Lindisfarne'. Care is now usually taken not to use episcopal titles already used by Orthodox or other bishops. Curial and diplomatic bishops also take titular sees but are not auxiliaries or coadjutors. In some countries in large metropolitan cities auxiliary bishops have been given unofficial 'area responsibilities', as for example in Westminster. In other places auxiliary bishops have sector ministry responsibilities and may also be Vicars General. In recent years the Roman Congregation for Bishops has shown some reluctance to agree to the multiplication of auxiliaries. There appears to be as

which a bishop today can, or should, hold his office 'in totality', that is, as a personal, collegial and communal office, where it is clearly an impossibility for a single individual to carry out all the traditional and modern functions of a bishop. In an episcopal Church certain of these functions cannot be delegated except to another bishop. So the suffragan no longer discharges the diocesan's episcopal office where he cannot do so himself because he is absent or ill. He stands in a permanent working relationship with his diocesan, as a bishop in his own right.

424. Questions both theological and practical are raised by the existence of large numbers of suffragan bishops. If it is true that the importance of episcopacy resides in the fact that the three planes of the Church's life intersect in the office of the bishop, it has to be asked to what extent the suffragan as distinct from the diocesan bishop represents and expresses the local, the collegial and the apostolic or continuing dimensions of the Church's life. If it is true that the demands of contemporary Church life are too burdensome for one leader to fulfil them, it has to be asked to what extent the creation of suffragan bishoprics is holding the Church of England back from a serious consideration of the problem of the size of dioceses.

425. Suffragan bishops in substantial numbers are likely to be with us - and in other parts of the Anglican Communion[39] - for the foreseeable future. Theological rationale and pastoral necessity may not always sit comfortably together, except insofar as pastoral necessity provides its own theological justification.

426. It is clearly unacceptable that a suffragan bishop should be seen either within his diocese, or within the wider Church, as an anomaly born of

---

much doubt about the theological status and the place in the Church's order of a bishop without designated jurisdiction within the Roman Catholic Church as is evidenced within the Anglican Communion in relation to suffragan bishops. There are also, in parts of Orthodoxy, Assistant Bishops functioning in a Diocese rather like Anglican suffragans. This is not uncommon in parts of the diaspora (e.g. in the USA and in this country) and in large cities such as Athens. (J. Zizioulas, *Being as Communion*, p. 197, n. 99, speaks of titular bishops in the Orthodox Churches as 'a grave anomaly'.) Over the centuries the restrictions placed on *Chorepiscopoi* where they have persisted have increased, until their ministry has become almost indistinguishable from that of presbyters. There are no territorial titles attached to the Chorepiscopate, which is now treated as an honorific.

39   Canterbury and York are, however, the only Provinces in the Anglican Communion where the number of suffragans exceeds the number of diocesan bishops.

pastoral necessity. There is ample evidence that the ministry of suffragan bishops is desired and valued. The questions relate to the consequences for our theology of episcopacy and our management of the mission of the Church if there is a continuing proliferation of bishops who are in some sense subordinate bishops, and who do not exercise the full jurisdiction of a diocesan bishop. While the term 'jurisdiction' is part of our ecclesiastical law in relation to bishops, its use in connection with what suffragans may or may not do distorts the idea of *episcope* which is essentially personal without being necessarily in all respects individual.

427. We do not envisage that suffragans could or would be dispensed with, but we think it appropriate that we should begin by considering the option of returning in the Church of England to dioceses which are presided over by one bishop.

i. One bishop, one diocese?

428. The continuing tradition of episcopal Churches from an early date has, as we have seen, maintained the principle that the diocese with one bishop is the fundamental unit of Church administration and also the fundamental pastoral unit. The diocesan bishop has a cathedral, in which stands the *cathedra*, or seat from which he teaches his people. A single place of worship and ministry of Word and Sacrament thus lies at the heart of the diocese.[40] This rule of monepiscopacy is enshrined in the Church of England's Canons, particularly Canon C 18. Every bishop is the chief pastor of all that are within his diocese, as well laity as clergy, and their father in God' (Canon C 18). The idea of 'Fatherhood', which is often used as an argument for monepiscopacy, is only a metaphor and should not be pressed in a literal sense. Both diocesans and suffragans can symbolise fatherhood.[41]

429. To follow the rule of monepiscopacy would present the Church of England with difficulties because of the size of many existing dioceses. The reluctance of the Church to countenance the creation of new dioceses in

---

40   'You cannot multiply Bishops in one place. One Bishop in one city was the patristic principle because the people of God related to a person and not to a committee. A community needs a single focus.' Canon Gareth Bennett, Proceedings of General Synod, November 1985, p. 1008, and see the 1938 Report of the 1922 Doctrine Commission. The Dioceses Commission has explored the subject fully by way of a questionnaire. See their Second Report, GS 697, 12 and 14.

41   Cf. Appendix III a, para. 24.

recent generations, despite the substantial increase in the population, has led to the pluriformity of practice in episcopal leadership which gives rise to a number of expressions of confusion and disquiet. Is it a practical possibility, or indeed desirable, to multiply dioceses so that we can dispense with suffragans altogether, and every bishop will be a diocesan? The idea of creating a large number of small dioceses, especially in urban areas, was rejected by the Report on Bishops and Dioceses (1971) on the grounds that, 'More and more these areas are administered economically and politically as single units, and in their pattern of life are socially single entities. Were the Church to divide them into small independent, or even semi-independent units, it could be ignoring the character of society in these areas'.[42] The debate on the Dioceses Commission's *Report* (GS 697) in the General Synod in November 1985 saw small dioceses with single bishops as 'attractive ... theologically',[43] but feared that they would create too great an additional administrative load and, in some respects, make the Church's mission less effective.[44] There is no evidence that the Church would welcome such a development in dioceses where Area schemes are most fully developed, although there are undoubtedly some situations where boundary adjustments might properly be made and the division of a large diocese might enable the Church's boundaries to relate more properly to the natural boundaries of community life.

430.   Many considerations will determine the size of a diocese, but some account is bound to be taken of geographical and sociological factors. A diocese will not invariably have a natural identity although with the passage of the years there will often be a growing awareness of a common 'life-story'. Some dioceses would lend themselves more readily than others to division; it is important not to cut across old loyalties. The point is also emphasized in one of the recommendations adopted by the Synod from the first Report of the Dioceses Commission: 'A Diocese should be of compassable size.' The ideal size is seen as one which will enable the Bishop 'to be known by clergy and people, available to them and able to perform episcopal functions throughout the Diocese'.[45] 'A bishop must have a manageable and recognisable community'.[46] That is in line with the

---

42   *Bishops and Dioceses: The Report of the Ministry Committee Working Party on the Episcopate* (1971), pp. 26-7.
43   *Proceedings*, p. 1004.
44   *Ibid.*
45   'Episcopacy and the Role of the Suffragan Bishop', G.S. Misc. 551, p. 10.
46   *Proceedings* of the General Synod, November 1985, p. 1008.

evolution of dioceses in the early Church, where the local city often provided the natural focus.[47]

431. We consider that it is undesirable artificially to seek to create dioceses of uniform size, but our Group would like to see serious consideration of the possibility of reduction in the size of some dioceses by the creation of more dioceses. This should have the effect of reversing the trend towards the proliferation of suffragan bishops. At the same time, we would hope to see dioceses remain of a reasonable size. A diocese which is too small is as undesirable as one so large that its bishop must seem remote to his people.

432. The early idea that every bishop holds within himself the totality of the office would be fulfilled through the creation of a large number of small dioceses each presided over by one bishop. Such a development would represent a return to what is judged to be a primitive model. It would have the advantage of providing a pattern of episcopal oversight which is free of anomalies. But the 'theological purity' would be purchased at the expense of the various practical disadvantages we have outlined here. It is for the Church to decide how these are to be weighed.

433. If some dioceses remain too large for the single bishop to exercise his episcopal ministry adequately, and the number of dioceses cannot be sufficiently increased for reasons of practical politics, we are left with the theological question how the concept of a unitary episcopate can cohere with the exercise of directly episcopal ministry by other bishops in the diocese on virtually a permanent basis. Early debate in the General Synod led to the conclusion that 'there is no one pattern of episcopal organisation to which the Church of England would wish to commit itself, to the exclusion of all others'.[48] It is perhaps in the nature of the Church of England that a variety of patterns of episcopal leadership and oversight should coexist alongside each other, reflecting the needs of different dioceses, the aptitudes of different bishops and the proper reluctance of the Church of England to embrace comprehensive schemes of radical change.

[47] But with the important proviso that our cities are, as enormous conurbations, significantly different from ancient cities, *Proceedings* of the General Synod, November 1985, p. 1012.

[48] GS 214, Report by the Standing Committee entitled Episcopacy: Follow-up of the Debate on Canon Welsby's Consultative Document (GS 167) - Episcopacy in the Church of England.

434.   In what follows we look at three ways in which the ministry of the suffragan bishop can be envisaged in the Church of England today.

ii.   Three models

I.   **A theology of episcopal collegiality of the diocesan and suffragan bishops within the diocese**

435.   One approach which has gained a measure of support is to see the ministry of the diocesan bishop with his suffragan or suffragans in collegial terms. Historically, episcopal collegiality has been understood in terms of the collegiality of bishops within a province or provinces or of the total episcopate of the whole Church. Suffragans might be said to share in any case in a collegiality of all bishops by virtue of their consecration; but the intention of this particular approach is to create a new category of episcopal collegiality: that of episcopal collegiality within a diocese. It is important to be clear that this is a novel extension of the concept of collegiality.[49] Collegiality is an expression of the universal aspects of the bishop's office. There is a risk that the appropriation of the word 'collegiality' to describe the shared leadership that a chapter of bishops offers in a diocese, might lead unwittingly to situations in which the primacy of the diocesan bishop is obscured. Collegiality of bishops in a diocese could at its worst be little more than committee episcopacy, with the diocesan bishop able to be out-voted. No less seriously, an uncritical use of the notion of collegiality may compromise the *episcope* that a bishop shares with his clergy.

436.   This understanding of episcopal ministry as collegial within the dioceses where there are suffragans was expressed in the Report of the Ministry Committee Working Party on the Episcopate (1971). Their solution was to see a college of bishops in a diocese as the most satisfactory form of episcopacy for the effective administration and mission of the Church in the large urban areas.

> The Church in urban society needs a variety of episcopal ministry which a single Bishop in a Diocese cannot provide. The complexity and variety of the problems and opportunities, which the Church and community face in metropolitan Areas, demand a level of integration between specialist knowledge and skills and the episcopate of a Church in a Diocese which only a group of Bishops can give.[50]

---

[49]   Cf. 'Personal, Collegial, Communal' in Chapter 9, section c; and sections C iv, and section D of this chapter.

[50]   'Bishops and Dioceses', p. 27, sec. 55.

437. This approach has the merit of emphasizing the corporate character of the specifically episcopal ministry of those who are duly exercising such ministry in a particular diocese; and some of us take the view that there is no reason in terms of theological development, if the diocese is the essential component in an episcopally ordered Church, why a collegial model cannot be adopted. However, we do not judge that this has been the mind of the Church.[51] That is not to deny that there are collegial elements in the relationship between a diocesan bishop and his suffragans, related particularly to their common episcopal office within the diocese, nor to disparage the importance of responsible and harmonious personal working relationships;[52] but to invoke collegiality in too precise a sense must mean a departure in principle from the norm of monepiscopacy and endanger the theology which sees the focussing of the three planes of the Church's life in the person of the bishop; and there is little evidence that that is desired.

438. Most of the members of our Group believe that the diocesan bishop's role as personal minister of unity and as pastor of the 'local church' of his diocese is of supreme importance in our own episcopal Church, and that legislative arrangements and provisions for the appointment of suffragan bishops must not violate that principle. Some of us, however, feel that while the provisions of ecclesiastical law in determining what suffragans may or may not do must not be allowed to distort the idea of *episcope* as essentially personal, that personal office is not necessarily 'individual'.

II.   A pragmatic solution: the Area system

439. The Report of the Ministry Working Party on the Episcopate suggests that in dioceses with suffragans, each bishop should have a territorial area, a sphere of community life, and representation in a House of Bishops in the

---

51   'Episcopacy and the Role of the Suffragan Bishop', GS Misc. 551, p. 3, para 5. In the Synod Debate in February 1983 this statement was questioned. But the Dioceses Commission overstated reaction in declaring 'that this novel and misleading idea' had been rejected by the Synod.

52   The report of the research programmes under the auspices of the Urban Ministry project and the William Temple Foundation in 1983 summarised the work of a bishop in practical terms under three main headings: the pastoral care of parishes and people and inter-parochial ministries: the organising and enabling of the diocese as a whole: and the addressing of the world. It could be argued that a balanced team of diocesan and suffragans, especially in the larger conurbations, is best suited to this task.

Diocesan Synod.[53] The Report was not, however, dogmatic in proposing such a system for all dioceses.

440. This approach retains the focal role of the diocesan bishop, but looks for defined areas of responsibility for the suffragan; areas which are delegated to him and in which he exercises the delegated responsibility collegially with his diocesan. This pragmatic resolution of the difficulty is clearly the intention of two of the recommendations of the Dioceses Commission *Report* approved by the General Synod in 1983, that where possible a suffragan should be attached to a defined geographical area; and that in all cases suffragan bishops should be given specific delegated episcopal functions. The General Synod also approved two years later one of the recommendations of the second *Report* of the Dioceses Commission on Suffragan Bishops of relevance in this connection: the need for clarification of roles, where a diocesan bishop works with only one suffragan.[54]   We have pointed[55] out that the provision in the Dioceses Measure 1978 for temporary delegation of functions by instrument can lead to lack of uniformity and uncertainty as to the role of the suffragan bishop. Whilst the working relationship between the diocesan and his suffragan or suffragans can be successful, and diversity of approach depending upon the requirements of the particular diocese, can be valuable, it does not always follow that the working relationship is satisfactory and lack of clarification of roles can only exacerbate such a situation. Where there is no instrument the suffragan, the parochial clergy and the laity can have no clear idea of what the division of responsibility is.   Viewed solely in terms of clarification of roles the Area system is to be preferred.

441. There remains, then, the difficulty that such delegation may be seen as departing from the principle that nothing can divest the bishop of the diocese of any of his functions.[56] It is therefore important to be clear that, in an 'Area' scheme, the diocesan retains direct pastoral oversight of the whole geographical area of the diocese, including his own (if any) and the suffragan's or suffragans' areas. Nevertheless, the suffragan has a 'title',

---

53   The question of the value of an Area Synod, envisaged as an 'elected body to support each Area bishop' has attracted mixed comment, cf. *Proceedings* of the General Synod, November 1985, p. 1006.

54   It was suggested in the same Synod that the Area scheme is 'a practical and limited attempt to deal with the problem of the multiplication of bishops in dioceses', *Proceedings* of the General Synod, November 1985, p. 1008.

55   See section c on 'Current Law'.

56   See Chapter 6 and Dioceses Measure, 1978, Sections 10 (3) and 11 (7).

while he exercises in his own person the *episcope* of his diocesan in his area.[57]

442. The Dioceses Measure of 1978 can provide territorial areas for the diocesan and his suffragan or area bishops. Such a development recognises the impossibility of one bishop's providing adequate episcopal oversight within a large diocese. It takes seriously the integrity of each bishop by virtue of his consecration, and the authority that belongs to his office. It provides a framework for mutual support at an episcopal level. We believe that in a number of dioceses this pattern is working well and we believe it to be welcomed by the people.

443. Area schemes exist at present in comparatively few but large and numerically significant dioceses, and are being explored elsewhere. They would not do everywhere. Not every diocese can be happily divided into natural 'neighbourhood' parts which coincide with an episcopal area to which the people can feel they belong (cf. *The Report of the Ministry Committee Working Party on the Episcopate* (1971), pp. 26 ff.). It is freely recognised that schemes under the Dioceses Measure can devolve substantial responsibilities upon the area bishops, but the growing tendency to differentiate between area and suffragan bishops, as though they were in different categories, has no authority in theology or in canon law. Moreover, if division into 'areas' became a standard pattern, a new level would appear to be created in the Church of England's hierarchy in which the existing diocesan has something of the role of a 'metropolitan', and it may not always be clear what constitutes the basic 'diocesan' unit of the 'local church'.

444. Whilst area schemes have made a bishop more readily available to his clergy and people, the corresponding need to maintain a loyalty to the diocese and to the bishop of the diocese may lead to confusion as the area seeks to establish an identity and to give to its area bishop the recognition and the network of support he may require.

445. It is clear from all this that the Church of England has not as yet adequately defined the episcopal relationships involved in this pragmatic solution in a theologically satisfactory way. Certainly, in its debate on the first *Report* of the Dioceses Commission in February 1983, the Synod did not think so. It rejected the recommendation that a distinct geographical

---

[57] He has an important measure of local jurisdiction and will preside at an Area Synod if provision is made for such a body in the scheme (Dioceses Measure, 1978).

area should be retained for a diocesan's personal oversight. It also rejected a recommendation in the Second Report of the Dioceses Commission that encouragement should be given to the drawing up of formal Area Schemes in the case of Dioceses with two or more suffragans. In both these instances it might well be said that in defining the role of suffragans the role of the diocesan was perhaps left without the necessary degree of theological clarity. If a diocesan needed a geographical area, that might seem to imply some diminution of his relationship with the rest of the diocese. It might also be asked, if dioceses were being encouraged to move towards formal Area Schemes, on what understanding of the episcopate they were doing so. In reply it can be said that inherent in this model of shared episcopal ministry is the desire to give formal recognition to the status of the suffragan as a bishop whilst at the same time retaining the overall leadership of the diocesan in the mission of the Church within and beyond the diocese.

III. The suffragan as episcopal vicar

446. We therefore offer a third approach for consideration, which provides in the view of most members of the Group a good theological basis, with sound historical precedent. This is to see the suffragan or area bishop in his relation to his diocesan as his specifically episcopal representative or 'vicar'. We suggest that the suffragan's presence enriches the episcopal ministry of the diocese because of what he personally brings to it in his gifts. He can be in the fullest sense an episcopal and focal minister in the example of personal holiness he sets, and in meeting the people's need for a special minister in whatever ways the Church locally requires of him.

447. The model of the 'episcopal assistant curate' is unacceptable, and we are arguing for something rather differently conceived; 'the bishop who acts in the place of his diocesan when delegation or occasion requires' is a better way of describing a suffragan's ministry. There are other 'vicarial' ministries of course. The archdeacon is the legal 'eye' of the bishop; generally speaking the senior staff of a diocese share in pastoral oversight. But representative ministry in specifically episcopal matters should be seen as the task of the suffragan. This is more than a sharing in ordination or confirmation or institution.[58] It is a sharing of identity. It is in a sense the exercising of the *personal* ministry of his diocesan. It may be too much to say that the suffragan is his diocesan's *alter ego*; but he might be described

---

[58]　Institutions may of course be carried out by Archdeacons as commissaries of the diocesan bishop.

as taking his diocesan's 'episcopal presence' with him as he exercises an episcopal ministry of oversight, of guarding the truth, of ministering the Word and presiding at the Eucharist, and of discipline. He and the diocesan may share ordinations or confirmations, or take them alternately; they may share out vacancy meetings, institutions, special festivals in parishes; the suffragan may have special responsibility for some aspect of diocesan work. In all this, and however he exercises his *episcope*, the suffragan is exercising the unitary oversight of his diocesan as his vicar. But that argues no diminution of his own episcopate. He is not *merely* an episcopal curate or assistant. He is himself fully a bishop. He exercises an episcopal and personal *episcope*, not the general *episcope* which the diocesan bishop shares with all his presbyters. We take the view that if the diocesan has divided the episcopal tasks between himself and his suffragans so that the *episcope* within the diocese is shared, it need not follow that the *episcope* of the diocesan is thereby impaired.

448. On this theological model the diocesan bishop remains the diocesan bishop and the suffragan has a full and authentic episcopal ministry as a bishop; but it is a ministry understood within a clear theological context.

iii. The practicalities

449. Such a model of episcopal vicariate needs to be worked out in good practice. The diocesan-suffragan relationship is rightly and unavoidably very personal, and must depend in some measure on a good working understanding and mutual loyalty. Even the best of relationships can run into difficulties and a change of diocesan, when a new bishop arrives with a different personality and priorities, may cause some tension. For this reason the clear definition of the suffragan's vicarial tasks or area responsibilities can be an important element in achieving a harmonious and fruitful ministry. It is, moreover, a means of enabling bishops and dioceses to see more clearly where they stand. The diocesan remains the diocesan. Whatever delegation has been made there should never be any 'no go' areas of diocesan life for him. On the other hand, in those parts of diocesan life which have been defined for the suffragan as his responsibility, the suffragan carries a representative authority in which he exercises an episcopal ministry in its fullness.[59] It also means that he is able to exercise

---

[59]   The Lambeth Conference of 1988 stressed that 'all bishops by virtue of their ordination share in the fullness of *episcope*' (*The Truth Shall Make You Free*, Lambeth Conference, 1988, Mission and Ministry Section, p. 157.).

that same representative ministry more widely within the diocese and in mission as priorities or pastoral needs require.

450.   In implementing a theology of the suffragan as episcopal vicar, some variant of the area system may well fit best in some dioceses; in some instances a less formal arrangement may be preferable.   It is questionable whether area schemes in the formal sense should always be normative in dioceses where there are two or more suffragans.   If any diocese were to wish to opt for Area Synods, care would have to be taken to ensure that these do not detract from the diocese's sense of unity, and the focal role of the diocesan.[60]   In dioceses with a single suffragan, a formal statement about an area or areas of responsibility may be of benefit; but again it is open to question whether formal arrangements should always be normative.[61]

i v   Wider episcopal collegiality

451.   There is also the question of the suffragan bishop's place in the wider collegiality of the episcopate in the Church.   It could be argued (on the theological premise upon which a theology of episcopal vicariate rests) that a suffragan's episcopal place is in the diocese.   But we have also argued that he exercises his episcopal office in its fullness; and although we have expressed reservations about the technically exact use of the term 'collegiality' as excluding its referring to the sharing of episcopal ministry within the diocese,[62] we would stress that the suffragan shares by virtue of his office in a wider collegiality.   We note here the 1988 Lambeth Conference Resolution that:

> all bishops active in full-time diocesan work be made full members with seat, voice and vote, of all provincial, national and international gatherings of Anglican bishops.[63]

---

60   Despite the favourable view of Area Synods expressed by the Dioceses Commission in its Second Report of 1985, we note that in the Diocese of Chelmsford the possibility of having Area synods has for the moment been rejected.

61   We recognise the significance of the 1988 Lambeth Resolution 46, which calls for the ensuring of a true *episcope* of jurisdiction and pastoral care for all bishops; but we see problems in some instances in too detailed requirements.

62   Cf. the opening paragraph on the first of our three 'models', and section D of this chapter.

63   Resolution of the 1988 Lambeth Conference 46A.   Compare *Proceedings* of the General Synod, November 1985, p. 1008, 'A bishop whose voice is not heard among other bishops in Council is not a true bishop at all'.

452. We do not comment on the appropriate response to that decision as far as the Lambeth Conference itself is concerned, although we should like to see review of regulations governing the invitation of suffragan and area bishops to the Lambeth Conference;[64] but it has to be frankly recognised that there are undoubted practical difficulties in implementing such a resolution within the synodical structures of the Church of England. It would, for example, be disproportionate to increase the number of bishops within the House of Bishops of the General Synod without a commensurate increase in the number of clergy and laity. Such an operation would be costly and there would seem to be a possibility of its having a negative effect on the role of the diocesan bishop. Nevertheless, it may be helpful to review the actual number of suffragan bishops who are to be elected.

453. If, however, suffragans are to experience a genuine collegiality with other bishops within the Church of England we take the view that there may be, quite apart from synodical considerations, a place for genuine theological reflection and the development of a corporate responsibility through a properly constituted residential meeting of diocesan and suffragan bishops, where they may give one another brotherly counsel and support and have time for extended spiritual and theological study together.

We make the following comments and suggestions:

454. The question of the appointment of suffragan bishops - together with other senior Church appointments - is the subject of review at the present time by a working party of the Synod; but it would seem to follow, from all that has been said in this chapter, that the diocesan bishop should continue to have the decisive say in the choice of suffragans, for they are in law his commissaries.[65]

455. Suffragan bishops, in their contemporary ministry, may be seen as exemplifying the adaptability and variety of the ways in which the needs of God's people are met by the Church's ministry. Pastoral need created and has sustained the office in the Church, without its presence threatening the

---

64   At present only suffragan and Area bishops who are members of the House of Bishops of the General Synod (9 in all) come to the Lambeth Conference. This would need to be looked at alongside provisions elsewhere in the Anglican Communion.

65   With due concern for the implications of the fact that suffragans may in due course become diocesan bishops. See, too, Chapter 12, section on the Appointment of bishops.

personal character of the episcopate of the diocesan. The diocesan exemplifies in his own person and at the highest level the principle that all ministry in the Church is shared. He shares with the suffragan the episcopal presence in the diocese. Yet we believe that it is of the greatest importance to ensure that a suffragan's ministry is seen as authentic in its own right, a ministry to which the Church may well feel that a bishop will often have a permanent calling.[66]

456. We would argue that diocesan autonomy rightly extends to a degree of self-determination in choosing a scheme which best fits local needs. The ancient rule of subordination of diocesan to provincial synods (and in today's Church of England, to the General Synod), in legislative matters ought to ensure, in practice as well as in principle, that the options allowed remain within a framework of common order.

457. With that proviso, we consider that Area Schemes, whether formal or informal, should have the Church's general approval. We are not all convinced however that a geographical area for the diocesan is necessary or always helpful, and most members of our group would see it as going against our theology of diocesan unity for a diocesan to have an 'Area' of his own within the diocese. This is, both theologically and practically, an issue of some importance.[67] But we agree that 'single' suffragans will have a more effective episcopal ministry if given a clearly defined area or sector of responsibility within their dioceses.

458. We do not think it appropriate for there to be fixed rules for the division of work in dioceses with suffragans, although the General Synod has given support to the view that the suffragan's responsibilities can and should be clearly understood within the diocese.[68] There is clearly a difference between the way in which a diocesan bishop and one suffragan can best work together, and the pattern which will fit a diocesan with a larger number of suffragan bishops. This seems to fall into the area of ecclesiastical order which is rightly left to 'human' disposal. There is room for team work and corporate pastorate without prejudice to a personal pastoral office.

---

[66]   But on the understanding that in some cases it may lead to appointment as a diocesan, cf. *Episcopacy and the Role of the Suffragan Bishop:* A Second Report by the Dioceses Commission, GS 697.

[67]   See *Proceedings* of the General Synod, November 1985, p. 1011.

[68]   See *Proceedings* of the General Synod (1985), pp. 1005 ff.

459. As we have argued, the ministry of the suffragan is the ministry of a bishop exercising a representative ministry in ways that pertain to episcopal office. We believe that if the episcopal character of this ministry is properly understood there is less likely to be confusion between the role of a suffragan and the ministry of an archdeacon. We recognise that archdeacons carry out to an increasing degree many of the pastoral tasks of a suffragan or Area bishop, with the exception of confirmation and ordination. But the difference between bishop and priest remains, and the experiment in some dioceses of combining the offices of suffragan and archdeacon has not commended itself to the Church at large. There has been virtually no support within our Group for the proposal that a revision of Canon Law should permit the bishop of the diocese to devolve upon his archdeacon the power to administer confirmation. The tradition of episcopal confirmation is so deeply established throughout the Anglican Communion that any adjustment is bound to provoke disquiet. It must be recognised that, even in a large diocese, the fact that *a* bishop is the minister of confirmation is an expression of the ultimate pastoral concern of *the* bishop and, therefore, of his role as the focus of unity. But this begs larger questions about the exercise of episcopacy and the extent to which an archdeacon already shares substantially at a senior level in the *episcope* of the diocesan bishop. The commonplace distinction between episcopal leadership in *mission*, with archidiaconal responsibility confined to maintenance, cannot always be sustained in the contemporary Church. It will often be the archdeacon who consults widely and enables parochial clergy and congregations to resolve issues relating to pastoral reorganisation, the redundancy of churches, the formation of team or group ministries, the establishment of local ecumenical projects, the development of extra-parochial ministries. These are all practical matters of significance in relation to the question of how best to use resources to further the mission of the Church.

460. In some dioceses, retired bishops or younger bishops who have returned from missionary dioceses[69] have been available to help the diocesan. By virtue of their consecration, they retain the power to confirm and to ordain, but they cannot exercise it except by invitation within another bishop's jurisdiction. They have no formal part in any diocesan scheme; they help where needed. Nevertheless, that help may be regular and substantial and amount to a more or less full-time service and it is of immeasurable value to those dioceses which enjoy it. No theological

---

[69]   GS 551, Dioceses Commission, 16.

justification can exist for ordaining to 'assistant bishopric' in this sense, for no 'title' and therefore no personal pastoral care is involved, but there is every reason to be grateful for the part assistant bishops play in episcopal diocesan ministry.

461. We have reservations about the concept of a 'House of Bishops' in a diocesan synod because it appears to compromise the unitary office of the diocesan bishop - with its personal, collegial and communal dimensions - within which the houses of clergy and laity have their proper place. It is, however, of the first importance to affirm the truly episcopal character of the ministry of suffragan or area bishops, and a 'House of Bishops' must in practice be the norm at present. The principle would seem to be secured by retaining to the diocesan in the power of veto[70] an episcopal leadership which is more than a 'presidency'.

462. The view that 'a community needs a single focus' remains central to our case. Because this is a near impossibility in large conurbations, we believe that the Church ought to explore the possible creation of some new dioceses; and at the same time that it ought to question too ready a proliferation of more suffragan or area bishops.

463. The institution of a properly constituted Bishops' Meeting for all the full-time bishops in the Church of England for the purpose of common counsel and theological reflection is a matter of some urgency.

464. We should like to encourage review of the eligibility of suffragan bishops for membership of the Church Commissioners. It would seem anomalous that no regular provision is made for the representation of suffragans and area bishops. Possible solutions would seem to be to provide that suffragan bishops elected to General Synod should during the lifetime of that Synod serve, together with all diocesan bishops, as Church Commissioners and should therefore be available for nomination by the House of Bishops to serve on the committees of the Church Commissioners; or for the inclusion of all bishops *ex officio*, with serving members on the Board of Governors or the Committees of the Church Commissioners chosen from among the suffragans by the General Synod; or for those suffragans elected to the General Synod, to serve for the lifetime of the Synod.

---

[70]   Synodical Government Measure, 1969, Schedule 3, 28 (e).

D.   Conclusions to (A), (B), (C)

465.   We conclude discussion of this connected group of issues arising in the Church of England today, with a few summary points.[71]   An early debate in General Synod strongly suggested that 'there is no one pattern of episcopal organisation to which the Church of England would wish to commit itself, to the exclusion of all others'.[72]   It is perhaps in the nature of the Church of England that a variety of patterns of episcopal leadership and oversight should co-exist alongside each other, reflecting the needs of different dioceses.   It is entirely right ecclesiologically that dioceses should vary in their expression of their life as 'local churches', and in England that variety is very marked.[73]   We have not wished to see any diminution of that proper pluriformity.

466.   Nevertheless, we reaffirm in our reflections in this Chapter the fundamental principle that the diocesan bishop is the personal focus and minister of unity in whom the three planes of the Church's life intersect. We have argued that under the pressures of the pastoral and missionary demands which are made upon bishops in the Church of England today (See Section A), that ministry must sometimes be shared in ways for which earlier generations set no exact precedent, although they must respect the traditional and fundamental division between those tasks which a bishop only may carry out and those which may be shared.   So there will be a sharing of *episcope* or oversight in tasks where oversight is not exclusively the function of a person in episcopal orders (See Section B), but we would press for a strict reservation to the bishop of those responsibilities which have traditionally been his, as we have outlined them in our first eight chapters.[74]

467.   Secondly, there will remain, in many dioceses, one or more suffragan bishops.   We have proposed that their ministry should be understood in terms of an episcopal vicariate, the diocesan retaining personal oversight of the diocese.   Within this framework, there is room for both the division of dioceses into areas and a variety of informal arrangements by which the Suffragan or suffragans can give general episcopal assistance throughout a

---

71   We have in mind points drawn to our attention by the Dioceses Commission.

72   GS 214. Report by the Standing Committee entitled *Episcopacy: Follow up of the debate on Canon Welsby's Consultative Document* (GS 167) - Episcopacy in the Church of England.

73   Cf. *Proceedings* of the General Synod, November 1985, p. 1005).

74   Dioceses Commission, *Memorandum of Evidence* to the Archbishops' Group on the Episcopate, 5 (a).

diocese. Neither option is incompatible with a theology of the suffragan as episcopal vicar.[75] We have sought to clarify the sense in which 'collegiality' ought to be used, that is, to refer to the brotherhood of diocesan bishops. We have admitted as a proper extension of that sense, a collegiality of all bishops in the universal Church. We have preferred to avoid the use of the term within the diocese, to refer to the relationship of the diocesan to his 'episcopal vicar', while stressing that that relationship is peculiar to those in episcopal orders and constitutes a sharing of *episcope* of a different kind from that which the diocesan bishop enjoys with other diocesan officers.[76]

468. In response to a point made to us by the Dioceses Commission, that 'as yet no proposal has been brought forward which would make use of the wide powers contained in the [Dioceses] Measure for creation and abolition of dioceses, and the sharing of administration',[77] we have pressed for more courage in this area, and for a reversal of this trend in favour of the attempt, where it is reasonable, to return to a pattern of 'one bishop, one diocese'.

469. We recognise that a conflict of opposing considerations continues to operate, with increasing demand for 'diocesan specialists' and 'men in episcopal orders' and at the same time a concern that 'there should not be so many bishops in the land that they cease to be "major figures" of standing nationally, regionally and locally'.[78] We see this as a healthy tension, which ought to prevent our having either too many or too few bishops to meet the Church's pastoral need. But for those who must make practical decisions, it presents difficulties. Regular periodic review of patterns of local social change may be helpful here as indicating where it may be necessary to think again about the size of a diocese, or its boundaries, or the deployment of areas within it. We see no objection to allowing some room for manoeuvre here. There is good precedent for adjusting the formal boundaries of the local diocesan Church as circumstances change. The proliferation of suffragans has arisen in part from its having seemed easier to staff existing dioceses in this way than to reappraise the distribution of the dioceses themselves.

---

[75] Dioceses Commission, *Memorandum of Evidence* to the Archbishops' Group on the Episcopate, 5 (b).

[76] *Ibid.*, 5 (c). And cf. 'Personal, Collegial, Communal' in chapter 9, section c; and Sections C ii I and iv of this chapter.

[77] For the most part, 'the proposals have been for more Suffragans and Area schemes'. The Commission suggests that this is 'in part ... an understandable reluctance to grasp politically thorny issues', *Ibid.*, 5 (d).

[78] *Ibid.*, 5 (f).

12

Episcopacy in the Church of England:

ii. Church and State

a. The history

i. The background [1]

470. The Church must always stand in a relationship to secular authority, which may at the least tolerate its presence and allow freedom of worship, or may, as it were, take it into partnership on some agreed basis for the benefit of the members of society. For many centuries the (forged) Donation of Constantine which purported to be a grant from the first Christian Emperor in submission to the Church, was pointed to by the Church as authorising the Church to regard itself as the senior partner. Notwithstanding that, in essence, the arrangement arrived at from late Roman times was that the Church should bow to the state where interest conflicted, saving conscience and the faith. At the same time, there was, from the conversion of Constantine in the early fourth century, a tendency for the Bishop of Rome to be regarded, and to regard himself, in parallel with the Emperor, as at least a twin, and by analogy increasingly a monarchical power. Constantine and Silvester (314-35) had their imitators in Charlemagne and Pope Hadrian (772-95), Otto III and Pope Silvester II (1000-1003); and Cardinal Wolsey looked wistfully after the possibility that he and Henry VIII might provide a not dissimilar model in wielding the two 'swords' of spiritual and temporal power in harness. The image of the two swords (Luke 22.49-51), used by Pope Gelasius I in the fifth century, depends for its force on the assumption that secular as well as spiritual authority is entrusted by God.[2] This regal and imperial theme and model is of the first importance in sixteenth century Anglican history. Much of the justification for a royal supremacy in the Church turns on its being in the hands of a divinely appointed ruler.

---

[1]   We should like to acknowledge the contribution of the late Reverend Canon Dr. Gareth Bennett especially warmly here. His work for the Group on Church-State questions has been most valuable to us, and we have made use of portions of his text.

[2]   Although there was extensive mediaeval debate as to whether the 'swords' were entrusted by God in the first instance to Church or State.

ii.   The Middle Ages

471.   Throughout the Middle Ages the Church had met society's spiritual needs, crowned kings, and, with royal permission, run ecclesiastical courts alongside the courts which dealt with secular offences.   There had been disputes about boundaries, and it cannot be overemphasised that these were unavoidable, because circumstances and political needs repeatedly threw up fresh problems.   Anselm of Canterbury (d.1109) was brought up sharply against the problem of the relationship of spiritual and secular authority in his relations with the two English Kings to whom he was Archbishop of Canterbury.   The broad principles of a ruler's treatment of the Church seemed to him clear and uncontroversial.   A monarch should honour the Church as the Bride of Christ, he explains to Matilda, Queen of England (Letter 243).

472.   The problem at the root of the 'investiture' contest in which Anselm unwittingly became embroiled was the question where the boundaries of jurisdiction lay between the spiritual and the secular.   Towards the end of the eleventh century Pope Gregory VII had challenged the practice, diffused throughout Europe, of secular lords, King as well as Emperor, investing new bishops not only with the temporalities but also with the spiritualities of their sees.   Gregory now claimed supreme power for the spiritual arm, and his arguments were taken up and developed by Bernard of Clairvaux in the twelfth century and others after him, until there emerged the full-blown doctrine of papal plenitude of power which gave rise to challenge: first in the late Middle Ages from those who looked for a 'conciliar' government, and then, in the sixteenth century, from the protestant reformers.

473.   While the theory grew more expansive, the constant irritant of disputes about the respective boundaries of jurisdiction of Church and State in the church courts made it impossible for the rivalry to cool.   In the later twelfth century in England Henry II and his Archbishop of Canterbury, Thomas Becket, quarrelled disastrously over the rights of the Church Courts under episcopal administration.   In England the Roman code of law did not operate and the claims of the Papacy and the canon lawyers were sometimes in conflict with the provisions of the 'common law' and Acts of Parliament. A series of legal writers from Sir John Fortescue (1394-1470) to Christopher St. German (c. 1460-1540) attacked the Church courts on the grounds that they had mixed the civil with the spiritual and denied the King his right to do justice to all his subjects.

iii.   The sixteenth century

474.   In the later Middle Ages the Papacy had pressed its claims to spiritual jurisdiction in England very hard. But the formal relation of the Church of England to the state was altered in the upheavals of the sixteenth century. The English Reformation was intimately bound up with questions of national identity, and it cannot be fully understood without reference to the Renaissance and Reformation politics and political theory of which it formed a part. The Reformation Statutes were Acts of a national Parliament and it was therefore by the authority of the Crown in Parliament that the new ecclesiastical settlement came into being. So at the Reformation arrangements were radically changed in an important particular. Statutes enacted by Parliament and bearing Royal assent substituted the monarch's jurisdiction over the Church of England for that of the Pope. Henry VIII assumed an ecclesiastical and temporal supremacy and became *de facto* the 'Pope' of the Church of England, though Henry VIII's new 'headship' of the Church was conceived of in jurisdictional rather than sacramental terms. It was not, therefore, a point for point replacement of papal power by royal power. The theory was that the king was uniting under himself the administrations, judicatures and legislatures of his kingdom.

475.   The Church was not, on this view, a separate *regnum* or realm; it was that part of the body politic 'which is called the spirituality'.   In ecclesiastical affairs there will still be the same institutions and the same law; the king will not ordain bishops though he will choose who shall be ordained; he will not sit in the Church courts personally but act through those learned in ecclesiastical law; he will not decide doctrine but will see that Convocation does not meet or proceed to make canons without his consent. There was indeed a continuing sense that it was appropriate to make the running of Convocation, with its Upper and Lower Houses, parallel with that of the Lords and the Commons in Parliament.[3] Behind this statutory change, however, lies a great deal of sixteenth century debate over the scope of royal power in matters spiritual. The Act of Restraint of Appeals (1533) claims imperial status for the English Crown, and with it all the 'plenitude of ecclesiastical power' (*plenitudo ecclesiasticae potestatis*)[4] of an Emperor conceived somewhat on the model of Constantine, the first

---

3   Cf. Cardwell, *Synodalia* II.421.
4   See O.P. Rafferty, 'Thomas Cranmer and the Royal Supremacy', *Heythrop Journal*, 31 (199
         133 ff.

Christian emperor. Cranmer himself took a most extreme view of the royal powers, at least during Henry VIII's lifetime.

476.   The theological debate about the meaning of this set of enactments began when the legislation was enforced. We give some space to it so as to make clear the theoretical foundations upon which Royal Supremacy came to be deemed to rest in the Church of England. Reginald Pole's *A Defence of Ecclesiastical Unity* (1539) went a great way in admitting that a national *regnum* had its God-given justification and purpose, and that there were many matters of Church organisation and property, and even of worship, which were best dealt with locally; but he underlined that the Church was universal and a gift of God to all humanity: there were some matters in which the local church was a very poor judge and in which its knowledge was limited. Thus the King of England cannot be Head of the Church of England because it is part of the universal whole.

477.   Thomas More's position is more complex. As a common-lawyer he was prepared to go to the very limit in conceding the power of the King-in-Parliament to be obeyed in any matters which could be described as temporal. He was willing to acknowledge that an Act of Parliament made Elizabeth heir to the throne though the Church had declared her illegitimate. He was prepared to see the properties of the Church confiscated and its administration rearranged by statute. He saw no basic objection to the king's controlling the operation of the Church courts. His sticking point lay in his belief that the Act of Supremacy destroyed the freedom of the English Church to choose to be part of the universal community of Christendom.

478.   More's critique was undoubtedly taken seriously by later defenders of the Royal Supremacy. Stephen Gardiner (1483-1555) was to be one of the leading figures in the so-called Marian reaction of the mid-1550s but in 1535 he had published one of the seminal defences of the title of 'Head of the Church'. His *Oration of True Obedience* was in many ways a canon lawyer's book. He accepted that in England there could be no real distinction between Church and State, and it was false to regard the Church with its officers, courts and Convocations as a purely spiritual sphere; there was a strongly temporal character to it, and this was properly the King's concern.   To distinguish the spiritual and temporal areas within the Church's jurisdiction Gardiner employed the canon lawyers' distinction between the *potestas ordinis* and the *potestas jurisdictionis*, the power of order and the power of jurisdiction. With the *potestas ordinis* the King did not interfere: he did not claim to be a bishop or a priest; doctrine, the

ministry, the sacraments, were those of universal Christian tradition and remained properly the concern of the bishops and the Convocations. On such matters the King would listen to the authoritative voice of those to whom such matters as preaching, ordination and the celebration of the Eucharist belonged. But their authority would be moral and pastoral in character. Where coercive jurisdiction was involved the case was quite different, and the *potestas jurisdictionis* was to be exercised under the Royal Supremacy. Gardiner offered the suggestion that the distinction between the two *potestates* was seen in those matters which a bishop must do personally and those which he could delegate to his Chancellor. Gardiner thus sought to combine the idea of a single *regnum* under one supreme administration with a freedom for the bishops to hold to the doctrine and practice of the universal Church in those things which were essential to unity.

479. There remained in Mary's reign a profound paradox. Mary restored Roman Catholic order by her supremacy and Cranmer found himself refusing to acknowledge the Pope because he believed in the supremacy of his Sovereign, who was ordering him to recognise the Pope's supremacy, not hers.

480. The Elizabethan Act of Supremacy of 1559 re-established, with minor variations, the Henrician form of the Supremacy. To avoid the controversial term 'Head of the Church', it was provided that henceforth the royal title should be 'Supreme Governor'.[5] Elizabeth's Proclamation of 1570 insisted that she did not 'either challenge or take ... any superiority' to herself 'to define, decide or determine any article or point of the Christian faith and religion, or to change any ancient rite or ceremony of the Church from the form before received and observed by the Catholic and Apostolic Church, or to assume the use of any function or office belonging to any ecclesiastical person ... being a minister of the Word and Sacraments of the Church'. There was therefore, in principle at least, no intrusion upon the spiritual jurisdiction of bishops in the Elizabethan Settlement.

481. Almost from the beginning the Elizabethan Supremacy came under fierce attack from two different quarters. English Puritans such as Thomas Cartwright represented an extreme version of Calvin's doctrine of the

5   Bishop Jewel tells Bullinger in a letter dated May 1559 'that the queen [Elizabeth] would not be styled "Head of the Church of England", giving this grave reason thereof, that that was a title due to Christ only, and to no mortal creature besides'. Strype, *Annals of the Reformation*, Vol. 1, p. 195, c.10; cited in Phillimore's *Ecclesiastical Law*, Vol. I.6.

Church as having Christ only as its Head and Lord; for them there could be no trespassing on the 'Crown rights of the Redeemer' and the courts and assemblies of the Church must be ruled by the Word of God alone. Cartwright argued for a complete separation of Church and State. In similar style Roman Catholics maintained that the Church of England was now a creation of the State, where bishops were royal officials without continuity with the historic Catholic episcopate; the English had rejected the authority of the Pope who by unbroken tradition had responsibility for the unity of the whole Church and subordinated spiritual matters to mere secular and political authority in a single nation.

482.   While John Jewel and John Whitgift provided a scholarly case for Anglican continuity in order and doctrine with the ancient and undivided Church, it was perhaps Richard Hooker who offered the most cogent theological defence of the Royal Supremacy. At the heart of *The Laws of Ecclesiastical Polity* is Hooker's insistence on the unity of human society. Tudor society was wholly Christian in profession, and it was possible on that assumption for apologists such as Hooker to describe an organic relation of Church to State as a desirable and proper expression of their unity in a Christian commonwealth.

483.   Both Puritans and Roman Catholics sought to make a separation between the realm of Christ and the realm of Caesar, as if these were two societies. But in Hooker's view, in a Christian nation commonwealth and Church must consist of the same persons: it is one realm with two 'aspects', civil and religious. A Christian polity *is* a Church, for the Church is not to be identified merely with its clergy or officers. The commonwealth is elevated to a moral and sacred character, and the Church is given the means to educate and form the life of the nation. To separate the Church from the commonwealth and make it a separate society is to make it a sect. Hooker saw the supreme Governorship as being regulated by the moral and religious ends of the society. Not least, it was confined by the 'laws' of ecclesiastical polity. These are the possession of the whole community and are well-known: they are the traditional Creeds, sacraments and institutions of Christendom. In the bishops, Convocations and the canonists the Supreme Governor has authoritative advisers who speak not only for the Christian people of England but for the whole Church of God. In effect, Hooker sought to make the exercise of the supremacy constitutional and conciliar in character. As kings were limited by the laws, institutions and the moral sense of their people, so the Supreme Governor operated within the laws of ecclesiastical polity and the religious sense of the community.

iv.   The seventeenth and eighteenth centuries

484.   Richard Hooker's judicious defence of the Royal Supremacy attained almost the status of an official Anglican *apologia,* but the reality of the English situation differed markedly from the ideal.   The Elizabethan Church was heavily under the thumb of state policy, even perhaps to its pastoral detriment and the endangering of its unity.   Widespread abuses belied its claim to be 'reformed'; its properties and revenues were plundered by the Crown and influential laymen; and its bishops were denied liberty to remedy glaring defects.

485.   It can be argued that the advent of James I marked in many ways the first real exercise in the Hookerian practice of the Royal Supremacy.[6]   The new King was genuinely interested in religious affairs; he appointed learned and active bishops and supported their endeavours; he worked for religious unity in England and among a wider Protestant community.   Such a Supreme Governor fulfilled the conditions of Hooker's theory and quickly became the focus of Anglican hopes for comprehensive reform and a recovery of the Church's revenues.   In the writings of Lancelot Andrewes and William Laud there is an almost mystically-framed view of the monarchy as God's representative, to whom obedience is due as a religious duty; and this is combined with a view of episcopacy as itself of divine institution.   The magnificent pioneering achievement of sixteenth and now seventeenth century Anglican scholars in new areas of patristic studies made plain the vital role which episcopacy played in the polity of the first four centuries of the Church, and the responsibility of the episcopate as a college for maintaining the tradition of faith.   James I's famous dictum 'No Bishop - No King' was a theological statement, intended to set forth the ideal of a union within a national church, of the local civil power and the representatives of the unchanging tradition of Catholic Christendom.   The danger of the Laudian position and its stress on the linking of monarchy and episcopate was that it would be seen as a threat to entrenched constitutional rights.   Such an enhanced notion of the Supremacy was clearly a major cause of the collapse of the monarchy and the episcopal system in the years from 1642 to 1660.

486.   The era after the Restoration in 1660 saw the beginning of a progressive retreat from a high theology of the Royal Supremacy.   For a

---

[6]   See Patrick Collinson, *The Religion of Protestants* (Oxford, 1982).

while there was a revival of Hookerian theory: a new stress on the religious or 'divine-right' character of Monarchy, and a conservative scholarship which attempted to show the adhesion of Anglicans to the patristic understanding of episcopacy. But in the Restoration period the union of Crown and episcopate was insecure, and we find Peter Heylyn asserting on the title-page of his *Aerius Redivivus* (2nd ed., 1672) the identity of 'episcopal' with 'monarchical' government, and the threat to the one posed by a challenge to the other. Archbishops like Gilbert Sheldon and William Sancroft found themselves interpreting the Supremacy in terms of the English Constitution, as subordinate to parliamentary control and legal enactment.

487.   After the Revolution of 1688 the conditions basic to the Hookerian theory gradually fell away. The theory of the religious unity of the church and nation was maintained but the passing of the Toleration Act of 1689 had the effect of allowing the existence of dissenting religious bodies. The mediaeval and Tudor understanding of the relationship of Church to State in the role of the bishop subtly altered as nonconformity grew louder in the seventeenth and eighteenth centuries. It was still broadly true that society was Christian. It was no longer true that it was only 'Church of England'. Kings and governments actively patronised dissent and resisted any restoration of the Anglican religious monopoly; bishops were often appointed for their political services; and legislation (like the appointment of bishops for the colonies) denied.

488.   For the first time there appeared among Anglican theologians a critique of the Supremacy which was cautious and hostile. This is shown pre-eminently in the famous Convocation controversy of 1697-1717 which resulted in the effective silencing of Convocation until 1852 (for Canterbury) and 1861 (for York).[7] William Wake in his *The Authority of Christian Princes over their Ecclesiastical Synods Asserted* (1697), argued for a high doctrine of royal power, deploying an arsenal of precedents from early Church history; but later writers like Benjamin Hoadly reduced the argument to the crude level of the need for civil rulers to restrain clerical pretensions and religious quarrels.

489.   It was the 'High-Church' writers, like Francis Atterbury, and Nonjurors like George Hickes, who moved towards a theory of the basic and necessary independence of the Church when matters of doctrine or pastoral

7   See para. 216.

need were at stake. Atterbury's *The Rights, Powers and Privileges of an English Convocation* (1701) was an attempt to prove that the Royal Supremacy could never prevent the Church from taking emergency action to protect its faith and order. His arguments were condemned by a meeting of the judges, as inconsistent with the Act of Supremacy.

490. The reality of the eighteenth-century Church was that it was subordinated to the secular power. The Royal Supremacy came to be exercised by politicians, who controlled all appointments and refused to allow the Convocations to do business after 1717. Parliamentary Statute became the usual means of regulating ecclesiastical matters. This situation was recognised by William Warburton in 1736 when he published *The Alliance of Church and State*, the only theoretical account of the Supremacy to be published in the middle years of the century. He spoke of a voluntary association of Church and State, entered into on both sides by consent for mutual advantage, not an organic unity. They agree to enter into a compact for their mutual advantage: the Church gives up its independent powers of appointment, legislature and judiciary, and receives in return endowment from the public property, legal privileges and public recognition. It was said at the time that Warburton had removed any possible theological justifications for the Royal Supremacy and made its continuance purely pragmatic; that he had, in fact, made out a case for disestablishment as much as for continued Establishment.

v.   The nineteenth and twentieth centuries

491. In the early nineteenth century, with the repeal of the Test and Corporation Acts in 1828 and the passing of the Catholic Emancipation Act in 1829, the formal relationship of the Church of England and the nation began to change significantly, though the sovereign had still to be 'in communion' with the Church of England. There gradually grew up a demand for greater freedom and independence from state control, although that was far from consistently the case. A Whig government's attempt in 1833 to abolish bishoprics in Ireland precipitated a crisis.

492. The Oxford Movement, with its sense of the Apostolic character of the Church and its early beginnings in the first century, could find little place for Royal Supremacy: it was seen as a local and temporary arrangement in which the Church of England as one part of the Catholic Church found itself involved by historical chance. Nevertheless, in return

for allowing bishops in the House of Lords and the association of clergymen with schools, the armed forces and the work of government, the State thought itself entitled to some say in appointments and some power of veto over ecclesiastical policy. Gladstone pleaded for restraint on all sides: for the State to allow synods to meet and for reforms to take place; for Anglican radicals to realise the opportunities which establishment brought; and for non-conformists to realise the importance of a permanent Christian witness in the state. And in a sense the Gladstonian solution was already being implemented, notably in the formation of the Ecclesiastical Commissioners, a body set up by Statute to allow Anglicans to re-order their own affairs.[8]

493.   The nineteenth century saw repeated attempts on the part of successive governments to recognise religious diversity and to secure the religious neutrality of the state: the removal of all restrictions on grounds of religion for election to Parliament and to public office; the abolition of the wide-ranging powers of Church Courts; the abolition of compulsory Church rates: the opening up of the ancient universities; the introduction of civil marriages; the provision of public burial grounds in municipal cemeteries; the establishment of parish councils that were to be separate from the parish church and its officers. The 'Establishment' principle grew weaker but was not abandoned. A warm nineteenth century sense of what it means to be a national Church is still to be found in F.D. Maurice's view that 'a national church should mean a Church which exists to purify and elevate the mind of a nation; to give those who administer its laws a sense of the grandeur of law and of the source whence its proceeds, to tell the rulers of the nation that all false ways are ruinous, that truth is the only stability of our time or of any time'. In the twentieth century, it has been the Church of England which has taken the initiative in securing an appropriate degree of independence, for example in the establishment of Synodical government,[9] the Worship and Doctrine Measure (1974), and the procedures of the Crown Appointments Commission.[10]

494.   Hensley Henson had become persuaded by the late 1920s that disestablishment was both inevitable and desirable. He thought the answer lay in 'not disestablishment but more Establishment'. By that he meant that the fellowship of the established Church should be widened 'to include the orthodox non-conformist', so that it would be 'more truly in fact what it

8   1835 - 1948, when the Church Commissioners succeeded them.
9   Synodical Government Measure (1969).
10   Set up after the publication of *Church and State*, the Report of the Chadwick Commission (1970).

was in theory, the corporate expression of the nation's Christianity'.[11] He touched on what remains the central dilemma of a 'national' Church. As Cosmo Lang put it in a debate of 1913 in the House of Lords on the disestablishment of the Welsh Church, 'It is a very serious thing for a state to take out of that corporate heart of its life any acknowledgement at all of its concern with religion'.[12] On the other hand, the Church cannot always find it easy to reconcile the duties which service to the State may from time to time impose, or an association with a sense of national identity, with the Catholicity which has always been a mark of Anglicanism.

b.   Bishops and Establishment

495.   Establishment provides the legal framework within which the Church of England continues to offer public ministry to the whole community. Canon law declares that the Church of England, which is 'established according to the laws of this realm, under the Queen's Majesty, belongs to the true and apostolic Church of Christ'.[13] This statement affirms the wider community of faith and order to which the Church of England belongs, but recognises the distinctive historical process whereby it has evolved. Establishment does not determine the fundamentals of faith and order - the Scriptures, the sacraments, the credal statements, the orders of ministry - but it has inevitably influenced the Church of England's self-awareness and the wider perceptions, public and private, which have facilitated or inhibited the exercise of ministry. Equally, Establishment does not determine the nature and function of the episcopate in the Church, but it has shaped to some degree the expectations that surround the office of a bishop in the Church of England. The Church of England is bound, therefore, to ask that those who are in communion with the See of Canterbury shall be sensitive to the special circumstances in which the Church of England finds herself.

496.   The English Reformation settlements bear testimony to the biblical conviction that religious faith and practice, and peace and good order in society are bound up together. It must be conceded that the reality of the English situation has consistently fallen short of Richard Hooker's ideal, although there has been on both sides throughout the last four centuries some recognition of the mutual responsibility and the mutual inter-

---

11   *Retrospect of an Unimportant Life* (London, 1942-50), I, p. 209.
12   Hansard, Fifth Series, iii (1925), 1195, 12 Feb.
13   Canon A1. On this principle and all that follows in this Chapter, cf. *Church and State*, Report of the Archbishops' Commission (1970).

dependence of Church and State. The Establishment of religion was defended - and especially in the early years of the nineteenth century - on the grounds that it provided amongst other things the foundation of a right civil obedience. Christian morality was seen as the basis of law and of political order. There has been no consistent and coherent theory of Establishment, but there has been throughout these centuries a general agreement concerning the importance of religion as one of the first conditions of a sound social order.

497.   The State has long since recognised the religious diversity and the religious neutrality of the English people. And there have been other changes - silent changes in the very bed and basis of modern society - that cannot be ignored: the growth of an international world order; the evolution of a multi-racial, multi-faith society; the pervasive influences of secular thought. These are some of the factors - fundamental and far-reaching - that compromise still further the exclusive claims that the Church of England justly made in earlier generations simply on the basis of her position as the Established Church.

498.   It can still be claimed, however, that the Church of England continues to touch the life of the nation at many points. She is the Established Church, and yet she functions day by day with a degree of independence which makes it possible to describe her as the most significant voluntary agency in the country. She possesses vast resources in plant, man-power, financial reserves, traditions of involvement, and personal and public expectations. Parochial ministry represents at its best the Church's concern to minister to the whole life of the nation. It recognises the identity and the needs of the local community and the primary importance of the worshipping congregation within that community. It attempts to hold in balance the Church's best traditions of worship, teaching, pastoral care and evangelism. Through her parochial ministry; through her liturgy, and not least the occasional offices and provision of services for public and state occasions; through her substantial involvement in education and social care; through an intimate connection with the Crown and with Parliament and with the leaders of national life; through ties that are legal and historical, public and personal, local and sentimental, the Church of England continues to have a special relationship with the people of England.

499.   In the face of indifference, of secularism, of increasing numbers of people who are almost entirely untouched by the traditional patterns of public ministry, the Church of England is still able to understand the

different degrees of association with the Church that people want and are capable of sustaining. The Church of England, while retaining her own identity and integrity, has provided a framework within which the religious aspirations of non-churchgoing people could find expression from time to time. Regular attendance at church has been in decline[14] for many years but the Church of England is not the only Church to have experienced this. Passivity does not mean that people do not still turn to the Church for the major events in their lives. Many people still look to the Church of England for baptism of their children, for the solemnization of their marriages, for the burial of their dead. It was the judgement of the Archbishops' Commission on Church and State in 1970 that, 'The people of England still want to feel that religion has a place in the land to which they can turn on the too rare occasions when they think that they need it; and they are not likely to be pleased by legislation which might suggest that the English people as a whole were going unChristian'.[15] It is in this way that the Church of England - and especially through the work of her cathedrals and parish churches - continues to be primarily a community Church. The comprehensiveness of the Church of England, the network of relationships into which bishops, priests and deacons enter on taking up their charge, the opportunities for ministry and the expectations of people, mean that there continues to exist within the life of the Church some appreciation of the need to interpret the range of religious experience, and the sometimes inarticulate religion which has something to say about human behaviour and human need.

500. In today's society the Church of England stands as one Christian body among many, with Christianity itself the faith of only a proportion of the population. Some Anglicans argue for disestablishment on the grounds that by Establishment the Church is to some degree unavoidably tied to the State's apron-strings and that Establishment may exert seductive pressures; that the Church is not free to be fully authentic in its witness and that its spiritual vitality is constrained. For Establishment it can be said that it has served both Church and nation; that civil order and religious order are deeply interconnected; that the special vocation of the Church to serve the nation has been kept alive; that Establishment enables the Church of England to carry the banner of the faith before society, and to be in some sense a 'holding body' for the whole Christian community; and that were it not to

---

14 Though in some dioceses there is a rise. Can we regard frequency of churchgoing as a straightforward index of religious commitment when audiences of eight or nine million people are reported as watching televised religious services?

15 Para. 215.

do and be so Christian religion might tend to disappear altogether from public life; that the Church has been required to keep in touch with thoughts and interests wider and deeper than her own; that the nation has had held up before it the conviction that 'the ultimate ends and sanctions of politics lie in the realm which is beyond politics'.[16] The important point here would seem to be that the relationship between Church and State extends in its implications far beyond any technical or formal considerations.

501.   Here the role of the bishop is central. He remains a national figure with a place in society which is still generally recognised and warmed to. Society may not always wish to hear what he has to say: and on occasion may question his social or political judgements or his place in expressing them. Nevertheless, he speaks from within society rather than from outside it. For many, the bishop's 'public' role is to be seen in something closer to the prophetic terms of the first centuries, and as an aspect of his ministry of the Word and guardianship of the truth; he is seen as a leader of the Christian community able to identify with those in need; and able to speak boldly when something politically unpopular has to be said. The fact that bishops sit *ex officiis* in the House of Lords can be seen by some as a form of secular aggrandisement which operates as a barrier to their role in mission. But we would argue that through their position as Spiritual Lords (constitutionally long pre-dating the Reformation) they have a privileged opportunity to speak for Christ to the nation and on behalf of the nation. The State has a moral conscience and the voice of religious leaders should be heard. There is every reason why other Churches in addition to the Church of England should be represented in the House of Lords in order to achieve this end. The Archbishops' Commission on Church and State recommended as long ago as 1970 that there should be wider representation of other Churches.

502.   We see that Church-State relations will continue to evolve and we would expect questions to be asked over the years ahead about legislative structures and procedures for appointments. We attach great importance to the position the Church of England has in the life of the nation. We are not suggesting that the Sovereign should not continue to have a special place in the Church of England or in any united Church. We see no reason to differ from the view expressed by the Archbishops' Commission on Church and State that the place of the Sovereign, as a symbol of national recognition and encouragement, gives rise to very little difficulty, 'is seldom resented by

16   F.R. Barry, *Church and Leadership* (London, 1945), p. 46.

non-Christians, would not be an obstacle to Christian unity, and is much valued by many persons'.[17] We also note the wider implications which will arise as the nation-states of Europe move closer together within the European Community. We cannot leave this topic without noting that ecumenical trends in our communities have a significant bearing here, in ways which are only now beginning to be glimpsed.

c.   The appointment of bishops

503.   The diocesan bishop is God's minister, exercising a ministry from Christ, and sent by the Holy Spirit. He also stands at the point of intersection of the three planes of the Church's life. He is chief pastor to the people of the diocese, clergy and laity, the head of their community on earth, with a duty of guardianship of Scripture, tradition, faith and morals. He must therefore be accepted by them as their minister, and they should have a say in his selection. He is to be brother-bishop to other chief pastors, at least three of whom must join in his consecration. And, standing in the line of episcopal succession in his diocese, he inherits from his predecessors a relationship with other bishops, a relationship of communion in which in his person and office he links his diocese with the Church universal.

504.   Crown Appointments are made in the case of officers of the Church other than bishops, as well as of diocesan bishops, and it is not part of our brief to look at the system of Crown Appointments as such.[18] But we offer one or two comments on the appointment of bishops in relation to the theological framework we have been sketching.

505.   The disjunction remains, and perhaps must now remain, between the interaction of the ecclesial relationships which must come into being to make a bishop; and the practical process of selection, which must answer to many other requirements. What bridges the two is the Church's responsibility to the nation, which, deeper than its public expression of the nation's formal Christian alignment, has to do with the necessity laid upon the Church to proclaim abroad the good news of God's Kingdom. The bishop to be appointed has to win souls as well as care for them: the souls of everyone in the diocese, Church-connected or not, are in his 'cure'.

17   *Church and State*, 8, p. 2.
18   They are at present being considered by the Working Party on Senior Church Appointments set up in 1988.

506. In primitive times we have seen bishops being chosen by popular acclamation, and then turning to other bishops for ordination. During the 'investiture' struggle of the eleventh and twelfth centuries, royal encroachments on the 'spiritualities' were restrained and attempts were made to see that a clear line was drawn between what a king or emperor could do and what only an archbishop and bishops could do in the making of bishops. In England, as elsewhere in later mediaeval Western Europe, there are traces of a system under which the right of clergy and people to choose their diocesan bishops had passed into the hands of the Chapter of clergy of the cathedral church. But the right thus acquired by the Chapter was challenged increasingly, and with ever increasing success, by Pope and King; with the Pope in some places, and in some instances, succeeding in securing the appointment of his nominee, and with the King succeeding in others. In 1363 Urban V tried to reserve to himself the right to appoint to all bishoprics. Yet Henry VIII provided by Act of Parliament[19] that a cathedral Chapter must have the royal leave before embarking on the electoral process, and only then must it proceed to elect the royal nominee. Ultimately, the king, having secured the election of his candidate, issued directions to the archbishop to confirm the election and consecrate the person elected. Provision thus made by Henrician Act of Parliament simply gave statutory force to practices which 'strong' kings had previously followed in England and elsewhere in Europe.

507. The machinery established by Henry VIII continues in all outward appearances to this day.[20] But the royal powers have long been exercised on the advice of the Prime Minister.[21] Since 1977 the Crown, on the Prime Minister's advice, has voluntarily accepted that the choice of name should lie between two names[22] submitted by the Crown Appointments Commission, a

---

19   Appointment of Bishops Act, 1533.
20   With an interval under Edward VI when some episcopal appointments were made by Letters Patent without *congé d'élire*.
21   It should be noted here that this would seem finally to take away the force of arguments advanced by Cranmer and others to the effect that, since princes rule by divine right, it is the authority to appoint which makes a bishop, not the consecration; and that the gift of the spiritualities thus lies finally with the monarch. See O.P. Rafferty, 'Thomas Cranmer and the Royal Supremacy', *Heythrop Journal*, 31 (1990), 130-4, and Cranmer, *Works*, Parker Society, II.115 note 1. It seems fair to add that 'the custom still pertaining in the Church of England is logically indefensible, but practically serviceable', N. Sykes, 'The Election of Bishops', in *Bishops*, ed. G. Simon (London, 1961), p. 64.
22   The appointment of suffragan bishops also requires the submission of two names, but the normal practice is for one to be the diocesan bishop's preference and the other to be in a sense a 'sleeping partner'. There is precedent, on an occasion when a young unknown was the diocesan bishop's choice and the second name that of a beloved suffragan bishop of proven excellence elsewhere, whom the Prime Minister happened to know very well and admire, for the second name having to be changed in order to secure the appointment the diocesan wanted.

body chosen by the Church.[23] When a diocese becomes vacant there is extensive consultation about the vacancy, and full participation of the diocese in the actual discussions of, and nominations by, the Crown Appointments Commission. The Church effectively determines the field of choice, and within the field the Commission may place the candidates in order of preference. Under this arrangement the Crown may not introduce names of its own choice: in the event of difficulty, the matter goes back to the Commission. But the Crown's agreement to the convention is voluntary, and could at any time be repudiated (though this seems unlikely to happen in the foreseeable future).

508. The method of choice of Church of England bishops should be compared with the arrangements in the Roman Catholic Church in England where there is no formal tie with the State.[24] Here also, when a bishopric becomes vacant there is extensive consultation in the vacant diocese and beyond it. The information is accumulated not by the Archbishop or the President of the Episcopal Conference of England and Wales, but, directly on behalf of the Holy See, by the Apostolic Pro-Nuncio. He reports on his findings to Rome. The final decision is that of the Pope, advised both by the Pro-Nuncio and by advisers in Rome. There is evidence of a vestigial consultation with the State. From the restoration of the English Roman Catholic hierarchy for as long as the Vatican archives are open to consultation, it appears that appointments to the Archbishopric of Westminster have always been 'cleared' with the British Government in advance through diplomatic channels. Rome having made its nomination, the local bishops must ordain and the diocese must receive the new bishop. Roman Catholic practice elsewhere varies according to the nature of Church-State relationships in the country concerned, but direct nomination by a Head of State is no longer considered acceptable.

509. Clearly, the arrangements consolidated in England at the time of the Henrician Reformation, and which applied also in Ireland and in Wales until

---

23   The Crown Appointments Commission consists of the two Archbishops, three clergy and three laity elected from and by General Synod, and four representatives elected from and by the Diocese to which an appointment is to be made. There are two non-voting members, the Archbishops' Secretary for Appointments and the Prime Minister's Secretary for Appointments. The Commission is chaired by the Archbishop of the Province in which a Diocesan appointment is to be made.

24   See Appendix II for fuller details of the general procedure in the Roman Catholic Church and for comments on Orthodox and Lutheran procedures.

the disestablishment of the Churches in those countries, could not apply where a Church, episcopal in character and Anglican in tradition, was not Established. First in Scotland (post 1688), then in the United States (after the War of American Independence), and then around the world in countries many of which were then under the jurisdiction of the British Crown but where the Church was not Established, means had to be found of providing a local see with a new bishop.

510. The solutions adopted in the wider Anglican Communion fall into three main categories. In the first, the choice is made by election within the vacant diocese, in which both clergy and laity participate, sometimes voting by houses, sometimes together. Often there is a requirement for a special majority. Invariably the choice of the diocese has to be confirmed - e.g. by the bench of bishops in the Scottish Episcopal Church, or by reference to the Standing Committees of the dioceses in New Zealand. A second major category comprises cases where the choice is made on a provincial basis. Thus in Wales, when a diocese becomes vacant, the provincial electoral college assembles, with representation from all six dioceses of the province, but with the vacant diocese doubling its representation for the occasion. A third main (but smaller) category is of dioceses which stand alone geographically. In such a case, the clergy and laity of the diocese make their choice, which must then be confirmed by the Archbishop of Canterbury. In all three categories there is usually in each case a 'reserve' power, providing for the case where the electoral body is unable to agree (or to obtain the required majority for any one candidate). In such a case the choice usually falls to the House of Bishops of the Province or (in the case of an extra-provincial diocese), to the Archbishop of Canterbury.

511. It will be observed that the relationship with the wider Church, through the participation of bishops from outside the vacant diocese, is well safeguarded. The voice of the diocese in accepting - or even directly in choosing - is normally well accommodated. In England that voice is heard now through the process of consultation but also through the participation in the Crown Appointments Commission of four representatives elected from the vacant diocese (of a total Commission membership of twelve).[25] The gift of the Holy Spirit is a gift of divine grace in a Church thus acting by common consent.

---

[25]   In addition, some see as a useful safeguard the requirement (still in force), that the cathedral chapter will still need formally to elect the eventual nominee.

512.   The Crown Appointments Commission represents one further stage in the evolution of Church-State relations in England.   There is undoubtedly a strong desire within the Church to secure the decisive voice in the appointment of all bishops.   However, we do not presume to intrude here upon the area of work of the Working Party on Senior Church Appointments.   In our view it is important that efforts continue to be made in the selection of candidates for the episcopate to ensure a balance of expertise and experience (including knowledge of the Church in the wider world), of background (pastoral and academic), of place of origin (geographically wide), of interest and sympathy, so that the Church's life may be enriched in every possible way.   We need bishops who can respond with authority in ecumenical endeavour, in education, areas of social concern, knowledge of cultural and scientific development, and we endorse the Crown Appointments Commission's continuing efforts to balance these wider needs with the special needs of a particular diocese in any given appointment.

d.   Jurisdiction and the State

513.   We have noted that the most conspicuous change brought about by Henry VIII was the transference of papal jurisdiction in England to himself. There were loose parallels in the Continental Reformation, where a prince often played an important role as magistrate and protector in a local reformed Church and was deemed to make it in some sense legitimate by his patronage.   There was precedent in the early Church for such protection, and for the calling of Councils by secular rulers.   But there had always been a clear distinction in principle between the jurisdictional functions which could be performed by a secular prince or magistrate and those which belong to bishops and, *a fortiori*, to archbishops and primates, although, as we have described, it had had to be spelt out and fought for in the 'investiture Contest' of the late eleventh and and twelfth centuries.[26]

514.   At the end of the Middle Ages, the Pope had had, in England as elsewhere, universal immediate jurisdiction in spiritual matters.   That is to say, he could act locally, anywhere in Western Christendom, without necessarily doing so through the local bishop, although it was understood that the bishop's own jurisdiction remained in normal circumstances.   As Giles of Rome had put it early in the fourteenth century, 'the bearer of a

26   See section a ii of this chapter.

plenitude of power can do directly and immediately himself, what he normally accomplishes through a secondary cause'.

515. This was a special case of the 'jurisdiction as ordinary' which all bishops had and have in canon law, inherent in their office, and making each principal minister in his diocese. It required them to punish, where necessary, any who needed correction. It gave them authority over the clergy in the dioceses, such that they granted licences to those who were to serve there and received in return their canonical obedience. It made them judges in ecclesiastical Courts, or able to appoint others to serve in their stead as presidents of such Courts. The position about episcopal jurisdiction in England had in fact been anomalous in the late Middle Ages in several respects. In some dioceses a bishop from elsewhere had jurisdiction over a foundation within another bishop's See. (The Bishop of Exeter had jurisdiction over a royal college in the diocese of Chichester, for example.) Some diocesans exercised multiple jurisdictions, ecclesiastical and even temporal. There was corruption and inefficiency in some ecclesiastical Courts.

516. There was, then, a need for reform of the system at the time when Henry VIII made his own claim to take over the Pope's higher jurisdiction in England. Some radical proposals were put forward by advisers of the King with reforming views. Between February and June 1535, most of the bishops surrendered their bulls of appointment by the Pope, and received commissions which empowered them to exercise jurisdiction during the royal pleasure. In September the bishops were suspended from the exercise of their spiritual jurisdiction pending a general royal visitation, and it was only gradually restored to them in a series of subsequent grants. In the summer of 1547, the powers of bishops in their dioceses were temporarily suspended while royal commissioners travelled the country publishing a series of injunctions (including the one which stipulated without reference to the bishop that each Church was to have a copy of the new Book of Homilies).

517. Discipline was imposed by means of rules which were laid down for bishops, insisting for instance that they preach in their dioceses at least four times a year, so that they could not be more or less permanent absentees. Edward VI's bishops had a generally good record in the performance of such duties as presiding in person over diocesan courts and making visitations. This firm royal hand on bishops' affairs was continued in Mary's reign, when the Council took a daily direct interest in episcopal

actions. Elizabeth demonstrated her Supremacy (in a manner which had ample precedent, it must be said, among mediaeval kings), by leaving Sees vacant at her convenience so that the Crown might enjoy the revenues. The effect of all this was to underline the dependency of bishops upon Royal Supremacy, not for the spiritual powers of their office in themselves, but for the right to exercise those powers in dioceses which were now also under the secular 'jurisdiction' of the Crown.

518.   Bishops continued to hold office in the State, as 'Lords spiritual' in the House of Lords (where, incidentally, some of Henry's new bishops were intellectually formidable, having formerly been members of religious orders where they had got an advanced university education in theology). They were also, in practice, still living a social life on a level with country nobles and gentry, and were therefore often no less lordly than their mediaeval predecessors had been. The style and standing of Tudor bishops was not greatly different from that of their immediate predecessors.

519.   Archiepiscopal or primatial jurisdiction internally to the Church of England remained substantially unchanged. English Canon Law at present is in line with the sixteenth century when it states that an Archbishop has metropolitical jurisdiction throughout his Province, 'as superintendent of all ecclesiastical matters therein, to correct and supply the defects of other bishops' (C 17). As the 'clergy who have received authority to minister in any diocese owe canonical obedience ... to the bishop of the same' so the bishop of each diocese owes 'due obedience to the archbishop of the Province as his metropolitan' (C 14 (1)). This formal oath of 'due obedience' (C 14) is technically distinct from 'canonical obedience' in the language of canon law, because it is due among 'equals in the structure' of the Church's order to one bishop who acts as a focus and sometimes spokesman of the college of bishops. It implies an equality of all dioceses in a province and thus of all local or particular churches. The metropolitan see has, as a diocese, no pre-eminence among them. But the Metropolitan or Archbishop has a personal ordinary inherent jurisdiction derived from the submission of his fellow bishops for the sake of preserving what we may call the regulative operation of love in the province.[27] Thus during, and only during, the time of his metropolitan visitation, the archbishop has 'jurisdiction as Ordinary' (C 17). There are implications for a wider primacy. It has not been usual in recent Anglican Canon Law or practice to

[27]   Cf. AR, 82.

define at all fully the obligation of obedience which rests on the members of the Christian community who are not ordained.

e.   The Oath of Allegiance and homage

520.   We have pointed out that in adopting the title of Supreme Governor Elizabeth I insisted that she was in no way intruding upon the spiritual jurisdiction of bishops.[28]   The fact that the method of appointment of bishops has since 1533 been under the Crown does not mean that the Crown confers spiritual jurisdiction upon a bishop.   The Crown permits the exercise of, but is not the source of, spiritual jurisdiction.

521.   The distinction between the civil or secular jurisdiction and spiritual matters is clearly drawn in the Thirty-Nine Articles.   Article 37 provides that:

> Where we attribute to the Queen's majesty the chief government ... we give not to our princes the ministering either of God's Word or of the Sacraments; ... but that only prerogative which we see to have been given always to all godly princes in Holy Scripture by God himself; that is, that they should rule all estates and degrees committed to their charge by God whether they be ecclesiastical or temporal ...

Once it is appreciated that the Sovereign does not purport to be the source of the spiritual jurisdiction of a bishop, it becomes easier to understand the significance of the Oaths which are made to the Sovereign by a newly appointed bishop.

522.   In England both legally and historically there has always been a clear distinction between the oath of allegiance and the act of homage, which are made to the sovereign by a newly appointed bishop.

523.   The feudal system was based upon a special oath of fidelity, or mutual bond of obligation between a lord and his tenant.   The Sovereign is and always has been the chief lord, and the oath of fidelity or fealty (Latin *fidelitas;* Norman French: *feaulté*) was the allegiance declared by a subject to his sovereign.   It was an affirmation of the natural allegiance which the law recognised as due from 'all men born within the British dominions immediately upon their birth' (2Bl. Comm. 369) or of the acquired allegiance obtained by naturalisation (Co. Litt. 129a).   The oath of

---

[28]   See section a iii of this chapter, and also a ii on 'spiritualities'.

allegiance, as it is now known, continues to be that affirmation of loyalty to the Sovereign.

524.   Every ecclesiastical office is an office under the Crown. All bishops, priests and deacons are therefore required by canon law to take at the time of their consecration or ordination and of their appointment to all offices the oath of allegiance:

> I will be faithful and bear true allegiance to Her Majesty Queen Elizabeth II, her heirs and successors according to law: so help me God.[29]

But where a bishop or clergyman is a subject of a foreign state, or is to officiate or minister solely overseas, the Canon recognises that allegiance to the Queen, who has no jurisdiction in a foreign state, would be inappropriate. Thus no oath of allegiance is required to be taken by any subject or citizen of a foreign state whom either of the archbishops consecrates to officiate as a bishop in any foreign state (Canon C13 (2)).

525.   The act of homage by contrast is an acknowledgement of tenure, and relates to the temporalities or secular possessions attached to a see, which can be granted to a new bishop only by the Crown and are held by him of the Crown.[30]   Temporalities are to be distinguished from spiritualities, which derive from the office of bishop and are not held by the Crown during a vacancy but by the guardian of the spiritualities (the dean and chapter of the cathedral church of the diocese or the archbishop of the Province (Canon C19 (2)).   It is the guardian who exercises spiritual jurisdiction and grants licences to marry and gives institutions to benefices. The guardian cannot consecrate or ordain but can give commissions for ordination when the see is vacant (*sede vacante*).

526.   The temporalities could in the past be of considerable value, being 'castles, manors, lands, tenements, tithes' and other revenues[31] which had been annexed to the see by kings and others.   The right to sue for or claim such temporalities was clearly spelt out in section 5 of the Appointment of Bishops Act of 1533 which is still in force, and provides that:

> every person ... being hereafter chosen, elected nominate, presented invested and consecrated to the dignity or office of (any archbishop or)

---

29   Canon C 13.
30   The temporalities are not now 'taken' by the Crown during the interregnum, a right regularly exploited during the Middle Ages, but are vested in the Church Commissioners.
31   See para 488, Vol. 14, Halsbury's Laws of England, 4th edition.

bishop within this realm ... and suing their temporalities out of the King's
hands his heirs or successors as hath been accustomed, and making a
corporal oath to the King's Highness and to none other ... shall have and
take their only restitution out of the King's hands of all the possessions
and profits spiritual and temporal belonging to the said ... bishopric
whereunto they shall be so elected.[32]

527.   The need to sue arises out of the common law principle that the
temporalities, being ecclesiastical property, reverted to the Crown during a
vacancy in the see and could not pass into the hands of an individual. There
they remained until a new bishop had been consecrated, when his right to
claim the temporalities then arose. The sequence of events was, and still is,
that the election of the new bishop is confirmed by the vicar-general on
behalf of the archbishop; he is then consecrated by the archbishop with the
assistance of two other bishops; he then does homage for his temporalities
and barony and is then enthroned.

528.   The only guidance as to the form of the 'corporal oath' (that is an
oath by the new bishop who is a corporation sole in his capacity as bishop)
given in section 5 of the Appointment of Bishops Act 1533 is that it should
be 'in forme as is afore rehersed'. The only form of oath 'rehersed' or
referred to in the Act is in section 4, which requires the bishop elect to
make 'such othe and fealtie only to the Kynges Hyghnes hys heires and
successors as shal be appoynted for the same'. It therefore appears that the
oath to be made at the time of homage is an oath of fealty or allegiance. By
the act of homage the bishop then kneels before the Queen putting his hands
between the hands of the Queen, sitting in her chair of State, and then
promises fidelity to Her Majesty and acknowledges that he holds his
temporalities of her.

529.   Implicit in the oath of allegiance prescribed by Canon C13 is the
recognition of the Sovereign as Supreme Governor of the realm having
temporal jurisdiction over the Church of England as well as the State.
Canon A7 expressly acknowledges

> that the Queen's excellent Majesty acting according to the laws of the
> realm is the highest power under God in this kingdom, and has supreme
> authority over all persons in all causes as well ecclesiastical as civil.

It is not now deemed necessary to include this acknowledgement in the oath
of allegiance (see paragraph 355 above). The relevant Canon in force from
1603 until 1865 (Canon 26), however, required any person being received

---

[32]   Set out here in modern spelling.

into the ministry or to any ecclesiastical function to subscribe to the following:

> that the king's majesty under God is the only supreme governor of this realm and of all other his highness's dominions and countries as well in all spiritual or ecclesiastical things or causes as temporal; and that no foreign prince, prelate, state or potentate hath or ought to have any jurisdiction, power, superiority, pre-eminence or authority ecclesiastical or spiritual within his majesty's said realms, dominions and countries.

The form of words still used at the time when the new bishop pays homage to the Queen bears a marked resemblance to the wording of this former Canon. We consider that it would be appropriate for such wording now to be replaced by the wording of the oath of allegiance contained in Canon C13. Our interpretation of the requirement in Section 5 of the Appointment of Bishops Act 1533 is that the new bishop should make his oath of fealty or allegiance directly to the Queen 'and to none other'.[33] The use of an old form of words can at the least cause surprise and give rise to misunderstanding, and we recommend that early consideration be given to modernising the wording of the oath.

530.   A further point arises from the wording which we understand is used by the new bishop in doing homage for his temporalities and barony. He acknowledges that he holds the bishopric, 'as well the spiritualities as the temporalities thereof', only of Her Majesty. Such wording could give the impression that the spiritual authority and jurisdiction of a bishop is derived from the sovereign, whereas the law makes it clear that the spiritualities are not held by the Crown during a vacancy but by the guardian of the spiritualities and that the spiritual jurisdiction passes from the guardian to the new bishop immediately after confirmation of his election. We believe that the wording of the acknowledgement may be based upon the use of the words 'spiritual and temporal' in section 5 of the Appointment of Bishops Act 1533 which refers to 'all the possessions and profits spiritual and temporal belonging to the said bishopric' [34] Here again we recommend that the wording should be modernised and clarified so that it does not give rise to any misunderstanding about the source of the bishop's spiritual jurisdiction. In an ecumenical age we consider it important that no impression should be given that acceptance of the spiritual jurisdiction of a universal primacy in a future united Church could not be reconciled with episcopacy in the Church of England.

---

[33]   He will already have made the oath in the form prescribed in Canon C13 before the archbishop's vicar-general at the ceremony of confirmation of his election.

[34]   Modern spelling used.

13

Women in the Episcopate

I. The history of the debate during the lifetime of our Group

531.   At the time when we held our first meeting in January 1986,[1] the issue of women and the priesthood had already been subjected to extensive consideration over a period of about twenty years. Women had been admitted to the presbyterate in various Provinces within the Anglican Communion, and it was obvious that with the passage of time the possibility of a woman being ordained to the episcopate was going to arise. As one of the background papers to the Lima Report pointed out:

> In some traditions *episcope* is already exercised by women and the possibility of women among the *episcopoi* is becoming an ever closer reality.

a. The essential issues on the priestly and episcopal ministry of women

532.   From the outset we recognised that our terms of reference required us to consider the fundamental question whether a woman may ever become a bishop, or whether the nature and function of the episcopate is such that a bishop must necessarily be male.

533.   Within those Provinces which had proceeded with the ordination of women, there had clearly been an acceptance that the admission of women to the presbyterate was a legitimate development in the historic ministry. Similarly, we inferred from the resolution of ECUSA[2] that the majority of their members did not intend to withhold consent to the election of a woman as bishop, an acceptance that the consecration of a woman as bishop was a further legitimate development in the historic ministry. But this was only one side of a continuing debate about the theological acceptability of the

---

1   See Preface to this Report.
2   The Episcopal Church in the United States of America.

233

ordination of women and, without casting any doubt upon the sincerity of the beliefs which had led some Anglican communities to admit women to the presbyterate and to contemplate admitting them to the episcopate, we could not treat their actions as in themselves constituting proof of the rightness of their decision. We started our deliberations by recognising that there were other, equally sincerely held views, that such a step was not theologically acceptable.

534.   The main lines of the arguments for and against are set out in the commentary to the Lima text of the World Council of Churches (BEM):

> Those Churches which practise the ordination of women do so because of their understanding of the Gospel and of the ministry. It rests for them on the deeply held theological conviction that the ordained ministry of the Church lacks fullness when it is limited to one sex. This theological conviction has been reinforced by their experience during the years in which they have included women in their ordained ministries. They have found that women's gifts are as wide and varied as men's and that their ministry is as fully blessed by the Holy Spirit as the ministry of men. None has found reason to reconsider its decision.
> Those Churches which do not practise the ordination of women consider that the force of nineteen centuries of tradition against the ordination of women must not be set aside. They believe that such a tradition cannot be dismissed as a lack of respect for the participation of women in the Church. They believe that there are theological issues concerning the nature of humanity and concerning Christology which lie at the heart of their convictions and understanding of the role of women in the Church.[3]

535.   Within the Church of England, the debate on the theological acceptability of ordination of women to the priesthood was continuing in 1987, and continues at the time of completion of this Report in 1990. It did and does so against a background of lack of consensus on the matter, both within the Anglican Communion and in the ecumenical forum. To put it in the terms of the Lima Text, there has been no 'theological conviction' expressed by the Church of England and hence no experience as yet among us of the ministry of women in the priesthood.

536.   The Faith and Order Advisory Group's Report on *The Priesthood of the Ordained Ministry*, the Church of England's most systematic recent treatment of the theology of priesthood, did not address the question whether theological considerations told decisively for or against the ordination of women to the priesthood. But it notes:

---

[3]   Baptism, Eucharist and Ministry, Commentary (18), *Growth*, p. 500.

that the ordination of women to the priesthood does raise acute ecclesiological and ecumenical questions which go far beyond the specific theology of the priestliness of bishops and presbyters.[4]

537.   We were very conscious of this wider background when we started to explore together issues relating to the question whether a woman may be admitted to the episcopate. We were also aware that, insofar as the debate had concentrated upon ordination to the presbyterate, it appeared to have been assumed that what applied to the presbyterate applied *mutatis mutandis* to the episcopate, and that a decision on one operated automatically as a basis for a decision on the other. It was for us to examine whether that was necessarily so, and in what respects the ecclesiological and ecumenical implications bore on this principle.

538.   Since the interpretation of certain texts of Holy Scripture[5] must underpin the whole debate, we started our work by looking at a number of key texts which have been used in the arguments for and against the ordination of women to see what assistance could be derived from them in relation to the question whether a woman can ever become a bishop.[6] Here we immediately found that there was serious disagreement amongst us about the meaning of the biblical material and its proper interpretation in the present day and in our contemporary society, reflecting the difference of opinion in the wider Church. There were some of us for whom the early chapters of Genesis and the New Testament texts, speaking of man as 'head' of woman and of the 'subordination' of women to men, revealed a male authority as part of the order of creation; which would preclude a woman from exercising a priestly, and *a fortiori* an episcopal, ministry involving the exercise of authority in the community. For others amongst us, the Genesis accounts of creation did not reveal a fundamental male authority, and any assumption of male authority was seen as a consequence of the Fall, and the issues of subordination and headship seen as debated by Paul only in

---

4   *The Priesthood of the Ordained Ministry*, Faith and Order Advisory Group, published for the Board of Mission and Unity of the General Synod of the Church of England (1986), para 128, p. 90.

5   Scriptural texts of particular importance are: Genesis 1-3; I Corinthians 11.12-16 (headship); II Corinthians 11.3 and I Timothy 2.11-15 (Eve first fell into sin); Ephesians 5.21-33 and I Corinthians 7 (husband and wife); Galatians 3.27-9 (in Christ no male or female); to which may be added I Timothy 3.2 (bishop's wife); Mark 16.19; John 20.1 (women the first witnesses to the resurrection); Philippians 4.3 (women Paul's fellow-workers in the Gospel); Titus 2.5 (be submissive to your husbands); Acts 21.9, I Corinthians 11.5 (women prophesy); Romans 16.1 (Phoebe the deacon); Romans 16.5 (Junia/Junios, who may have been a woman).

6   See, too, *The Ordination of Women to the Priesthood, A Second Report by the House of Bishops of the General Synod of the Church of England* (1988), p. 49 ff.

the context of marriage. It followed that this interpretation of Scripture would not preclude a woman from exercising a ministry of authority either as a priest or a bishop. These differences of opinion remain unresolved among us.

539. When we turned to the question of the functions of a bishop, a preliminary helpful guide was before us in the Lima Text, which was to prove entirely in harmony with our evolving theological principle of the intersection in the episcopal ministry of the three planes of the Church's life:

> Bishops preach the Word, preside at the Sacraments, and administer discipline in such a way as to be representative-pastoral ministers of oversight, continuity and unity in the Church. They have pastoral oversight of an area to which they are called. They serve the apostolicity and unity of the Church's teaching, worship and sacramental life. They have responsibility for leadership in the Church's mission. They relate the Christian community in their area to the wider Church, and the universal Church to their community. They, in communion with the presbyters and deacons and the whole community, are responsible for the orderly transfer of ministerial authority in the Church.[7]

540. But whilst it was necessary for us to look at functions in order to work towards a theology of episcopacy, we were at pains to stress that these functions should not be regarded as mere practicalities. That would have been indicative of a failure to comprehend the spirituality of the early Christian concept of ministry and the mystery to which it points:

> Because of the integral nature of Gospel and Church, the body of Christ was believed to be a sign and instrument of communion with God. That is to say the outward form of the Church was expressive of the inner life of the invisible community where Christ reigns supreme. Moreover, the bishop's role as a pastor of the local church was seen as a visible sign and an instrument of the community in the heritage of the apostles.[8]

541. On the basis of these agreed points, we took it at this stage that the issues of apostolicity; unity and collegiality; and authority were the matters deserving of special attention in considering the arguments for and against the possibility of the ordination of women to the episcopate.

i   Apostolic continuity

542. The fact that Jesus was male, the Apostles were male, and their successors in the historic apostolic ministry for two thousand years have

---

[7]   BEM, M29, *Growth*, pp. 489-90.
[8]   See Appendix III (a).

been male created, for some in our Group, a view of the ordained ministry in which maleness is fundamental. Others in our Group have responded that it is 'humanity' and not 'maleness' that Christ assumed. Ascended now to God, Jesus bears not just male but full humanity in his Person. Since he represents all, he can be represented by either sex. Some of us want to respond, as our Memorandum put it, that:

> if any weight is to be placed upon the bishop representing the total community he can only do this because of the humanity he shares with us all and not because of a 'maleness' he shares with Christ.[9]

The issue here is whether the inclusion of women in the priesthood and episcopate makes a break in the apostolic continuity of a male ministry.

ii Unity and collegiality

543. We all recognised that the bishop is a focus and sign of unity of the whole Church and has a role in representing the universal Church to the local and the local to the universal. It was forcefully argued amongst us that if a woman were to be consecrated bishop and her orders were not recognised by other bishops in her Province, or indeed by other Provinces of the Anglican Communion, the unity of the Communion would be impaired.[10] It was equally forcefully argued that *koinonia* or communion can be said to be impaired by the exclusion of women from priestly and the episcopal ministry. That is to say, there is a disunity created by exclusion; a presbyterate and an episcopate inclusive of men and women would be a sign to the world of the unity of men and women given in Christ.

iii Authority

544. We considered the authority of the bishop as being twofold. Firstly, that in the office of bishop is focused the Lord's authority in the community. 'Aspects of this will inevitably include his authority expressed in terms of discipline.'[11] Secondly, the pattern and model of the exercise of episcopal authority is that of Christ the Servant, the awesome ministry of service in which love, humility and gentleness are enshrined. Once again we were divided in our views. For some of us it is essential for the authority of

9   See Appendix III (a).
10   Such consecrations not then having occurred.
11   See Appendix III (a).

the bishop, as exemplifying this twofold authority of Jesus Christ in the Church, to be exercised by a man. Some base this principle on a theology of headship which they find in Scripture and others on a theology of apostolic continuity. Common to both these approaches is a view of ministry which forbids the exercise of the episcopal function of oversight by a woman on the ground of gender.

545. Others amongst us, taking a different view of the theology of humanity, were firmly of the opinion even at this preliminary stage in our examination of the issues relating to the ordination of women to the episcopate, that a woman could indeed exercise episcopal authority in the Church. They argued that a male bishop does not exercise his ministry and authority as a 'male' but by virtue of an office which is not limited to one gender. The authority of a woman bishop, like that of a male bishop, would derive from her holding of the office of bishop and would be exercised by virtue of her office. The sex of the holder of the office is on this view irrelevant.

546. We have summarised the arguments put forward by members of the Group on these three issues to demonstrate why our divergence of views made it impossible for us to offer in a memorandum to the House of Bishops in 1987 any common response to the question of whether a woman may ever become a bishop.

547. The value of our early debates and painful disagreement was that it highlighted within our Group the difficulties which are encountered when there are some who favour a new development, whilst others resist it and consider it wholly misconceived. Whilst we agreed that we were united in our concern that women should find fulfilment in the service of Christ, we were totally divided over the question whether a woman could be allowed to find that fulfilment by way of ordination to the presbyterate or the episcopate.[12]

548. The common ground which emerged at that stage in our discussions was the following:

• that most of the theological issues raised in connection with the question of the consecration of women as bishops are the same as those which

---

12   Ordination to the diaconate does not raise the same difficulties because it does not involve the same issues of representation and headship. See *Deacons in the Ministry of the Church* for a full discussion of the diaconal ministry of women.

relate to the question of ordination of women as priests

- that apart from ecclesiological considerations there are no other theological distinctions between the presbyterate and the episcopate[13] which would preclude women from being ordained to the episcopate once they had been accepted for ordination to the presbyterate[14]

- that the ordination of women to the episcopate cannot be justified simply by reference to the fact that women nowadays frequently hold positions of authority and leadership in society or because they are already exercising certain ministries in the Church

- that because of the special role of the bishops as focus of unity and the collegiality of the bishops with other bishops, there could be a case for a Province to exercise restraint in relation to consecrating a woman as bishop in order to allow for wider participation in the decision-making process and to avoid making the office of bishop a centre of dispute.

549.   At this point we turned to consider other matters relating to the nature and function of the episcopate which in due course led to the writing of the remaining chapters of this Report. We intended to return later to the question of whether a woman may become a bishop. In the meantime, however, we have taken careful note of the events which have since taken place. The first of these was the response of the House of Bishops to the Primates' Working Party.

b.   The submission of the English House of Bishops

550.   In July 1987 the House of Bishops in England passed the following resolutions, which were sent to the Primates' Working Party to be put together with the responses from other Provinces:

> 1. The House of Bishops welcomes the statement on *Women in the Episcopate* agreed by the Primates' Meeting, Toronto, March 1986, and endorses its request to the Archbishop of Canterbury for consultation on this matter between the Provinces of the Anglican Communion.
> 2.   The House of Bishops recognises the inter-relatedness of the theological issues raised by both the ordination of women to the presbyterate and episcopate, but it also notes that the question of the ordination of women to the episcopate is only likely to become a live issue in a Province if and when that Province has a mature experience of women priests otherwise suitable for consideration for the episcopate.

---

[13]   On parity of ministry, see paras. 70, 121, 139, 185. This of course classifies issues of continuity, authority, unity and collegiality as ecclesiological.

[14]   On this point we agreed with the House of Bishops' Report, *The Ordination of Women to the Priesthood*, GS 764.

3. The House of Bishops considers that within the theological issues - e.g. 'headship' and 'representation' - ecclesiology is especially relevant to any consideration of women in the episcopate; it draws particular attention to para 42 of the House of Bishops' Report, *The Ordination of Women to the Priesthood* (GS 764):

> Although not strictly within our remit, the question of the consecration of women as bishops was seen to be closely related to the ordination of women to the presbyterate and to the considerations relating to that legislation. It is very difficult to sustain an argument for any essential sacramental distinction between the presbyterate and the episcopate such as to put in doubt the possibility of a woman's admission to the episcopate once the presbyterate has been granted. However, on grounds of the authority of jurisdiction which belongs to a bishop and the scriptural issues of headship, some might want to argue against such consecration. Further, because of the ecclesiological role of a bishop as focus of unity within his local Church and his role as symbol and link of communion between his Church and the universal Church, it might be considered by some as inappropriate to consecrate a woman as long as some Provinces remain opposed in principle to the ordination of women. There might be considered sufficient ecclesiological reasons for caution and restraint on the question of the consecration of women to the episcopate while there is no consensus on the issue. While it is possible to legislate in the case of priests diocese by diocese, the episcopate, as bond of unity and communion between dioceses and Provinces, could not be so legislated for. Were bishops not able to recognise each other's ordination and therefore not able to act collegially, that would lead to a serious rupture in communion. We recognised that such considerations are being looked at by the Archbishops' Group on Women and the Episcopate.[15]

The House of Bishops went on to encourage the Archbishops' Group on the Episcopate and the Primates' Working Party:

> a. to continue to explore these issues, together with a consideration of the positive and negative implications for women in the Episcopate for *koinonia* within the Anglican Communion, within the developing ecumenical fellowship, and within the wider unity of humanity.
>
> b. to consider how change or development in order is received by Anglicans within the universal Church.
>
> c. to examine the implications of one Province admitting women to the episcopate in advance of other Provinces.

c.   The Grindrod Report[16]

551.   The next major event was the publication of the Report of the Primates' Working Party, *The Grindrod Report*. The first part of this Report, 'Listening as a mark of communion', summarises the responses from seventeen Provinces, including the English House of Bishops. The

---

15   That is, our present Group under its earlier title.

16   *Women and the Episcopate*, Report of the Working Party Appointed by the Primates of the Anglican Communion (Anglican Consultative Council, 1987).

evidence in 1986 showed that the Provinces were at very different points in their thinking on the issue. For some the matter was immediate and pressing; for others it was hardly as yet beginning to feature on their agenda at all. The Report illustrated the considerable diversity and the wide range of opinion in the Anglican Communion - 'it is not a simple matter of those in favour clamouring for immediate action and those against threatening a rupture in communion and demanding the issue be dropped. Amongst those against there are some eager for further discussion and exploration and even a suggestion that it might be possible to provide pastoral guidelines which would make it possible for those in favour and those against to remain in communion. Amongst those in favour there were differing views on the appropriate time scale for action. What is clear, however, from the responses is the value every Province places upon consultation and listening to other Provinces.' There was also evidence of a general acceptance of the need for restraint, at least in the period which was to elapse before the Lambeth Conference in 1988. It was accepted, too, that the Lambeth Conference itself could not decide the matter and legislate for the wider Communion. The concern of all the respondents for unity and communion was clear, as was the recognition that bishops 'hold the communion together' and that any non-recognition of episcopal ministry would inevitably mean the impairing of communion. But those who wished to proceed to consecrate a woman believed that it was necessary for the sake of mission and for their witness to the unity of men and women in the Kingdom that they should go ahead when the time seemed right locally in each Province.

552.   The main section of the *Grindrod Report* sets out five issues that any Province would need to have considered before proceeding to consecrate a woman:

- is the ordination of women to the threefold order of ministry a legitimate development of the theology and practice of ministry?
- the episcopal ministry and its relationship to the communion or fellowship of the Church
- the process of consultation and decision-making in the fellowship of the Anglican Communion
- the process of consultation and decision-making when there is division in the universal Church
- the nature of the Church and of the unity we seek as a credible sign of the Kingdom in a divided world.

553.   The Working Party was not asked to make recommendations; nor did it. But it recorded that it had been constantly struck by the importance of the theological concept of reception in the process of forming and

articulating the mind of the people of God:

> The episcopate is not the possession of an individual Province but belongs
> to the Church. Therefore any decision regarding the fundamental
> expression of the episcopate would need ultimately to be affirmed by the
> Church. Those Provinces which are convinced that it is right to
> consecrate a woman as a bishop may wish to exercise restraint because of
> the possible disruptive effects upon the Communion. Alternatively, they
> may be persuaded by compelling doctrinal reasons, by their experience of
> women in ordained ministry and by the demands of the mission of the
> Church in their region to proceed to the ordination of a woman to the
> episcopate. This would only be done with overwhelming support in the
> dioceses concerned. Such a step could only be taken within an over-
> riding acknowledgement of the need to offer such a development for
> reception, or indeed rejection, by the whole Communion and by the
> universal Church and with care and support for the women so ordained.

554.   Were a Province to ordain a woman as bishop, the Working Party
stressed:

- The development should be offered to the Anglican Communion in an
  open process of reception
- The development could not be expressed as the mind of the Church
  until it had been accepted by the whole Communion. Even then there
  would necessarily be a tentativeness about it until it had been accepted
  by the universal Church
- Consideration of the ordination of women to the presbyterate and
  episcopate within the Communion would need to continue with
  Provinces listening to one another's thoughts and experience, aiding
  one another in theological reflection and exercising mutual sensitivity
  and care
- Debate in the wider fellowship of the Churches ought to be
  encouraged, particularly within existing bilateral and multi-lateral
  dialogues.

d.   The Lambeth Conference 1988

555.   Although it had initially been anticipated that we would report in time
for the Lambeth Conference, the extension of our terms of reference and
the sequence of events to which we have already referred made this
impracticable.   We realised that the Conference itself would be of
importance not only in relation to the question of collegiality, but also in
respect of the way in which the Conference handled the subject of
maintenance of communion within the Provinces in the event of a woman
being consecrated as a bishop.

556.   In addition to the evidence contained in the *Grindrod Report,* the
bishops assembled at the Lambeth Conference heard a presentation on the
question of the ordination of women which included views of both

proponents and opponents. They also spent a day debating Resolutions on the matter brought to the Conference from the section on Mission and Ministry, designed to avoid division as far as possible and to maintain the highest possible degree of communion amongst Anglicans.

557. The Conference passed the following Resolution:[17]

This Conference resolves:

1. That each Province respect the decision and attitudes of other Provinces in the ordination or consecration of women to the episcopate, without such respect necessarily indicating acceptance of the principles involved, maintaining the highest possible degree of communion with the Provinces which differ.

2. That bishops exercise courtesy and maintain communications with bishops who may differ, and with any woman bishop, ensuring an open dialogue in the Church to whatever extent communion is impaired.

3. That the Archbishop of Canterbury, in consultation with the Primates, appoints a commission:
   a. to provide for an examination of the relationships between Provinces of the Anglican Communion and ensure that the process of reception includes continuing consultation with other Churches as well;
   b. to monitor and encourage the process of consultation within the Communion and to offer further pastoral guidelines.

4. That in any Province where reconciliation on these issues is necessary, any diocesan bishop facing this problem be encouraged to seek continuing dialogue with, and make pastoral provision for, those clergy and congregations whose opinions differ from those of the bishop, in order to maintain the unity of the diocese.

5. Recognises the serious hurt which would result from the questioning by some of the validity of the episcopal acts of a woman bishop, and likewise the hurt experienced by those whose conscience would be offended by the ordination of a woman to the episcopate. The Church needs to exercise sensitivity, patience and pastoral care towards all concerned.

The Resolution was passed by 423 votes in favour, 28 against and 19 bishops abstaining.

558. We noted that the effect of the Resolution was to leave open the possibility of different views being held upon the theological acceptability of a woman being consecrated as bishop, because it was said that respect did not 'necessarily' indicate 'acceptance of the principles involved'. Similarly, the Commission set up by the Archbishop of Canterbury in accordance with the request made in the Lambeth Resolution was not asked to adjudicate between or within Provinces on the question of the ordination of women to the priesthood and episcopate as such. Rather, its mandate was to discover

17   Resolution I.

how Anglicans can live in the highest possible degree of communion with differences of principle and practice on the ordination of women to the episcopate.[18] The bishops of the Anglican Communion did not, therefore, as a forum assembled in a collegial way at Lambeth, seek to give any definitive guidance on the subject of the theological acceptability of the ordination of women. Their concern was ecclesiological, and to do with the maintenance of communion. This has left the Church of England and the Churches of the Provinces within the Anglican Communion with freedom to make up their own minds on the subject but with the knowledge that any decision, whether for or against the ordination of women to the presbyterate or the episcopate, will have implications in respect of the shared communion between the churches.

e.   A woman bishop

559. By the time that the Commission, under the chairmanship of the Primate of All Ireland, the Most Reverend Robert Eames, held its first meeting in November 1988, the possibility of women among the *episcopoi* had become a reality. The Reverend Barbara Harris had been elected an assistant bishop in the diocese of Massachusetts: that election awaited confirmation. By the time of the second meeting of the Commission in March 1989, the election had been confirmed and Barbara Harris was consecrated the first woman bishop in the Anglican Communion on 11th February 1989. There has since followed the consecration of a woman as a diocesan bishop in New Zealand. The Reverend Dr. Penelope Jamieson was consecrated and installed as the seventh Bishop of Dunedin on 29th June 1990.

f.   The Eames Commission

560. The Eames Commission, like our Group, had a membership which reflected differing views on the subject of women in ordained ministry, and there has indeed been an overlap of membership. The difficult task of the Commission was to try to discover the language and context in which Anglicans can continue to live together, and they recognised that the study of communion - *koinonia* - was therefore central to their work.

---

18   *Report* of the Archbishop of Canterbury's Commission on the Communion and Women in the Episcopate, 1989 (Eames Commission), p. 7.

561.   Just as we have felt the pain of bitter disagreement within our Group, so the Commission has experienced and been conscious of the pain generated by the present state of disagreement within the Anglican Communion. But its members were able to see ground for hope that the spirit of courtesy and respect spoken of by the 1988 Lambeth Conference 'will create a profound unity and communion beyond that which the world knows', even in the midst of 'tension, debate and pain':

> If those who find the *exclusion* of women from the priesthood and episcopate contrary to an understanding of God's justice and the meaning of the Incarnation, and those who find their *inclusion* an unacceptable development of the apostolic ministry, can come together to share each other's burdens and sufferings, then the Anglican Communion will have learned something of the meaning of communion with the God who suffers. And we shall have something to say about the unity of Christians and the unity of all humankind.[19]

562.   The Eames Report explores the nature of the communion of the Church, a communion grounded in the mystery of God's own life of communion and love, and maintained and served by various elements of visible communion, the gifts of the risen Christ to the Church. The Report recognises the ministry, and particularly the episcopal ministry, to be a special bond of unity working together with other bonds of communion. It makes the point that ecclesial communion has never been perfect. From the beginning of the Church there have been strains on communion and breaks in communion. The modern ecumenical movement, with its attempts to re-establish ecclesial communion, has contributed the insight that, in spite of disagreements leading to divisions, the Christian churches as they work towards unity still have much which binds them together in their common baptism and its implications; they are not 'out of communion' but share a communion which is only partial. Moreover, in a divided Church, all ministry lacks the fullness which would pertain to a single ministry in a united Church and may therefore in some sense be described as 'provisional'.[20] The growing awareness in the wider ecumenical debate that we are not 'out of communion' with our brothers and sisters of other churches is an important lesson to apply to internal Anglican communion and unity. In a situation in which it is clear that there is division of opinion and now of practice over the consecration of a woman as bishop, the Eames Report seeks to chart ways in which Anglicans may live together in love and in the highest possible degree of communion where there has been a failure of mutual recognition of ministry.

19   *Ibid.*, p. 8.
20   On 'provisionality' see later in this chapter, under 'Decision-making and reception'.

g. Provincial Autonomy and Interdependence

563.   With a view to encouraging that spirit of 'respect' and 'courtesy' and
the continuing communication called for by the Lambeth Resolution, the
Commission produced guidelines related to key elements in the exercise of
episcopal ministry.[21]   In doing so they touched upon the key technical
questions of parallel jurisdiction, Episcopal Visitors and collegial
participation in ordinations.

(i) Parallel jurisdiction
The Commission considered the question of episcopal care provided by the
creation of non-territorial 'dioceses' for congregations unwilling to receive
the pastoral care of a woman bishop or priest.   Because such proposals
would set up a separate and parallel episcopal jurisdiction within a single
diocesan territory, the Commission firmly rejected them, emphasizing the
importance of the bishop as a symbol of unity.[22]

(ii) Episcopal Visitors
Within Provinces where women have been made bishops while there
remains a body of Anglicans opposed to the move, the Eames Commission
suggested that Episcopal Visitors should be appointed to minister to those in
a diocese unable to accept either the ministrations of a woman bishop, or the
ministrations of a diocesan who has himself taken part in the consecration of
a woman bishop.[23]   As envisaged, there was to be a transitional arrangement
under which the Presiding Bishop had a discretion to designate members of
the House of Bishops to act as Episcopal Visitors to provide episcopal,
sacramental acts for congregations upon the request and under the authority
and direction of the Ecclesiastical Authority of a Diocese.   The Eames
Commission defended such a scheme from an ecclesiological perspective 'as
a necessary and strictly extraordinary anomaly in preference to schism'.

21   Reproduced in full in Appendix III (b).
22   The unity of the diocese as 'the Church in each place with its bishop' is paramount here.
     As the Report points out, successive Lambeth Conferences have set their face against
     parallel Anglican jurisdictions. 'Suspicion of parallel jurisdictions seems soundly based in
     an ecclesiology of "communion" which sees the bishop as the sacramental representative of
     the whole local ecclesial community, and that community itself as truly grounded in its
     social context and culture. The classical definition of schism was indeed the setting up of
     rival episcopal thrones in the same community', *Eames Report*, 38.
23   A proposal for Episcopal Visitors had already been debated in the Episcopal Church in the
     United States of America. For different reasons, it had met with opposition from both
     sides.

(iii) Collegial ordination

It was clear to the Commission that some people may feel unable to recognise the validity of ordinations by a woman bishop; and in some Provinces it is not at present possible to give canonical recognition to those ordained elsewhere by a woman bishop. To protect the interest of the ordinands, the Commission recommended that for a certain period a male bishop should participate in ordinations carried out by a female bishop.

h. The Primates' Meeting, May 1989

564. The Eames Report was well received by the Primates of the Anglican Communion at their meeting in Larnaca, Cyprus in May 1989, and they commended it to the Provinces for study. The Primates supported the Commission's rejection of parallel jurisdiction. They were in favour of the proposal that the provision ECUSA sought to make for Episcopal Visitors should be looked at sympathetically. However, they rejected the suggestion that male bishops should participate in ordinations involving a woman bishop, on the ground that such a suggestion was 'demeaning to women'. The practical consequence of this rejection is that not even all male presbyters in the Anglican Communion in future will share a mutually recognised ministry.

i. The Eames Commission's Report of March 1990

565. The main thrust of the Report produced by the Eames Commission at what is expected at present to be its final meeting, has been to seek to provide in more detail for the needs which are arising now that the first woman diocesan bishop has been consecrated. The aim is to 'hold the minority in communion, even though that communion be restricted'. Practical provision in the form of Episcopal Visitors is envisaged. These would 'have authority from the Primate within the collegiality of the House of Bishops'.[24] Implications for the maintenance of collegial fellowship in Provinces with women bishops are also considered, with the understanding that full collegiality may in some places give way to restricted collegiality. It is pointed out that in all cases of the making of a woman bishop correct

---

24 It should be noted that this proposal has a number of implications for the authority of the Primate. Cf. on primacy, paras. 83, 102, 124-5, 127, 147, 281, 321 ff.

canonical procedures will have been followed.[25] We note finally that the Eames Commission asks for restraint in two ways: that 'dissenting priests and congregations' shall 'recognise and maximise all that they continue to share' with other Anglicans; and that individuals should refrain from making personal statements about the breaking of Communion, but should leave such statements to be made at provincial level.

II.   Our reflections

566.   We have referred at some length to recent events in their context within the Church because of the encouragement we received from the House of Bishops to consider the ecclesiological implications relating to the consecration of women to the episcopate. It is to these ecclesiological considerations that we now turned in our work as a Group.

567.   We take as a basis here the list of key elements in the exercise of episcopal ministry cited by the Eames Commission from the Mission and Ministry text of the 1988 Lambeth Conference Report. The bishop is said to be:

(a)   a symbol of the Unity of the Church in its mission;
(b)   a teacher and defender of the faith;
(c)   a pastor of the pastors and of the laity;
(d)   an enabler in the preaching of the Word, and in the administration of the Sacraments;
(e)   a leader in mission and an initiator of outreach to the world surrounding the community of the faithful;
(f)   a shepherd who nurtures and cares for the flock of God;
(g)   a physician to whom are brought the wounds of society;
(h)   a voice of conscience within the society in which the local church is placed;
(i)   a prophet who proclaims the Justice of God in the context of the Gospel of loving redemption;
(j)   a head of the family in its wholeness, its misery and its joy. The bishop is the family's centre of life and love.[26]

To these we would add the two further elements of the bishop's role as a link to the universal Church by holding communion with the episcopate as a whole, and as one who symbolizes and effects continuity as a link in a

25   There are questions here about the 'bindingness' of legislative decisions in matters of faith and order, which we touch on in section c iii following.
26   Already quoted, para. 270.

historic chain. For reasons which emerged in our earlier debate, some of our Group would regard these key functions as precluding a woman, at least at present, from being a bishop, whereas for others amongst us there is no reason to be found among them why a woman should not exercise this episcopal ministry.

a. Communion and episcopacy

568. The debate in the Anglican Communion so far has illustrated the importance of setting the question of women and the episcopate within a wider understanding of the fundamental nature of the Church as communion, a communion grounded in the mystery of Trinitarian life. The ordained ministry, in particular the episcopal ministry, needs to be seen as one of the bonds of that communion.

569. The bishop as personal focus of unity is crucial here. Any decision taken on the consecration of a woman as bishop must therefore consider the effect such a development has upon the unity and communion of the Church. We have already pointed out that the consequence of non-recognition of the validity of ordinations conducted by a woman bishop is that certain presbyters within the Anglican Communion will not for the foreseeable future share a mutually recognised ministry. Exchange of ministries in ecclesial communion is consequently restricted and weakened, even though the fracture in the unity of the ministry cannot destroy at its deepest level the communion which exists between those baptised into the life of God.

570. Within our Group and elsewhere it is clear that both those who favour the consecration of women and those who hold to the tradition of the Church have a regard for unity: both the unity of the Church in the world and the unity of the Kingdom of which the Church is sign, instrument and foretaste. In this perspective, it cannot properly be asserted that those who press for development are disregarding the importance of maintaining unity, and those who refrain are safeguarding unity. It is essentially a difference concerning the aspects of unity which ought to be given priority. On one side there are those who emphasise the gravity of fragmenting further an already divided Church and of slowing ecumenical progress towards a future united Church. On the other side are those who believe that the episcopate would gain a wholeness, and would necessarily become a more convincing sign of the unity of the Kingdom, if women were included.

b.   The bishop as focus of unity and continuity

571.   The essential task of the episcopal office, we have argued throughout this Report, is to maintain the Church in unity, a task carried out and symbolised on 'three planes': first in relation to the local community; secondly in relating the local community to the wider Church; and thirdly in relating the local community to the Church throughout the ages.

572.   The bishop is the *representative person in the local eucharistic community*, focussing and guarding the unity of that community. Some maintain, within our Group and elsewhere, on the basis of the 'icon of Christ' argument which is sometimes drawn from Scripture, that a woman could never fulfil such a role as head of the eucharistic community, and *a fortiori*, as bishop. The argument in favour of a headship which sees man as head over woman as Christ is head of the Church, would also, for some, preclude a woman from acting as head of the local community. There remains a question at the sacramental level. A sign or symbol if it is to convey something of the reality it represents, must bear a clear resemblance to it. The celebrant at the Eucharist (the focal act of unity of the community), who is the bishop or the priest as his delegate, acts 'in the name of Christ'.[27]   Some would argue that this precludes Eucharistic presidency being confided to a woman. However, if none of these arguments is thought to carry weight, then it is difficult to find any reason why a woman should not represent a local community in just the same way as a man may do.

573.   On the level of the second plane, *the bishop is the link between the local community and other local communities*, representing his people to the wider Church and the wider Church to his people. We fail to understand why, if the cultural context does not militate against it, a woman should not fulfil this function just as adequately and ably as a man. Moreover, some would argue that when the bishops gather together collegially to guard the faith and guide the Church, there is something anachronistic in the late twentieth century about an all male episcopate, particularly when the matters under discussion concern the ministry of women, or certain areas of human sexuality. This is not to say that men may not represent women (any more than that a woman cannot represent men) but to suggest that a balance and

27   Cf. II Corinthians 2.10, and cf. para. 29.

wholeness of experience is excluded from the debate when those who take part in it are all of one sex, be that male or female. On the other hand, whilst neither all the bishops in the Anglican Communion nor the episcopates of the great Episcopal Churches of East and West can recognize the consecration of a woman as bishop, it is *de facto* the position that a woman bishop cannot link her community fully to all others.

574. In this 'second plane' of *episcope*, the bishop has a profoundly important role in relating the gathered people of God in the diocese to the secular community in which they are set. Here the bishop is the spearhead of mission, and the key issues concern whether the good news of the Kingdom is more powerfully expressed and more truthfully proclaimed by an episcopate which includes women, or the reverse. Some would say that a Church which excludes any on grounds of gender from the most authoritative roles of leadership, by its own example vitiates the authenticity and credibility of the news it proclaims, that God has made a bridge between the divided and healed the fractures of the world. Others would say that to consecrate women to the episcopate would be further to fracture the Church and therefore to act against the spirit of unity and healing which is God's gift: thus too the power of the Church's proclamation might be seen as vitiated, and her mission undermined.

575. No internal debate even on such an important issue as the ordination of women should be allowed to deflect the Church's energy from pursuing the primary calling of proclaiming God's saving purposes. Unity and mission are obverse and reverse of the same calling.

576. The bishop also focuses the *continuity of the Church from the Apostles* through the ages. It is obvious that because the Apostles were all men, to include women in the episcopate would be to make a change in, or at least to modify, the sign of continuity. A view as to the significance of this must be taken. As we have pointed out, some see the change as a fundamental and unacceptable break with the tradition; others believe the inclusion of women in the episcopate would strengthen the sign of apostolicity, making the representation of all humanity more whole and more credible in the mission of the Church for which the bishop has a special ministry. Since the inclusion of women in the episcopal order creates large problems of non-recognition both for major partners in ecumenical dialogue and also for the internal unity of the Anglican Communion, it must be taken for granted that the issue will require a very long time to reach a resolution.

c.   Decision-making and Reception

577.   An important part of the discussion on women and priesthood and women and the episcopate, has concerned the manner in which the Church can arrive at decisions on the subject.   The matter is a complex one not only because Anglican structures of decision making are still evolving but also because the Anglican Communion is only one part of the universal Church, attempting to form a mind on the ministry which belongs to the whole Church.   The concept of reception (on which we have touched in Chapter 10)[28] is one on which serious reflection will be needed by the Church of England in forming its mind on women and the episcopate.   We therefore give it further space here.

578.   While legally binding decisions[29] can be made at the level of a Province, there has also been recent growing recognition that decisions on matters of faith and order must take into account the interdependence of the Provinces of the Anglican Communion and the position of all the Christian Churches.   It is in this recognition that, in the recent debate on the consecration of women as bishops, much has been made of the need to see the legislative decision of any particular Province within a much wider, longer and more complex process of reception.

579.   What we must not lose sight of here, of course, is that 'reception' has been a process over centuries, and in trying to resolve points of difference in faith and order between the Churches we have all been painfully engaged on it since the enduring divisions of the fifth century.   This particular issue of the reception of women's ministry is but one further aspect of the difficult process by which we are slowly seeking to move towards 'receiving' each other's ministry, in the Churches.

i.   Acceptability

580.   Particularly at issue here are the theological appropriateness and the acceptability to the Christian community of women in performing the tasks of priests and bishops.   There can be reception only of what is acceptable, although it is not necessarily the case that what is unacceptable in a given age will always be unreceived.   Development is possible here.   Some would

---

28   See Chapter 10, section on 'The bishop as guardian of faith and order'.
29   See paras. 264 and 272 ff.

argue that sharing in the teaching ministry of the Church should be distinguished from discharging its teaching office; yet women have, for example, come to play a comparatively uncontroversial role in sharing in the teaching ministry of the Church, although, according to one school of Biblical interpretation, St. Paul thought they should not speak in Church.

581. The theological questions we have to answer concern the weight to be placed upon the acceptability to the community at a given time, (i) of decisions on this matter of order which will affect the whole community; and (ii) of the actual ministry of the women who are placed, by the implementation of such decisions, in a new role in relation to that community. These are distinct issues. The first has to do with what makes decision-making in the Church 'binding', that is, received and accepted by the community of the faithful. The second is sacramental, and has to do with the validity of acts of the Church through a minister who cannot be accepted by the whole community as having been placed in the necessary special relationship to that community.

582. It is at present the case that a woman is not acceptable to many members of the Anglican Communion as a priest or bishop.[30] As we have indicated,[31] the validity of ordination normally depends upon the action of the Holy Spirit in conveying the gift of oversight; the faithful transmission of the Gospel within the Christian community; the acceptance of the community; and the transmission, by those authorized for the task, of the commission for ministry which Christ gave to the apostles. While the first, second and fourth of these conditions may to many be self-evidently present in the consecration of a woman bishop (as in America and New Zealand), there must clearly be, in the present circumstances, questions for some about the validity in such cases of the consecration of a woman bishop, because of the problems which attend acceptance by the whole community, even locally. For many, the fact that such a consecration cannot have a pure 'universal intention' (that is, of creating a bishop 'in the Church of God'), undermines its validity. For others the fact that there is not at present universal mutual recognition of ministry in the Church means that no such 'universal intention' is possible; for the recent impairment of communion among Anglicans has to be set in the context of the existing lack of full

---

30   This poses in more acute form some of the difficulties which already exist because of the inability of some Churches to recognize the orders of some other Churches, thus making universal mutual recognition and reconciliation of ministry impossible at present. See the following Chapter on *Ecumenical Progress*.

31   See paras. 174 ff.

communion and mutual recognition between divided Churches.[32] For those who look at the matter in this way, the validity of a woman bishop's consecration is therefore as complete as that of any existing bishop.[33]

583. Against this indication that there must be some uncertainty over the validity of an episcopal ministry commissioned in these circumstances, may be set a principle touched on in Article 26 of the Thirty-Nine Articles. In keeping with Western tradition since Augustine, this Article states that it is 'Christ's institution and promise' which makes the sacraments 'effectual'. As Augustine puts it, 'it is Christ who baptises', and this would seem to imply that God acts to ensure a true sacramental life for his people even where the ordinary safeguards have in part broken down and their ministers are imperfect in their ministry. So if a woman bishop, even of exemplary character, and duly administering the sacraments, might by some be deemed to require in present circumstances some such special intervention in order that her ministry of the sacraments may not be invalidated by the incomplete acceptance of the community, it is patently arguable that this is guaranteed by God. Ministries clearly of the Spirit (the Old Testament prophets; the charismatic ministries of the early Church) have come to be accepted even though they were not regularly commissioned within the community. In a rather different way, ministries instituted in what was seen at the time as an 'emergency situation' (as, for example, Luther's proposed arrangements for the Bohemians), have come in time to be accepted in the wider Church as blessed by the Spirit.

584. Fruitfulness is a sign of the Spirit's commissioning.[34] It may be - and there are indications in the Episcopal Church's experience of women priests in the United States of America and Canada over more than a decade that this could happen - that this evidence of the blessing of the Spirit will help to resolve the questions which face us in time by making the ordained ministry of women acceptable to the whole community.

585. We come to the test of time. Here we have to take a long view. The apostolic warrant can and must be seen not only in terms of derivation from the beginning, but also in terms of the eschatological hope of the Church. 'The ecclesial ministry ... will ... be apostolic because the eucharistic

---

32 'Impaired communion' has come to have the clear and limited meaning of the impairment of a state of full communion existing up to now.
33 On 'universal intention' see further under 'legislative decisions' in section iii following.
34 ORC, 5.

assembly at which the minister presides is an anticipation of the final community with Christ'.[35] That is the final test of acceptability, for as ministry in the Church reveals Christ's presence and the Spirit's work and looks to the coming of the Kingdom[36] it wins acceptance. Validity cannot be a matter of assertion, still less of self-assertion. Acceptance cannot be compelled. It is bound only 'to the eschatological reality of the Kingdom'[37].

ii.   Provisionality

586.   The Eames Commission speaks of 'provisionality'. The term seems likely to be much used in the continuing debate, and so we offer some reflections on it here. We must begin by distinguishing three applications of the term 'provisionality':

   a. The 'provisionality' of an imperfect ministry in the present divided state of the Church.
   b. The 'provisionality' of legislative decisions made where there is not a settled consensus.
   c. The 'provisionality' of a ministry whose validity may subsequently be brought into question as development in the Church proceeds.

587.   Within the community of faith, where there is divided conviction, matters must be open either to subsequent affirmation or to subsequent rejection. That has always been the Church's way. Talk of the provisionality or openness of the process of reception refers to the fact that the community under the Holy Spirit has the continuing opportunity of deciding upon the acceptability of a particular development. In the meantime, a synodical decision 'must be respected on all sides as a considered judgement of that particular representative gathering'.[38] It is provisional only in the sense that any legislation can be revoked and replaced by further legislation. In matters of faith, mistakes can be put right. In matters of order, such as the ordination of women to the priesthood and especially to the episcopate, the possibility of subsequent rejection or alteration of a legislative decision raises peculiar difficulties, for an ordained woman is a fact not a belief. If ordination is for life, as Anglicans believe,[39] an ordained woman cannot be deemed to be ordained priest or consecrated bishop 'provisionally', even if the legislation which

---

35	ORC, 14
36	Cf. ORC, 10
37	ORC, 11, cf. 22
38	*Report* of the Archbishop's Commission on Communion and Women in the Episcopate (1989) (Eames Commission), 29.
39	See para. 173.

permits her ordination is itself deemed 'provisional'. A woman can hardly be ordained on the understanding that her ordination, and therefore the sacraments she administers, are in some way uncertain. Nor would it be easy to unravel the problem of ordinations by a woman bishop of priests (male or female) whose ordination is not recognized by some of their flock.

iii.   *Legislative decisions*

588.   The decisions of general or universal Councils may be seen as points of formal articulation of what has been heard and agreed; they have been tested by time and consent, and, in the case of the first four General Councils, their decisions on matters of faith have continued to be accepted by Christians of every tradition.[40] The decisions of Provincial or national synods or councils present a different problem because they are not necessarily made with universal reference,[41] and sometimes not with universal intention.[42] This is unavoidably the case where one Anglican Province acts unilaterally in deciding to ordain women to the priesthood or to the episcopate, in the knowledge that other Provinces do not yet do so and may decide against doing so.

589.   Where such a decision is upon a matter of order rather than of faith, it presents the further problem that the local legislative decision creates a breach of mutual recognition in the ordained ministry. The common sacramental life in which all Anglicans have hitherto been able to share is impaired, where not all Anglicans are able in conscience to accept the ministry of all those ordained within the Anglican Communion. A further task is added to that of listening to the Holy Spirit and forming a common mind: that of discovering means of reconciling ministries and restoring mutual recognition.

590.   Some members of our Group believe that the room for dissent is small and that reception is not so much an 'open' process but a pathway to acceptance of a synodical decision into the life of the Church. On this view, once a legislative decision has been made it must then be respected. Others

40   With the exception of the non-Chalcedonian Churches which were unable to endorse the Christological formula of the Council of Chalcedon in 451.
41   The first Provinces, which came into being in the fourth century, were an administrative convenience, allowing regional conciliar meetings of bishops to legislate for local needs in matters of purely local concern.
42   Intention and consequence may be two different things, and it is of course possible to act with universal intention but find that divisive consequences follow.

of us would wish to set legislation within the context of the theology of reception we have been outlining, and to emphasize that ecclesiastical law is capable of amendment.

vii. Room for dissent

591. We note that the Eames Commission was careful to limit the extent of the expression of dissent which would be permissible.

> Dissenting priests and congregations must, for their part, not go as far as to refuse canonical recognition to their diocesan bishop or to say they are not in communion with their ordinary. This would mean that their position would have to fall short of maintaining that the Church could never admit women to the priesthood or episcopate.[43]

Many of us feel that such a distinction between total and partial dissent would be undesirable and unworkable in practice in this country. Furthermore, its original context was the position of male bishops who were ordaining women to the priesthood and taking part in their consecration to the episcopate; the position of a woman diocesan bishop raises further issues. Others amongst us, while recognising that the scope for expression of dissent must be limited, hold that with a matter which involves the ministry of the universal Church, any provincial decisions necessarily have to be received within the wider Anglican Communion and within the universal Church, and that until a consensus is reached in this wider Christian fellowship provision for dissent must be made. For them a system such as that of the 'Episcopal Visitor' would be a way of providing space for continuing dissent within the open process of reception. For some of us the special relationship of the bishop and the local community which we have emphasized, and our very different geographical situations in England makes the concept of an Episcopal Visitor unacceptable on practical grounds, but other members of our Group would regard Episcopal Visitors, with due safeguards, as a helpful provision.

592. Like the Eames Commission, we see a number of objections to any suggestion of parallel jurisdiction, or the creation of 'non-territorial' bishops. In both cases the idea runs counter to the concept of the bishop as

---

43   Cf. para. 42 of *Report* of 1989. This point has been repeated in the Supplementary Report issued by the Commission in April, 1990, para. 5 (f).

the representative of the whole local community within his diocese.[44]

d.   The role of the Archbishop of Canterbury

593.   In the most recent letter of Pope John Paul II to the Archbishop of Canterbury, the Pope drew attention to the 'delicate nature' of the Archbishop's position. 'As Archbishop of Canterbury', he wrote, 'you also represent the Anglican Communion in its relations with the Catholic Churches. He observed that 'a highly problematic situation could certainly arise for those Provinces opposed to women's ordination if there were women priests in the Church of England'. The Roman Catholic Church is, of course, in dialogue with the entire Anglican Communion and not just with the Church of England; but we recognise the anxiety of the Pope over the Archbishop of Canterbury's special position in relation to the Church of England itself.

594.   The Archbishop of Canterbury, then, has a special role in relation to the Church of England, the whole Anglican Communion and within the ecumenical movement. Each of these roles needs to be safeguarded. We regard as wise the suggestions of the Eames Commission in relation to the present situation: namely, that like all other bishops the Archbishop of Canterbury 'should conform as much as possible to the customs of a Province which he is visiting, while at the same time, he should uphold the canonical position of his own Church as well as the common mind of the House of Bishops of the Church of England on the matter'. However, we recognise that if the Church of England were to ordain and consecrate women as bishops it is unthinkable that the Archbishop of Canterbury should not recognise those women bishops.

e.   In conclusion

595.   We have explained earlier in this chapter that we were able to agree that many of the theological issues arising in connection with the question of the consecration of women as bishops are the same as those which arise in relation to the question of the ordination of women as priests. The issue of women and the episcopate is therefore inseparable from the debate on

---

[44]   There do, however, exist precedents within the Anglican Communion, for example in New Zealand's provision for Maori bishopric, and bishops for the Armed Forces in the Church of England.

women and the priesthood. It is also in practice the case that only when a decision has been made that the admission of women to the priesthood is a legitimate development of the historic ministry that there can be experience of women in the priestly ministry.[45]

596. We must return finally to this aspect of the question. If the Church of England were to make a decision to admit women to the priesthood, then members of our Group agree with the House of Bishops that it is difficult to sustain an argument for any distinction between the presbyterate and the episcopate of a kind which would put in doubt the possibility of a woman's admission to the episcopate once the presbyterate has been granted. In any case, should the Church of England ordain women to the presbyterate we would expect that after some years of experience of women ministering as priests a woman would come forward for consecration as a bishop. However we recognise that there are some who, on the grounds of the authority of the jurisdiction that belongs to a bishop, or the responsibility that rests pastorally with an incumbent, would be unable in the light of their interpretation of Biblical passages about male headship to accept women as bishops or incumbents, even if they might be willing to accept them as priests.[46]

597. We have made it clear that when we first considered the question of women in the episcopate we found that we were divided on the question of women and the priesthood and hence inevitably divided on the question of women and the episcopate. Returning in the concluding months of our work together to the question of whether a woman may ever become a bishop, we find ourselves still divided.

598. Some of us, having worked through the long process of study and discussion, and accepting that the ecclesiological considerations are part of the theological argument, wish to affirm that we see no sustainable theological arguments against the consecration of women as bishops and that we consider that any woman consecrated through prayer and the laying on of hands with the authority of any Province of the Anglican Communion would be as truly and fully a bishop in the Church of God as any man so consecrated. We recognise that this conviction in itself does not justify the consecration of a woman but it is one fundamental element in the process by

---

45   The Church of England has, of course, good experience already of women deacons.
46   In principle it is of course possible to pass legislation at one time allowing both for the ordination of women as priests and their consecration as bishops (cf. Canada and Ireland).

which a Province would come to the decision that it was the right time for it to take such action.

599. Amongst those of us who take such a view, there are differences of opinion about whether women priests and bishops should at the present time be allowed to exercise their ministry when visiting this country. Some of us believe that they should be so allowed. Others hold that it is right, despite the pain which may be inflicted by non-recognition of such ministry, to maintain the General Synod's decision not to allow such ministrations, so as to give time and space in which the Church of England can make up its own mind.

600. Others amongst us see no theological objections to the ordination of women but argue that until the Church as a whole reaches a consensus in favour of ordination we ought not to go ahead.

601. There are others of us who remain opposed to the ordination of women in the episcopate on the grounds set out in the House of Bishops' *Second Report on the Ordination of Women to the Priesthood*.[47] The arguments against women as priests are also seen, in an ecclesiological context, as arguments against consecrating women bishops.

602. For some of us who are opponents on these grounds, a decision to make women priests or bishops ought only to be made within a much larger consensus. Whatever other Provinces may choose to do, they believe that the Church of England ought not to take a decision on its own, without the widest ecumenical consensus, to change the tradition of the Church. To others of us the ordination of women to the episcopate will always be wrong, on theological grounds.

603. Although we have been unable to reach a common mind, we have valued the fact that we have been involved in a debate which is being taken so seriously in the Anglican Communion, and with a determination on the part of all involved to maintain the highest degree of communion in spite of differences of opinion and also practice, in respect of women and the episcopate. We have been struck by how much both sides hold in common, how much agreement they share on the ministry of the Church and particularly upon the episcopal ministry as an essential bond of communion, focus of unity and sign of continuity.

---

[47] See earlier in this chapter.

604.   We have been encouraged to note the role that the bishops are playing in discerning and guiding the mind of the Church in this matter, a role which properly belongs to bishops in an episcopally-led Church. The referral of the matter to the Primates' Meeting by ECUSA in 1986, the subsequent reflection of the Grindrod Working Party, the leadership of the College of Bishops at the Lambeth Conference, the setting up of the Eames Commission, all show the bishops in the Anglican Communion taking a lead, while the Report of the English House of Bishops and their role in framing legislation on the ordination of women to the priesthood, and of a Code of Practice in England, shows us an episcopate performing what we believe to be their proper role in seeking to discern and articulate the mind of their people and in guiding the Church.

14

Ecumenical progress

605. We spoke in an earlier chapter about the convergence which is emerging ecumenically in the Churches' thinking about *episcope* and episcopacy, and the remaining areas of incomplete agreement. We believe it to be important that ecumenical conversations should continue to work towards removing old stumbling-blocks. We should like to see full continuing commitment of the Church of England, and of the whole Anglican Communion, to the study of the ministry of oversight in conversation with other Churches at every level; and especially of the role of episcopacy in enabling the restoration of communion in a future united Church.

606. In this connection, we turn now to a series of practical moves of recent years towards the consummation of a unity which will allow Christians to come together in a shared Eucharist in one Body of Christ.

a. Mutual Recognition and Reconciliation of Ministries

607. Christians can meet at the Lord's Supper only where they share ecclesially a ministry of Word and Sacrament led by an ordained ministry all can recognize to be authentically commissioned. Mutual 'recognition' of ministries involves the acceptance by one ecclesial community of the commissioning of the ordained ministries of another. Such recognition may be full or only partial. But even where it is unequivocal it does not necessarily lead to the reconciliation of ministries which unites separated Churches.[1] We must look not only to recognition, then, but also to reconciliation.

608. The role of the episcopate in ordination has been a major focus of all conversations between Anglican and both episcopal and non-episcopal Churches designed to bring about mutual recognition of ministry, with the possibility of reconciliation to follow. Non-episcopal Churches have been

---

[1] The Roman Catholic and Orthodox Churches are a case in point.

anxious to ensure that no defect in their existing ministries is implied; Anglicans, that they do not lose the historic episcopate in union with non-episcopal Churches. Proposed resolutions of these difficulties have usually involved the non-episcopal Churches taking episcopacy in some form into their system. With other episcopal Churches the issues are different. The Roman Catholic Church has not recognised the validity of Anglican orders since the sixteenth century, although in recent years the old objections to their doing so have begun to disappear.[2] In the case of the Orthodox Churches the problems are deeper and ecclesiologically more complex. With neither of these Communions have any practical steps yet been taken towards the reconciliation of ministries. We therefore concentrate in what follows upon a series of attempts, so far unsuccessful, to achieve such reconciliation between Anglicans and other Churches.

i.   *Attempts to achieve reconciliation of ministries within England*

609   In the proposed Service of Reconciliation between Anglican and Methodist Churches in England in the early 1960s the intention was to achieve 'formal reception of the members and ministries of each Church by accredited representatives of the other, performed in such a way as will enable each member to communicate and each bishop, priest and minister to officiate in either Church'. But the statement of intention was thought ambiguous, as, to some degree, were the actions to take place in the Service. Both groups of ministers were to 'submit' themselves to God, 'praying that our Lord Jesus will renew the gifts that he has given to us all, and will enable each of us to enter into that which he has given to the other', defined as 'the spiritual heritage' of the Methodists and 'the spiritual heritage and continuity of commission' of the Anglicans, respectively.[3] The Anglican bishop was to lay his hands on the head of each minister and say 'Take authority to exercise the office of a priest'. This could certainly be interpreted as an act of ordination; but it need not be so interpreted. And any implication of deficiency in either or both ministry might be taken to be redeemed in the humble submission of all present to the will of God for their united ministry, without being read as a failure of respect and

---

2   Cf. paras. 229 ff.
3   Conversations between the Church of England and the Methodist Church, *Report* (London, 1963), p. 38.

acceptance of the other's ordained ministry by either Church.[4] It was stressed that 'no denial of any gift or grace already received is intended on either side'. 'The [proposed] Service of Reconciliation proceeds on the assumption that' neither Church 'wishes to call in question the reality and spiritual effectiveness of the ministry of the other Church'.[5]

610. The assumption that each ministry represents and embodies a distinctive heritage which could be given to and received by the other presents a further difficulty. If this is taken to mean that each style and pattern of Church life makes a valuable contribution to the whole, the claim is uncontroversial. Any other construction put upon it would seem to imply that the ministries to be reconciled were formerly something less than fully ministries 'in the Church of God'.[6] And that, in turn, would have implications for the two Churches' acceptance of one another as ecclesial communities within that one Church.[7]

611. These three points: the role of episcopal ordination in a service of reconciliation of existing ministries; the question of implied defect in existing ordained ministries; the question whether full mutual ecclesial recognition ought to imply both the ceasing to exist of either Church as a distinct ecclesial entity and the automatic recognition of ministries duly and regularly commissioned in each by the other, remain crucial.

612. Some lingering sense of the importance of the participating Churches retaining separate identities in a scheme of reunion was perhaps still to be found in the Covenant proposals of 1980. There, it was suggested that those exercising oversight in non-episcopal Churches were to be 'identified by their Churches at the time of Covenanting' and thereafter to serve 'as colleagues with bishops'. They were not to be deemed to stand 'immediately' in the 'historic episcopate'.[8] Episcopal ordination was to be

---

4   On both these points, cf. Dissentient View, *Report*, p. 59 and *The Church of England and the Methodist Church: A Consideration of the Recent Anglican-Methodist Report*, ed. J.I. Packer (Abingdon, 1963), pp. 37-9, essay by C. Buchanan.

5   *Anglican-Methodist Conversations, Report* (1963), p. 37.

6   Both this scheme and the Covenant (see following paragraphs) were concerned with the English scene only.

7   See Buchanan in *The Church of England and the Methodist Church*, ed. Packer, p. 40, on the problem of 'unifying' Methodist or Anglican ministers returning from abroad after the United Church had come into being.

8   Defined as 'an episcopate which is exercised by persons ordained to that office and which is in continuity and communion with the historic episcopate', cf. *Proceedings* of the General Synod (July, 1980), p. 663.

introduced from the time of reunion. In ordinations such ministers of oversight as were not bishops were always to 'share ... in collegiality with others who have been ordained bishop'. Freshly appointed or re-appointed ministers with oversight were to be ordained bishop 'in joint services conducted by the proper authorities of all the Covenanting Churches' (5.4.4.3, p. 50). The purpose of such joint services was 'to ensure that the persons so ordained are acknowledged by all the Covenanting Churches as participating in a single ministry, and that regular public witness is given to this fact' (5.4.6.1, p. 51).[9] The question of defect in either existing ministry was not systematically addressed.[10]

613. The Covenant text[11] envisages the forming of a single ministry as implying the coming into being of a single united Church:

> Ordination is an act of the whole community of the Church universal in its continuity with the apostolic Church and an act of fellowship of the Covenanting Churches ... in the ordination of a bishop other bishops lay

---

9 The Right Rev. Eric Kemp, Bishop of Chichester, pointed out in the General Synod debate on the proposals that 'It has not been too difficult [in schemes for Christian unity] to get episcopal and non-episcopal Churches to agree upon a structure for the future upon invariable episcopal ordination. The sticking-point has come every time at what is to happen to the existing ministers, and unless we can find a way through that ... we are not really going to get very far in the region of interchangeability of ministers' ... 'The Union of the Churches in North India and Pakistan included a sacramental act integrating the ministries at the outset, an act of such a kind that this Synod nine years ago was able to say that bishops and presbyters taking part in such an act had received grace and authority for the office and work of bishops and priests in the Church of God' (*Proceedings*, pp. 686-7).

10 Things had not substantially changed since representatives of the Archbishop of Canterbury and the Evangelical Free Churches produced the *Report* on *Church Relations in England* (London, 1950), in which it was noted that 'the Free Churches ... have repeatedly stated that they are not able to countenance the re-ordination of their Ministers. There would probably be reluctance on the part of the Free Churches to accept a distinction within the ranks of their Ministers, even for an interim period' (p. 40) [that is, to distinguish between those commissioned within the new United Church and those made Ministers in their own Churches before it came into being].

11 The bishop's tasks were outlined in the Covenant proposals of 1980 in terms which won general acceptance:
The bishop:
   - represents the unity and continuity of the church, thus enabling it in each place and time to relate to the Church universal;
   - exercises leadership and oversight in the worship and witness of the Church, to ensure that the faith is safeguarded, the word proclaimed and the sacraments rightly administered;
   - carries pastoral responsibility for the people committed to his charge, and especially for the presbyters and other ministers of whom he is given oversight;
   - presides at ordinations;
   - shares in the councils of the Church, with a special concern for those matters which relate to its life at regional, national and international levels. (*Towards Visible Unity: Proposals for a Covenant*, The Report of the Churches' Council for Covenanting (1980), p. 49.)

hands on him as they request the gift of the Spirit for his ministry. Thus they signify that they receive the new bishop into their ministerial fellowship, and that the new bishop and the people entrusted to his charge belong within the communion of Churches, and stand in continuity with the apostolic Church (5.2.3, 4, p. 47).

Nevertheless, bishops thus commissioned were to continue to serve principally in and for their own Churches. 'Immediate episcopal responsibility' was to 'be exercised within their own Church and only in another Church jointly with the bishop (moderator, etc.) of that Church and on his invitation' (5.4.6.6, p. 50). Only in the area of guardianship of faith and order in decision-making do we see the clear aim of acting 'in common' and 'together' and the promise 'to honour the authority of shared decisions' (8.1.1).

614. Both the Anglican-Methodist and the Covenant schemes failed; they did so for a number of reasons, the uncertainty over the role of the bishop in future ordinations[12] and of the ecclesial autonomy of the participating Churches after reconciliation perhaps the most prominent among them, theologically speaking.[13] These ought not to be separated, if, as we have been arguing, it is his calling to be the minister of unity and continuity which is constitutive for the bishop's office and which makes him the proper and fitting minister of ordination in the episcopal Churches. By episcopal ordination the ordained minister is commissioned to serve not only in the local, but (within the structures of the Church's order), also in the wider Church, wherever he may be given pastoral responsibility.

ii. The Anglican-Lutheran proposals

615. These two issues and their interdependence were clearly of some importance in the framing of the most recent proposals for bringing about mutual recognition and reconciliation of ministries, this time with Churches of the Lutheran tradition which regard themselves as in part episcopal, and which see the acceptance of the historic episcopate as no bar to union.[14] We

---

12   Speeches in the General Synod debates on the Covenant proposals in particular showing a
       huge preponderance of concern about the issues surrounding episcopacy.
13   Cf. a comment in the General Synod debate on the Covenant proposals by the Bishop of
       Guildford (D.A. Brown), that 'unity discussions are not concerned with the incorporation of
       one Church into another' (*Proceedings*, p. 649), and Bishop Montefiore of Birmingham's
       warning that the proposals would be likely to 'proliferate parallel episcopates' (p. 667).
14   Cf. *Pullach Report* (1972), Statement of the Lutheran participants:
       'The Lutheran Churches have practised full fellowship with each other regardless of the
       forms of *episcope* (or even of the episcopate). With ecumenical developments this freedom

give some space to these, because they are perhaps the most advanced and ambitious of the attempts being made at the moment to frame, with Anglicans, proposals which may lead to an ecclesial act of reconciliation together, followed by practical steps towards unity.

616.   In an attempt to set the question of succession fully in its Gospel and ecclesial framework, the Anglican-Lutheran *Niagara Report* of 1987 takes up the theme of *episcope* and episcopacy in the context of the nature of the Church and its mission. The bishop in the early Church is seen as linking the local community to the universal in his own day and over time:

> The symbolic position occupied by the bishop had two dimensions, the spatial and the temporal. The connections between the local and the universal, the present and the past, are both aspects of the one *koinonia* or communion. On the one hand, the bishop 'is responsible for preserving and promoting the integrity of the *koinonia* in order to further the Church's response to the Lordship of Christ and its commitment to mission' (ARCIC *The Final Report*, Authority I, 5); ... On the other hand the bishop as confessor of the faith links the church with its foundation in the prophetic and apostolic scriptures (Eph 2:20).
> What is essential to the life and mission of the Church is that the connection between the universal and the local should be made, and that it should be effective   (52, 53)

But it is argued that the mere presence of a bishop in continuity will not guarantee the preservation of *koinonia*; nor will the absence of such a bishop necessarily entail its destruction.[15]

617.   The *Niagara Report* affirms the comprehensive agreement which exists between Anglicans and Lutherans in matters of faith and order.

---

for fellowship has allowed Lutheran Churches to enter into fellowship with non-Lutheran churches with various forms of church government'.
Since full fellowship has been retained between some Lutheran Churches which have not preserved the office and name of bishop and other Lutheran Churches which have retained the historic episcopate in a form similar to the Anglican and since the particular form of *episcope* is not a confessional question for Lutherans, the historic episcopate should not become a necessary condition for interchurch relations or Church union. On the other hand, those Lutheran Churches which have not retained the historic episcopate are free to accept it where it serves the growing unity of the Church in obedience to the gospel.
The Lutheran participants in these conversations recognise the churches of the Anglican Communion as true apostolic churches and their ministry as an apostolic ministry in unbroken succession, because they see in them true proclamation of the gospel, and right administration of the sacraments. As would be true for any church which proclaims the gospel in its purity and administers the sacraments properly, the participants regard the historic episcopacy as it has been retained in the Anglican Communion as an important instrument of the unity of the Church (83-91).

15   Cf. again paras. 52-3.

Amongst the points of agreement is listed a shared belief in a ministry of pastoral oversight (*episcope*), exercised in personal, collegial and communal ways, and seen as a necessary witness to, and safeguard of, the unity and apostolicity of the Church (69). *Niagara* proposes mutual recognition of ministry without reordination on either side, on the basis of existing mutual ecclesial recognition and the conviction that ministers regularly commissioned within their own Churches ought to be received by other Churches on that basis. This is envisaged as, at the very least, a major step towards reconciliation:

> Because of all that we share, we concur with the conclusion of the Anglican-Lutheran European Regional Commission; 'There are no longer any serious obstacles on the way towards the establishment of full communion between our two Churches'. We 'acknowledge each other as true Churches of Christ preaching the same gospel, possessing a common apostolic ministry, and celebrating authentic sacraments' (*Helsinki Report*, 62-63). (71)

On the basis of this follow practical suggestions designed to lead to full mutual recognition and reconciliation of ministry in organic union.[16]

618. Both Lutheran and Anglican traditions face demanding challenges here. Lutheran Churches are asked to concede the following:

- that bishops should be elected for the same tenure of office[17] as other pastoral ministers.
- that the installation of bishops be revised so that there is laying on of hands by at least three other bishops and that one should be from a Church in the Anglican Communion.
- that it should become an unfailing practice that only bishops (including Suffragans) should preside at ordinations.

Anglicans for their part are asked to make these changes:

- canonical revisions should be made to recognise the full authenticity of the existing ministries of Lutheran Churches.

This is acknowledged to require a major change in Anglican practice, and some revision of theological assumptions concerning continuity of succession in the 'historic episcopate'.

- regular invitations should be made to Lutherans to participate in Anglican consecrations.

---

16   *Niagara*, 88 ff. Present conversations with the Nordic-Baltic Churches seem likely to result in proposals in line with these.

17   It should be understood here that 'office' contains for Lutherans something at least of which Anglicans would understand by 'orders'.

There is thus significant rapprochement, but we would suggest that some of the continuing unresolved difficulties we have been outlining are not perhaps fully solved here.

619. The most important of these is whether ordination of bishops must be carried out in the historic succession if there is to be full mutual recognition and reconciliation. This kind of difficulty was addressed in the case of the Church of South India. The basis on which reconciliation of ministry was achieved there was that 'those Bishops, Presbyters, Deacons and Probationers who have assented to the Basis of Union and accepted the Constitution of the Church of South India' were accepted as bishops, presbyters and deacons of the United Church. The laying-on of hands of bishops-elect was to involve the presiding bishop with two brother bishops, so as to fulfil the requirement for three bishops in the historic succession, but the SIUC and Methodist presbyters were to join in the act as representatives of their communities.[18] In North India and Pakistan there was a sacramental act at the outset which integrated the ministries.[19] We would urge that where the end in view is, as we believe it should be, full organic union in one Church, mutual recognition and reconciliation of ministries in schemes involving a variety of polities should always proceed, as was attempted in these cases, on the basis of the fullest possible explicitness about what is being done and the clearest possible theology.

620. The Meissen Report *On the Way to Visible Unity* (1988) is the result of a series of conversations between delegates of the Church of England and delegates of the Federation of the Evangelical Churches in the then German Democratic Republic, and of the Evangelical Church in Germany. The Report, speaking as it does for Reformed and United, as well as Anglican and Lutheran Churches, sees greater difficulties over the form of a future common episcopate than the *Niagara Report:*

> Lutheran, Reformed and United Churches, though being increasingly prepared to appreciate episcopal succession 'as a sign of the apostolicity of the life of the whole Church', hold that this particular form of *episkope* should not become a necessary condition for 'full, visible unity'. The Anglican understanding of full, visible unity includes the historic episcopate and full interchangeability of ministers. 'Yet even this remaining difference, when seen in the light of our agreements and convergences, cannot be regarded as a hindrance to closer fellowship between our Churches' (16).

18   Bengt Sundkler, *The Church of South India* (London, 1954), pp. 342-3.
19   Cf. note 7.

Accordingly, although there is an affirmation of a form of mutual recognition of ministries in the Report, reconciliation of ministries is seen as a hope for the future:

> We acknowledge one another's ordained ministries as given by God and instruments of his grace, and look forward to the time when the reconciliation of our churches makes possible the full interchangeability of ministers ((17) A (iii)).

621. Restoration of mutual recognition and reconciliation of ministry among Anglicans,[20] and the achievement of mutual recognition and reconciliation of ministry with Christians of all other Communions, depend upon the resolution of difficulties concerning the episcopate which are common to both endeavours. For that reason, theological conversations working towards these two goals need to be co-ordinated. The underlying questions concern the nature and function of the pastoral ministry and the authorities in the Church competent to act under God to commission for such a ministry.[21] It is our view that an episcopate whose function is supremely to act as the ministry of unity, is the appropriate competent authority to act here, with all due safeguarding of the freedom of the Spirit and the liberty of the people of God. But, *ipso facto*, such a ministry of unity must be universally recognised, or it cannot discharge its function.

b.   United Churches

622. We turn now to the question of the role of an episcopal 'polity' in the existing United Churches, that is, to the ways in which some form of working solution has been implemented already. There have been several attempts in addition to that in South India, some successful, to bring together, in a single polity in a united Church, what are in origin 'congregational' and 'presbyteral' structures with 'episcopal' ones. The Reformed Episcopal Church in the United States (which had its English counterpart in the 1870s) recognised episcopacy as valuable but not of divine institution; insisted that there is only one 'order', that of the presbyterate; and that bishopric is an office to which the Church's Council

---

20   See our previous chapter on *Women in the Episcopate*, on new difficulties arising here as a result of the consecration of women to the episcopate in some Provinces of the Anglican Communion.

21   We refer the reader here to Chapter 5 for discussion of the main differences amongst the Churches.

elects, and not an order.[22]   The proposed solution here was to move away from the historic episcopate altogether. That has not been the direction in which most solutions have looked in this century. In the United Churches of the Indian sub-continent solutions have been found under the pressure of missionary need. The Tranquebar Manifesto of 1919 envisaged a congregational element, a 'delegated, organised or Presbyterian element, whereby the Church could unite in a General Assembly, Synods or Councils in organised unity' and a 'representative, executive or Episcopal element'.[23] The view that the episcopate could best be treated as 'a fact not a theory' was current in the debates of the 1920s, and attempts were made to avoid defining its character too closely. But it was still felt by many from Churches which did not retain the historic episcopate, that in a system which was to involve an episcopate, they would be making all the concessions; and the Reformed and Methodists who joined the South India scheme did so by accepting episcopacy as a fact and insisting that this acceptance must not be tied to any particular doctrine of episcopacy.[24]   That had the effect of throwing somewhat into question the acceptability of the resulting united ministry among Anglicans.

623.   It was clearly seen that a problem would arise in maintaining communion between the new United Churches and the Churches from which their elements had come. As the Encyclical of the 1948 Lambeth Conference put it, 'Reunion of any part of our Communion with other denominations in its own area must make the resulting Church no longer simply Anglican, but something more comprehensive'. (This question has now been happily resolved. The United Churches are in communion with the Anglican Churches, and the United Churches of Bangladesh, North India, Pakistan and South India send members to the Lambeth Conferences.)

624.   Yet the very scheme of unity which paradoxically disturbed the 1948 Lambeth Conference by its implications, proved in South India itself a means of uniting congregations in a way which had never been possible before. 'Each congregation, like the village of which it was a part, was very much a world of its own', commented Bishop Lesslie Newbigin, 'But the continual visiting of each congregation by the bishop was the first way in

22   Annie Darling Price, *A History of the Formation and Growth of the Reformed Episcopal Church, 1873-1902* (Philadelphia 1902), p. 150.
23   Sundkler, p. 101. See, too, the Lausanne Conference of Churches of 1927.
24   Cf. *The Church of Pakistan: Today and Tomorrow*, Report of an International Consultation, ed. Michael Nazir Ali (Lahore, 1985).

which their unity in one Church became a reality to them'.[25]   A truly episcopal ministry of unity undoubtedly emerged in the Union, then, although the question of its identity and continuity with the historic episcopate has perhaps remained imperfectly resolved.

625.   Although there are differences in the manner of the reconciliation of ministries, between the Church of South India on the one hand, and the Churches of North India, Pakistan and Bangladesh on the other, they are fundamentally at one in the bringing together of the 'Congregational' with the Reformed synodal principle and with the Anglican episcopal principle. As a result, a constitutional episcopacy, with the bishop-in-synod, is the hallmark of all the United Churches of the Indian sub-continent.   The constitutional framework of the United Churches nevertheless leaves much to each local bishop and diocese to evolve in the light of local traditions and experience.   The actual working out of the office of bishop has therefore varied considerably from diocese to diocese.   The problem - as Bishop Lesslie Newbigin has expressed it - 'was to find the proper relations which should exist between the local congregation, the councils and committees, and the bishop'.[26]   The United Churches would be far from claiming that they have yet achieved this.   The search for a proper balance between episcopacy - local and collegial - and centralized official structures remains part of the continuing agenda of these Churches.[27]

626.   Bishops, in the United Churches, must always carry the synod with them.   They must do this by holding in balance polarizing tendencies towards episcopal autocracy or ecclesiastical democracy.   Evangelism is a prime duty of a bishop.   This is often fulfilled by the bishops of the United Churches personally as well as by giving pastoral support and encouragement to the Church as a whole in its mission.   The bishop is also called to be a teacher of the faith - though, as elsewhere in the Church, the relation between the bishop and theological institutions has not been fully resolved.   Above all, the bishop is seen as the focus of diocesan unity.   Here, episcopal leadership is focused in the central work of the Church: worship, of which the bishop, in the United Churches, is the chief celebrant.   The bishop, while not primarily seen as an administrator, cannot give proper leadership without administration.

25   In *Bishops, But What Kind?*, p. 150.
26   'Bishops in a United Church', in *Bishops, But What Kind?*
27   Cf. Bengt Sundkler, *The Church of South India* (London 1954), Chapter VIII.

627.   The episcopate in the United Churches is also increasingly seen as the means of expressing locally the growing unity of Christians throughout the world. Episcopacy in the United Churches has helped congregations to think of themselves as not so much mission out-stations as local embodiments of the universal Church - not least by the provision of a truly local ministry of Word and Sacrament. The desire of the United Churches to be fully part of the Lambeth Conference of bishops is in part a reflection of this. Such a desire for collegial and conciliar unity naturally complements the conception of the episcopate as the visible expression of local unity, even if this is not fully expressed in the constitutional documents of the United Churches.

628.   Above all, for the United Churches as for all episcopal Churches, a bishop must be a man of God. Episcopacy is a symbol, a service, a cross to carry. The bishop is the focal point of the fellowship of the Church. Through his life and example people accept him and recognize him as a man of God and follow him with love and respect. But if marks of godliness and concern for the people are not to be found in the bishop, the people do not accept and follow him.[28]

c.   **United Churches in Microcosm: The local ecumenical scene**

629.   There will always be a tension between local and universal expressions of the one Church of Jesus Christ. The New Delhi Assembly of the World Council of Churches (1961) stressed that the Church 'is made visible as *all in each place* who are baptized ... and who at the same time are united with the whole Christian fellowship in all places and all ages ...'. At the Nairobi Assembly (1975) this description was further refined. The Assembly spoke of 'a conciliar fellowship of local churches which are themselves fully united', and pointed out that 'in this conciliar fellowship each local church possesses, in communion with the others, the fullness of catholicity'. Such an ecclesiology is also strongly expressed in the bilateral ecumenical dialogues.[29] At a Consultation on Ecumenical Episcope in 1986 it was accepted that 'personal', 'collegial' and 'communal' forms of *episcope* should always be held together, and that all three needed to be found in any model of local ecumenical oversight. Against this background Local Ecumenical Projects in our own country have properly seen themselves as

---

28   As Bishop Anandaro Samuel has written, Faith and Order Paper, 102, WCC p. 46, quoted in *Bishops: But What Kind?*, p. 161.

29   For example Anglican-Reformed and Anglican-Roman Catholic.

authentic manifestations of the universal Church of Christ rather than unofficial experiments. But this recognition has itself posed questions about the nature of the oversight by which they are linked to the universal Church in a divided Christendom.

i. Personal Ecumenical Episcope

630. (a) A study was made in Swindon in the 1970s of the possibility of setting up a system of ecumenical oversight. The working party examined various forms of *episcope* and eventually produced a report which recommended 'A Bishop for all churches in Thamesdown' (Thamesdown is the civic area in which the town of Swindon is located). The bishop was to exercise personal oversight of all the churches in the area and to be the President when the Eucharist was celebrated. He was to be a bishop-in-council having the support of a 'mission council'. The report owed much to the experience of personal *episcope* as exercised throughout the area unofficially but *de facto* by the then Bishop of Malmesbury, the Rt. Revd. Freddie Temple, Suffragan to the Bishop of Bristol. The scheme foundered because of a number of factors, among them the problem of the structural relationship with the Diocese of Bristol; difficulties in making real the relationship of the Ecumenical Bishop with the collegial leadership in other churches; and the reluctance of a few congregations (Anglican as well as Free Church) to adopt the idea.

631. (b) In Milton Keynes the Presidency, which comprises the several church leaders with oversight of the new city, elects one of its number to be 'pastoral President' for two years. The Pastoral President then acts in a representative capacity for all the Church leaders (and of the Christian Council) as far as may be accepted by the congregations, thus embodying the principle of the personal focus of unity.

632. (c) The development of the role of the Ecumenical Officer should also be considered under the heading of ecumenical oversight. Where a full-time, ecumenically appointed ecumenical officer serves the Churches, part of his/her role is thought of as to give ecumenical and in some sense a pastoral oversight to Local Ecumenical Projects and to their clergy and ministers. This is not seen as undermining or detracting from the authority and caring exercised by denominational leaders, but often as providing them with a joint representative. Examples of this may be seen in Merseyside, Telford and Milton Keynes. Ecumenical Officers are not, however,

necessarily ordained ministers, and caution is needed in the use of the terms 'pastoral' and 'oversight' here.

ii.   *Collegial Ecumenical* Episcope

633.   (a) The growth of Sponsoring Bodies over the past twenty years reveals a developing pattern of collegial ecumenical *episcope*. This has commonly been exercised imaginatively; and it has often enjoyed widespread local acceptance.   Sponsoring Bodies were originally set up to monitor individual Areas of Ecumenical Experiment (as Local Ecumenical Projects were then known).   But these organs have developed in many places into bodies made up of church leaders who now exercise some form of corporate oversight of a growing number of Local Ecumenical Projects.   In a number of cases when a member of the Sponsoring Body is present, that member is seen as in some sense representing the rest.   At a joint confirmation in an Anglican/Free Church Local Ecumenical Project, where Bishop and Free Church minister jointly lay hands on the candidates, it has been argued that the Bishop acts in such a case not only as a representative of the Church of England but also (as a member of the Sponsoring Body), the wider Church.

634.   (b) In Milton Keynes the Presidency is written into the constitution of the Christian Council in such a way that ecumenical *episcope* is seen to be corporate.   Its purpose is described as being to 'enable our communion in the Spirit to find expression in the life of our churches and communities ...' and to 'exercise leadership and guidance; and among its duties to 'confer leadership over pastoral appointments and movements as they affect the Borough'.

635.   (c) In Merseyside the Church Leaders have effected a Covenant for the search for unity.   Constitutionally this large group is said to 'provide a tripartite Presidency for the Assembly [which is both personal and collegial], consisting of the Anglican Bishop of Liverpool, the Roman Catholic Archbishop of Liverpool, and the President of the Free Churches ... These persons shall individually and together represent the Assembly'. Similar regular meetings and at least one Covenant are to be found in other parts of the United Kingdom.[30]

---

30   Cf. *Living Stones*, 4.1.

iii.   **Communal Ecumenical Episcope**

636.   In several of the foregoing examples the element of communal *episcope* is present implicitly or explicitly.   (a) In the case of the ecumenical bishop for Thamesdown (Swindon) the scheme envisaged a bishop-in-council bringing together personal and communal forms of *episcope*.   The council was to be drawn from the several congregations in the area and would comprise clergy and laity.   (b) In both Milton Keynes and Merseyside the Assembly has a role of oversight which is shared with it by the Presidency in each case, and the Presidency cannot be understood apart from its relationship with the Assembly.

d.   The Anglican Bishop and Ecumenical Oversight

637.   Bishops of the Anglican Communion are ordained to a ministry in the Church of God.   In microcosm at local level they are beginning to meet, in these and many other ways, some of the practical questions about oversight which arise as Churches move towards unity in the inter-Church process. New Ecumenical Instruments[31] are providing guidelines, but unforeseen issues both profound and more trivial will need to be resolved as they arise.

638.   Any revision of diocesan boundaries must take account of the need to form common areas ecumenically with other churches.   At present in England there is a *de facto* parallel episcopal jurisdiction of Roman Catholic, Orthodox and Anglican bishops, acting alongside the *episcope* of the non-episcopal Churches.   There are significant differences of style and approach.   Co-operation may be very successful and helpful to the ecumenical cause (as, for example, it has conspicuously been in Liverpool). But systematic thought needs to be given to the ways in which not only brotherly charity and mutual help, but also a shared understanding of the task of oversight are to be advanced.

639.   The Anglican bishop has a responsibility to be sensitive to the views of those who are sharing oversight in his area; to witness in his own discharge of his office to the understanding of episcopacy which is his heritage; and to look courageously towards the commitment of Anglicans to unity in a future united Church.   We believe that the Anglican bishop should, by his presence whenever possible at ecumenical services and on

---

31   *Churches Together in Pilgrimage*, British Council of Churches (1989).

ecumenical occasions, seek to be a visible sign of Anglican commitment to the ecumenical endeavour. We should like to see the bishops of the Church of England participating with full commitment in local ecumenical schemes.

640. The bishop acts, however, not as a private individual but as his Church's representative, and therefore, for the sake of long-term success in the ecumenical cause, it is important that he does nothing which goes beyond the Lund rule of 'doing together all that we can'. This is particularly a concern in confirmations and ordinations. We should like to see clarification of theology and practice here.

15

Looking forward

641. It was clear to the first Christians that the Church on earth was the Gospel made present, active and effective. Its calling was to go into all the world and preach the good news. There was a strong sense that the visible Church was a sacramental sign of the Kingdom of the reign of Christ over all things in glory. It was to be a sign and an instrument of communion with God and, in Christ, with all the faithful. It was there to be a part of the world, so as to challenge it and invite it, through the power of the Crucified and Risen Lord, to receive forgiveness for sin and a place in the Body of Christ. Thus the ministry of oversight, as it serves and nurtures, is closely related to the Church's most fundamental message and mission, and in this way it is part of its 'givenness'.

642. We have been a good deal concerned in our Report with what may be thought of as the domestic concerns of the Church: questions of its internal relationships and order. That has been unavoidable, because that is largely where the areas of traditional and continuing controversy lie. But we have tried to make it plain that all these practicalities of the Church's life must always be set in the context of the Gospel imperative which sends the people of God out in mission to the world. We look forward now in our concluding chapter to the place of episcopal ministry in today's Church and the Church of the future, both in that Church's inner life and in its work in the world.

The local church

643. We have argued that order in the Church is not mere organisation; it is certainly not simply a matter of government. It is a way of being in which the relationships of the persons united in Christ, and of the local Churches to which they belong, are enabled to reflect, even though in a limited, creaturely way, the relationship of the Persons of the Trinity.

644. The Church in each place is completely and perfectly the Church just as each of the Persons of the Trinity is fully God; at the same time, just as

the Persons are one God, so the local Churches are inseparably one Church. Orthodox tradition has kept alive with special vividness this understanding of unity in the Church. The mediaeval Western tradition has placed a stronger emphasis perhaps upon the formal, structural patterns which provide the Church with its visible shape. But both East and West have always recognised that right order in the Church embraces both the inward and spiritual and the outward and visible.[1]

645. The protracted debates of many generations in the West about what is of divine institution and what is of human arrangement in the order of the Church have chiefly concerned the outward and visible. There has been less concern over the spiritual character of oneness in order because that has not been a divisive issue for Western Christians. As a result, the theology of that spiritual and mysterious oneness in order has been less fully spelt out over the centuries. We stress its importance here, because unless the spiritual relationship of 'the Church in each place' to the one Church is seen to underlie all structural provisions for oversight in the Church, we shall not get beyond the differences which have divided us.

646. We have also argued that there is strong, if not conclusive, New Testament warrant for the pattern of 'one Church, one shepherd'. Whatever weight we may wish to give to the practice of the Church through the ages, it cannot be questioned that there has been a consensus here. In all Christian traditions, 'the Church in each place' has had a pastor.

647. On two related points, however, there has not been consensus: the definition of the 'local Church' or 'Church in each place'; and the precise nature of the relationship in which the pastor stands to his people. These are in fact inseparable, if, as we have argued, the sense of 'being a Church' requires a focussing of life and worship within the community which enables it to act as one body sharing a common life. It is this focussing and representing function which may be seen as God's distinctive gift to the Church in the pastoral office; and which we would see as being of God.

648. A sense of 'being a Church' must be a real and lively characteristic of the Church's life for the people of each local Church; and they must be able to recognise themselves as acting with their pastor in all that they do together.

---

[1]   Cf. paras. 99 ff. and 117.

Pastor and people

649. Churches influenced by the Reformation, amongst which the Church of England places herself, as Catholic and Reformed, have traditionally emphasised the centrality of the Ministry of the Word; they have seen this as constitutive for ministry in the Church. That is to say that the Church does not derive its authority from its ministry but from its apostolic character of faithfulness to the Gospel, which ministry serves; ministry loses authority if it ceases to be faithful to the apostolic tradition embodied in Scripture.[2] But it has equally always been the Church of England's view that if that authority of the living Word is not expressed in the mystery of the Church's sacramental life, the people of God cannot truly be one with their Lord. So order in the Church, both in its inward and spiritual being, and in its visible manifestation of that inward unity, must be expressed through the instrument and service of a ministry commissioned to maintain the community both in faithfulness to the Word and in its sacramental life. These elements of Church structure have always been found in Churches obedient to the Word of God.

650. It seems to have been everywhere the case, even in the divided Church, that such a ministry is commissioned within the community in a manner whose details are agreed by that community. The precise pattern has varied, but there has always been an acknowledgement of the ministerial authority of all the people of God, for all are commissioned for ministry through their Baptism and share in the priesthood of all believers. So all the people of God must join in the further commissioning of the ordained ministry through their assent, and through their representatives, who themselves have the apostolic commission, and who perform the laying on of hands with prayer in token of the gift of the Holy Spirit for the pastoral ministry which leads the community in acting as one.[3]

651. Thus commissioned, the pastor can take the community with him, both in the sense that he helps to enable it to act as one body, and in the sense that he can act and speak on its behalf in council with leaders of other communities.[4]

---

2   Cf. O. O'Donovan, *On the Thirty-Nine Articles*, p. 119.
3   Clericalism and anti-clericalism are equally distortions of a right view of ministry in the Church.
4   Cf. Jalland, *op. cit.*, pp. 320-3, 326.

652.   Churches which have not retained the historic episcopate share an understanding of oversight as a ministry of unity. But they have not, as a rule, seen the minister appointed to that responsibility as being thus permanently altered in his commission in relation to the worshipping community.

A personal office

653.   We have placed a great deal of emphasis upon the episcopate as a personal office. We would stress again here that the word 'personal' needs to be understood in two senses. It is of the first importance what kind of 'person' the bishop is. His personal holiness, the example he sets, the qualities of mind and character, the skills and experience he brings to his office, will rightly be reasons for his appointment. They will mark his episcopate and make his diocese and its people spiritually richer. But, paradoxically, because the episcopal ministry makes the pastor a corporate person in relation to the community, there is a sense in which his individual personality ceases to be of importance. He is, in a sense, emptied out of self in service to God and the people of God. It is important that this 'emptying' should be more than symbolic, and should be reflected in the bishop's life and work.

The balance of our life together at home and in the world

654.   The Church of England needs to develop a conscious sense of the 'every-member ministry' of the community and of the active participation of all the people of God in their pastor's leadership, as in his commissioning. It has always been a responsibility of pastors to 'enable' the ministry of others, and that task takes on fresh aspects in the intellectual and social climate of our own time, when there is an increasingly high sense of 'community' in the secular world, and a call for full participation and involvement in many kinds of activity.

655.   The Church of England embraces both the Protestant heritage of a sense of the local church as the 'gathered' congregation; and the heritage of the Church of the first millenium and a half (and of episcopal Churches since), which regards the diocese as the local church. Here Anglicans need to develop a livelier sense of the diocese as the 'local church', if episcopal ministry is to fulfil its purpose at the heart of corporate life and worship.

In many dioceses there is already a good sense of the bishop as pastor of the fellowship of parish churches. But there is clearly a need for development of his role and for rethinking of some of our assumptions about it.[5]

656. In particular we would stress the importance of the bishop's being seen and known by his people as their pastor, teacher, and leader of the mission of God's people in that 'place' which is their ecclesial home.

657. The bishop must respond to his people's needs, and to what his fellow bishops and the General Synod require of him. To him come the problems which it has not been possible for others in the diocese or the wider Church to deal with. This ministry of response is that of the shepherd who walks behind his flock as he guards and guides. But a shepherd may also go in front as his flock's leader, and as he answers the call to mission, the first task Christ entrusted to his disciples, he must be seen in active leadership. True episcopacy is rooted in apostolicity, and the bishop must make it a matter of priority to be an active leader in mission.

658. We believe that the Church of England at present faces a number of difficulties over the need to keep in balance the personal authority of the bishop and his role as bishop-in-synod, where he must honour the work of the whole people of God in their ministry. As we strive to find the right balance of 'every member ministry' with the special responsibilities entrusted to the ordained ministry, we too easily fall into the habit of convening new committees and setting up fresh meetings, until those who serve on them find their time and energies disproportionately committed to planning and discussion. Personal leadership gives scope for initiative, and it must be an important part of the bishop's task to lead in a way which frees himself and others to witness with vitality and directness.

659. The question 'What is the local Church?' takes on a new dimension in the ecumenical experiments which are taking place as 'Churches together in England' comes into being as successor to the British Council of Churches. A sense of 'being the Church in that place' may well develop in an ecumenically active area, such as Swindon, to a stage where local Christians

---

5   It should not, for example, be the case that parishes feel that they are not listened to in the choice of their parish priest, with the bishop perhaps imposing his own candidate upon them; it should be possible for the people and their bishop to work together as pastor and people in deciding upon the minister with whom the bishop is to share his pastoral responsibilities in that church and whom the local people are to have among them as his vicar. [Provision is made for this in the *Patronage Benefices Measure* (1986) recently brought into operation.]

feel that they belong together rather than to their separate denominational congregations. That is entirely to the good, if we are seriously looking to a future united Church. But that means that in the interim - and it may be a lengthy interim, of perhaps several generations - pastoral oversight cannot be unitary but must involve the working together of bishops and moderators and superintendents and chairmen of Methodist Districts and presidents and ministers of the various participating Churches. We believe it to be important for leaders of Churches in such local schemes to take seriously the implications of the temporary character of this provision, and to work together towards a personal pastorate of the whole gathered local community, to be entrusted ultimately to a minister drawn from any of the Churches, but commissioned within the united community to an episcopal office which will stand in the historic succession. We do not intend here to gloss over the difficulties inseparable from such a suggestion, but merely to indicate that this should continue to be the Church of England's vision.

Out of our hands?

660. Certain developments are going to affect the Church of England whether or not we take steps to meet them. The two most conspicuous of these are the ordination of women to the episcopate in other provinces of the Anglican Communion; and the ecumenical advances which are taking place locally in England. We have discussed what we believe to be the Church of England's proper response to these at some length in the two previous chapters of our Report. We emphasise here what seem to us to be the key aspects on which we need to concentrate in our thinking as a Church, as we go forward into a future in which our sense of 'identity' as Anglicans in England is challenged by these events.

661. Where there is impaired Communion among Anglicans as a result of a breakdown of mutual recognition of ministry at the episcopal level, with consequent non-recognition not merely of priesthood conferred on women, but also of any ordinations by bishops who ordain women as well as men to the priesthood, we strongly endorse the recommendation of the Lambeth Conference of 1988 and of the Eames Commission that Anglicans should act in mutual charity to sustain communion as far as that may be possible. Without in any way seeing it as a mitigation of the disaster of impaired communion, we see it as helpful ecumenically that recent events have sharpened the recognition that in fact impaired communion is nothing new, but has been a stumbling-block and an offence throughout the centuries

during which the Church has been divided. We believe that present developments in the Anglican world-wide Church are part of the larger problem, and that therefore seeking a solution with care and mutual charity may well help the larger endeavour for unity.

Pluriformity

662.   What are we to regard as a permissible degree of pluriformity in the structures of Church government and, more importantly, in the understanding of the mystery of the spirituality of episcopal pastoral office? In what can the Church of England regard itself as free to experiment with episcopal ministry as we go forward into the twenty-first century? The Holy Spirit has fostered diversity in the Church from the beginning, but always within an order which is also harmony. The constraints upon all Christians, we have argued, are those of mutual charity and what may be called 'universal intention', that is the intention to act for the good of the whole body of Christ and not merely for local benefit.

663.   We have argued that it is proper for dioceses to decide for themselves how the personal pastoral ministry of their diocesan bishop is to be shared and delegated, with the proviso that there are functions only a bishop may discharge (confirmation,[6] ordination). This, we believe, is a means of strengthening diocesan life and enabling each diocese to realize itself increasingly fully as 'the Church in each place'.

664.   There remains the question of pluriformity in the 'polities' which Churches may legitimately adopt in their pattern of government. Richard Hooker and others among the sixteenth and early seventeenth century Anglicans argued that the external and visible structures of the Church are 'indifferent', or 'accessories'. That is to say, salvation does not depend upon them. Of course God can work without them. But that does not mean that they are unimportant or that they may legitimately take any form at all without restriction. We have argued that the form matters because the ministry of oversight must be an instrument of unity in its leadership in the Church's ministry of proclamation. It is possible for there to be fellowship in apostolic faith with other Christians and a sharing in a variety of ways in life and mission when the sign of a single episcopal ministry is not present,

---

6   Normally. Anglicans have been prepared to recognize presbyteral chrismation and confirmation as practised in the Roman Catholic and Orthodox Churches, where the chrism has been blessed by a bishop.

although such communion cannot be expressed in its fullness in the presidency of the Eucharist. We have seen the sign of the historic episcopate, when fully integrated into the total apostolic life of the Church (but never as a thing in itself apart from that whole life), as a fitting expression of that oversight which is a gift of assurance and grace belonging to the catholicity of the Church, and the episcopate as in this way an institution shaped by the Gospel itself.[7]

665.   The bishop in the Church discharges his office within a transcendent frame of reference in which he is in his person an appropriate sacramental and visible sign of God's grace. Apart from the Church the sign of the episcopate can only be empty: but in the Church now and in the community succession through the ages, it witnesses to, serves and safeguards the community's unity, which must be grounded in God's own Trinitarian being. It points in a clear and eloquent way to the continuing ministry of Christ in and through the Church, helping the Church to be an effective sign of the Kingdom of God in the World.

Independence and interdependence in love

666.   We live in an age where personal freedom is highly valued, and with it the right of communities of various sorts to be 'self-determining'. Christians rightly support those who are striving by peaceful means to achieve liberties which will help them to fullness of life, for Christ came to set the captive free. But he also taught us to love one another, and in a balanced Christian polity and economy, mutual charity and concern for the welfare and well-being of others ought to be interdependent with the expression of personal and community freedom.

667.   It is always controversial for bishops in the Church of England (or indeed anywhere else at any time in Church history) to speak on social issues. We take the view that it is part of their role, though learning and experience may well make some better qualified to do so than others. The spiritual lives of their people cannot be separated from their general well-being. Jesus fed the multitude with loaves and fishes; he fed their minds and souls with his teaching. We would, however, encourage the placing of a particular emphasis upon the need to keep in balance, in pressing for

---

7   'It was the pressure of gospel truth concerning Christ and his work that caused the Church to feel for the need for episcopal office once the uniquely comprehensive and authoritative oversight of the Apostles had ceased ...', *Growing into Union*, p. 75.

economic, social and political reform, the claims of individual liberty and the duty of mutual charity.

668. In the wider arena of the Church of England's relationships with the other provinces of the Anglican Communion, the right to provincial autonomy has become a matter of urgent concern. We would urge the Church of England to give careful thought to the ecclesiological implications of allowing an imbalance to arise between independence and interdependence here.

669. Similar questions present themselves ecumenically, as uniting Churches struggle to maintain what is precious to them in their own traditions and styles of Church life, while at the same time entering together into a new common life. We believe it important to stress that the Church of England need fear no loss here, but only gain, and we should like to encourage Anglicans in England to go forward openly and in confidence in the Lord, as we learn to live a common life with other Christians.

670. Episcopal and non-episcopal Churches have learned a great deal from one another in recent decades. Churches with a congregationalist tradition bring a lively sense of local community and a warmth of relationship between people and pastor to local ecumenical schemes. Churches in the presbyterian tradition have tested experience of corporate oversight. The episcopal Churches have, in their bishops, a pastorate which embodies elements which some formerly non-episcopal Churches are now seeking to take into their own systems, notably certain aspects of the mystery of that relationship of pastor and people which helps to make the local Church a microcosm of the universal Church.

671. We would wish to encourage such 'learning from one another' at every level. We see it as the best way to overcome prejudices. Above all, it appears to us the most appropriate means by which the Churches may discover together what is God's will for episcopal ministry in a future united Church. We have sought to demonstrate in these pages what has seemed to us the characteristically and in every sense personal value of the historic episcopate. We have also striven to emphasise that Christians must remain open to the will of the Holy Spirit for the future of episcopal ministry, as we participate in the forming of the mind of the Church under his guidance.

Continuity and looking forward

672.   We believe that it is of the first importance that our bishops should be
strong teachers of the faith who are both deeply engaged in the continuing
education of the people of God within the community of the Church, and
powerful defenders of the faith and winners of souls in the world. Such
evangelism and guardianship of the faith involves a diversity of gifts, not all
of which can be looked for in every bishop, but which we must seek to
ensure are present in their fullness in the episcopate as a body. There must
be well-balanced expository preaching of the Scriptures; teaching about the
two thousand year life-story of the Christian people; sensitive and hopeful
response to the challenge of our society, and to human need in our time,
rooted in the confidence that Jesus Christ, through his victory over sin, will
save his people from death, physical and spiritual; a steady endeavour to fill
minds and souls with the greatness of a vision which looks to an eternal
future. The diocesan bishop has rich opportunities of speaking and writing,
in the media as well as directly to his people, on matters of both faith and
morals; and of reaching in this way those who have not as yet had a real
opportunity of hearing the Gospel.

673.   We see the bishop's special responsibility as guardian of the faith
together with his fellow-bishops as requiring great care in maintaining a
right balance between teaching the faith delivered to the Apostles and
speaking to the world of today. Here he must be a good listener as well as
an interpreter. Bishops

> are to guard, expound and teach the faith as they have received it. They
> are also to be 'apostolic pioneers'. As such they are guardians of the
> process of exploration as well as of received truths. They need to listen
> not only to the Church but to the world, to give courage and support to
> those who are engaged in proclaiming afresh, and to respond creatively to
> new knowledge and new opportunities.[8]

So the bishop must strive to show his flock the way in times of controversy,
when currents of academic debate trouble the faith of some:

> As teachers of the faith themselves, bishops need to be in sympathetic
> touch with those in the vanguard of knowledge. ... A bishop may
> properly enter into questionings on matters of belief, both because as a
> man of integrity he will feel any force there is in such questionings, and

---

[8]   *The Nature of Christian Belief*, Statement by the House of Bishops of the Church of
England (London, 1986), 67.

also because as a leader part of his responsibility on behalf of the Church is to listen honestly to criticisms of its faith and life. But in all he says he must take care not to present variant beliefs as if they were the faith of the Church; and he must always make as sure as he can that his hearers understand what that faith is and the reasons for it.[9]

That will mean speaking collegially with his fellow-bishops and with the consensus of the faithful through the ages.

674. He must himself be a teacher, then, and also an overseer of the continuing process of theological education for all the ministers of the Church, clerical and lay. The history of the Church is nothing else but the story of its life. We should like to encourage the placing of a greater emphasis on the study of the Church's life-history in schools and universities and especially in theological colleges, so that Christians may grow up with a sense of their fellowship with Christians in every age and of every tradition. We see this as ecumenically indispensable, as a means of growing together. The bishop's teaching must look forward along the line of time as well as back to the apostolic origins and so he must exercise a prophetic ministry, speaking to the world in the challenging situations of his own time in ways which will keep ever before society the hope and promise of the Kingdom.

675. The bishop is also the guardian of continuity in the Church's order. That is most readily visible in the episcopal ministry in ordination; but, as we have argued in our previous two chapters, it is a responsibility which has taken on a new seriousness in the light of recent developments. It presents perhaps the greatest challenge to the Church of our time, and the one in which bishops must take a courageous lead in love.

676. It is a salutary lesson in humility in a late twentieth century climate where it is readily assumed that humanity has grown out of the simple-mindedness of its infancy and is breaking new ground, to discover from the past that nothing proposed today is altogether without precedent in the history of Christian theology. We would argue that Christians need to enter into their heritage for this reason, too, so that they may be able to take an informed view of the implications of today's debates.

677. The continuities of which we have spoken in this Report are important because they bind us together in the one Body of Christ with all

9   *Ibid.,* 70.

God's people through the ages. Nothing speaks so directly to the present as the Gospel of Christ; nothing offers us hope for the future as the Gospel does.

———————

'As the Father has sent me, even so I send you.'   John 20.21.

'Receive the Holy Spirit.'   John 20.22.

'Feed my sheep.'   John 21.17.

'Go then, to all peoples everywhere and make them my disciples: baptize them in the name of the Father, the Son and the Holy Spirit, and teach them to obey everything I have commanded you. And I will be with you always, to the end of the age.'

                                                        Matthew 28.19-20.

Appendix I

The corporate person in law

1.   The Christian understanding of the nature of the relationship between the ministry of unity and the community has always had to be expressed in terms familiar in secular, social and political contexts as well as in those of Scripture, which depend in their turn upon such borrowings. The leader of the Old Testament community in his sacral kingship could already be seen as in some sense a 'corporate person', a 'centre of power' extending throughout the body and beyond it, stretching through time as well as space, 'so that the mystic bond which unites society may be conceived retrospectively ... and progressively'.[1] Roman law, Germanic law in the centuries after the fall of the Roman Empire, and developing canon law, all tried to give working definitions of the notion of the 'corporate person', the leader or representative through whom a body acted as one. Roman society recognised cities, colleges, corporations as bodies in which this was possible, with the emphasis upon the corporate possession and transmission of property through the agency of the representative who could speak in court and conduct legal business. The Church was early recognised as such a body, certainly the local Church, and arguably the universal Church too, although it was always seen as exceptional in certain respects. The corporate person was a legal fiction, but the personal representative was a fact, and the body represented consisted of real persons, so that the relationship between representative and represented involved real tensions of authorisation and accountability.[2]

2.   From the late twelfth century procedure in the West became relatively settled. A *bona fide* representative acting as corporate person must demonstrate his authority by producing a mandate from his *dominus* the body, authenticated by the corporate seal and showing that the body he represents will ratify his action and accept decisions with which he concurs or to which he submits.

1   A.R. Johnson, *Sacral Kingship in Ancient Israel* (Cardiff 1967), pp. 2-3.
2   P. Gillet, *La personnalité juridique en droit ecclésiastique* (Malines 1927); Gaines Post, *Studies in Mediaeval Legal Thought* (Princeton 1964), both discuss these issues.

3.   Behind these legal requirements in the case of the Church lay a complex of assumptions, not all held everywhere and equally. In the case of a cathedral chapter, the seal used might in fact be that of an archdeacon, dean or canon who allowed his personal seal to be used because he was a member of the body concerned. In such a case the authority was, in part at least, personal in another sense and only by extension that of the 'corporate person'. In about 1149, the glossator Rogerius sees the representative of the Church as acting in the capacity of steward (*yconomus*).[3] Connected with this view of the representative function is a mass of legal literature in both East and West on the theme economically stated in Justinian's *quod omnes tangit* (C.5.59.5.2). What touches everyone must be referred to everyone for approval; there is a common good in which everyone has a legitimate interest, a *utilitas* which no private interest must be allowed to override. The representative of the community has an obligation to act for the common good and with the common consent with arguably, in the case of the Church, the duty to perceive that common good universally and not just at the local level where he is directly commissioned to act. That implies the existence of a relationship between local and universal which is not simply one of part and whole, but closer to Galatians 3.28: 'You are all one in Christ Jesus'. It also requires, in the case of the Church, a relationship of local representatives to one another which will enable them to act for the good of the whole.

4.   In law, the mandate given to the representative as 'corporate person' implied a contract. Its details might vary. His commissioning might be for life or for a period. He might be elected by the body he represented, or deemed to be appointed from above (by God or king), and his appointment recognised by the body he served. In the community of the Church until the end of the Middle Ages, in East and West, the commissioning is always seen as permanent and as involving both the Holy Spirit and the local and universal community. It was clearly understood that office is conferred for specific purposes - a principle strongly reinforced by the assimilation of Aristotelian notions of teleology from the thirteenth century.[4]

5.   The purposes might vary according to the task in hand. The representative 'corporate person' acted for the body, but he might not always do so in a manner binding upon its members; there might have to be

---

3   The notion of stewardship is of importance in relation to the concept of *economia*.
4   Cf. ARCIC A II, 16.

some referring back. He might be given plenipotentiary powers (*plenitudo potestatis*) or limited powers. He might be given authority (*auctoritas*) to shape legislation or to participate in its making, or merely *potestas*, power to execute what is already decreed.[5] But at the point where he acted as representative two things were true of the corporate person: he was both 'with' his people, because notionally they were all acting together, and 'over' them, because he had powers as an individual to act on their behalf, and to commit their obedience by his act. And secondly, he became the organ or instrument of their unity. This was supremely true in the high Middle Ages of the papacy, which made mediaeval Christendom in the West one body in a way nothing else could have done.[6] But it was also, at another level, the function of the bishop.

494. The use made by the Church, by local Churches, and by other ecclesiastical bodies such as monastic communities, of the legal principles of corporate personhood was not limited to bishops by any means. But the bishop was supremely the 'corporate person',[7] theologically speaking and within the order of the Church.

---

5   W. Ullmann, 'Frederick's Opponent Innocent IV, as Melchisedek', *Atti del convegno internazionale di Studi Fredericiani*, 1950 (Palermo, 1952), p. 63.

6   W. Ullmann, 'The Mediaeval Papacy, St. Thomas and Beyond', Aquinas Society of London, 35 (London 1960), p. 2.

7   See J.M.R. Tillard, *The Bishop of Rome*, tr. J. de Satgé (London, 1983), pp. 157 ff. on corporate personality and primacy and pp. 159 ff. on communion.

Appendix II

The normal procedure for the appointment of bishops

i.   In the Roman Catholic Church of the Latin rite

1.   The normal procedure is established by the canon law of the Roman Catholic Church, promulgated on 25th January, 1983.

a.   The Provision of Ecclesiastical Office

> Provision of an ecclesiastical office occurs by the free conferral of a competent ecclesiastical authority, or by installation by the same authority if presentation preceded it, or by confirmation or admission granted by the same authority if election or postulation preceded it, or, finally, by simple election and acceptance by the one elected if the election does not require confirmation.   Canon 147

2.   This canon provides a summary introduction of the ways in which acquisition of an office can occur.   In general, an office is acquired by *appointment*, which may entail prior presentation of a candidate, or by *election*, which may require subsequent confirmation by a higher authority, or by the substitute for election known as postulation.

3.   Free conferral is by far the most common way in which offices are acquired in the Church. Thus, diocesan bishops are freely appointed by the Roman Pontiff unless a collegiate body has the right to elect someone, in which case the Supreme Pontiff confirms the nominee (see Canon 377).

4.   The Holy See has asked those heads of state who have traditionally had the right to present candidates for diocesan bishoprics to relinquish that right, and most have by now done so. This was asked for by the Second Vatican Council Decree on Bishops, *Christus Dominus*, 20. ('Since the apostolic office of bishops was instituted by Christ the Lord and is directed to a spiritual and supernatural end, the sacred Ecumenical Council asserts that the competent ecclesiastical authority has the proper, special, and, as of right, exclusive power to appoint and install bishops. Therefore in order to safeguard the liberty of the Church and the better and more effectively to

promote the good of the faithful, it is the desire of the sacred Council that for the future no rights or privileges be conceded to the civil authorities in regard to the election, nomination or presentation to bishoprics. The civil authorities in question, whose good will towards the Church the sacred Synod gratefully acknowledges and highly appreciates, are respectively asked to initiate discussions with the Holy See with the object of freely waiving the aforesaid rights and privileges which they at present enjoy by agreement or custom.') It is confirmed in Canon 377 (5).

b. Bishops: Their Designation and Installation, Canons 375-380

5. These canons deal with some general notions about the office of bishop and in particular with the designation of individuals as bishops. Canon 375 deals with the divine institution of the episcopate, the sacramental basis of the episcopal ministry and the reality of hierarchical communion. Canon 376 states the two types of bishop in general, diocesan and titular. Canon 377 clarifies certain aspects of the process whereby bishops are designated. Canon 378 establishes the specific qualifications for episcopal office. Finally, two obligations of the bishop-designate are specified: the reception of episcopal consecration before taking possession of a diocese (Canon 379) and the making of a profession of faith and the taking of an oath of loyalty to the Holy See (Canon 380). A brief commentary on some of these canons may help to clarify the legal process by which an individual is designated bishop.

1. The Supreme Pontiff freely appoints bishops or confirms those who have been legitimately elected.

2. At least every three years the bishops of an ecclesiastical province or, if circumstances suggest this, the bishops of a conference of bishops are to compose in common counsel and in secret a list of presbyters, including members of institutes of consecrated life, who are suitable for the episcopate and send it to the Apostolic See; each bishop retains the right to make known to the Apostolic See on his own the names of presbyters whom he thinks worthy and suitable for the episcopal office.

3. Whenever a diocesan bishop or a coadjutor bishop is to be named, then (unless other provisions have legitimately been made), it is the responsibility of the pontifical legate to draw up what is called the *terna*, that is, a list of three candidates to be proposed to the Apostolic See. In doing so he is to seek out individually the suggestions of the metropolitan and the suffragans of the province to which the diocese to be provided for belongs or with which it is joined and of the president of the conference of bishops and to communicate them to the Apostolic See together with his own preference; moreover, the pontifical legate is to hear some members of the college of consultors and of the cathedral chapter, and if

he judges it expedient, he shall also obtain, individually and in secret, the opinion of other members of the secular and religious clergy as well as of the laity who are outstanding in their wisdom.

4. Unless other provisions have legitimately been made, a diocesan bishop who judges that an auxiliary bishop ought to be given to his diocese is to propose to the Apostolic See a list of at least three priests who are suitable for this office.

5. No rights and privileges of election, nomination, presentation, or designation of bishops are hereafter granted to civil authorities.

Canon 377

6. Certainly, one of the most significant administrative acts in the life of the Church is the designation of a bishop, and this important canon deals with various aspects of the designation process. It should be noted that the process of becoming a bishop involves several interrelated steps. The first is the designation of a particular person for the episcopal office, which can take place in various ways - the present canon deals almost exclusively with this initial stage of the process.

7. The first paragraph reaffirms the 1917 Code's emphasis on the pre-eminent role of the Pope in the designation of bishops. The present law refers not simply to the free nomination or appointment to office by the Pope but also to his confirming candidates who have been legitimately elected in virtue of particular law. Thus, there are two means by which the Pope designates a priest bishop - by nomination and by confirmation.

8. Free nomination (or appointment) means that according to law the Pope chooses episcopal candidates without the necessary involvement of others in the process even though he will conduct a process of gathering information most especially through his advisers at both the local and international level. Paragraphs 2, 3 and 4 of this canon outline the prior consultation process whereby the Holy See examines the merits of such candidates in the light of the general qualifications for office specified in Canon 378, and other specific requirements relating to the office in question.

9. Confirmation is a more complex and involved process. In various places throughout the church, such as Germany and Switzerland, certain groups, such as chapters of canons, have long enjoyed electoral rights established by law and custom concerning candidates for the episcopate. They have the right to elect and present candidates for the office of diocesan bishop. The legal procedure to be followed by the electors (e.g. the canons)

and the consequent confirmation by the Pope of the person(s) elected is controlled by the particular law of the chapter, the diocese or country concerned, as recognised by the Holy See. In addition, the procedure may be equally controlled by the concordat which may exist between the Holy See and the country in which the diocese is found.

10.   A typical, but not necessarily uniform, procedure would be as follows: Normally, the chapter will send to Rome the names of three candidates it has elected, indicating its first choice for the vacant bishopric. The Pope then has the right of confirming the first choice or one of the other nominees.   On the other hand, he can, depending on the rules governing this particular election, reject all three and ask the chapter to reconsider and re-elect and may, in certain circumstances, have the right to suggest his own candidate or candidates from whom the chapter is to elect. If there is an *impasse*, then the Pope may confirm no-one and he has the right to appoint an Apostolic Administrator for the diocese until the problem is resolved. This has happened most especially in Eastern Bloc countries where civil interference in the procedure has been frequent. It must be added that this 'normal' procedure is further complicated by specific concordats that may exist, as is the case in certain cantons in Switzerland. One would have to refer to the specific concordat and its regulations concerning the appointment of bishops in the diocese of the canton concerned.

11.   In general the rules governing the election of diocesans by specific corporations in the Church have to be studied individually, as they differ, at times considerably, from one another, but the general outline given above is an indication of what could be considered a 'normal' procedure.

12.   It is true that the pre-eminent role of the Pope reflects a gradual historical and theological centralisation that was at least in part an attempt to cope with certain abuses. It also reflects his mission to promote the common good of the universal Church and the particular good of all Churches (*Christus Dominus*, 2). On the other hand, the continued existence of the rights of particular groups to elect their bishop, is not only a reflection of earlier practice but also an indication that centralisation does not necessarily mean uniformity.

c. Qualifications for Episcopate

1. In order for a person to be a suitable candidate for the episcopate it is required that he be:

i. outstanding for his solid faith, good morals, piety, zeal for souls, wisdom, prudence and human virtue and endowed with the other talents which made him fit to fulfil the office in question;
ii. in possession of a good reputation;
iii. at least thirty-five years of age;
iv. ordained a priest for at least five years;
v. in possession of a doctorate or at least a licentiate in sacred scripture, theology or canon law from an institute of higher studies approved by the Apostolic See or at least truly expert in these same disciplines.

2. The definitive judgement concerning the suitability of the person to be promoted belongs to the Apostolic See.   Canon 378

13. Paragraph 2 is a further confirmation of the special role of the Holy See in the designation process and it largely restates Canons 331 and 333 of the 1917 Code regarding the judgement as to whether a particular candidate meets the legal requirements of the episcopal office. A point worth noting is the fact that the Holy See expresses the 'definitive judgement', which implies that other judgements are also relevant during the process.

14. When reference is made to the Holy See in the canons on the designation of bishops, it usually means the Sacred Congregation for Bishops unless one is dealing with the missionary churches when the competent congregation is the Sacred Congregation for the Evangelization of Peoples. When the selection of bishops involves negotiations with civil governments, the Council for the Public Affairs of the Church is competent.

d. Requirement of Consecration

Unless he is held back by a legitimate impediment, whoever is promoted to the episcopate must receive episcopal consecration within three months from the reception of the apostolic letter and before he takes possession of his office.

                                                                Canon 379

15. In requiring consecration prior to the taking possession of office (*Lumen Gentium*, 21), the present canon reflects the conciliar emphasis on the significance of episcopal consecration for the conferral of the power of government. One might note also Canon 1013, 'No bishop is permitted to consecrate anyone a bishop unless it is first evident that there is a pontifical

mandate', and Canon 1014, 'Unless a dispensation has been granted by the Apostolic See, the principal consecrating bishop in an episcopal consecration is to associate to himself at least two other consecrating bishops; but it is especially appropriate that all the bishops who are present should consecrate the bishop-elect along with the bishops mentioned.' Also, relevant, given the Lefebvre Affair, is Canon 1382 excommunicating a bishop consecrating another bishop without a papal mandate. This is one of the few excommunications whose remission is reserved to the Holy See - an indication of the seriousness with which the legislator takes this legal violation. 'A bishop who consecrates someone a bishop and the person who receives such a consecration from a bishop without a pontifical mandate incur an automatic (*latae sententiae*) excommunication reserved to the Apostolic See.' (Canon 1382).

e.   Profession of Faith and Oath of Loyalty

> Before he takes canonical possession of his office, the person promoted is to make a profession of faith and take an oath of fidelity to the Apostolic See in accord with a formula approved by the same Apostolic See.
>
> Canon 380

16.   The demands of ecclesial communion as emphasised by the canon seem to underlie the twofold obligation of a profession of faith and an expression of loyalty, by oath, to the Holy See on the part of the bishop-designate.

ii.   In the Orthodox and Oriental Orthodox Churches

17.   We speak more generally about the appointment of bishops in Orthodox and Oriental Orthodox Churches, where there is a degree of variation.

18.   Bishops in the Orthodox Churches are elected.[1] The election may have to be confirmed by a 'secular' figure - the tsar, the sultan, the minister of cults, for example.

---

[1]   Cf. C. Konstantinides, 'The Episcopal Order and the Bishop in the Orthodox Church', in *Bishops*, ed. G. Simon (London, 1961), p. 80.

19.   Those eligible to vote in such an election vary from Church to Church, and this eligibility has varied slightly at different times in the history of the Orthodox Churches. In some it is the Holy Synod (which is of course exclusively of bishops - the ecclesiology being that the laity and clergy are represented in their bishop). In some Churches there is a degree of lay involvement. The majority would probably say that this was theoretically at least a desirable, or perhaps even essential, element. The proportion of lay involvement varies. In the Indian Orthodox Church it is substantial, requiring a majority vote of the equivalent of the House of Laity of the General Synod.

20.   All the Orthodox and Oriental Orthodox Churches at present will elect only unmarried men to the episcopate, for in principle a Bishop must be a monk, because bishops are to be models of godliness and spirituality, free from worldly involvement. In practice nowadays the candidate is not always a member of a monastic community but will be a celibate priest. The Byzantine Orthodox will accept a widower as a bishop though not all the Oriental Orthodox will do so. In the past married men were validly and canonically elected as bishops and the point is occasionally made that an Ecumenical Council could restore this situation.

21.   In most of the Orthodox and Oriental Churches candidates for episcopal office are selected from a particular monastic class - Archimandrites (the Byzantine Orthodox), Vartopeds (the Armenians), Rambans (Indian Orthodox), etc. An elected candidate not in one of these groups may be admitted to it prior to his episcopal consecration.

22.   Practice differs concerning the chorepiscopate. For the Copts, the *chorepiscopos* must be a celibate. The Indian Orthodox treat the chorepiscopate as largely an honorific title with no powers of ordaining, and will admit married men to the office.

23.   The election to the office of bishop may itself take a quasi-liturgical form in some of the Orthodox Churches. Popular ratification of the election is liturgically expressed in most traditions by the shouting of *axios* ('worthy') at the actual consecration. In most of the rites currently in use, however, this acclamation does not take place until after the laying on of hands has occurred. It cannot therefore strictly be viewed as a potential veto of the election.

iii. In Lutheran Churches

24. It is difficult[2] to give a clear or comprehensive picture of current developments in Lutheran practice in the appointment of bishops because there is no uniform pattern of procedure. The consistent principle, however, is that they should be elected. In Denmark the assumption of absolute power by the King in 1660 led to some acceptance of the view that it was lawful for the King to appoint bishops on behalf of the laity, because he was the first member of the Church.[3] In Sweden the Church Order of 1571 created an organ for the election of bishops, consisting of clergy (and sometimes laymen) experienced in church affairs. The electors took an oath, and made their election by majority vote. The person thus chosen then went in person to the sovereign to have his election confirmed.[4] In Germany[5] the Landesherrliche Kirchenregiment, or system of church government derived from the sixteenth century practice of asking local 'princes' or 'lords' to provide a secular patronage and protection, came to an end with the First World War. This was replaced by a local leadership shared between bishop and synod. The Landesbischof now shares authority with a synod which can 'appoint' him by electing him, or remove him from office.

It is suggested in the Niagara Report that Lutheran Churches may 'want to revise the procedures for identifying and nominating candidates for election to the ministry of bishop so that God's gifts of leadership and governance (I Corinthians 12.28) are properly recognized and called to office' (90), as part of a process of change in which constitutions are revised 'so that bishops are elected to the same tenure of office as are congregational pastors, chaplains, and other pastoral ministers in the Church' (*ibid.*). The point of substance here is that the mode of appointment of bishops is unavoidably and properly a function of the understanding of the character of the episcopate to which they are to be appointed; and this is itself at a stage of crucial development in the Lutheran Churches.

---

2   The subject is barely touched upon in the papers of the Anglican-Lutheran Consultation on *Episcope* (1987) or in the Niagara Report.

3   *Episcopacy in the Lutheran Church?*, ed. I. Asheim and V.R. Gold (Philadelphia, 1970), p. 122.

4   *Ibid.*, p. 128.

5   See *Niagara Report*, Appendix IV.

Appendix III (a)

WOMEN AND THE EPISCOPATE

An Outline of the Theological Issues

bearing upon the Ordination

of Women to the Episcopate

by

George Carey

5.6.1987

Introduction

1.   I have sought in this paper to identify the principal issues bearing upon the ordination of women to the episcopate and the differences of opinion in relation to those issues.   I have received contributions and suggestions from various members of the Archbishops' Group on the Episcopate which I have incorporated into the paper, but it is essentially my work and, although written in the plural, does *not* emanate from the Group as a whole.

2.   The paper is divided into a number of different sections, as follows:

a.   The use of scripture

b.   Theological issues relating to the episcopate
    (i)   Bishop as focus of unity
    (ii)   Bishop as focus of authority and mission
    (iii) Images of ministry

c.   Ecumenical factors

d.   The experience of women in the world

a.   The use of scripture

3.   By starting with the interpretation of scripture we recognise its normative role in regulating and guiding theological truth. Whilst Anglican theology has always attempted to hold together scripture, tradition and reason as essential and complementary sources of faith, the primacy of the Bible is accepted by us all.

4.   This traditional Anglican understanding of the way we do our theology is placed under stress, however, when radical changes in society or Church introduce factors which challenge our assumptions and received theology.   In addition to the issue of the ordination of women to the priesthood and the episcopate, there are also ethical and political questions which involve the same dilemma. How does the community of faith listen to the faithful witness of its foundational documents, learn from the experience of the Church past and present, as well as respond to the world in which its ministry and mission is located?

5.   The Church must not approach challenges which call for change or development by simply reiterating biblical texts as if they are self-evident. Hermeneutical consideration requires that we take into account the social and cultural presuppositions and the systems of thought which separate the biblical world from our own. These two worlds need to be brought into engagement with each other. It is only in this way that we can begin to discover the meaning of the original text and what application it might have to our contemporary situation.   How do we decide what are the eternal values to be retained and what are the secondary factors which simply mark out social elements which belonged to the mores of a past society? For example, what does it mean to say that women are made in the 'image of God' in the setting of contemporary society? Even if we are persuaded that the Pauline injunctions ruled out full participation of women in ministry in the first century, we would still need to ask whether and on what grounds we consider that these have authority and relevance for us today.

6.   It was with these questions in mind that we began our work together by looking at a number of key texts which have been used in the arguments for and against the ordination of women.

The Genesis accounts of creation: women and men made in the image of God

7.   We are agreed that women as much as men are made in the image and likeness of God. Both accounts in Genesis, while differing in certain respects, are at one in showing that male and female share a special relationship with God in which each express his image and enjoy his love. Each is made for the other in a relationship of unity.

8.   We all agree that God is a God of order, and that there is order in the creation relationship between men and women. Our disagreement centres on our understanding of that relationship. For some of us there is an inherent equality and complementarity between the sexes, and any assumption of male authority is to be seen as a consequence of the fall. Others of us, while asserting an equality of nature and essence between men and women, would distinguish this from an assumption of equality of function. They would see a male authority as part of the order of creation.

The position of women in the New Creation

9.   We recognise that Christ's salvation has a significance which extends far beyond a spiritual relationship with God. Any doctrine of the Kingdom which refuses to acknowledge social and political consequences is seriously deficient. A theology of humanity made 'in the image of God' and the Kingdom 'breaking in' has profound repercussions upon our understanding of poverty, social order and the sharing of resources. Similarly, there are many clues in the New Testament to indicate that the writers understood that the powerful impact of the gospel affected relationships in society and in family life. A gospel shaped by sacrifice and love is clearly going to influence concepts of authority and hierarchy. Thus we see that Paul's injunctions to the family in Ephesians - to love, submit, obey - are expressions of life lived 'as to the Lord'.

10.   Our understanding of the position of women in the new creation must begin with Jesus's own relationship with women and his acceptance of their ministry to him. Their place at his side in death, and in the first moments of the Resurrection, reveal a ministry which their presence in the Upper Room at Pentecost suggests does not come to an end with his Ascension.

Indeed, the Spirit falls on all flesh and women are among the recipients of
the Spirit of Christ.

Pauline teaching

11.   It is true that this data has been variously interpreted. Paul's
instructions concerning the use of gifts in ministry (I Corinthians 12) surely
have implications for our discussion. Some of us believe that the out-
pouring of the Spirit's gifts raises the question: How can a 'ministry' be
refused if a 'charism' has been given? So some of us see women among the
prophets. This memorandum must do justice to those among us who have
been just as keen as the rest of the group to see women's gifts exercised in
the Church but feel that the evidence does not lend support to women
exercising episcopal authority over men. New Testament scholarship
emphasises the different strands in Paul's statements concerning the role of
women in the Churches. Some interpreters claim that there is a clear gospel
message in Pauline theology which is radical in its implications. For
example, they argue that Galatians 3.28 is a radical charter of human
freedom and equality which affects profoundly the place of women in the
new society of the Church. Others, on the other hand, believe that the thrust
of this and similar texts refers to our spiritual freedom and unity in Christ
conferred by baptism. Whatever the correct interpretation may be, it is true
that the great number of references to women among his close workers and
friends, show that Paul affirmed them strongly, and that they made a major
contribution to the spread of the Christian faith.

12.   Nevertheless, there are other aspects in the Pauline letters which
appear to some of us to point in a different direction. His acceptance of
women prophets in the churches (I Corinthians 11.5) is puzzling alongside
his 'Let your women keep silence in the churches' (I Corinthians 14.34).
Although this may be interpreted as Paul's instructions to maintain order in
assembly (especially if women were separated from men on the synagogue
pattern), it seems to breathe a disapproving attitude which appears to clash
with the picture noted earlier. In this connection we have to note the
strongly worded statement in I Timothy 2 where the apostle or writer
forbids women to 'teach or have authority over men'. Recent scholarship
suggests that *authentein* should be understood as 'domineering' and may
have reference to the nature of the particular heresy enjoying favour at
Ephesus at the time. The entire passage, of course, bristles with exegetical

problems when we try to relate it to the place of women in society and Church today.

13.   Some of us believe that issues of submission and headship are only debated by Paul in the context of marriage; while others of us believe that I Corinthians 11 provides a wider setting in relation to the creation ordinance. (We must note that Paul's mention of headship in 11.2 does not relate to his observation of women as prophets but to seemly behaviour.)

Conclusion on the biblical data

14.   Very much reflecting the difference of opinion in the wider Church, we discover among us disagreement concerning both the original meaning of the biblical material and its interpretation today. While on the one hand we are united in our concern that women should find fulfilment in the service of Christ, we differ in our evaluation of the pertinent scriptures. However, we have valued the open and honest discussion and we perceive an urgent need in the Anglican Communion within the context of the wider Church for a forum in which exploration of the text may be done not polemically but sympathetically, openly and in a spirit of Christian love.

b.   Theological issues relating to the Episcopate

15.   Most ecclesiologists agree that no one single Church order is found in the pages of the New Testament. On the contrary, the profusion of ministries in all their variety expresses the vitality of the infant Church. But towards the end of the Apostolic era a two-fold local ministry of presbyter-bishops and deacons became the dominant Church order. A further development took place in the second century as a three-fold order of ministry in the local Church emerged of one bishop, assisted by presbyters and deacons.

16.   The history of the growth of the Church might suggest to some that the emergence of the episcopate was but a matter of pastoral administration. While the first Christians were concerned for the good news of Jesus Christ, crucified and risen, to redeem humankind, this did not mean that the Church through which the message of salvation came was a mere functional entity. Because of the integral nature of Gospel and Church, the body of Christ was believed to be sign and instrument of communion with God. That is to say,

the outward form of the Church was expressive of the inner life of the invisible community where Christ reigns supreme. Moreover, the bishop's role as a pastor of the local Church was seen as a visible sign and an instrument of the community in the heritage of the apostles.

17.   The theology of ministry as expressing apostolic continuity is enshrined in three important early witnesses: Ignatius of Antioch, Irenaeus of Lyons and Cyprian of Carthage.

(a) *The bishops as the centre of unity.* The Church for Ignatius is at heart a eucharistic community. In his seven letters the picture of the local Church gathered around a table where its bishop presides is an inspiring and interesting vignette of the life of the early Church. The bishop as leader, and by his role as the one who presides, acts as the visible centre of the unity of the local Christian community. It seems that Ignatius saw a remarkable link between the work of the Father and that of the bishop. Just as Christ is the focus of salvation and draws people into fellowship with God, so the bishop focuses on earth the unity which was its reality in heaven. Indeed, the bishop according to Ignatius is a 'type' of the Father. As such he represents the authority of the Father and deserves to be followed as 'Jesus Christ did the Father', for 'Where the bishop is, there is the Church'.

(b) *The bishop as a sign of apostolic continuity.* Writing against Gnosticism towards the end of the second century Irenaeus was led to attach to the episcopal office another sense. Because of the Gnostic claim that divine truth had been 'handed down' by their own teachers, Irenaeus countered this argument by insisting that the true Christian 'paradosis' was evident in a continuity of apostolic teaching in those very Churches which had been founded by the apostles. Irenaeus' attention, of course, was on the truth of the gospel but it has this important corollary that he considered the episcopal office to be rooted in the apostolic faith.

(c) *The conciliar and collegial character of the episcopate.* Arising from controversy with Rome and issues within his own diocese, Cyprian of Carthage emphasized the collective and collegial aspects of episcopacy. The theological issue he wrestled with was the relationship of the local Church to the Universal Church. He insisted that the fullness of the faith was to be found in each local Church as it is united to its bishop around the eucharistic celebration. Although never independent, each Church is a Church in its own right, a full expression of the totality of the Catholic faith. For

Cyprian, therefore, each bishop received the fullness of the episcopal *charisma* and in his office he focuses the unity of the universal Church.

18. Whilst we recognize that Ignatius, Irenaeus and Cyprian do not either singly or corporately express a full theology of episcopacy, the insights they contribute are most valuable for the modern Church as we struggle to clarify our understanding of the nature of the episcopate. The issue concerning whether and under what conditions a woman may be appointed bishop is related to some of the theological principles touched upon above. The following topics are central to our study.

The bishop as focus of unity

19. As we have already noted, the attention of the three patristic writers was upon the nature of the bishops as ecclesial centre of unity; as witness to continuity because through his teaching office he is faithful to the teachings of the apostles; and as manifesting and maintaining the collegiality of the Church by episcopal ordination. Therefore, the bishop is a *focus* and a *sign* of the unity of the local Church and of its place in the Universal Church. He is a *focus* of a gathered people around a common table and in continuity to a common gospel and as such he is a *sign* of the *oneness God wills for his people*.

20. The question that concerns us as we explore the issue of *Women and the Episcopate* relates to the nature of the unity of the Church: Are there any factors at the heart of apostolic continuity and collegiality which either contest the ordination of women to the episcopate or which reinforce its desirability at some point?

21. *Apostolic continuity* is sometimes used as an argument against the ordination of a woman to the episcopate on the grounds that such an appointment would constitute an even greater break with past traditions than that of the ordination of women to the priesthood. This conclusion is based upon the bishop's role as President of the presbyteral college, and, more significantly for some of us, the argument that because the bishop is a *sign* of the fidelity of the apostolic teaching, to change the sign is to endanger the link with the past. There is little doubt that this would be perceived by many as a break with the received pattern of Christian ministry, but those who support the ordination of women to the episcopate remind us that there have been many contested developments in Church history which later

generations of Christians considered to be the will of God for his Church. Tradition, according to this view, is never static. Rather, controlled by the apostolic kerygma, led by the Spirit of God and interpreted by godly men and women in the Church, it may break forth into new forms of truth which were only dimly perceived by earlier generations.

22.   Whilst we must conclude that tradition by itself is not absolute, any doctrine of development implies organs of critical discernment, and we must acknowledge that there have been false developments in Church history. Our Anglican tradition, however, attempts to hold together two lines of approach. On the one hand, the possibility of new actions through which the Spirit of God leads his people into new appreciation of truth. And on the other hand, that same tradition reminds us that we are not *'the* Church', not the *only* place where God's truth is to be found; hence our awareness of the essential 'catholic' and conciliar dimensions of the Christian faith.

23.   Mention of the conciliar dimension of the faith reminds us that closely related to the understanding of the bishops as a 'focus' of unity is the notion of *Collegiality*, which as we saw earlier was prominent in the patristic understanding of the episcopate. The bishop is not merely consecrated for his own see. He is a sign of the unity of the whole Church and has a quasi-sacramental role in representing the universal Church to the local and the local to the universal. Although each bishop is a bishop in his own right as each Church is fully a Church in its own right, no bishop of a Church is independent of the body of which he is a part. The sign of collegiality is the bishop acting in union with his brother bishops in maintaining the faith 'once delivered to the saints'. If a woman were to be consecrated bishop and her episcopate were not recognised by other bishops of her Province or indeed by other Provinces of the Anglican Communion, the unity of the Communion would be greatly impaired. The non-recognition of the orders of women priests is already placing a strain on the unity of the Anglican Communion. The non-recognition of bishops who are called to be the focus of unity and continuity would be an even more serious matter. Further, not only would a woman bishop be unacceptable to such provinces who have not taken this step, but the orders of priests (male as well as female) ordained by her would be put in question. It appears to be the case, then, that the ordination of women bishops at the moment would constitute a fundamental fracture in the collegiality of the Anglican Communion; the *koinonia* of which, already impaired by women priests, would be further damaged if provinces took this step by themselves. Yet equally for others of us that same *koinonia* could be seen as already

impaired by the exclusion of women from the priesthood and ultimately from the episcopate, and for these therefore a maintaining of the status quo threatens that same unity just as powerfully if more subtly. For such, unity is not maintained by the exclusion of women but rather progressively diminished.

The bishop as focus of authority and mission

24. Central to the episcopate is *authority*. The authority of the bishop resides in two important areas of ministry. First, in the fact that in his office the authority that is focused is God's authority in the community. Christianity is a corporate faith; we need the Christian community to live as Christians; and we stand under the authority of ministry which conveys God's word and his sacraments to us. The bishop represents to us the universal Church in its faithful adherence to the apostolic teachings. As a 'Servant of the servants of God' the authority offered to us in him is a way in which the harmony and health of the family is fostered. Aspects of this will inevitably include his authority expressed in terms of discipline. Further, as placed over those 'in the Lord' he represents the fatherly care of God to the people of God and mediates to the community the wisdom and love which is pre-eminently expressed in the ministry of Christ. That pattern of authority is the awesome ministry of service in which love, humility and gentleness are enshrined.

25. To some of us the question: *'Can a woman exercise episcopal authority in the Church?'* invites the response, Yes, of course, because the Christian notion of authority transcends issues of sexual differentiation. No male bishop exercises his ministry as a 'male' and in our judgement the authority of a woman bishop would not stem from her sex but from the office conferred upon her.

26. However, we have to recognise that the issue of episcopal authority for some is rooted in a theology of humanity in which issues of gender are integral to a theology of oversight and representation. Some base this on a theology of headship which they find in Scripture and others on a theology of apostolic continuity, both of which we have considered briefly. Common to both these approaches is a view of ministry which forbids the exercise of the primary episcopal function of oversight in any authoritative sense. Therefore to argue from function to office is beside the point; women are precluded from exercising authority as a bishop on grounds of gender.

27.   A further factor arises in relation to the acceptance of authority in a Church divided over the nature of its ministry. If one function of ordination is to confer authority, we have to ask whether a woman bishop would be recognized as expressing that authority on behalf of the whole Church. Unfortunately, it does seem likely that in a Province divided over the admission of women to the episcopate, the leadership of a woman bishop would be greatly challenged and her office called into question.

28.   *The Mission of the Church.* We have already noted the close connection between the unity of the Church focussed in the office of the bishop and the mission of the Church in the world. As we see it, there appear to be two aspects to the bishop's missionary role: he is to be the 'public face' of the Gospel and he is to ensure that the people of God in his care live up to their missionary calling. For some of us, the Church's mission will be hindered if women are ordained to the episcopate.

29.   For others of us, a decision against ordaining women to the episcopate could seriously hinder the proclamation of the good news in Christ Jesus. It is claimed that the presence of women on the episcopal bench would make available at that level of leadership the particular contribution of women, thus manifesting complementarity as an episcopal reality and also expressing to the world that unity between men and women in service to each other and to Christ.

30.   *Images of Ministry.* For many people the issue of 'maleness' is at the heart of the problem of the ordination of women to the priesthood. An 'iconic' representation of God (and later the *imago Christi*) is a fundamental feature of episcopal and presbyteral ministries in patristic sources. There are those who believe that such theological sources suggest that 'maleness' is not an optional extra but an indispensable element of ministry. However, we do not have to reject an 'iconic' feature of the episcopal office to affirm the possibility of women becoming bishops. If as we have seen, the source of the image was originally the eucharistic celebration, we can only say that a woman cannot represent Christ if we hold, as many do, that the maleness of Jesus is an inherent feature of the economy of salvation. Some who would not want to press this argument at the level of logic can see that psychologically there is a fittingness in preserving the tradition that the ministers in the sacrament of our redemption acting 'not in their own name but Christ's' (Art. 26) are masculine. Others of us, however, would want to assert that if maleness is essential to Christian ministry, at that very point many women would feel excluded from the eucharistic celebration.

31. The theological argument above raises theological questions which relate to the significance of the maleness of Jesus and its congruence with the economy of salvation. What weight do we place on the particularity of Jesus' maleness as compared with the particularity of his Jewishness? Does 'maleness' correspond to the divine nature in a way that 'femaleness' does not? Some of us want to respond that if any weight is placed upon the bishop representing the total community he can only do this because of the humanity he shares with us all and not because of a 'maleness' he shares with Christ.

32. The last paragraph raised sharply the issue - is it 'maleness' or 'humanity' that is appropriate in imaging Christ and the continuity of male apostles? There are those amongst us who, whilst rejecting the argument based on Christ's 'maleness' are very sensitive to the link between the office of bishop and the cluster of masculine images and metaphors which undergird the office. We therefore addressed ourselves to the question: 'Would the admission of women to the episcopal office destroy something essential in the theology of episcopacy which is enshrined in masculine terms, such as 'Father in God'?' Some of us feel this issue very keenly and argue that a concept such as 'Father in God' is more than an image. It is deeply integrated with the work of God and the representative functions of the bishop. Those who press this point are well aware of the analogical use of theological language but they believe that more than language is at stake here, because to change the image comes very close to shattering the truth the image enshrines.

33. On the other hand, others among us argue that theological and biblical language is rarely univocal and assert that while exclusively masculine terms would have to be removed from the concept of bishop if women were appointed, this would not mean that anything of real substance is lost. It is probable, they argue, that other images would very quickly be found for an office now shared by men and women.

34. *Reception.* Although we acknowledge that provinces at the present time have the constitutional right to admit women to the episcopate, some of us question whether they have the theological right to do so if collegiality is essential to the notion of the episcopate. That is to say, the process of consultation is not complete at the stage when a Province has made up its own mind. A decision that a province believes to express God's truth for its own life has to be tested and confirmed by the wider Church of which it claims to be a part. So that failure to consult, or unwillingness to heed the

advice of other member Churches in its communion, will indicate that it does not take the consultative process seriously.

35.   Moreover, a true doctrine of reception cannot be elaborated by Anglicans in isolation from the whole Church. Some of us will wish to give more emphasis to the experience of women ministers in many protestant Churches while others will wish to pay regard to the official attitudes of the Orthodox and Roman Catholic Churches with which Anglicans claim to share the historic episcopate.

36.   Yet, others of us again the group would wish to question whether the capacity of the Church to 'receive' a new development without breach of communion should be one of the tests by which we assess the appropriateness of development. If that were the case, many of the things we value within the Church as symbols of truth and therefore of unity - two-natures in Christ, credal statements, secured after long periods of controversy, would hardly stand up to that criterion. The history of doctrinal development hints at the opposite viewpoint that Churches which refuse to entertain the possibility of radical change may be equally guilty of failing to heed the principle of collegiality.

c.   Ecumenical Factors

37.   The significance of the ecumenical movement is that no Church lives in complete isolation any more. The contribution of the multilateral and bilateral texts together with the work currently being done by English ARC on Anglican/RC Ordinals are signs of encouragement. We need to bring into focus just as strongly as the Anglican/RC links, however, particularly those with whom we share in local ecumenical projects in this country where the contribution of women to the ordained ministry is harmonious and extremely positive. In non-Episcopal Churches where the ordained ministry of women has been a fact for many years the experience of ordained women in leadership has not led to the division and conflict that some fear.

38.   On the other hand, while it is important to do as much theology as possible together with other Churches, so that our dialogue may strengthen our growing unity, we cannot do our theology wholly constrained by the traditions and discipline of other bodies. Our theology, especially in the area of ministry and mission, must be true to ourselves and to the character

of Church life that mirrors our experience of God's grace. Within a fractured Church, Churches can only work out for themselves the balance between what it is essential to do together, what they can legitimately do apart and what they should do apart. We recognize, however, that what we decide and how we decide to do it will often have implications for unity with other Christian bodies. Great sensitivity too, and awareness of, the wider Christian community must guide the internal structuring of a Church's life.

39.   While we have asserted that a Church must have some autonomy over its own life, the irony is that a change which will be welcomed by some member Churches of the WCC,[1] will be regretted by others. We have to recognize that there will be implications for our dialogue with Rome and the Orthodox Church and to our existing relationship with the Old Catholics, if the Church of England ordains women as priests. The problem will be compounded if women are admitted to the episcopate. We considered the two sides of this question. On the one hand, communion with Rome is nearer now than at any other time since the Reformation, opening the way to the reconciliation of the ministries of our two Churches. Surely, some argue, it is reckless to brush aside the sensitive ecumenism which has been going on for the last fifteen years, Recognition of one another's ministry would mean that both Churches could then address the issue of women's ministry together.

40.   Against that, the counter argument is put that it would be wrong to sacrifice on the altar of unity a widespread desire in our Church that women should play a full and equal part in the ministry of God's people. Indeed, some would argue, the very move towards greater openness to each other in the Church arises from the same movement of the Holy Spirit in our hearts as he breaks down the barriers between male and female.

d.   **The experience of women in the contemporary world**

41.   During this century there has been a social revolution which has gradually emancipated women from their previous role definitions. With increasing freedom in society to follow their chosen careers and interests, women have made their impact in many areas of life. In this country

---

[1]   World Council of Churches.

legislation designed to ensure equality of treatment in the workplace has been an indicator of the tide of feeling in society. But it is not by Acts of Parliament that the transformation has really been brought about but by the acceptance within the community of the equality of status of men and women. It has become generally accepted that domestically there is a sharing of responsibility and division of tasks between them. Within numerous professions, commerce, industry and government, men and women work alongside each other, respecting the contribution which each person is making within his or her own sphere, irrespective of sex.

42.   Young women can now confidently expect to be able to make use of their skills and abilities on equal terms with men in most areas of life. They have already seen women in positions of responsibility and exercising leadership in government and other professions.

43.   Within the Church there have also been changes. We bear in mind that many of the Churches around the world owe a debt to women in the past who carried out missionary, teaching and pastoral functions. In some of those Churches there are now women priests, and it is a growing acceptance of their ministry and leadership in their congregations which has given rise to the possibility of a woman becoming a bishop. As the Lima Report notes:

> In some traditions *episcope* is already exercised by women and the possibility of women among the *episkopoi* is becoming an ever closer reality.

Within our own Church there have not been such major changes, but women have been engaging in greater numbers in positions of leadership. Women deacons have been given pastoral charge of parishes. Many have the same qualifications as their male contemporaries, but they are not at present able to become priests.

44.   Having noted the experience of women in the contemporary world, both within as well as outside the Church, we are agreed that the ordination of women to the episcopate has to be justified on theological grounds and not simply by reference to the fact that women nowadays frequently hold positions of authority and leadership in society or because they are already exercising certain ministries in the Church. Nevertheless, what is happening in society poses a number of questions to our theological assumptions. To a certain extent it is nothing new in the history of the Church to see women in positions of authority when we recall the pre-Reformation Abbess. We have

to consider whether we are now being pointed towards a new break with tradition. For those of us who consider maleness essential to episcopal and presbyterate ministry this is not an acceptable approach to the question. But for others the fact that women have demonstrated their ability as leaders in society, and are doing so in various ways within the Church, is very relevant to our quest to interpret God's truth at the present day.

Appendix III (b)

Pastoral Guidelines

from

The Report of the Archbishop of Canterbury's Commission on Communion and Women in the Episcopate, Eames Commission (1989), 56 - 78

56.   The Mission and Ministry Section of the Lambeth Conference Report, 1988, page 61, outlines key elements in the exercise of episcopal ministry. Among other things, the bishop is:

(a)   a symbol of the Unity of the Church in its mission;
(b)   a teacher and defender of the faith;
(c)   a pastor of the pastors and of the laity;
(d)   an enabler in the preaching of the Word, and in the administration of the Sacraments;
(e)   a leader in mission and an initiator of outreach to the world surrounding the community of the faithful;
(f)   a shepherd who nurtures and cares for the flock of God;
(g)   a physician to whom are brought the wounds of society;
(h)   a voice of conscience within the society in which the local Church is placed;
(i)   a prophet who proclaims the justice of God in the context of the Gospel of loving redemption;
(j)   a head of the family in its wholeness, its misery and its joy. The bishop is the family's centre of life and love.

Each of these elements of episcopal ministry has implications for relationships between dioceses and Provinces as the bishop has a particular responsibility to foster the communion and interdependence of local Churches.

a.   A symbol of unity

57.   The bishop is an embodiment and agent of unity and continuity in the Church. Where bishops minister in dioceses and/or provinces in which there is strong division of opinion on the question of the ordination of women to the episcopate, they should exercise special care lest they cease to be agents of unity by becoming focal points of dissension. Since the bishop is a symbol

319

of unity the idea of parallel jurisdictions is inappropriate. The ECUSA model for Episcopal Visitors could be looked at sympathetically.

b.   A teacher and defender of the faith

58.   Bishops   should place the matter of the ordination of women to the priesthood and episcopate within the overall context of reflection on Scripture, Tradition and the development of doctrine and practice. Given differences of opinion on this matter, however, bishops should take every opportunity to emphasise their fundamental agreement on matters of faith, practice, and the received understanding of apostolic ministry to which they all steadfastly adhere.   Both those who support and those who are opposed to the ordination of women are motivated by the common desire to preserve and remain faithful to the historic threefold ministry of bishops, priests and deacons.

c.   Pastor of the pastors and of the laity

59.   Bishops should take particular care to minister to all clergy and laity in their pastoral charge, especially to those who may disagree with them on this issue. Clergy and laity who disagree with their diocesan bishop should be encouraged to take every opportunity to express their point of view sensitively and clearly and enter into a full dialogue, so that mutual trust and respect may grow. Provision for Episcopal Visitors is a way of exercising pastoral care.

60.   In the exercise of any aspect of episcopal ministry in a diocese other than their own, visiting bishops should act in accordance with Resolution 72 affirmed by the Lambeth Conference, which reads as follows:

This Conference:

1. Reaffirms its unity in the historical position of respect for diocesan boundaries and the authority of bishops within these boundaries; and in light of the above

2. Affirms that it is deemed inappropriate behaviour for any bishop or priest of this Communion to exercise episcopal or pastoral ministry within another diocese without first obtaining the permission and invitation of the ecclesial authority thereof.

d.   Enabler in the preaching of the Word and in the administration of the Sacraments

61.   1. Where visiting bishops accept invitations to exercise the ministry of the Word they should do so in ways which foster the overall edification of the whole Church. Visiting bishops should exercise sacramental ministry in the following way:

> Where there is agreement among Provinces in the matter of the consecration of women to the episcopate, visiting bishops would be free to participate fully in any sacramental act.

Where there is disagreement among Provinces,

> i. Bishops should uphold the canonical position of the Province from which they come, out of respect for the local Church which they represent.   In order to foster the highest degree of communion canonically possible, however, they may be present at sacramental acts, recognising that 'presence' is indicative of a degree of communion.

> ii. Care should be taken that such 'presence' should not become an occasion of divisive demonstration.

62.   2. The growing practice of admitting children to communion on the basis of baptism and prior to confirmation, along with the provision of the Confirmation Rubric of the *1662 Prayer Book* for those 'desirous to be confirmed' to be admitted to communion prior to confirmation, there seems little, if any, possibility of an occasion arising where a person confirmed by a woman bishop would legitimately be excluded from communion in the diocese of a bishop who is yet to be convinced of the propriety of women's ordination and consecration.

In the light of the above observation, the Commission strongly discourages any suggestion of re-confirmation.

In Churches where confirmation is understood as a commissioning of a person for adult responsibility in the life and ministry of the Church or where confirmation is canonically required of those who desire to hold office in the Church, the local discipline should be re-examined and revised, so that a bona fide communicant in good standing in one Province is not excluded from participating as fully as possible in the life and ministry of another.

63.   3.   It is already clear that some people may feel unable to recognise the validity of ordinations presided over by a woman bishop. Also, in some Provinces it is not at present possible to give canonical recognition to those ordained elsewhere by a woman bishop. During the process of reception, at least for a certain period, it is recommended that ordinations be carried out collegially. The collegial participation of a male bishop does not question the validity of a woman bishop's consecration nor her capacity to confer orders but rather protects the interests of the ordinand and the communities in which he or she may minister in the future.

e.   A leader in mission

64.   The mission of the Church is to restore all people to unity with God and each other in Christ. The ability of the world to learn and understand the message of reconciliation is related to the Church's capacity to live that message out in community.

65.   Bishops should take the initiative to listen and to interpret opposing views so that the Church's witness to reconciliation, peace, and concord is not obscured.

f. & g.   A physician for wounds and a shepherd for nurture

66.   In being a healer of wounded persons and shepherd for nurture of people, the bishop deals not only with hurt resulting from a breakdown in inter-personal relationships, but also with various conflicts within the ecclesiastical institution as a whole. In exercising a ministry of reconciliation, the bishop will often use resources of consultation and advice beyond the episcopal office.

67.   In Provinces in which there is continuing controversy over the ordination and consecration of women it is desirable that specific action be taken in the resolution of conflict. For example, it may be creative for a Province to invite facilitators to visit from another Province of the Communion for 3 or 6 months to foster communication between polarized groups and to encourage reconciliation where communication has broken down.

h. & i. Prophecy and conscience

68.   In addressing matters of conscience and prophecy bishops should take account of the multiplicity of social and ethical issues confronting Church and society and not focus exclusively on the single issue of the ordination of women.   A detailed account of such issues is found in the chapter entitled 'Christianity and the Social Order' in the Lambeth Conference 1988 Report *The Truth Shall Make You Free*, pp. 155 ff.

j.   A centre of life and love

69.   In Churches in which it is not canonically possible for visiting women priests and bishops to be invited to exercise sacramental functions, it is desirable that positive opportunities should be created for mutual encounter and dialogue.   The meeting of Anglicans from different Provinces, for the mutual exchange of views in a spirit of fellowship and charity, is an expression of the communion we enjoy by virtue of our common baptism and shared history and tradition.   Dialogue is important for living together through tension and is a means of deepening our communion despite acknowledged differences of opinion and practice.

70.   Provinces should, therefore, welcome and foster visits of overseas women priests and bishops; this is particularly desirable where Provinces have decided against the ordination and consecration of women or have yet to resolve the matter.   In this way the people of God in the Provinces concerned will have at least a limited experience of the ministry of women, and some opportunity to understand and appreciate developments elsewhere in the Communion.   The fostering of such visits should be taken up as a particular responsibility of the primatial leadership in each Province. Bishops should be encouraged to license ordained women to those orders to which they are allowed to by Canon.

71.   There is a mutual responsibility for the giving or, and responding to, invitations to participate in acts of episcopal ministry.   Therefore, those responsible for the issuing of any invitations so to participate, especially in the consecration of a woman as a bishop, should exercise courtesy and respect for the position of the diocese and/or Provinces from which that person is invited.   Likewise, persons responding to invitations should be sensitive to the position of their own dioceses and/or Provinces.   Such

mutual sensitivity and interdependence in the giving and receiving of invitations is in itself a realisation of communion.

72.   Within this context the Commission would reiterate the advice given prior to the consecration in Boston, Massachusetts:

> If invitations are issued to bishops outside the Episcopal Church we recommend that both invitations and responses should be co-ordinated through the Presiding Bishop and the Primate of the particular Church concerned. A decision should be made in accordance with the canonical position of the Province and within the collegiality of its bishops.

The Archbishop of Canterbury

73.   What has been said in the guidelines about all bishops, applies to the Archbishop of Canterbury as well. In view of his role as a focus of unity for the Anglican communion, the Archbishop of Canterbury has to be sensitive to the positions of all the Provinces in determining his response to particular situations.

74.   1. It is recognised that the Archbishop of Canterbury, like all other bishops, would conform as much as possible to the customs of the Province which he is visiting, while at the same time, he should uphold the canonical position of his own Church as well as the common mind of the House of Bishops of the Church of England on a particular matter.

75.   2. While allowing for consultations between the Archbishop of Canterbury and the provincial authorities concerned, in the current developing situation in the Anglican Communion, it may be wise for Provinces to invite the Archbishop of Canterbury to preside at celebrations of eucharists which he attends, at least in situations where controversy is a possibility.

76.   3. In responding to invitations to consecrations it is recommended that the Archbishop of Canterbury acts in accordance with the Canons of the Church of England.

*   *   *

77.   In reviewing the situation the Commission has come to the conclusion that it is likely that there will be continuing developments over the question

of the ordination of women to the priesthood and episcopate. This is entirely consistent with what we have said about the dynamic view of communion and also the open process of reception. The evidence which has led the Commission to suggest the above pastoral guidelines prompts the members to recommend that a way should be found to monitor the implications and consequences of future developments.

78. It is the hope and prayer of all involved in the work of the Commission that this Report may in time become an instrument for further understanding and for deepening the *koinonia* of the Anglican Communion.

Appendix IV

The role of the 'Anglican Formularies' and the question of confessional autonomy

1.   There have been several attempts by Anglicans and others since the framing of the Thirty-Nine Articles to set out what is basic to the faith. The notion of a hierarchy of truths, some not 'necessary to salvation', was already current in the late Middle Ages. It needs handling with care, as seventeenth and eighteenth century Anglican divines discovered in attempts to identify 'fundamentals'.

2.   Each Communion affirms its catholicity by joining with the whole Church in authorising the great central truths of faith. But, as William Laud put it, the Church of England 'is not such a shrew to her children as to deny her blessing, or denounce an anathema against them, if some peaceably dissent in some particulars remoter from the foundation'.[1] It has been an Anglican habit to speak of 'comprehensiveness' and to identify as characteristically Anglican the pursuing of 'a middle way, not as a compromise, but as a positive grasp of many-sided truth'. This is seen by the Lambeth Conference of 1968 as a 'richness' enabling Anglicans 'to live, both in fellowship and in tension, with those who in some points differ from us'.[2] The 1978 Lambeth Conference put forward arguments for not defining too rigidly in matters of faith. Nevertheless, 'a limit ... there must be to freedom of opinion within a communion which possesses a definite creed'.[3] Comprehensiveness must have definable bounds. There is a question of the limits of tolerance to be extended to those who would be joined in a single Communion. Here the apparently peripheral may prove to be more central than it seemed. The lesson would seem to be that it is important to seek the fullest possible consensus.

3.   If we may take it, then, that life and worship in the Church, though locally variable, are ultimately inseparable from questions of unity of faith with the whole believing community of the universal Church; that fundamentals cannot be separated from the fullness of Christian believing;

1   Laud, *Fisher*, pp. 59-60.
2   Lambeth, 1968, p. 141.
3   J.B. Mozley, *Subscription to the Articles* (Oxford, 1863), p. 32.

327

that the truth once for all delivered (and thus 'standard') is also maintained and living and growing in the Church, we can begin to set in context the question whether it can be right to speak of an 'Anglican' as distinct from a 'Christian' faith. The Lambeth Quadrilateral of 1888 lists Scripture, the Creeds, the Sacraments and the Historic Episcopate[4] as the four standards. The intention was ecumenical. That is to say, it was envisaged that upon these four fundamentals a future united Church might be constructed. Nevertheless, the Conference of 1888 distinguished between 'the standards of doctrine of the Universal Church which the whole Anglican Communion has always accepted' and 'those which are especially the heritage of the Church of England, and which are, to a greater or less extent, received by all her sister and daughter Churches'. These are listed as the sixteenth century formularies, 'The Prayer Book with its Catechism, the Ordinal, and the Thirty-Nine Articles of Religion'. It is the position of documents which claim to be the special source or standard for a particular ecclesial body, as distinct from a valued part of its heritage or tradition, with which we have to be concerned here, because it raises the question of their authority.

4.   The 1922 Doctrine Commission says that the Anglican Formularies 'should not be held to prejudge questions which have arisen since their formulation, or problems which have been modified by fresh knowledge or fresh conceptions'.[5] We must, therefore, if we are to use the term 'standards', work with some sense of the term which allows for restatement and growth in a living community. It is easy to see that process at work in the history of Anglican reflection on the Thirty-Nine Articles. Richard Hooker (c.1554-1600) put forward his trio of Scripture, tradition and reason in the context of contemporary debate about the need for any guide at all but Scripture. Carey in 1682 was chiefly anxious to differentiate the Thirty-Nine Articles from 'the doctrine of those commonly called Presbyterians' on the one side, and the tenets of the Church of Rome on the other, because he saw that as the way to stress something which is distinctively and constitutively Anglican. It is a strong mark of ecumenical progress that that now seems to many a false goal and the wrong way to go about it. William Beveridge in 1710 had the idea of 'consonance' in wanting to show that the Articles were 'consonant to Scripture, reason and the Fathers'. Henry Cary in 1835 supplied 'Testimonies of the Fathers of the first four centuries to the doctrine and discipline of the Church of England

4   See *Quadrilateral at One Hundred*, ed. J. Robert Wright (Ohio, London and Oxford, 1988), for a recent series of essays.

5   *Report* of the Doctrine Commission (1922) (London, 1938), p. 37.

as set forth in the Thirty-Nine Articles', in an endeavour to show the continuity of the Church of England with the early Church. Richard Bentley Porson Kidd listed 'testimonies and authorities, divine and human' in confirmation of the Articles (1848). Joseph Miller (1878-87), E. Tyrrell Green (1896), B.J. Kidd (1899), W. Goode (1845), placed emphasis upon the witness of history. In short, we find in Anglican tradition a good deal of development in the view which is taken of the place and weight of these texts.

5.   The Lambeth Quadrilateral speaks of 'articles', but the Chicago version of 1886 which served as its model describes its clauses as 'inherent parts of this sacred deposit'. The word 'parts' undoubtedly fits the grammatical form and the meaning of the Quadrilateral clauses better. In neither the Chicago nor the Lambeth version are they strictly 'clauses' at all; there is no verb. The focus is actually upon a series of things: Scripture, the Creeds, the Sacraments, the Historic Episcopate. In each case the noun is qualified by a phrase explaining how it is to be understood (the Creeds 'as the sufficient statement of the Christian faith', for example). This is not a point of grammatical pedantry; the difference is crucial. Of one of the Thirty-Nine Articles one may say, 'I believe that ...', and make by quoting it a propositional statement of a doctrinal position on the issue in question. Of one of the clauses of the Lambeth Quadrilateral one must say, 'I believe in ...'. So in the Quadrilateral's clauses we have something much like the sixteenth century 'notes of the Church', or their ancient equivalents, four things which when present are taken to indicate that we have a 'true Church'. As the Lambeth Quadrilateral sees it, it is a living community within which Scripture is active, underpinning the Creeds, ministered in the sacraments, guarded and preached under the oversight of the episcopate.

6.   With a slightly different emphasis in mind, the 1922 Doctrine Commission lists Scripture, the Church, the Creeds and the Anglican Formularies. Here Scripture is taken as the bedrock of revelation, which keeps authenticating itself by 'continuing to mediate to individuals the revelation which it records and by nurturing their spiritual life'. But again it is being seen in the context of the life of the believing community of the Church and in harness with the Creeds.[6] The key difference - and it is of great importance - is the emphasis on the Anglican Formularies as defining 'the position of the Church of England in relation to other Christian

6   *Report* of the Doctrine Commission (1922) (London, 1938), p. 31.

bodies'.[7] That strikes a disjunctive note deliberately omitted from the Lambeth Quadrilateral, and surely out of tune with its central ecumenical purpose.[8]

7.   Yet there must be proper spheres of authorising within the Anglican, or any other Communion, and arguably within Provinces. It may be argued that in a divided Church it is the place of each ecclesial body to word the truths of faith which belong to and are apprehended by the community of the universal Church, in ways comfortable and natural and appropriate to the style and character of that Church, and which may be used in its life and worship; but always with care not inadvertently to set up a barrier to other Christians. But it must also be the duty of each body to correct error and misunderstanding in its midst, and to work always towards unanimity with the *consensus fidelium*. We must therefore carefully separate a sense of corporate identity based on common norms of worship and on common life within a Communion, from the expectation that Anglicans will share a common faith which somehow distinguishes them from other Christians. That cannot be right. Everything we know about faith endorses the view that it unites us to the whole Body of Christ's faithful people through Christ, and is thus a corporate believing with the universal community. Matters of doctrine are always the responsibility of the universal Church and never at the disposal of a local community without reference to the whole under Scripture.

8.   All this has implications for authorising in matters of faith and practice within individual Provinces, and within the particular churches, or individual dioceses, and, with certain restrictions, for individual congregations, insofar as these may be deemed ecclesial bodies. An ecclesial community may, within the limits set by orderliness, legislate for its own people. It may do so relatively freely in matters which cannot be divisive in relation to other Communions or communities, provided its actions are consonant with Scripture, causing no difficulty to tender consciences. In all matters of faith and worship where there is known to be imperfect consensus as yet in the universal Church, we would take the view that the diocese or Province or Communion must seek in charity to 'defer to the common mind'.[9] In matters of order, too, there should never be any attempt to force others into conformity with a *fait accompli*. No

---

7   Cf. G.R. Evans, 'Permanence in the Revealed Truth and Continuous Exploration of its Meaning', *Quadrilateral at One Hundred*, pp. 111 ff.
8   *Ibid.*, p. 36.
9   Lambeth Conference, 1948.

Communion, province or diocese should respond to another's actions in anger, or in any manner likely to lead to division. Solutions must be sought which reconcile and foster the growth of common life. Where this purpose is paramount, and anger and resentment not allowed to confuse the real issues, we may go on in faith that the Lord, whose intention for his Church is that it should be one with him, will bring about a right resolution of differences. Deference to the common mind means a willingness to accept that one may be wrong and to grow in understanding, as well as a pooling of the special insights into the fullness of the truth which have been vouchsafed to each Christian Church.

SELECT BIBLIOGRAPHY

A People Belonging to God: Report of the Bishop of Chelmsford's Commission on Diocesan Strategy (1988).

Anglican-Methodist Conversations, Interim Statement (London, 1958).

Anglican-Methodist Conversations, Report (London, 1963).

Anglican-Reformed Conversations, *God's Reign and our Unity* (London and Edinburgh, 1984).

Authority in the Anglican Communion, ed. S. Sykes (Toronto, 1987).

Bacon, F., *Church Administration: A Guide for Baptist Ministers and Church Officers* (Bristol, 1981).

Barry, F.R., *Church and Leadership* (London, 1945).

Baxter, Richard, *Vindication of the Church of England* (London, 1682).

Becon, T., *Catechism,* ed. J. Ayre, Parker Society (1843-4).

Beveridge, William, *Ecclesia Anglicana, Ecclesia Catholica, Works,* Vol. 11 (Oxford, 1840).

Bishops, ed. G. Simon (London, 1961).

Bishops: But What Kind?, ed. P. Moore (London, 1982).

Bowmer, J.C., *Pastor and People* (London, 1975).

Bradshaw, P.F., *The Anglican Ordinal* (London, 1971).

Butler, B.C., *The Theology of Vatican II* (London, 1967).

Canons of 1604, in E. Cardwell, *Synodalia* (London, 1842), 2 vols.

Cardwell, E., ed., *Synodalia* (London, 1842), 2 vols.

Carpenter, E., *The Protestant Bishop* (London, 1956).

Celestine I, Pope, *Epistolae et Decreta, Patrologia Latina,* 50, and ed. E. Schwarz, *Acta Conciliorum Oecumenicorum,* 7 (Strasburg, 1929).

Chadwick, Henry, 'Ministry and Tradition', *Teologia de Sacerdocio,* 21 (1990), 69-77.

----- 'Episcopacy in the New Testament and Early Church', *Preparatory Articles* for the Lambeth Conference, 1978, ed. J. Howe (London, 1977), pp. 206-14.

----- 'The Status of Ecumenical Councils in Anglican Thought', *Orientalia Christiana Analecta,* 195 (1973).

Cheney, C., 'The Earliest English Diocesan Statutes', *English Historical Review,* 75 (1960), 1-29.

----- 'A Group of Related Synodal Statutes of the Thirteenth Century', *Mediaeval Studies Presented to Aubrey Gwynn, S.J.,* ed. J.A. Watt *et al* (Dublin, 1961), pp. 114-32.

Chronicle of Convocation (Canterbury) (1847 -).

333

Church and State, Report of the Archbishops' Commission (the Chadwick Commission) (London, 1970).

Church Government, London Yearly Meeting of the Religious Society of Friends (London, 1968).

Church Relations in England (Conversations between representatives of the Archbishop of Canterbury and representatives of the Evangelical Free Churches in England) (London, 1950).

The Church of Pakistan: Today and Tomorrow, Report of an International Consultation, ed. Michael Nazir Ali (Lahore, 1985).

Churches Respond to BEM, Official responses to the "Baptism, Eucharist and Ministry" text, ed. M. Thurian (Geneva, 1986) vol. 1 - .

Collinson, Patrick, *The Religion of Protestants* (Oxford, 1982).

Communion and Episcopacy: Essays to Mark the Centenary of the Chicago-Lambeth Quadrilateral, ed. J. Draper (Cuddesdon, 1988).

Cranmer, *Remains*, ed. H. Jenkins, Parker Society (1833), 4 vols.

Cyprian, Bishop of Carthage, *Opera, Corpus Christianorum Series Latina* (1972).

Davidson, R.T., *Origin and History of the Lambeth Conferences, 1867 and 1878* (London, 1888).

Deacons in the Ministry of the Church, A Report Commissioned by the House of Bishops (London, 1988).

Dix, G., *Jurisdiction in the Early Church* (*Laudate*, 1938, repr. London, 1975).

Dolan, G.E., *The Distinction between the Episcopate and the Presbyterate according to the Thomistic Opinion* (Washington, 1950).

Dombes, Les, Group of; see also p. 336.

Eames Commission, see *Report of the Archbishop of Canterbury's Commission on Communion and Women in the Episcopate* .

Echlin, E.P., *The Story of Anglican Ministry* (Slough, 1974).

Episcope and the Episcopate in Ecumenical Perspective (prepared as a background text to BEM).

Episcopacy and the Role of the Suffragan Bishop: A Report by the Dioceses Commission, GS 551 (1983).

Episcopacy and the Role of the Suffragan Bishop: A Second Report by the Dioceses Commission, GS 697 (1985).

Episcopacy in the Lutheran Church, ed. I. Asheim and V.R. Gold (Philadelphia, 1970).

Evans, G.R., *Authority in the Church: A Challenge for Anglicans* (Norwich, 1990).

Field, Richard, *Of the Church* (1606, repr. Cambridge, 1854), 4 vols.

Gathered for Life: The Official Report of the Vancouver Assembly, World Council of Churches (Geneva, 1983).

General Synod Report of Proceedings (1970 -).

Gerson, Jean, *De Concilio Generali*, ed. P. Glorieux, *Oeuvres Complètes* (Paris, 1960 -).

Gillet, P., *La personnalité juridique en droit ecclésiastique* (Malines, 1927).

God's Reign and our Unity, see Anglican-Reformed Conversations, 1984.

Gogan, B., *The Common Corps of Christendom* (Leiden, 1982).

Greenslade, S.L., 'The English Reformers and the Councils of the Church', *Oecumenica* (1967), 95-116.

Grindrod Report, The, see *Women and the Episcopate*.

Growing into Union, ed. C.O. Buchanan, E.L. Mascall, J.I. Packer, G.D. Leonard, (London, 1970).

Growth in Agreement, ed. H. Meyer and L. Vischer (New York/Geneva, 1984).

Halliburton, J., *The Authority of a Bishop* (London, 1987).

Hamer, J., *L'Église est une communion* (Paris, 1962).

Hanson, R.C.P., *Groundwork for Unity* (London, 1971).

Headlam, M., *Bishop and Friend* (London, 1944).

Henson, H. Hensley, *Retrospect of an Unimportant Life* (London, 1942-50), 2 vols.

Hinschius, P., *System des Katholischen Kirchenrechts mit besonderer Rücksicht auf Deutschland*, II (Berlin, 1878).

Hippolytus of Rome, *The Apostolic Tradition*, ed. G.N. Bonwetsch and H. Achelis, *Werke* (Leipzig, 1897-).

Historic Episcopate, The, ed. K.M. Carey (London, 1954).

Hooker, Richard, *The Laws of Ecclesiastical Polity*, ed. G. Edelen, Cambridge, Mass. (1977-).

Ignatius of Antioch, *Works*, in *The Apostolic Fathers*, ed. J.B. Lightfoot (London, 1889- 90), vol. I2; *Works*, tr. A. Roberts and W.H. Tambaut, *Ante-Nicene Christian Library* (Edinburgh, 1868-9).

Inskip, James, *A Man's Job* (London, 1948).

Irenaeus, *Adversus Haereses*, Sources Chrétiennes (Paris, 1974), pp. 210, 211.

Islington Conference Papers. Bishops in the Church (London, 1966).

Jewel, John, *Works*, 4 vols., ed. J. Ayre, Parker Society (1845-50).

Johnson, A.R., *Sacral Kingship in Ancient Israel* (Cardiff, 1967).

Kemp, E., *Counsel and Consent* (London, 1961).

Kirk, K.E., ed., *The Apostolic Ministry* (London, 1946).

Lambeth Conference *Reports* are quoted from:
Five Lambeth Conferences (London, 1920) [1867-1908]

The Lambeth Conferences (London, 1948) [1920-1948]
The Lambeth Conference *Reports* for 1958, 1968, 1978.
The Truth Shall Make You Free: Report of the Lambeth Conference (London, 1988).
Lambeth Essays on Unity, ed. A.M. Ramsey (London, 1969).
Lathbury, T., *A History of the Convocation of the Church of England* (London 1842, 2nd ed. 1853).
Latimer, Hugh, *Works,* ed. G.E. Corrie, Parker Society (1844-5).
Laud, William, *Works,* ed. W. Scott and J. Bliss (1847-60), 7 vols.
Legrand, Manzanares and Garcia, eds., *The Nature and Future of Episcopal Conferences* (English version in *The Jurist,* 48 (Washington, 1988).
Les Dombes, Group of, *Towards a Reconciliation of Ministries* (1975).
----- *The Episcopal Ministry* (1976).
----- *Pour la communion des Églises* (Paris, 1988).
Liturgical Commission of the General Synod, *Ordination Services, Series 3,* (1977).
Longley, Charles Thomas, *Charge Addressed to the Clergy* (1861).
----- *Charge intended for Delivery to the Diocese of Canterbury* (1868).
Lossky, Y., *Mystical Theology in the Eastern Church* (tr. London, 1957).
Lutheran Understanding of the Episcopal Office, Lutheran World Fellowship (Geneva, 1985).
Many Gifts, One Spirit, Report of ACC-7, the seventh meeting of the Anglican Consultative Council, Singapore, 1987 (London, 1987).
Mascall, E.L., *Theology and the Gospel of Christ* (London, 1977).
Moore, E. Garth, *An Introduction to English Canon Law* (Oxford, 1967).
Moravian Unity Church Order.
Mozley, J.B., *Subscription to the Articles* (Oxford, 1863), p. 32.
Nairobi, 1970, Proceedings of the Uniting General Council (Presbyterian and Reformed) (Geneva, 1970).
Nature of Christian Belief, The, A Statement and Exposition by the House of Bishops (London, 1986).
Neill, S., 'The Historic Episcopate', in *Bishops,* ed. G. Simon (London, 1961).
Newman, John Henry, 'The Catholicity of the Anglican Church', in *Essays Critical and Historical* (London, 1890).
----- *Letters and Diaries,* ed. I. Ker and T. Gornall, III (Oxford, 1979).
Niagara Report, The, Report of the Anglican-Lutheran Consultation on Episcope 1987 (London and Geneva, 1988).
Norris, Richard, 'The Bishop in the Church of Late Antiquity', Papers of the Consultation, *Episcope in Relation to the Mission of the Church Today,* prepared as background for *The Niagara Report* (1987).

O'Donovan, O., *On The Thirty-Nine Articles* (Exeter, 1986).

Ordination of Women to the Priesthood, The: A Second Report by the House of Bishops, GS 829 (1988).

Phillimore, R., *Ecclesiastical Law of the Church of England* (2nd ed. London, 1895).

Piepkorn, A.C., *Profiles in Belief* (New York, 1978), Vol. II.

Poschmann, B., *Penance and the Anointing of the Sick*, 2 vols., tr. F. Courtenay (Frieburg, 1967).

Post, Gaines, *Studies in Mediaeval Legal Thought* (Princeton, 1964).

Price, Annie Darling, *A History of the Formation and Growth of the Reformed Episcopal Church, 1873-1902* (Philadelphia, 1902).

The Priesthood of the Ordained Ministry, Faith and Order Advisory Group (London, 1986).

Proceedings of the Church Assembly (London, 1922 - 1969).

Quadrilateral at One Hundred, ed. J. Robert Wright (Ohio, London and Oxford, 1988).

Rafferty, O.P., 'Thomas Cranmer and the Royal Supremacy', *Heythrop Journal*, 31 (1990), 130-4.

Rahner, K. and Ratzinger, J., *The Episcopate and the Primacy* (tr.) (Edinburgh/London, 1962).

Report of the Doctrine Commission (1922), *Doctrine in the Church of England* (London, 1938).

Report of the Archbishop of Canterbury's Commission on Communion and Women in the Episcopate (London, 1989).

Rogers, Thomas, *Works*, ed. J.S. Perowne, Parker Society, 1854.

Roman Catholic-Orthodox Conversations, *The Sacrament of Order in the Sacramental Structure of the Church* (New Valamo, 1988).

Rousseau, O., 'La vraie valeur de l'Épiscopat dans lÉglise d'après d'importants documents de 1875', *Irénikon*, 29 (1956), 121-50.

Santer, M., ed., *Their Lord and Ours* (London, 1982).

Saltet, L., *Les réordinations* (Paris, 1907).

Samuel, A., *Faith and Order Paper*, 102, World Council of Churches.

Study of Anglicanism, The, ed. S. Sykes and J. Booty (London, 1988).

Suenens, Cardinal, *Co-responsibility in the Church*, tr. F. Martin (London, 1968).

Sundkler, B., *The Church of South India* (London, 1954).

Tappert, G. (tr.), *The Lutheran Book of Concord* (Philadelphia, 1959).

----- *Lutheran Confessional Theology in America*, 1840-80 (New York, 1972).

Taylor, Jeremy, *Episcopacy Asserted, Works* 10 vols., ed. C.P. Eden (London, 1847-54), Vol. 5.

Tillard, J.M.R., *The Bishop of Rome* (London, 1983).

Thurian, Max, *Priesthood and Ministry* (Mowbray, 1970).

Tyndale, William, *Works*, ed. H. Walter, Parker Society (1848).

Ullmann, W., 'The Mediaeval Papacy, St. Thomas and Beyond', *Aquinas Society of London* 35 (London, 1960), p. 2.

----- 'Frederich's Opponent Innocent IV, as Melchisedek', *Atti del convegno internazionale di Studi Fredericiani*, 1950 (Palermo, 1952).

Vatican Council II: The Conciliar and Post-Conciliar Documents, ed. A. Flannery (Leominster, 1981).

von Campenhausen, H., *Kirchliches Amt und geistliche Vollmacht in den ersten drei Jahrhunderten* (Tübingen, 1953).

Ware, T., *The Orthodox Church* (London, 1963).

Welsby, P., *Episcopacy in the Church of England* (London, 1973).

----- *Bishops and Dioceses* (London, 1971).

Whitgift, John, *Works*, ed. J. Ayre, 3 vols., Parker Society (1851-3).

Wilberforce, Samuel, *The Letter-Books 1843-68*, ed. R.K. Pugh (Oxford, 1970).

Wilson, Thomas, *Sacra Privata*, in *Works*, ed. J. Keble, V (Oxford, 1860).

Women and the Episcopate, Report of the Working Party Appointed by the Primates of the Anglican Communion (Anglican Consultative Council, 1987).

World Council of Churches, *Baptism, Eucharist and Ministry* (BEM) (Geneva, 1982).

Wright, J. Robert, 'The Authority of Chalcedon for Anglicans', *Christian Authority: Essays in Honour of Henry Chadwick*, ed. G.R. Evans (Oxford, 1988).

------ *Quadrilateral at One Hundred* (Cincinnati/London, 1988).

The York Journal of Convocation (1874-).

Zizioulas, J., *Being as Communion* (London, 1985).

----- 'The Institution of Episcopal Conferences: An Orthodox Reflection', *The Jurist* 48 (1988).

Index

The index refers to page-numbers